D1442884

The Burning Fountain

Dust to the dust: but the pure spirit shall flow
Back to the burning fountain whence it came,
A portion of the Eternal, which must glow
Through time and change, unquenchably the same . . .

SHELLEY, Adonais

THE BURNING FOUNTAIN

Philip Wheelwright •

A Study in the Language of Symbolism

Bloomington
INDIANA UNIVERSITY PRESS

SECOND PRINTING 1959

Copyright, 1954, by Indiana University Press

LIBRARY OF CONGRESS CATALOG CARD NUMBER: 54-6206

Manufactured in the United States of America

TO

MAUDE

(without whom, not)

Acknowledgments

Acknowledgment is made to the following publishers who have graciously granted permission to quote from the books indicated: The John Day Company, Alan Porter *Signature of Pain;* Duell, Sloan & Pearce, Dilys Bennett Laing *Birth Is Farewell;* Harcourt, Brace and Company, I. A. Richards *The Principles of Literary Criticism* and T. S. Eliot *Gerontion, Ash Wednesday,* and *Four Quartets;* Harvard University Press, Susanne K. Langer *Philosophy in a New Key;* John Murray, Avery and Heath-Stubbs (trans.) *Poems of Hafiz of Shiraz;* W. W. Norton & Company, Bertrand Russell *An Inquiry Into Meaning and Truth;* Princeton University Press, Allen Tate *The Language of Poetry;* Rockliff Publishing Corporation, Jean Louis Barrault *Reflections on the Theatre;* S.P.C.K., M. A. Ewer *A Survey of Mystical Symbolism.*

Acknowledgment is also made to *The Sewanee Review* and its editor Monroe K. Spears, to *The Kenyon Review* and its editor John Crowe Ransom, and to *Philosophy and Phenomenological Research* and its editor Marvin Farber, for permission to use in modified form certain articles and parts of articles originally published in those quarterlies.

Chapters V and XII have been developed out of lectures given at Indiana University in 1951 on the Mahlon Powell Foundation. Acknowledgment is made to the University and the Foundation for the use of this material.

Preface

VIRTUALLY all of this book was written (and twice rewritten) in the private study in Baker Library which I was privileged to occupy during the sixteen years (1937 to 1953) that I was a member of the Dartmouth College Faculty. I am warmly grateful to members of the library staff for their generous coöperation and help. My thanks go also to the President and Trustees of Dartmouth College, to Dean Donald H. Morrison, and Professor Maurice Mandelbaum, for assisting me, by a leave of absence and a reduced teaching load, toward the completion of the book; as well as to the Mahlon Powell Foundation of Indiana University and to the University of California at Riverside for financial grants covering part of the cost of publication.

The number of colleagues, students, and others from whom I have drawn ideas, or by whose criticisms I have profited, exceeds my power to enumerate. If I single out for special mention such good friends as Lydia Hoffmann Behrendt, Elizabeth Drew, Francis Fergusson, F. Cudworth Flint, René and Erika Fülöp-Miller, Edwin A. Halsey, Abraham Joshua Heschel, Bernard C. Heyl, William Ernest Hocking, Fritz Kaufmann, Julián Marías, A. Hyatt Mayor, John Crowe Ransom, Richard Rogin, Monroe K. Spears, Frederick W. Sternfeld, Vernon Venable, and Don José Vasconcelos, it is because they indicate the points at which my consciousness of intellectual indebtedness is most acute. My interest in symbolism was first stimulated some forty years ago by my aunt, Elizabeth D. Meeker, and in the subsequent years I have profited frequently from her researches and interpretations, particularly in the field of religious archetypes. A group of criticisms offered by Preston Carter has been of help in rearranging the materials of the early chapters. My remaining acknowledgment is reserved for the Dedication.

P. W.

The University of California at Riverside

Contents

The Burning Fountain

Foreword

Tʜᴇʀᴇ ɪs a legend in Estonia that the god of song Wannemunne once descended onto the Domberg, and there, in a sacred wood, played and sang music of divine beauty. All creatures were invited to listen, and they each learned some fragment of the celestial sound: the forest learned its rustling, the stream its roar; the wind caught and learned to re-echo the shrillest tones, and the birds the prelude of the song. The fish stuck their heads as far as the eyes out of the water, but left their ears below the surface; they saw the movements of the god's mouth and imitated them, but remained dumb. Man alone grasped it all, and therefore his song pierces into the depths of the heart, and mounts upwards to the dwellings of the gods.[1]

The present book is concerned with ways in which men have aspired to imitate the god worthily and sing the full song. The majority of human utterances are thin pipings, as though (Nietzsche remarked) the Eroica Symphony were to be scored for two flutes. The language of the full song may be called *expressive language* or *depth language,* and one of my aims in the early chapters will be to distinguish its nature and potentialities from those of literal language, or, as I shall sometimes call it for brevity's sake, *steno-language*— the language of science, and in general of precise logical de-

3

notation. Man's everyday intercourse employs both kinds of language to some degree, often in uncritical conjunction, besides mixing them up with phatic modes of utterance, which is to say emotional or merely conventional vaporizings. The greater uses of depth language, as exemplified in religion, in poetry, and in myth, represent approximately the scope and focus of this book; whose central thesis, which I shall clarify and defend in the early chapters, is that religious, poetic, and mythic utterances at their best really mean something, make a kind of objective reference, although neither the objectivity nor the method of referring is of the same kind as in the language of science.

Our contemporary vision tends to be limited and prejudiced by certain prevalent habits of interpretation and expectancy. I don't say there haven't been other limitations and prejudices at other times; that, however, is not especially our business. The task of a rational being is to see beyond his own prejudices, not to deride the prejudices of another. An age of technosophy—an age, that is to say, in which our ways of interpreting and appraising experience tend to be influenced more and more by the streamlined methods and glittering results of technology—encourages us to think in certain ways and inhibits or dissuades us from thinking in other ways. Take as example an inspirational dream—where, say, a man has gone to sleep with a problem bothering him and awakes with a happy awareness that the solution has clicked. How to explain it? Aeneas awakening in Carthage had no doubt that Mercury had brought him the command to put to sea. Such an explanation, even if we were to substitute Christian mythic symbols for Roman, would hardly receive wide credence today, whereas an explanation in such terms as "incubation" and "delayed response" would at least seem inherently plausible. At the moment I am not arguing for either interpretation as against the other; I am only pointing

out the obvious fact that there are characteristic differences
between the types of explanation which an ancient man and
a twentieth century man would normally regard as reasonable, and the obvious but very important corollary that our
way of explaining things sets marked limits to our acceptable ways of directly envisioning reality. Our current intellectual mores permit us to envision a world of ego and id, of
synapses and conditioned reflexes; they do not permit us to
envision—at least not with an equal degree of seriousness and
public accountability—gods and demons, fairies and elves, or
(in anything like a firm sense) inspiration by the Muses.
They restrict us, by and large, to the naturalistic point of
view, allowing few or no beliefs save such as can be validated in the last resort by scientific method.

The inquiry upon which I am embarking is partly ontological, partly semantic. Let ontology be understood to mean
the study of the major ways in which anything can be said
to really *be*. When Jesus speaks of our Father in Heaven,
or when Prometheus in Aeschylus' play denounces the tyranny of Zeus, in each case something is being spoken about.
Neither Jesus nor Aeschylus is just vaporizing; each of them
has a certain beliefful attitude towards that which he is characterizing. On the other hand, neither of them is speaking
about that Something Other in literal everyday terms. Jesus
does not mean that God is a father in quite the same sense
as an earthly father; Aeschylus does not mean that God is a
tyrant in quite the same sense as an earthly monarch. Both
are using the language of analogy—or, in the most adequate
sense of the phrase, the language of poetic vision. Each is
speaking about something which he regards as very real, but
of a different order of being from that of common familiarity.
And we, as readers and hearers, if we want to understand
such teachers instead of imposing our own conceptualizations
upon them, must try to find our way back into their onto-

logical perspective—into that way of confronting the world and asking questions about it which is the realizing medium of their mode of thought and utterance—i.e., the medium through which and in terms of which the object spoken about is real. The discipline of grasping such a viewpoint, of effecting such a translation of basic intellectual reliance, is an ontological discipline—a discipline with respect to the way in which Being is grasped and interpreted.

Now ontology is closely involved with semantics—which is to say, with the study of meanings and of how they can be expressed and communicated. Being, in its various modes, has to be articulated by language, and the habits and customs and styles and limitations of language set barriers to the ways in which Being can be understood. Thus, substitute the word "psyche" for "soul," and how differently the entourage of problems tends to shape itself! Or again, consider with how much more innocence it was possible to use the word "God" a few centuries ago, when Christian assumptions permeated every stratum of daily life, than in these days of the locust and the dry wind. The two factors—our intimations of what *is* and our limited ways of saying it—affect each other mutually. A critical method must examine them as complementaries: it must try to report the radical character of things so far as a disciplined exercise of philosophical intuition can discover it, and at the same time, with a touch of irony, acknowledge that this discovery, too, is conditioned and limited (we never know just how far) by the linguistic resources which are at once the instruments of expression and largely also the conditioning media of thought itself.

Accordingly, the purpose of this book is to inquire into the character of both language and existence, so far as they mutually affect each other. Since, however, the words "language" and "existence" are used homonymously, in more than one sense, it is necessary to remind ourselves again and again in what sense we are using them and in what sense we are not. My primary emphasis with respect to both terms is humanistic. By "existence" I mean not the abstract concept of existence but the living reality of it to us whom it engages. This will be the theme of Chapter I. Thereafter I shall approach by various means the complementary question, to which most of the book is devoted—the nature of expressive language; more specifically, the semantic characteristics which enable the language of religion and myth and poetry, at their best, to speak in a way that truly "mounts to the dwelling-place of the gods," and testifies to the reality of that dwelling.

ONE

Man's Threshold Existence

MAN LIVES always on the verge, always on the borderland of a something more. He is the only
animal, apparently, who has built restlessness into a metaphysical principle. Even in the practical sphere he is restless
in ways that mark him off, for good *and* for ill, from his fel-
low-animals. Human desires, winged by imagination, fly beyond the scope of natural instinct and mock at our efforts to
satisfy them. Such is a favorite theme of moralists. But even
when—perhaps especially when—we succeed in allaying the
grosser forms of uneasiness, the sense of a beyond and the
urge to wonder about it remain.

Indeed, the intimation of a something more, a beyond the
horizon, belongs to the very nature of consciousness. To be
conscious is not simply a fact or event like those determinate
facts and events which make up our physical world. If we
call it a fact, or event, or process, or function, we do so by
analogy, and in any analogy the differences are at least as
important as the resemblances. To be conscious is not just to
be; it is to mean, to intend, to point beyond oneself, to testify
that some kind of beyond exists, and to be ever on the verge
of entering into it.

That is why there can be no science of man. You can study

a man scientifically to just the extent that you can grasp and systematize his thinglike characteristics, which form an ontological substructure of every one of us; but the man in his wholeness, which is to say in his distinctively human character, eludes every network of rational concepts that is thrown out to cover him. In our technosophic age it is especially important to remember and reaffirm this inalienable first principle of the human condition. For when we sink back into the passivity and complacency of the Nothing Else But, and ignore the radically threshold situation that is our birthright —at once the glory and tragic finitude of being human—we throw away the one chance, however small and fragmentary, of fulfilling our destiny as rational and (in the sense that I hope will gradually become clear in these chapters) spiritual creatures.

There are three major respects—three dimensions of awareness—in which the presence of a something more makes itself felt. To exist humanly is to exist in all three of them, but with greater or less conscious awareness. There is the time dimension: we move continually from a past that is vanishing into a future that is not yet. There is the mundane dimension: we are aware of, and by sound instinct we accept the independent existence of, other persons and things as realities constituting our potential (never fully realized) world. And there is the "vertical"—or, without thunder, the religious dimension: we are forever (one might say) reaching up to grasp the gates of Heaven while one foot is slipping off the edge of the Abyss.

The threshold of time. All existence, as we can humanly know it, is in process of change: an unremitting passage out of *what just was* into *what is just about to be.* This familiar truism has a deeper significance than might appear at first glance. Our minds tend to minimize time's radically destructive power by forming a concept of time: of ourselves existing "in" the present, with the past behind us and the future ahead. The conceptualization has its uses. We employ it whenever we write a history or prognosticate tomorrow's events. But it distorts the reality of the one kind of time we can ever directly know—the present.

What is this present "in" which I find myself? What does it mean to be "between" past and future? Both "in" and "between" connote spatial relations, and our readiness to use them confirms Bergson's theory that a concept of time, as distinguished from pure experience of it, is always built on a model of space. Present does not stand in the same relation to future and past as Indiana to Ohio and Illinois. To think of it so is to substitute an artifact for the fact as directly known. The present moment as experienced is not distinct from what immediately follows and from what immediately precedes. Herein it differs from an intermediate area in space. Time future and time past interpenetrate to form the present moment. Julián Marías writes: "Man is not simply *in* a situation. He is in it only in the respect that he is just emerging out of one situation and into another." Marías accordingly defines the human situation as "intrinsically historical," in the sense that "it consists simultaneously of what it is emerging out of and what it is moving into." The emphatic term here is "consists of." The very substance of the present is the interpenetration of the Just Was and the Just About To Be.[1]

Each moment of time is thus a dying to the past and a being reborn to the future. But if that were all, we could not know ourselves; the "I" of one moment would have no identity with the "I" of the next. It is man's prerogative to be conscious of time's passage. To be conscious that the present moment is but a moment, that passage into the future is a death and a birth, is to transcend the bondage of the moment in the only way that is humanly possible to us. Memory and imagination give the past and future a shape; contemplative awareness of them reduces their power over us—or at any rate over that part of us which matters most. Thus metaphorically we can say that human existence, so far as we live it on the human level, is an interweaving not only of moment with moment, but of the transiency of moments with the permanency of that which sustains us in their passage, and which we can only know "as through a glass, darkly."

The threshold of the world. A second way in which man transcends himself is in relation to the persons and things which make up his everyday world. One's relation to the world is ambivalent: there is certainly a world out there, other than I; yet its nature, as I know it, and my nature as knower of it, seem at once different and yet intimately involved with each other. In this dimension, too, there is interpenetration. On the one hand I am part of my world, in so far as I live and breathe in it, act on and am affected by it. On the other, and in another sense, my world is part of me—in so far as I know it through the perceptions and ideas which I have of it. By stressing either of these interpenetrative aspects to the exclusion of the other, philosophers have produced one or other of the two perennial types of philosophical system—materialism and idealism. The materialist forces to its utmost the insight that each mind is somehow a part of, a function of the material world; he understands mind, soul, and personality entirely in the light of that function, and therefore believes them to be exhaustively explainable (if one were sufficiently clever and well-informed) in terms of how the material world behaves. The idealist (in the metaphysical, not ethical, sense of the word) forces to its utmost the insight that matter can be known only through the ideas of it that the mind entertains: thus he envisages the material world as merely a conceptual construct out of mental experiences, whether man's or God's. Both the materialist and the idealist can make out a strong case for their respective positions, but only by a willingness to belittle half the evidence. Each of them backs a single kind of insight to the limit, believing consistency of interpretation more important than fullness of reference. Their contrasting positions can be made to look logical, but they are not humanly reasonable.

Better a reasonable paradox than a cantankerously one-sided syllogism! To explain away the self in terms of not-self, or not-self in terms of self, may produce a clean-lined thought-structure, but it does no justice to the amplitude, the varied subtleties, and the paradoxical realignments of actual and possible experience. A person's total relation to his world is neither simple nor monological. Partly he stands over against his world, confronted and confronting; partly he finds himself immersed in it, continuous with it, more or less identified with it. Continuity vs. distinction, oneness vs. duality, same vs. other: in the living flow of experience these antitheses do not stay fixed.

Let it be granted at once that you can, if you force the issue hard enough, regard any component of experience—the greenness of a grassplot, or its oblong shape, or the molecules of which it is composed, or the gay and washed and friendly aspect that it wears after a spring rain—as either subjective or objective, either an experience of your mind or an aspect of the world confronting you. Some of the grassplot's characteristics—its measurable length and breadth, the mass of its particles, etc.—are extremely stubborn and, like a man with only one idea who declaims it again and again, they give repeated evidence of ontological rigidity: they are just what they are, and while we can often exploit their characteristics and turn them to our uses, they maintain their own kind of existence in apparent disregard of how we choose to think about them. Other characteristics are ontologically more flexible, more adaptable to varying moods, to differ-

ences of perceptual and emotive response. What presents itself to one man as a gloomy and hostile landscape may seem
mysteriously inviting to another, perhaps even friendly and
promising to a third; and a painter can even train his eye to
see shapes and colors differently from the way in which they
initially impressed him. Doubtless it is reasonable, then, to
say that the grimness of a gray weatherbeaten cliff is a *more*
subjective characteristic of it than its height above sealevel
or the percentage of silicon in its chemical make-up. But to
call it "merely" subjective is to ride a partial insight too hard.
In the moment of living experience the grimness and grayness appear as real qualities out there, in the rock itself and
not in the knower of it. It is only when we fear the testimony
of the burning moment and take refuge in a currently fash-
ionable thought-pattern, that we can deny such qualities as
grayness and grimness their place in the world that confronts
us. Partly, indeed, we shape those qualities by being the kind
of persons we are (not color-blind, for instance, and not entirely phlegmatic) but partly too they shape us, our minds
and souls, by being just such qualities as they are. There is
paradoxical interplay here, and no philosophy that reduces
it to black-and-white simplicities is being faithful to the integral human vision.

We stand, then, on the verge of the circumambient world.
We interpenetrate that world; for "no man is an island," and
in the epistemological no less than in the social sphere a wise
man claims nothing—not even a dream—for his utter own. In
every instance of real as opposed to nominal knowledge we
are partly insiders with immediate awareness of what it is to
be, and partly outsiders looking at surfaces. The dual role,
the in-and-out movement of the mind seeking to penetrate
its object, frames every experience with the irony of its own
finitude. In the distractions of practical life and in the security of theorizing alike we may lose sight of that irony, and

not the least of the poet's important tasks is to bring us back to ourselves, and to it, by an evocative image or cadence, or by the jolt of an unexpected metaphor.

The important thing is not explanation but perspective. Why are we all so convinced that Berkeley was wrong, despite the bright cogency of his arguments? Because it is unnatural, and unreasonable, for the mind to maintain its rationality in so isolationist a way. One's mind becomes partly identified with an object at the moment of knowing it, and feels instinctively sure that there is more to the object than ever meets the eye. Dr. Johnson in kicking the stone did not refute Berkeley, who had foreseen that kind of objection and had answered it in advance.[2] But although his logic was inferior to the Bishop's, his perspective was more reasonable.

The threshold of the unseen. There is a third dimension of human experience, a third persistent paradox of man's ontological situation, and here we enter the borderland where more than ever our everyday language must flounder. I have put it that man is ever reaching upward to grasp at Heaven's gate while one foot is slipping into the Abyss. How adequately this mode of speech reflects each reader's peculiar way of seeing man's moral and spiritual predicament I do not know. Some will doubtless criticize the symbolism as needlessly oblique. Why not say simply (they may ask) that man entertains lofty ideals which he repeatedly and sometimes tragically fails to realize? My answer is that there is more to the full intended meaning, the depth insight, of man's predicament than the language of secular ethics is able to convey. For the predicament is not simply ethical but, in the most basic sense, religious. It is constitutional, not remediable. Ethical remedies are but patches, which never mend the rip down the center of our natures—the tragic discrepancy between the faulty creatures we are and the high destiny to which we are repeatedly called. The theological symbols of Heaven and the Abyss (they are symbols, of course, and not place-names) and of man's Creaturehood connote more and are truer to the full human situation than the mere ethical admission that we often fail to carry out our ideals in practice.

Consciousness then in its religious dimension, as in its temporal and mundane dimensions, stands on a threshold. Here as there, one may sense the dark presence of a Something More, and a devoted seeker may be rewarded with occasional clues to Its nature, but never with full knowledge. Our insights, dim at best, have to be expressed by analogies drawn from the everyday world. And all such analogies are faulty, for the plain reason that what they refer to is not the everyday world from which they are drawn, but a Something More with which we and our world mysteriously and never quite adequately interpenetrate.

The Threshold, in each of its three aspects, is a primordial situation from which no human creature ever entirely withdraws. But a threshold implies a mansion beyond, and how can we know that the mansion is real if we are unable to enter and take up abode in it? The "how" may be ultimately unanswerable; but the fact (and this is where I believe we should firmly start) is that we can and do have direct intuitions of that beyond—intuitions which can err in details but can never be proved to err in the major assurances of a Something More which they yield. The word "intuition" in its proper sense (shorn of the meretricious associations and exaggerated claims that sometimes get attached to it) is perhaps the best way of denoting man's threshold awareness; for the Latin verb *intueor* meant "I look at, behold directly, rather than through intermediaries," and to intuit thus means to be directly aware of more, in any experience, than the immediate sensuous content.

I repeat that intuition, exercised in any one of the three dimensions, can err in detail. Whether we intuitively foresee a pattern of coming events, or intuitively size up a man's character, or intuitively submit to the holiness of a higher will than our own, we should recognize that error of interpretation is possible and should take what precautions we can against it. An intuitive person is not necessarily a jackass. And in any case everyone exercises intuition to some degree or other; for everyone gets, and secretly depends on, glimpses of reality that go beyond the purely inductive probabilities of sense-experience. The seer, the saint, and the poet are not freaks; they are we, and we are they potentially; but they have learned to concentrate and intensify the insights which the rest of us habitually dissipate or ignore. Or (shifting the metaphor from eye to ear) it is they who have learned, and can sometimes teach us, the art of creative listening. To listen for the voice of Wisdom, or the Muse, or Wannemune, or Conscience, or Christ, means standing ready to be guided by an imperative not wholly of one's own making, yet to which one's psyche responds at a level of depth. It is an apprenticeship in singing the full song.

Symbol, Language, Meaning

THE THRESHOLD character of human existence is reflected in the character of our attempts to express it. For the classical truism that man is a rational animal does not mean, at least not primarily, that he is able to contrive syllogisms and manipulate mental counters. The heart of the axiom concerns man's ability to reach "intentively" beyond the here-now. Such intentionality is of two basic kinds, corresponding to the familiar Aristotelian distinction between Practical and Contemplative Reason. On the one hand, man is the decision-making animal: he alone, presumably, is able to reflect upon the ultimate ends of life and remake himself in the light of that examination. On the other hand, man is the symbolizing animal: he is able to hold some particular patch of experience, sensed or imagined, up to contemplative attention, not for what it is but for what it indicates or suggests. In these two kinds of rational activity lie the possibilities, broadly speaking, of ethics and metaphysics respectively. In the one there is intention in the popular and dynamic sense of the word—a reaching out toward the future in an act of deliberate choice, a striving toward a still unrealized possibility which lies somehow within our power to effect. In the other there is "intention" in the more technical

17

and static sense of the word which has come into contemporary philosophy largely through the influence of Brentano and Husserl[1]—where the mind's outreach is not in the time dimension but from the sensuously grasped particularity to the something more which it is taken to symbolize or adumbrate. The ethical use of reason, except for incidental comparisons, lies outside the scope of this book; the question at issue being rather the nature of man's symbolizing activity, particularly in its more expressive and humanly significant manifestations.

The primacy of the human urge to symbolize is acknowledged allegorically—an unconscious allegory, no doubt—in the Biblical account of man's first recorded act. Directly after the Lord God had put man in the Garden of Eden to till it and preserve it, and even before offering him woman as a helpmeet and companion, it is recorded that He brought the beasts of the field and the birds of the air to the man to see what he would call them; "and whatever the man called every living creature, that was its name. The man gave names to all cattle, and to the birds of the air, and to every beast of the field. . . ."[2] As an account of the origin of language the passage leaves much to be desired, but there is a hidden truth in it nevertheless. Not God, but man, gave names to things. That is to say, there is no inherent necessity for the name of anything to be what it is; but man, the creature endowed with reason, did the naming, out of his inherent need to symbolize and so to make reference to things when they are no longer sensuously present. Man's primordial act, as a contemplative being, is the act of symbolization.

DEFINITION OF SYMBOL

A symbol, in the broadest sense of the word, is *that which means;* and the ways in which a symbol can mean are po-

tentially as many as the ways in which one thing can stand
for and lead the mind to something else. As Mary Anita Ewer
has written:

> A word is a symbol, because it stands for its meaning. The sign
> + is a symbol, because it stands for the operation of addition.
> A lily, in religious art, is a symbol, because it stands for purity.
> The creature which, in some terrifying dream, threatens to de-
> vour the dreamer, is a symbol, because it stands for some situa-
> tion in the environment or some conflict in the inner life which
> threatens to engulf the personality. The flag in battle is a symbol,
> because it stands for the ideals and the honour of the mother
> country. In theology, the Creed is a symbol, because it stands for
> a truth which its words cannot completely express.[3]

There are plain and fancy symbols, private and public, emotional and intellectual, verbal and pictorial, serious and playful, religious and scientific, symbols in art and symbols in
everyday life. What they all have in common is the property
of *being more in intention than they are in existence.* A symbol points beyond itself, means more than it is. In the words
of an older vocabulary it is ideally self-transcendent.

What the symbol means, when definite enough to be pointed to or otherwise clearly identified, is called the *referend;*
when the main thrust of its meaning is a conception entertained by the mind about some referend or class of referends
it is called the *reference.* The word "meaning" can denote
either the referend or the reference or the process of referring; on most semantic occasions, however, the three aspects
are by no means distinct. In certain contexts it will be convenient to borrow Professor I. A. Richards' terms "vehicle"
and "tenor" as expressive names for the symbol, or organization of symbols, and its referential thrust.[4]

Another way to define the nature of a symbol in the broad

sense I am starting out with is by distinguishing it from other types of indicator which the mind can apprehend. First, there are natural signs. A rapidly clouding sky points to the prospect of a storm; the sky is here a sign of the oncoming storm, but not a symbol. It signifies or indicates the likelihood of a storm purely by virtue of its causal connection with stormy weather, to a mind which has learned of that connection through previous experience. A natural sign is not used with any purpose or intention of communicating; it works by causal efficacy alone.

Again, a symbol is not merely a signal. The difference between symbol and signal has been stated clearly by Susanne K. Langer:

> Man, unlike all other animals, uses "signs" not only to *indicate* things, but also to represent them. To a clever dog, the name of a person is a signal that the person is present; you say the name, he pricks up his ears and looks for its object. If you say "dinner," he becomes restive, expecting food. You cannot make any communication to him that is not taken as a signal of something immediately forthcoming. His mind is a simple and direct *transmitter* of messages from the world to his motor centers. With men it is different. We use certain "signs" among ourselves that do not point to anything in our actual surroundings. Most of our words are not signs in the sense of signals. They are used to talk *about* things, not to direct our eyes and ears and noses toward them. . . . "Signs" used in this capacity are not *symptoms* of things, but *symbols*.[5]

A dog either ignores a spoken word altogether or reacts to it in bodily expectation of something appropriate to come. But let an eighteen-month-old baby hear the word "Mummy!" and frequently without any attempt to seek its mother or any show of expectation that she will appear the child simply becomes interested and repeats the word in pleased contemplation of the suggested idea. And since the use of symbols appears to be confined to man, Professor Langer offers the highly suggestive hypothesis that man's basic need, the one function that most truly distinguishes him from beasts, is the need of *symbolization*, the need to form conceptions of things. Unfortunately her use of the word "symptom" in this connection veils the distinction which I am maintaining between what characterizes a signal and what characterizes a natural sign; for a symptom is in general a species of natural sign. The scent of a hare which sets a fox in pursuit is at once a natural sign and a signal. But a red traffic light is a signal without being a natural sign. And to a reflective physician a symptom of an interesting disease in someone who is not his own patient and therefore does not require that he act, is a natural sign without being a signal.

Natural signs (including symptoms) and signals are both signative, which is to say indicative. They may be spoken of indifferently as signs and indicators. But they signify or indicate in different ways. Thunder, for example, may simultaneously function as a natural sign (as indicating the probability that lightning and perhaps rain will follow), as a signal (so far as it warns us to seek shelter), and as a symbol. Although in popular idiom we sometimes say that the thunder "means" that a storm is coming up, it is more accurate to reserve the words "mean" and "meaning" for the functioning of symbols, and to say that non-symbolic signs signify or indicate. Thunder (like anything else) may come to function symbolically also: as when, in the *Brihad-Aranyaka Upanishad*,[6] it represents the voice of Prajapati issuing divine commands to gods, to asuras, and to men. In the context of Vedanta philosophy, as in many another religio-cosmological context, the sound of thunder not only indicates but means.

Often natural signs are part of the thing they indicate. We see a familiar face and gesture: they indicate the presence of a friend, while at the same time they are components of the friend's total personality. It is only by an effort of abstraction, or by habituation to the idea of a disembodied soul, that I can regard the friend as existing quite apart from his face and visible actions. Signs which indicate by standing in the relation of part to whole may be called participative or threshold signs. Whether the thunderclap which indicates a storm is to be regarded as part of the storm or as an indicator external to it, and whether a rash which indicates measles is to be taken as part of the measles or not, will depend upon the current practices of thought and language. At any rate the importance of threshold signs for our present study is to be found in the interesting forms which the threshold function can take when such signs are used as symbols: a matter to be developed in later chapters.

Finally, a symbol should be distinguished from an *associative stimulus*. Cloudy weather may by its gloom stir thoughts of death, without being taken either as an indication that death will occur or as a symbol by which the idea of death can be communicated. A landscape seen from a train window may stir one's mind to childhood recollections: perhaps because of some resemblance, obvious or hidden, to a place which one knew as a child. Here again, the landscape is simply an associative stimulus: the memories are evoked either by reason of objective similarity or contiguity (since what is *like* something else or *next to* something else in space or time has a general tendency to elicit an idea of that something else) or by reason of some more obscure and personal psychic connection. Since no expectancy is involved there can be no error as in the case of a signal. And since the stimulus merely acts upon the observer by the propulsions of psychic association and is not taken by him to stand for anything, it does not have the status of a symbol. However, such stimuli are related to problems of symbolism in two ways. They may sometimes be traced by psychoanalytical techniques to a depth situation in the psyche that experiences them, which can then be interpreted (by analogy with consciously symbolic acts) as unconsciously symbolizing its disturbances in this way. Freud's use of the term "dream symbolism" is justified only on the basis of such analogy. Associative stimuli are further interesting because of the ways in which they can be developed, through the arts of poetry and painting, into deeply expressive and sharable symbols. The madeleine dipped in a cup of tea was originally an associative stimulus in Proust's private experience, but through his memorable account of its effects, and his contextualization of the incident as a theme in the orchestration of his novel, the taste of madeleine in tea was made into a symbolic vehicle whereby Proust could communicate expressively and concretely something of his personal discoveries about memory.

The nature of a symbol can now be stated more precisely, in contradistinction to the related functions just discussed. As distinguished from a signal it invites consideration rather than overt action. As distinguished from an associative stimulus it is accepted by its observer as standing for something; which is to say that the observer is also an interpreter. These two characteristics are widely agreed on as essential to the symbol. A third characteristic is more debatable. Some will have it that as distinguished from a natural sign the symbol does not merely happen, but is used with intention to communicate. This would be true of most types of symbol, but the use of the word "symbol" in depth psychology—where, for instance, the dream of appearing naked in public is spoken of as a "symbol" of repressed fears and shames[7]—would then have to be justified by the hypothesis of unconscious intentions, and it is controversial whether the meaning of "intention" should be broadened to that degree. Perhaps it is just as well not to insist on too sharp or doctrinaire a definition; such definitions involve the risk of ignoring or distorting borderland concepts which do not readily fit into a given scheme. It is enough for our purposes that we understand a symbol as that which means or stands for something more than (not necessarily separate from) itself, which invites consideration rather than overt action, and which characteristically (although not perhaps universally) involves an intention to communicate.

Let it be noted in passing that popular usage does not ordinarily admit the term "symbol" in the broad sense here defined, as coextensive with any ascription of meaning whatever. Most people would doubtless say that the three-letter word f-o-x "stands for" or "means" but does not "symbolize" the animal with the bushy tail, but that the animal in turn "symbolizes" the quality of cunning. In this more special sense a "symbol" is not just anything that has meaning, it is that which carries a hidden or less obvious or more transcendent meaning in addition to the surface one. The fish as an early Christian symbol of Christ, the flag as a symbol of national unity, Moby Dick as a symbol of the evil latent in dark sub-human forces, are recognizable examples. The term "symbolism," too, is popularly employed in this more restricted sense; whereas "symbolization," being a word of later and more deliberate invention always carries the broader reference which I have been defining. But while I have thought it more consistent to *define* "symbol" in the broader sense, the symbols which it is my purpose to study are for the most part of the oblique and latent kind which the popular usage connotes. I call them *expressive* or *depth symbols*.

TWO STRATEGIES OF LANGUAGE

Language, in the broadest sense, is any intelligibly related system of symbols; more narrowly it may be regarded as confined to word-symbols. While there are those who speak loosely of the language of music, the language of architecture, or the language of lovers' glances, it is more exact to identify language with verbal language together with those symbolisms which like mathematics have developed out of verbal language by hyper-refinement. For undoubtedly verbal language with its relational syntax offers greater opportunities of richness and energy combined with clarity and exactitude than any other form of symbolic activity. Music may on occasion express more energetically, and to the intuition of a musical creator it may even seem more adequately adaptable to subtleties and shifts of mood. The technical symbolism of mathematical logic, on the other hand, is an instrument of unsurpassed precision within its field of relevance. But what music "says"—what it expresses and communicates—is vague and perhaps for the generality of men slight; while the perfect clarity of mathematics and mathematical logic is of so strictly technical an order that it has no direct bearing upon poetry, politics, religion, love, moral choice, or the poignancy of sheer nonsense. In fields of such major human concern as these the instrument of verbal language, whatever its defects, is indispensable both for thought and for speech.

Semantically considered—i.e., with respect to what it *means*—language may be conceived as having two main complementary uses: to designate clearly as a means to efficient communication, and to express with maximum fullness. Although reconcilable and effectively combinable in some instances, these aims pose a problem in others. When they conflict, which shall be given precedence? Granted that the semantic ideal should be to combine logical precision and richly vigorous expressiveness both to the highest degree, yet the achievement is a hard one, which even the most accomplished writers strive for with but fluctuating success. The question of precedence will be answered differently of course according to the nature and dominant purpose of the occasion. And so far as we set primary importance either upon wide-scale communicability or upon associative depth and fullness, we tend to engage in one or other of the two basic types of semantic strategy: to employ steno-language (the language of plain sense) or to employ depth language (the language, broadly speaking, of poetry). Correspondingly we may distinguish symbols as either steno-symbols or depth symbols, regardless of whether they are connected with a verbal form of language or not.

The distinction between these two modes of language should not be oversimplified as a distinction between the objective and the subjective, nor as a distinction between the precise and the vague. Subjective vs. objective is a relative not an absolute differentiation, and shifts somewhat according to the occasion and the point of view adopted. We reach out toward the objective in one way or another, but our grasp of it is never as firm as we like to think, for our vision is always colored by some degree of subjectivity, whether privately obtruded or publicly agreed on. There are, to be sure, limiting cases. At the one extreme there are symbols which are taken by an individual as goad or prop to his private contemplation. A bereaved lover may keep a lock of his beloved's hair or a batch of her letters as symbols of the happiness that has vanished: they are private symbols, inasmuch as he cannot fully share their meaning for him with anyone else, and probably does not want to. Indeed, they are perhaps on the border of what I have called associative stimuli, differing from them only insofar as elevated to symbolic status by a kind of ritual observance. At the other extreme there are the sharply objective symbols of logic and mathematics. Within the framework of mathematics the meaning of any number is determined solely by its place in the homogeneous numerical series. The most drastic limitations have been imposed before mathematical thought even begins. "2" and "3" have perfectly objective meanings just because of our willingness to abide by these limitations and not inject questions about the special qualities of what is being counted. Apples or atoms or love affairs or days of the week—it does not matter. Two of them plus three of them always make five of them. But between the extremes of subjective soliloquy on the one hand and mathematical objectivity on the other there lie most of the areas of large human concern. Objectivity in matters of religion, of poetry, of moral judgments and personal relationships is something to be constantly striven for rather than securely attained, and is hazardous and tentative at best.

With respect to precision vs. vagueness, too, the question is one of degree—and of price. Effective depth language' strives toward its own kind of precision, but never at the cost of expressive fullness. Macbeth's "Tomorrow and tomorrow and tomorrow" speech contains some vagueness, to be sure—a kind of deliberate *soft focus;* but Shakespeare, after all, is representing his protagonist's state of mind and soul when shaken to their depths, and if he had imposed such logical clarities as Davenant saw fit to substitute a century later,[8] his representation of that state of mind would have been much less precise than as it stands. Similarly, although Beethoven's *Eroica* Symphony offers a musical depth statement about (let's say roughly) heroism and human destiny, any attempt to translate its meaning into words (including of course this one) is bound to be crudely inaccurate. The semantic distance here between tenor and vehicle (the critic's words and the musical meaning) is wide and gross, whereas when the music is performed the vehicle of orchestral sounds and their meaning fuse into an aesthetically and ontologically firm unity. Analogously in a religious context, a worshiper's sacrificial and penitential acts are doubtless a more accurate index of his real belief in God than the most ingenious theological exposition could be. Precision, then, is nothing absolute, for precision of a wrong kind turns out, when examined in context, to be flagrantly imprecise.

No doubt there is a fairly plain respect in which steno-language does have *somewhat more* objectivity and precision than depth language. This is particularly so when the problem of communication is foremost. Language can function communicatively to the extent that it carries the same meaning for more than one individual. Its objectivity in this sense is a question of its public character—of the number of individuals for whom the meaning is substantially the same; its precision, of the verifiable accuracy with which such sameness may be predicated. Two friends may communicate to each other by special words or gestures which no one else understands, a scientist writing for fellow-scientists may employ technical expressions that are meaningless to the layman, and a poet may be content to follow Milton's wish and "fit audience find, though few." Other uses of language have a very wide range of communicative power. Familiar class-words, in particular, like "cat" and "tree" can communicate the same relevant meanings to all who understand the language in which they occur; and there are certain symbols, such as gestures of amity or entreaty, which apparently possess a communicative range as wide, or nearly so, as humanity itself. Often, however, as language becomes wider in its communicative range it becomes correspondingly more stereotyped in the meanings which it so publicly conveys and thus it loses connotative depth; or it may come to do double service, carrying a relatively simple and overt meaning for the many and retaining a fuller set of connotations for some few—a duplicity which all great art practices to some extent. There is a tendency in a self-consciously

democratic age to regard the most publicly shared meaning
of linguistic or other symbols as the "real" meaning, and to
deny therefore any semantic validity to the largely unshar-
able meanings ascribed to them by more sensitive or better instructed minds; but this, as I shall argue in the next
chapter, is an arbitrary and unwarranted limitation of the
meaning of meaning. The more objective procedure is to
recognize that various linguistic usages show interesting differences of *communicative range,* and to investigate such
differences as one major aspect of the general problem.

THREE

The Limits of Plain Sense

When people stammer together that is thinking. GERTRUDE STEIN[1]

THERE IS no more ironic illusion than to suppose that one has escaped from illusions. So subtly do the real and the illusory interpenetrate that their difference is never finally clear. Mind is by nature a meddler, and there are no self-evident criteria by which to discriminate its insights from its commentaries. Still, the quest for certainty persists. The history of philosophy, save for sceptical interludes, is a record of men's shifting intellectual stratagems by which to secure some firm line of demarcation between truth and error.

In the everyday business of living we do indeed establish convenient rules of thumb to indicate, for practical convenience, what can be handled and by what laws it may be expected to operate. Such public operables, actual and potential, constitute our physical world; the study of their regularities of operation is empirical science, and the practical exploitation of those regularities is technology. From time to time, but especially in our day, certain theorists, impressed by the science and technology and wishing a short-cut to first principles, advance this study of public operables as the one valid form of cognition, the sole way of escape from illusionistic muddle, and the system of public operables themselves as the only genuine kind of reality. Such postulation generates the philosophy known variously as materialism, naturalism, and positivism. The last name, positivism, being freest of adventitious connotations, is the one I shall mainly employ: it may be defined precisely as the philosophy which identifies "reality" with the public operables which can be scientifically determined (space-time events and their correlations), and "truth" with the system of empirically verified propositions about such operables and their interrelations, together perhaps with propositions established by deduction from mathematical and logical axioms.

Positivism in the twentieth century goes beyond older forms of materialism: not only because of its recognition of revolutionary new scientific developments, but also—what pertains to the theme of this book—by virtue of having worked out a semantic, which is to say a theory of meaning, of its own. Positivism in this guise may be called *semantic positivism*. Whereas a positivist in general is anyone who identifies reality with the system of public operables that constitutes the physical world, and truth with the system of verifiable propositions describing that reality, a semantic positivist takes the yet more drastic step of identifying *meaning* with such terms and propositions as denote such operables. In other words, the semantic positivist starts off with a judgment about *language*. The only language that really means anything, he declares, is language which refers to things, events, and relations in the physical world. If it does not refer to the physical world, it does not refer to anything (for nothing else exists), and is therefore, strictly speaking, meaningless. By this bold stratagem the positivist gains an enviable advantage: instead of having to argue with dissenters he need only declare that the terms in which they formulate their opposition do not conform to the conditions of meaningfulness which he has set up; in short, he dismisses them as talking nonsense.

As a matter of fact, semantic positivism only puts in plainer and more uncompromising form, with a more explicit statement of its postulates, an attitude which is shared by many so-called hard-headed realists—people who are fond of saying, "It all boils down to this"—and which may be called the Dogma of Plain Sense. Such an attitude represents, on its affirmative side, the excellent intention of promoting intelligibility and avoiding confusion. It proceeds from the principle that we ought to be as clear as possible about the meaning of our utterances, and be able to know when we are speaking sense and when we are just vaporizing. With this general aim every candid thinker will agree. The question is, where the line between sense and vaporizing is to be drawn. Semantic positivists have no difficulty in drawing it. Language may, on the one hand, they declare, assert something in the form of a proposition about what is "actually the case"; on the other it may, in the words of Rudolf Carnap, "express the emotions, fancies, images, or wishes of the speaker, and under proper conditions evoke emotions, wishes, or resolutions in the hearer."[2]

It is instructive in this connection to have another look at the much discussed theory once espoused by I. A. Richards. Since Professor Richards is one of the most alert of contemporary thinkers, it might not seem fair to saddle his present reputation with views which he expressed over twenty-five years ago. His more recent writings have shown a tendency to liberalize and soften the hard semantic postulates which he advocated during the 'twenties. Nevertheless the influence of those early books has persisted, and the point of view which they advocate is still very much alive. Inasmuch as that point of view, consistently developed, destroys the very basis of that poetic vision of the world which alone can give human life its transcendental significance, there is as much pertinence now as there ever was in subjecting it to critical scrutiny.

In *The Meaning of Meaning* (written in collaboration with C. K. Ogden), *Principles of Literary Criticism,* and *Science and Poetry* Richards struck virtually the same note of semantic positivism which receives fuller technical development in writers like Carnap:

> A statement may be used for the sake of the *reference,* true or false, which it causes. This is the *scientific* use of language. But it may also be used for the sake of the effects in emotion and attitude produced by the reference it occasions. This is the *emotive* use. The distinction once clearly grasped is simple. We may either use words for the sake of the reference they promote, or we may use them for the sake of the attitudes and emotions which ensue.[3]

The distinction is simple enough, to be sure; indeed, far too over-simple. What follows from so uncompromising an "either-or"? The consequences for poetry and religion had been stated frankly enough in *The Meaning of Meaning* a few years earlier, where it was argued that as poetry and religion do not employ words scientifically, so neither of them employs words referentially—that is to say, neither of them is capable of speaking *about* anything: the one plain test of whether a given use of words is essentially symbolic and referential or essentially emotive being the question, "Is it true or false in the ordinary strict scientific sense?"

The ontological basis of Richards' semantic position became clarified in his article, "Between Truth and Truth," published in 1931. Two years earlier, in *Practical Criticism,* he had pursued more fully the question of communication in literature. From that standpoint he now reformulated his position. A poem, he now declared, describes and communicates something, but what? "Two alternatives, and not more I think, are before us, two main senses of 'describe' and 'communicate.' . . . The first sense is that in which a form of words describes or communicates the state of mind or experience of the speaker; the second is that in which it describes or communicates some state of affairs or fact which the speaker is thinking of or knowing (something in all but one case, that of introspection, *other than* the experience which is his thinking of it or knowing it). . . . To take an extreme instance, when a man says 'I'm damned!' he may be saying that eternal judgment has gone against him or showing that he is surprised or annoyed."[4]

Richards then turns to John Clare's description of the primrose—

> With its crimp and curdled leaf
> And its little brimming eye,

about which, in a previous article, J. Middleton Murry had remarked that it "is surely an accurate description, but accurate with an accuracy unknown to and unachievable by science." Richards complains: Mr. Murry "does not say explicitly whether he takes it as a description of an object (the primrose) or of the experience of seeing one." And he adds: "It seems to me not likely that there will be widespread disagreement with the view that the description applies to the experience of seeing or imagining a primrose rather than to actual primroses."

But how absurd! Surely any observant flower lover, unless constrained by loyalty to a preconceived theory, will disagree. Neither the lexicographer's definition of the primrose as a "plant or flower of the genus Primula" nor a botanist's or biochemist's analysis of it into scientifically discoverable elements and processes can describe the perceived primrose in its full living actuality as adequately as Clare's lines have done. If we are willing to consider such words as "crimp" and "curdled" in their descriptive function (as Richards has done in formulating his complaint against Murry above), then clearly it is not the *experience of* a primrose that is being described (for it is not my experience that is crimp and curdled!) but *the primrose as experienced.*

The trouble is that Professor Richards had fallen here without realizing it into the trap of metaphysics. The defection is particularly noticeable in a footnote to the article just mentioned, where he distinguishes the "sensed or imagined primrose" from the "inferred or constructed common or gardener's primrose" on the ground that the former lacks such scientifically determinable characteristics as weight! The distinction does not stand up under examination. The very same primrose which I see as crimp and curdled I can also pick up and feel as having a trifling bit of weight. Such visual and such kinaesthetic experiences refer to what I naturally and reasonably regard as constituting a single object. So, too, but less directly, do the experiences of looking at the notches of a scale on which the primrose is being weighed. On the basis of this latter type of experience (mine or another's) the primrose is assigned a numerical figure which we call its "objective weight"—bearing some relation no doubt, but not a strictly determinable one, to the kinaesthetic experience of lightness which I feel when I take the flower in my hand. Now the fallacy of the semantic positivist is to reject the "crimp and curdled" kind of experience, and the kinaesthetic kind of experience ("Why, this flower weighs practically nothing!") for the kind of experience which consists in looking at notches on a scale or some other measuring instrument. For the notch on the scale to which the pointer turns can be securely agreed on by everyone who is not blind; and such agreement is unlikely in the case of the other qualities mentioned.

When I say "reject," of course I do not mean that a semantic positivist wants nothing to do with the more colorful and feelingful qualities of things. He may indeed, as Mr. Richards explicitly does, consider them more "valuable" for the larger human purposes than a knowledge of such abstract properties as length and weight. His rejection is not practical but ontological. He asserts that only *abstract objects,* like the scientist's primrose with its numerical length and weight and its chemical properties, have real existence; whereas concrete objects, like Clare's primrose with its plenitude of warmly experienced qualities, are not really objects at all. He asserts, therefore, that when a poet or anyone else appears to be speaking about such qualities he is not really speaking *about* anything, but is merely ejaculating the history of his mind, "his feelings and attitudes in the moment of speaking, and conditions of their governance in the future." Naturally I do not deny that poetry does and should express in some degree the poet's feelings, nor that it may and should have for a reader the beneficial and equilibrating effects described in Richards' *Principles of Literary Criticism.* These things have their own kind of importance, but from the standpoint of interpreting what the poem *says* they are strictly secondary and sometimes quite irrelevant. Every science has its proper object; and the object of poetic interpretation, rightly conceived, is the poem under consideration, and not either the poet's supposed feelings or the reader's expected benefits. An adequate study of the meaning of poetry, then—what I shall call *the semantics of poetry*—must first establish unhampering postulates and find a suitable language whereby the nature and reference of poetic utterance can be indicated, without evasion into fields of discourse peripheral and sometimes alien to poetry.

The position which Mr. Richards adopted a quarter of a century ago has produced some quaint monsters in subsequent poetical theory. Consider, for example, Bertrand Russell's analysis (arrived at quite independently of Richards, to be sure) of the experience of witnessing a drama:

We experience "Hamlet," not Hamlet [Lord Russell declares]; but our emotions in reading the play have to do with Hamlet, not with "Hamlet." "Hamlet" is a word of six letters; whether it should be or not is a question of little interest, and it certainly could not make its quietus with a bare bodkin. Thus the play "Hamlet" consists entirely of false propositions, which transcend experience, but which are certainly significant, since they can arouse emotions. When I say that our emotions are about Hamlet, not "Hamlet," I must qualify this statement: they are really not about anything, but we think they are about a man named "Hamlet." The propositions in the play are false because there was no such man; they are significant because we know from experience the noise "Hamlet," the meaning of "name" and the meaning of "man." The fundamental falsehood in the play is the proposition: the noise "Hamlet" is a name.[5]

There are only two ways of taking Lord Russell's odd pronouncement, so far as I can see. Either he is saying something significant about the way in which to respond to the play in question; or else he is saying something trivial about the way in which he chooses to delimit the word "experience." On the former interpretation I believe he is plainly wrong; it is neither necessary nor desirable to focus our experience upon a noise and a six-letter word while allowing our emotions to expend themselves upon we know not what. Serious emotional experience is better integrated than that. The feelings we entertain toward Hamlet grow out of the experience we have of him in reading the play or seeing it performed; take away the experience of Hamlet and his sea of troubles and my emotions about him will either vanish or fall into confusion and bathos. A fit response to the play and to the predicament of its main character involves experiencing and feeling as inseparable aspects of one and the same response.

If, on the other hand, Lord Russell is only intending to prescribe how the word "experience" should be employed— i.e., that it should be limited to sensory data such as visible letters and audible noises, and the act of apprehending them, then I would reply that such a linguistic procedure has no backing in the common idiom, nor can it be justified on logical grounds as clarifying the relevant situation. It is both vapid and needlessly confusing. When someone speaks of a play as "a moving experience" no one takes him to refer primarily to the quality of noises which proceed from the actors' larynxes, but to the dramatic action which those noises (aided by gesture, staging, etc.) reveal. Moreover, there is a worse evil than the negative ones of violating common practice and failing to clarify. For to insist that the word "experience" denote only the mechanics of seeing and hearing is to prejudice the issue in advance. Other readers think that in some important sense they experience Hamlet; the semantic positivist rules out that possibility by arbitrary definition. Thus upon either interpretation of Lord Russell's remarks there is the radical vice of critical irrelevance; a kind of self-imposed obtuseness to the poetic and dramatic meaning of the play and the characters in it. The positivist assumptions and vocabulary are as inapplicable to poetry as an axe would be to wood-carving. The result in either case is splinters, not significant shape.

Nor does the problem of poetry stand alone. For the issue which I have been discussing amounts to this: whether there is such a thing as *poetic vision,* or whether the only true vision of things must be ultimately scientific. If you accept the latter alternative—the position of semantic positivism—

then the consequences, provided you carry them out vigorously, will be utterly destructive for religion, for metaphysics, and even for ethics as independent disciplines; and that is to say, for the very mainsprings of significant human living. The truth-claims of these three disciplines necessarily transcend the reach of scientific methods of validation; therefore (so the positivist's argument runs) they cannot be validated at all, and so have a merely subjective status. Metaphysics is either preëmpted as an organon of the sciences— a critical instrument by which the methods of the individual sciences may be brought into greater unity with one another—or else is dismissed as presumptuous vaporizing and word-play. Religion and ethics are explained away as mere projections of personal or group emotions; and, when they seem to give any real insight into the nature of reality, they are denounced as shams.

Now ethics is important for everybody; for while there are individuals who think they are able to do without religion, metaphysics, and poetry (I am not now discussing whether they are self-deceived), it is obvious that human life cannot be lived in anything like a human way without some implicit acknowledgment of moral principles. The alternative, as Hobbes has memorably said, is a life "nasty, brutish, and short." Yet as we ponder the assumptions of positivism we are forced to the realization that on the basis which they set up there are no real moral issues. At least one eminent positivist, Alfred Ayer, faces the consequence frankly, and accepts it. An apparent moral statement, such as "You acted wrongly in stealing that money," is really, he maintains, nothing more than the simple factual statement, "You stole that money." The first sentence does not *mean* anything different from the second; it merely "evinces" the speaker's emotional disapproval—as if one had said "You stole that money" in a peculiar tone of horror.[6]

So extreme a form of positivism as Ayer's is not hard to refute. Two weaknesses are quickly apparent. We might first appeal to the testimony of reflective experience that moral issues do exist. We might argue that deliberations, disputes, and decisions about right and wrong, good and evil, are at least as real a part of human life as any of the sensory and the scientifically determined data on which Ayer bases his position. We might conclude that a philosophy which writes off the evidence of mankind's experience in such a high-handed manner is grossly over-simplified and rather foolishly naïve. But we can also attack Ayer's argument on its home territory. If the ethical element in the sentence, "You did wrong in stealing that money"—i.e., the element which differentiates it from the factual statement, "You stole that money"—were *nothing more than* an expression of horror, it would follow that our judgment of the immorality of the act must increase and diminish in exact ratio to the changes in the feeling-tone of horror. This, however, is obviously not what actually happens. Horror or no horror, we can still raise and consider the moral issue. We can ask, "Is our horror or repugnance in this case *morally justified?*" Ayer would have to take this to mean, "How much horror do I feel at myself for feeling horror?"—which is plainly not what we mean when asking whether the original horror is justified. Ayer's theory of meaning is too black-and-white an affair to be capable of handling the moral dimension of human experience.

A more intricate theory than Ayer's, which leads however to substantially the same conclusion, is that of Charles W. Morris. In his much discussed essay "Science, Art and Technology"[7] Professor Morris has gone so far as to classify ethics under the head of technology: as a "technology of technologies, consisting of those techniques which a community has available for the satisfaction of its interests." While it is possible indeed for the community to be wrong in its beliefs as to which techniques best perform the desired function, Morris contends that the question is still technological in essence, since the end—what the community takes to be its ultimate interests—is "undisputed" (alas, if it only were!), and that the only ethical questions therefore have to do with the means that will most effectively attain it. The moral element in thinking, then, Morris conceives as hyper-technological, or "simply the development" of the everyday language-function of *controlling behavior;* an affair solely of techniques, of means. The reëxamination and revaluation of ends, the redemptive quest which many would regard as the very core of adult morality, he is compelled by the framework of his theory to reduce to "art."

Now I agree that the crucial part of any moral valuation is hyper-technological, and that it has a good deal in common with art. But that is because I regard religion, morality, and art at their best as sharing something of that poetic vision of life with which the present book is most radically concerned. Consequently, when Professor Morris defines art as "the language for the communication of values" and adds that its method of communicating them is iconic—i.e., by concrete embodiment rather than by abstract reference—I am more in agreement with the second statement than with the first. I grant that whatever it is that art communicates, its essential method of communication is by concrete embodiment, not abstract reference. When art functions as a language—by designating and communicating—it does so iconically: which is to say, it designates by resembling, embodying, or participating in the ideas designated. But to characterize the ideas so designated and embodied by art as "values" seems to me misleading for two reasons.

In the first place, even if art does communicate values iconically, it cannot be *defined* by that characteristic. For there are other linguistic media than those we normally identify as "the arts," which can also communicate iconically and participatively. The story of Damien among the lepers, or of Gandhi's use of non-resistance as a political weapon, or of Schweitzer's self-dedication in equatorial Africa, may communicate iconically with a power and a specificity that ethical verbalizing could never effect; yet such actions are not, in any usual sense of the term, art. Religious worship, except where it becomes perfunctory and automatic, communicates values among the participants and possibly in a transcendental direction as well, and, as distinguished from theology, it does so iconically: here too it could be said that the values represented—reverence, self-deflation, and self-redirection, adulterated no doubt with a bit of illusionistic self-complacence (the rose windows and organ tones that poison the silences)—are embodied in the worship-service itself. The worship-service is thus an iconic symbol (Morris would prefer to say "iconic sign," reserving "symbol" for scientific use) and is communicative of values, yet it is not, in any usual sense, a work of art. It thus appears that to define art as the language by which values are communicated iconically is too loose and inexact a piece of categorizing.

My second and more important objection to Morris' view of art is that it involves, in effect, the same sharp dualism between referential and non-referential language as vitiates the thought of semantic positivists generally. This consequence of his view is somewhat plainer in his book, *Signs, Language and Behavior*,[8] than in the essay I have just been discussing. In the book he follows Charles Peirce in giving the overall name of *semiotics* to the general science of signs— "whether the signs be those of animals or men, . . . whether they are signs in science or signs in art, technology, religion, or philosophy"; and he subdivides this general science into three sub-sciences: *pragmatics* (study of the origin, use, and effects of signs), *semantics* (study of significations), and *syntactics* (study of the mutual relations of signs). Since Professor Morris believes that what art "designates" is only values, and since he further believes that the meaning of a value must be interpreted behaviorally, his avowed aim is "to push semiotic as rapidly as possible in the direction of a natural science," and therefore to describe all the principal classes of signs "in terms descriptive of behavioral processes"; hoping thereby to point a way to overcoming the cleavage between science and the humanities.

Now it is a fine thing to seek ways of overcoming, or at least of mitigating, the opposition between science and the humanities; but at whose expense? The naturalistic and behavioristic way of overcoming opposition is totalitarian: peace by assimilation. Pragmatics is made a *Gauleiter* over semantics and syntactics. The distinctive characteristics of symbolism as employed in humanistic studies become blurred, because the only symbolic differences taken seriously are those which evince some behavioral effect that can be verified (in principle) scientifically. The result is that although Mr. Morris has spread his naturalist's net wide, which is to say, that his naturalistic categories are dexterously chosen and ingeniously applied, his often keen insights about the nature of art in its significative aspect are not developed into that full analysis of artistic signification which might have been his major contribution to contemporary aesthetics.

Take an instance. He tells of having asked a number of persons what kind of situation Stravinsky's *Rite of Spring* appeared to them to signify. He reports: "The answers are various: a herd of wild elephants in panic, a Dionysian orgy, mountains being formed by geologic processes, dinosaurs in conflict. But there is no suggestion that it might denote a quiet brook, or lovers in the moonlight, or the self's tranquillity. 'Primitive forces in elemental conflict'—such is the

approximate signification of the music, and such conflict is
presented iconically in the music itself." This is a thoroughly
pertinent point to make and is well stated so far as it goes.
But nothing is concluded from it other than the quite general and already announced principle that art is a "language"
which "builds its material into iconic signs and these into a
single compound icon." One could wish that the relation between the component icons and the total compound icon—
between component and total statement—as well as the relation between what is agreed on and what is disputed as
to the signification of any work of art—illumined center vs.
shadowy penumbra—had been further explored. Indeed, it
is perhaps a commentary on the relevance of Mr. Morris's
semiotic analysis of art that there are so few concrete instances of art mentioned in his book, and that of those few
the significative interpretation is not developed.

Poetry, because its medium is verbal language, is a better test than music of the adequacy of a positivistic type of
analysis. Mr. Morris is particularly unsatisfying here; for in
order to uphold his doctrine that poetry is "an example of
discourse which is appraisive-valuative" and that "its primary aim is to cause the interpreter to accord to what is
signified the preferential place in his behavior signified by
the appraisors," he quotes five lines from Walt Whitman's
A Song of Myself, beginning "I believe in the flesh and the
appetites"—the only poetic quotation in the entire book! Obviously the example has not been chosen impartially, but as
a passage well fitted to bear out Morris's own behavioristic-
valuational theory of poetry. Whitman's uninhibited narcis-
sism in the last three lines which Morris quotes—

> Divine am I inside and out, and I make holy whatever I
>   touch or am touched from.
> The scent of these arm-pits aroma finer than prayer.
> This head more than churches, bibles, and all the creeds.

—does, on the surface, invite a behavioristic-valuational interpretation and very little else; but is the signification of all poetry equally limited? Even *A Song of Myself* turns out to mean a great deal more when its entire imagistic pattern and referential thrust are considered, than when a single passage is judged out of context.

My objection to the theory which I have been examining under the general name of "semantic positivism" may now be summed up. It requires, in effect, that the truth of a poem, or of a religious belief, or of a philosophical insight—of anything, in short, which is not a scientific statement of verifiable fact—be judged ultimately by its emotive and conative affects. Hence it may be aptly spoken of as the Affective Theory of poetic, religious, and philosophical truth. From its standpoint the existence of poetry can be justified only on one or other of two grounds: either on the hedonistic ground that it gives pleasure to those who like it, or on the clinical ground defended by the earlier Richards and implicit in Morris that it tends to promote a healthier equilibrium of attitudes in the reader and therefore possibly in the society wherein he moves. Even religion can be given no firmer justification than one or the other of these, if the Affective Theory is true. There are, however, two grave flaws in that theory, one in the flower and one in the root. Experientially, the theory does not do justice to the full nature of either poetic or religious experience; and logically, it rests upon an arbitrary (and I believe false) presupposition.

On the first count let it be considered that neither the pleasurable nor the therapeutic effects of poetry or religion are fortuitous. While those of poetry may partly proceed from the direct propulsions of rhythm and imagery upon the physio-psychic organism, they most characteristically involve something more. A poem affects a mature reader as it does partly because it seems to him, notwithstanding its

fantasies and pseudo-statements, to be offering a kind of genuine insight and thereby to be revealing, however obscurely
and elusively, a kind of truth. In *King Lear,* for example, the
language and imagery and character developments and story
are inseparable aspects of the total poem and legitimate factors in its appeal. But *King Lear's* principal claim to greatness transcends these components: it is great because in and
through such poetic devices it reveals depth-meaning—it adumbrates truths and quasi-truths of high importance about
such matters as human nature, old age, false seeming, and
self-confrontation through suffering. The depth-meaning of
Lear—the "poetic truth" to be discovered in the play—is what
mainly accounts for and justifies the Fit Reader's full response, an inseparable blending of emotive and intellectual.
If the depth-meaning is not at least dimly and subconsciously adumbrated—and perhaps too sharp a focus of it is generally undesirable—the reader's response will hardly be the
same. Impoverishment or distortion of the intellectual response will involve some impoverishment or distortion of the
emotive. To regard the specifically poetic response as purely
emotive, then, is a naïve way of psychologizing.

The shallowness of the positivistic interpretation of religion is even more evident. For in religion the depth-meaning is *all* that matters. If you ignore the depth-meanings of
Sophocles or Dante or Shakespeare, something of the nature
of poetry still remains in them; and those whose response is
limited to story, imagery, and versification may still be responding in a way proper to poetry, though but limitedly
so. But if you ignore the depth-meanings of religion, what
you have left is not religion at all, but sabbatical play-acting.
Prayer and worship can be justified as psychic therapy only
if the postulant and worshiper believes that his utterance is
somehow heard and somehow responded to. Now it is possible of course—I mean it is *logically* possible—that the reli-

gious believer is mistaken, and that his conviction of entering into a responsive relationship with a Power or Powers transcending the human condition is illusory. Whether transcendental existence and men's intercommunication with it are real or illusory is, as Pascal demonstrated, the most important question of all; and it cannot be settled by ruling out all answers but one as "meaningless." An adequate semantic organon should make it possible to formulate *both* theses— the religious and the anti-religious—intelligibly. A semantic theory which denies meaning to any and all specifically religious affirmations thereby prevents us from inquiring and discussing whether particular religious affirmations are true or false. Its denial of their meaning is a disguised way of rejecting their truth-claims *a priori*, and thus of prejudging the question of religious truth wholesale.

The other and more analytic objection to the Affective Theory concerns the presumed dichotomy on which it rests. Two types or modes or uses of discourse are sharply distinguished: typically called the referential and the emotive. Referential statements, as the previous exposition has shown, are postulated or defined to be true insofar as they correspond with, and truly describe, what is actually the case, false insofar as they do the contrary; and it is further postulated that in all instances of a referential statement it is possible to specify the empirical conditions under which it could be verified or disproved. Emotive discourse, on the other hand, is taken as expressing some emotive-conative state of the writer (or speaker) or as aiming to arouse such a state in the reader (or hearer), and therefore as not being intrinsically referential. The unguarded inference from "intrinsically emotive" to "not intrinsically referential" reveals the main logical presupposition of the Affective Theory: that language which is intrinsically the one cannot be intrinsically the other; that the terms "referential" and "emotive" (or their synonyms) constitute a natural dichotomy. This is a presupposition which must now be challenged.

For clarity it should be noted that ordinary "mixed discourse," which semanticists of all schools admit as a familiar possibility, is not what I am speaking about. A cry of "Fire!" for instance simultaneously conveys information—i.e., refers to an actual state of affairs—and expresses and communicates an emotive attitude. But the relation here between the two functions is extrinsic. The test of its extrinsicality is a simple one: the referential meaning can be explicated in propositional non-emotive form without loss. "A fire has broken out in this building," perhaps with some such corollary as "There is danger" or "There is need of immediate action"—this conveys virtually the same information as the original outcry, and indeed conveys it more exactly. In the case of poetic, and more generally of expressive discourse, on the contrary, such prosaical restatement is not possible without essential loss. My thesis is that truly expressive symbolism—in a poem, for example—means, refers, awakens insight, *in and through* the emotions which it engenders, and that so far as the emotion is not aroused the full insight is correspondingly not awakened. Granted that irrelevant emotions may be aroused, still the problem of learning to know and understand a poem is largely also the problem of distinguishing the relevant from the irrelevant—of distinguishing, that is to say, the responses aroused by the whole poem's intrinsic emotivity from the incidental responses aroused by isolated parts and fortuitous associations. In religious insight, too, (as distinguished from blind acceptance on the one hand and from theological ratiocination on the other) emotion may play a legitimate role. But it is of utmost importance to distinguish the quality of emotion which reveals some aspect of the Divine from the quality of emotion which obscures and confuses; the clarifying act of self-transcending reverence from the muck and muddle of self-deluding religiosity. In short, I am asserting that poetic and religious emotions, when they are depth-oriented, may have or come to have distinctively ontological bearings of their own. Whether one agrees or disagrees with this thesis, it is not a new or trifling one, and it ought not to be ruled out by the apriori maneuver of setting up a dichotomy that leaves no room for it.[9]

Let us therefore reopen the logical possibilities of the situation by conceiving "referential" and "emotive" not as contraries but as independent variables. The negative of *referential* is not emotive but *non-referential;* the negative of *emotive* is not referential but *non-emotive.* This logical truism enables us to construct a two-dimensional graph in which the vertical axis has "referential" (R) and "non-referential" (non-R) as its poles, the horizontal axis "emotive" (E) and "non-emotive" (non-E).

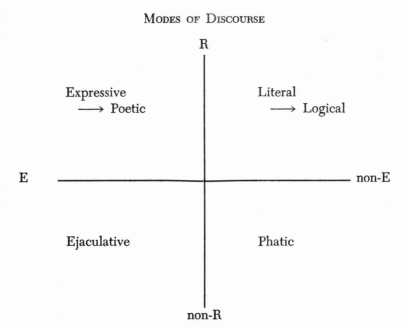

Modes of Discourse

Four areas are thus established, representing four modes of discourse:

R, non-E: *Literal discourse:* ordinary everyday language in its referential mode. *Logical discourse* is its ideally perfected form.

Non-R, non-E: *Phatic discourse:* "Good morning," etc.

Non-R, E: *Ejaculative discourse:* "Damn!" etc.—where, as distinguished from phatic discourse, something is really felt. For clarity's sake we must avoid the practice of some semanticists, of applying the word "expressive" in this connection.

R, E: *Expressive discourse:* language which is referential and emotive at once—not by incidental conjunction as in the cry of "Fire!" but in the more organic sense that the referential function, the proper meaning, takes at least some of its essential character from the emotivity of the language, and changes therefore as the emotivity changes. *Poetic discourse* is a species of expressive discourse, in which the main part of the meaning is controlled by the poet's art rather than by social custom and fortuitous association.

What I am proposing, in short, is a sort of Copernican Revolution in semantics. Or perhaps non-Euclidean, or trans-Euclidean, would offer an apter analogy. For whereas Euclidean geometry was once regarded as the be-all and end-all of geometrical truth, modern mathematicians are able to regard a world in which the postulate of parallels holds true, as merely a *limiting case* (perhaps also an actual one) in the universe of possibilities. Analogously, we may regard the semantic positivists as residing too doggedly in a Euclidean-like world. The aim, the instrument, and the presuppositions of logical discourse, as developed by the formal and experimental sciences, they accept without serious question. And my belief is that they are wrong, dead wrong—not of course in the contributions they have made to logical clarity in fields where it suitably belongs, but in their refusal to admit the possibility of other kinds of semantic objectivity—the possibility of meanings other than those which logical language can formulate. Such metalogical meanings are of dominant importance in religion, in poetry and expressive prose literature, in all the arts that "say" anything, and in moral wisdom as distinguished from moral rules; they are present helter-skelter in the vagaries of daily experience; and they even, I suspect, play a bigger role than is usually admitted in science, particularly when it comes to the discovery of fresh hypotheses. Accordingly, what any adequate theory of semantics should include, and what has not yet been systematically attempted so far as I am aware, is an exposition of the basic principles of metalogical signification. One such exposition, so far as the nebulous nature of the material allows, is the purport of the next chapter.

FOUR

The Logical and the Translogical

LET ME try to set down what I take to be the main assumptions which underlie the logician's view, and in general the scientist's view, of what language at its best should be. Of course no man is purely logical all day long, and even a logician will find many human occasions when it is wise to depart from professional usage. But the danger is that he tends to take the properties and laws of logical language as his standard, his point of departure for interpreting and evaluating language in general; and when he does this his view of the humanistic employments of language—in literature, art, religion, and expressive discourse generally—may become gravely distorted.

The method I am employing in this chapter is dialectical, in the sense practiced by Socrates in the earlier Platonic Dialogues and tersely formulated in the Scholastic formula, *Omnis determinatio est negatio.* That is to say, all definition involves exclusion; in determining exactly what a thing is, we thereby implicitly determine what it is not. To define a concept is to declare by one and the same act what it does mean and what it does not mean. Likewise when we define a belief, we therein define by implication what that belief opposes, and hence what contrary belief could be held about the matter without self-contradiction. This last point is of greatest importance for the understanding of dialectical method as employed in this chapter, and more generally for spiking the claims of any dogma that parades itself as the only possible way of looking at a matter. For with respect to any belief that one holds there must be the logical possibility of holding some opposite belief; if not, then one's belief is a mere tautology, which is to say no real belief at all but only a verbal imposture. To believe in God is to recognize the logical possibility of atheism; indeed, to believe in God with any intellectual and moral vitality is to recognize that the position of atheism has grounds, that it offers a challenge, that it is a redoubtable antagonist to the belief which one has elected to hold. Again, in order to believe intelligently in the law of universal physical causation one must be able to understand what a reasonable opponent or doubter of this belief can mean by his heresy. Analogously, then, if we set down the basic assumptions of logical discourse and clearly understand what they affirm, we can thereby discover what they deny and hence what counter-assumptions, non-logical or rather trans-logical in character, it is possible to postulate as a basis for expressive discourse.

The main assumptions of logical discourse have been traditionally given as four: the Law of Identity ("A is A"), the Law of Contradiction, or more accurately of Non-Contradiction ("A is not at once B and non-B"), the Law of Excluded Middle ("A is either B or not B"), and the Law of Sufficient Reason ("Whatever is true must have a sufficient reason why it is true"). These traditional laws of logic need interpretation, however, if they are to disclose anything about the nature of logical language. To say without qualification "A is A" is to utter a tautology and therefore to say nothing really at all. The Law of Identity in its traditional form silences dissent by its sheer nothingness; it cannot be significantly denied, only because it cannot be significantly affirmed. On the other hand, if we interpret it as saying that a logical term, A, should have a clearly defined meaning and should keep that meaning unchanged throughout a given investigation or discourse, then the Law does say something: it sets up a procedure to be followed, hence indicates by implication that there are contrary procedures to be avoided; and so it now becomes possible, from the new form of the Law, as it was not from the old, to deduce certain apriori characteristics of non-logical, non-literal language.

Now there is a most essential difference between the postulates which steno-language requires, and postulates of non-logical or trans-logical language which are dialectically derived from them. The postulates of logic say "must," the postulates of expressivity say "may." This is evident both analytically and experientially. Logic has to operate by fixed laws from which it cannot depart without losing its logical character. Its laws, therefore, involve a "must," or, obversely, a "cannot." It declares, "If you wish to be logical you *must* avoid contradiction"; which is to say, "You *cannot* contradict yourself and still remain logical." Now what is involved in challenging the absolute validity of the Law of Non-Contradiction? Surely not that one must contradict himself at every turn; but that there *may* be elements of radical paradox in expressive discourse, which cannot be reduced to perfect logical consistency without distorting the meaning which they connote. "Must" and "cannot" belong to the world of *Anangkê,* of iron necessity. Their real antitheses, belonging to the world of freedom, are "need not" and "may." In short, the two uses of language are not on a par. Steno-language represents a set of limiting cases, so to speak, in a universe of infinite semantic possibilities.

Of course we should not rest content with the bare apriori possibilities of the case. Language does not automatically become expressive just because it is non-logical. We are in-

terested in non-logical possibilities only because they leave
room for the operation of language that is genuinely expressive. Dialectic can vindicate such language; only the awakened sensibility can create it. Accordingly three steps, not
two, are called for. It will be necessary, first, to reëxamine
the main assumptions of steno-language without blind ad-
herence to the way in which they have been traditionally
formulated and understood. There are eight such assumptions which strike me as the most essential, and in any case
the ones most relevant to our purpose. Following that, I shall
proceed to deduce, by strict dialectic, the eight counter-
postulates which are *logically allowed for* by our refusal to
accept the laws of steno-discourse as absolutely binding. The
third step is a passage from the abstract possibility to the
concrete instance. Our eight counter-postulates must be *experientially confirmed* by the way in which depth language
is found to actually function; and thus the third and most
decisive step consists not in argument but in choice of illustrations.

ASSUMPTIONS OF LITERAL LANGUAGE

1. *Assumption of semantic discreteness:* that a linguistic
symbol is always distinct, or at least distinguishable, from
its referend. Symbol and referend are, so to speak, non-inter-
changeable. There is nothing of twoness about the figure
"2". And although mathematicians do find it useful to employ iconic symbols in geometry—e.g., a blackboard triangle,
which at once means the concept "triangle" and is a particular instance of that universal meaning—yet the character of
a geometrical drawing, being governed by considerations of
propaedeutic convenience, does not affect the nature of the
geometrical entities it refers to. Steno-symbols therefore are
dispensable; their usage is by stipulation. Any of Euclid's
theorems is as true, though perhaps not so readily appre-

hended, when expressed in words or in algebraic equations as when represented by a diagram. Similarly in the more general uses of literal language, every literal meaning is assumed to be translatable without essential loss into another language. Dr. C. K. Ogden, the founder of Basic English, once remarked that he conceived it possible to construct an ideally perfect Basic English into which all authentic meanings could be translated; and that whatever apparent meanings should get unavoidably lost in the translation would thereby reveal themselves to be not real *meanings* at all, but merely embellishments.[1]

2. *Assumption of univocation:* that on a given occasion of its use a symbol has one meaning only; or else a plurality of meanings so distinguishable that they can be stated separately and represented by distinct symbols without semantic loss. Overtones of meaning, secondary implications, innuendo, irony, humorous or tragic suggestiveness and such, are treated as materials for explicit restatement in univocal language.

3. *Assumption of definiteness:* that on a given occasion of its use a symbol has a definite and ideally definable meaning. Vagueness is always a fault, a lapse from the logical ideal. The limiting nature of this requirement becomes evident to anyone capable of honest introspection. For none of us is perfectly clear about every aspect of a matter; and he who says, "I understand perfectly," is either deluding himself or parroting a phrase or (what is often a practical necessity) limiting his attention to certain skeletal and formal properties. Steno-language always presumes such limitation and builds upon it.

4. *Assumption of semantic invariance:* that a given sign must keep the same meaning throughout the course of a given argument or a given science. Hobbes speaks as an honorable logician in declaring that "in all discourses where-

in one man pretends to instruct or convince another, he should use the same word constantly in the same sense. If this were done (which nobody can refuse without great disingenuity), many of the books extant might be spared."[2] The requirement is essential where the aim of the discourse is "to instruct or convince."

5. *Assumption of bidimensional significance:* that the referend of any sign is characterized by either of two kinds of integration, possibly in combination: logical universality, established by definition, and existential particularity, established by space-time continuities. These two familiar types of meaning are what Santayana has called concretions in discourse and concretions in existence;[3] the one is expressed through common names ("horse," "green," "above"), the other through proper names or particularized common names ("this horse," "the position in which I am now sitting").

The five preceding assumptions pertain to the *term*, which some logicians have called (long before 1945) the "atomic" constituent of literal language. The next two assumptions have to do with the *proposition*, the "molecular" constituent.

6. *Assumption of truth-value equivalence:* that any true proposition is equally true with any other true proposition, and hence (from Postulate 7) that any false proposition is equally false with any other. Judgments of probability, far from violating, rather confirm this law: for a probability is a degree of approximation to truth, and there could be degrees of approximation only if the truth approximated were regarded as ideally determinate. When we judge, for instance, that the proposition "Man has evolved from lower animal species" is *more probably* true than the proposition "Mars is inhabited by rational beings," we mean that the evidence for the truth of the first proposition is more adequate than the evidence for the truth of the second; we do *not* mean that the first proposition if actually true is any truer than

the second proposition if actually true. The propositions differ not in degree of truth but in the degree to which the available evidence suffices to establish a valid judgment of truth.

Definition and corollary. A *statement* may be defined as any unit of language such that the predicates "true" and "false" may be asserted of it without complete absence of meaning; and a *proposition* as the type of statement used in literal language—i.e., consisting in an assertible relation between *terms,* as defined above. From these definitions taken in conjunction with Assumption 7 we may derive the theorem (traditionally called the Law of Excluded Middle) that every unitary proposition, when adequately stated, is either entirely true or entirely false, and the theorem (traditionally called the Law of Contradiction) that no such proposition can be both true and false.

7. *Assumption of contradictories:* that for every proposition (p) there is another proposition (non-p) such that the truth of either implies the falsity of the other and the falsity of either implies the truth of the other. The assumption as here formulated contains the germs both of the Law of Contradiction and of the Law of Excluded Middle. The present formulation lays bare the postulational character of these "laws," which in their usual formulation appear axiomatic and tautological. It also distinguishes between their sense as indicated in the corollary to Assumption 6 (as limiting the truth-values of any single proposition) and their sense as indicated in Assumption 7 (as involving the interrelation of two assertible contradictory propositions).

8. *Assumption of ideal explicability:* that every true proposition has an intelligible and assignable place in a system of true propositions, to at least some of which it is related by strict implication. The so-called Law of Sufficient Reason in its strictly formal (non-cosmological) interpretation is iden-

tical with this postulate, which refers beyond the atomic and molecular levels of semantic complexity (terms and propositions respectively) to what may be called the organic level (relations among propositions).

The eight foregoing assumptions are operative in all logical discourse, and therefore in all literal discourse so far as it is free from logical imperfection. But that they are implicitly postulational, not axiomatic, is proved by the fact that it is possible to question, doubt, or deny each one of them in turn without necessarily talking nonsense. The method of dialectic can go only so far: having formulated the hidden postulates on which semantic positivism rests, and having discerned them to be non-tautologous, it can formulate their logical antitheses and assign them a postulational role of their own.

Pure dialectic suffers, therefore, from the disability that the postulates which it thus establishes by logical negation are (i) still hypothetical, since they are in no way declared to be more than bare possibilities, and (ii) so broadly and abstractly negative as to be unoriented with respect to any realm of experience to which they might apply. Although it can demonstrate the apriori possibility of other types of language than the type defined by the eight postulates of logical discourse, it offers no experiential clue to their positive nature. Formal dialectic must therefore be supplemented by *ontological intuition:* whereby the opposing principles are drawn not merely out of the thin air of logical possibility but out of actual semantic procedures with respect to certain realms or qualities or aspects or functions of experience. By this double method we are enabled to posit provisionally the following eight principles of expressive discourse as at once dialectically opposed to the eight postulates of literal language and as experientially derived from actual semantic operations. So far as their derivation is experiential—and this

must be judged by the character of the concrete illustrations
—they are not merely postulates but *principles;* and it is by
this name therefore, although not forgetting their postula-
tive character, that I shall designate them.

PRINCIPLES OF EXPRESSIVE LANGUAGE

1. *Principle of iconic signification:* that there are symbols
which, although they may point beyond themselves, have a
largely self-intentive reference as well.

Non-symbolic signs may also have something of this double character; in fact, they normally do so except where the
situation has become exclusively practical. Each thing in nature that stirs us deeply seems at once valuable in itself and
a kind of gateway or threshold to an unexplored Something
More. A fetish or a totemic animal probably has such a
character when it first strikes a wondering savage as important. It is charged with otherness—not only an otherness with
respect to the savage himself, which makes the object inherently fascinating, but a potentiality of otherness that indefinitely exceeds the mind's objective grasp, and suggests
infinite unnamed possibilities. Thus the blue stone or the
totemic brown bear becomes a thing of mystery, acquires a
numinous quality, and the tribesman confronts it with an
ambivalent attitude of confidence and dread. The confidence
is helped by sacraments, but the dread remains to keep the
total experience ambivalent and vibrantly alive. Later, as
the dread is drained away, familiarity and fancy transform
the original mythic intuitions into mythologies, and ambition
degrades the sacraments into magic.

Fortunately the development is not exclusively desiccat-
ing. The symbols which develop are, in every healthy culture, still partly iconic—i.e., they mean by resembling—and
this shows itself in the love for the medium. Not only what
is said but the way of saying it counts; not only the god who

is supplicated but the ritual of supplication itself. This is the aesthetic element in experience and in communication, the valuing of a thing for its own sake, without which as a terminus no utilitarian values would have any eventual justification. At its ultimate stage it becomes mysticism—where not only symbol and referend, but also knower and known, merge into one self-intentive whole. Aesthetic contemplation, however, is and should be but a halfway house to mysticism, keeping the self-identification and the discrimination in fairly even balance. An aesthetic icon thus bears the double characteristic of being more than ordinarily itself and yet the adumbration of a something further that is unspoken. The double aspect produces a tension which, at its best, is a harmony in diversity and the very life of the aesthetic situation.

Unlike logical symbols, therefore, it is impossible to substitute one expressive symbol for another without destroying or radically transfiguring the texture of meaning. Expressive meanings, in short, are not stipulative; they are given not by definition but mainly by contextualization.

2. *Principle of plurisignation:* that an expressive symbol tends, on any given occasion of its realization, to carry more than one legitimate reference, in such a way that its proper meaning is a tension between two or more directions of semantic stress. When we say that poetry uses charged language, we mean that the poetic symbol tends characteristically to be plurisignative in this sense: that its intended meanings are likely to be more or less multiple, yet so fused as sometimes to defy any attempted analysis into monosignative components, and always to produce an integral meaning that radically transcends the sum of the ingredient meanings. In these last respects plurisignation differs from simple punning. A brief example is Faustus' agonized cry: "See, see where Christ's *blood* streams in the firmament!"[4] Re-

ligion—as distinguished from theology on the one hand and superstition on the other—regards plurisignation as not merely a human technique but as the inevitable articulation of divinity, which can speak to men only through "signatures" that combine sacred with secular modes of significance.

3. *Principle of soft focus:* that there are meanings which do not have definite outlines and cannot be adequately represented by terms that are strictly defined. Strict definition is possible only to those who agree upon a semantic convention, which involves the systematic omission of whatever meanings or elements of meaning cannot be commonly shared. Such a common nucleus of meaning establishes a denotation to which a given steno-symbol (verbal or other) may refer. But over and above its denotation every symbol bears a connotative fringe, which is not likely to be altogether the same for everybody. With some words and in some contexts (e.g., the word "square" in geometry) the connotative increment is unimportant and may easily be dismissed as irrelevant to the science in question. Thus if during a mathematical demonstration a blackboard square strikes one of us as ugly and another of us as a well-balanced arrangement of lines, this obviously has no bearing upon the problem of discovering the square's geometrical properties. To the ancient Pythagoreans, on the other hand, the harmonious character of the square was an intrinsic part of its nature, and hence an intrinsic part of what was meant by the figure (an iconic, participating symbol) and by the word designating it (a conventional, potentially stipulative symbol). Now even though all members of the Pythagorean cult may have agreed that the square was a harmonious and noble figure, it is hardly likely that they all thought of these aesthetic and moral properties in exactly the same way. Exactitude in such matters cannot be verified, for exact designation is not possible to anything like the same degree as with the

geometrical properties. The Pythagoreans used the verbal and iconic symbols for "square" in a plurisignative manner: the geometrical meaning was a sharply focused semantic nucleus, while the metaphysical meaning was a softly focused semantic fringe.

The recognition of soft focus as a genuinely semantic characteristic of certain situations throws light upon the problem of obscurity in poetry. Ignoring such instances of obscurity as proceed from either incompetence or snobbishness, we can accept certain poetic utterances as obscure for either or both of two valid reasons: (1) because the subject matter itself is too subtle and elusive to allow of exact delineation— as in the portrayal of mature human emotions; or (2) because the poet can produce his effect more fully by producing an ambivalent impression upon the reader's mind. In great as distinguished from transient poetry the ambivalence is justified because it corresponds to a real ambivalence in the nature of things; and thus the second valid reason for ambivalence tends to reduce to the first.

Poetry and expressive language in general have, to be sure, their own kind of precision, but it is essentially different from the precision of literal language. We cannot ask whether one type of language is *more* precise than the other; we can only try to understand and accept their differences. The precision of expressive language is paradoxical, for sometimes it can represent its object most precisely by a sort of controlled vagueness. There have been endless disputes about the character of Hamlet, or, in semantic terms, about what the poetic and dramatic indications of Hamlet's *dramatis persona* "really mean." There are virtually no such disputes about Polonius. Would Shakespeare have represented Hamlet more precisely by giving as definite indications as he does of Polonius? Obviously not, for the very nature of Hamlet as a "character" or *dramatis persona* is ambivalent—an aura of highly significant obscurity around a bright, focused center—and one cannot say of him, as of Polonius, "This, just this and not something else, is what Shakespeare meant."

4. *Principle of contextualism:* that an expressive symbol is a controlled semantic variable, the full meaning of which, although identical throughout all instances *on some level of analysis,* tends to shift about within moderate limits. The reason for this limited non-identity is found partly in the iconic, partly in the plurisignative nature of the expressive symbol. On the one hand, life itself is in continual flux, and the expressive symbol, being iconic, will tend somewhat to reflect that never-ceasing flow in itself. On the other hand, since the plurisign, unlike the monosignative terms of logical discourse, cannot be semantically controlled by explicit definition, its fused multiple meaning must be determined afresh on each occasion—in part by a relatively persistent core of meaning which unites or relates the various semantic occasions together, in part by the entire relevant context which the particular occasion gathers up and generates. In poetry the relevant context of a symbol is controlled to a large degree by the poet's individual manipulation of his medium; in religion it appears to depend more upon the elusive factors of social and individual sensibility to the signature of divinity in the experienced world.

5. *Principle of paralogical dimensionality:* that there are other dimensions or nodi of meaning than those of logical universality and existential particularity, which latter constitute the coördinates of logical discourse. A nodus of meaning is designated a universal when its specificable references are related by virtue of some *publicly verifiable similarity,* of whatever degree of abstraction; it is designated a particular when its specifiable references are related by virtue of some *publicly verifiable space-time contiguity and continuity.* If we examine these two kinds of connection semantically, as nodi

of meaning, we discover that they do not exhaust the possibilities of semantic grouping. They constitute two pragmatically important ways in which possible here-nows of the experienceable world are grouped and represented by a symbol. The general concept "horse" represents one kind of grouping, based mainly upon publicly understood similarities relating one horse to another; "Butch" (the name of a horse I once knew) represents another kind of grouping, based mainly upon the partly observed and partly inferred spatio-temporal continuity of the parts and moments of which the horse named Butch is composed.

But clearly other bases of association are possible. Any aesthetic experience is such an alio-dimensional grouping. An artist's characteristic attempt, in its semantic aspect, is to express and communicate an experience comprising a grouping of experiential moments—that is, of perceived and imagined here-nows—for which there is no publicly accepted word, formula, or other symbol already available. In the words of Ezra Pound: "The error of making a statue *of* Night or *of* Charity lies in tautology. The idea has already found its way into language. The function of the artist is precisely the formulation of what has not found its way into language, i.e., any language verbal, plastic or musical."[5] What Pound says of Night and Charity is true both of horseness and of any individual horse: each finds its adequate expression in a language of word concepts—a common noun in the one case, a proper noun in the other—and an exact undistorted reformulation in terms of painting or sculpture is neither possible nor worth attempting. Horseness shoots through experience in a given direction and "means" a grouping of certain qualities and functions that are conventionally conceived as belonging together; the flesh and blood horse now clanking along the pavement outside my window "means" another grouping—in this case, of physically contiguous qualities; whereas the horses of say Donatello, or of deChirico, or of Kenneth Shopen "mean" a more novel and still unconventionalized grouping of qualities, some of which are shared with the dictionary concept "horse," others with the perceptual qualities of live horses that the artist has seen, while some have closest affinity with subtle forms of emotion otherwise inexpressible.

Thus the platitude that great art is universal, although true in a special sense, is misleading: for the integral meaning of a work of art (whatever its component meanings may be) cuts across experience in a different dimension from that of any logical universal whatever, and establishes its own quality of universality—a more concrete and more alive universality than that represented by any dictionary definition. An analogous distinction may be observed between the concrete universality of the Cross as an integral religious symbol and any theological exposition of what the Cross represents; or between the ideal of justice as it appears to men who are sacrificing their lives to uphold it and the idea of justice as employed in a discussion of theoretical ethics.

6. *Principle of assertorial tone:* that statements—for we here consider the molecular order of meanings—vary with respect to the manner in which they are susceptible to affirmation and denial, ranging all the way from "heavy" assertorial tone—which characterizes the literal statement, the proposition—to "light" association or semi-affirmed tension between two or more symbols. A poetic statement differs from a literal statement not, as Dr. Richards used to maintain, in that the one has a merely subjective, the other an objective reference—at least this is an unnecessary and generally irrelevant difference; but in their manner of asserting. There are differences of what may be called *assertorial weight.* A literal statement asserts heavily. It can do so be-

cause its terms are solid. It must do so because we are practical busy creatures who want to know just where we stand. A poetic statement, on the other hand, consisting as it does in a conjunction or association of plurisigns, has no such solid foundation, and affirms with varying degrees of lightness.

A stanza from Carl Rakosi's *A Journey Far Away* offers a syntactical illumination of the principle.

> An ideal
> like a canary
> singing in the dark
> for appleseed and barley

Is the poet making a statement here or is he not? If so, the syntax is not quite adequate: the copula "is" is needed for its completion. But try inserting it, and see how fatally that little word destroys the original quality of affirmation! "An ideal is like a canary singing in the dark for appleseed and barley." Note what has been done. Not only has the reader-response been altered through a lessening of the pleasure with which the utterance is received: more than that, the very nature of the affirmation has been changed. This prose version, we feel, overstates its case, it affirms too heavily: no ideal can be so much like a canary as all that! Rakosi's way of singing the matter did not belabor the point; it suggested only that between an ideal and a canary there might be a slight and lovely connection, too tenuous to be expressed by the harsh little word "is." So delicate an affirmation does not seriously jostle our other beliefs; we can accept it as true without mental inconvenience. But the literal statement, by reason of its assertive heaviness, falsifies.

Assertorial weight should not be confused with the strength or force of a poetic statement. Take, for instance, Christina Rossetti's well-known quatrain:

My heart is like a singing bird
  Whose nest is in a water-shoot;
My heart is like an apple-tree
  Whose boughs are bent with thick-set fruit . . .

If some literal-minded reader should object to the second
comparison on the ground that the differences between
hearts and apple-trees are more pronounced than their resemblances, we might justly dismiss him as unduly obtuse.
In terms of the present analysis he would be making a statement of full assertorial weight which is nevertheless ridicu-
lously weak, contrasting painfully with the simple eloquent
force of Miss Rossetti's assertorially lighter statement.

Suppose, again, that the graceful compliment to a lady expressed implicitly by Herrick—

Her eyes the glow-worm lend thee,
The shooting stars attend thee . . .

were made explicit and that the lady's charms were set forth
with descriptive literalness. Not only the grace, but more
subtly the central poetic meaning of the utterance, would be
destroyed. Herrick's own statement is by indirection. It is
offered more lightly than its prose counterpart would be, but
partly for that reason it is all the more forceful and suggestive. Generally speaking, the combination of poetic delicacy
and poetic strength is one of the prime distinguishing marks
of authentic poetry.

A poetic statement, then, does not usually assert its claims
so heavily as a proposition. Its truth is more fragile, and it
asks no guarantee. For a poem can be regarded, from a semantic standpoint, as a complex tension among variously related plurisigns. Some phases of the poetic tension have more
of a declarative character than others; and as this declarative

character becomes more pronounced a phase of the poetic
tension may approximate the character of literal statement,
yet without quite totally attaining it. Frequently enough a
phase of the poetic tension may contain a literal statement
as one of its aspects. When Macbeth cries, "If it were done
when 'tis done, then 'twere well/It were done quickly," his
words contain an unmistakable literal meaning. This literal
scenario meaning could be expressed equally well, from a
logical standpoint, in another arrangement of words, such
as: "If the effects of the deed could but terminate with the
performance, it would be well to finish the matter off as
quickly as possible." But the literal meaning is only one aspect of the full poetic meaning, and to restate it in the second phraseology is to wrench it away from the associated
poetic meanings of the original. The principal poetic meaning in the passage is expressed in the thematic use of the
word "done," repeated three times like the tolling of a dirge.
Directly and literally the passage asserts the logical proposition I have just formulated; such is its meaning to the reader's
clear-cutting intellect. But if the reader reads with his intellect and sensibilities working in collaboration he will hear
in that insistent repetition of the word "done" a tragic reminder of the irrevocability of a deed once performed. The
reminder is expressed obliquely, but in some mysterious way
it gains in power by its very indirection. Now in much the
same manner that Bach so often passes from a theme in a
minor to a final chord in the major key, Shakespeare again
and again in his plays marks the close of an emotional sequence by passing from an oblique to a correspondingly literal statement. Thus after a number of variations have been
played upon the "done" theme, Lady Macbeth concludes the
matter by declaring explicitly (III. ii) "What's done is done,"
and again in the sleep-walking scene (V. i) "What's done
cannot be undone." In the word "done" as used suggestively

throughout the play we have a plurisign, which in these two quasi-literal remarks of Lady Macbeth approximates but does not quite reach the character of a monosign. Correspondingly, Lady Macbeth's two statements approximate but do not quite reach the character of propositions.

7. *Principle of paradox:* that two statements which by the canons of strict logic are mutually contradictory, may sometimes be jointly acceptable. It is not the maneuvered, expository type of paradox that is relevant here—such as Chesterton's "Darwin was no Darwinian," and Lord Russell's analogy between the paradox of physical ether and the paradox of Homer: "We know who Homer *was*—he wrote the *Iliad* and the *Odyssey;* only we don't know whether he *existed.*" The aim of such paradoxes is to startle, amuse, and suggest a fresh perspective. They can be cleared up easily enough by anyone who takes the trouble to make the appropriate logical distinctions—between Darwin's views and those of his self-professed followers, and between the abstract conception of "authorship of the *Iliad* and *Odyssey*" and the historical question of whether they were or were not written by a single man. The paradoxes of expressive language are something more than this.

Generally speaking I would say there are three main uses of paradox in poetry: I may call them the paradox of surface, the paradox of depth, and the paradoxical interplay of statement and innuendo. The first is exemplified, perhaps even a little crudely, by the conventional oxymoron of Romeo's opening comment upon the brawl between the two noble houses:

> Why, then, O brawling love! O loving hate!
> O any thing, of nothing first create!
> O heavy lightness! serious vanity!
> Mis-shapen chaos of well-seeming forms!

Feather of lead, bright smoke, cold fire, sick health!
Still-waking sleep, that is not what it is!
This love feel I, that feel no love in this.

So far as these conceits are anything more than courtly rhetoric—which is to say, so far as they may be conceived to
function expressively and not only decoratively—they are
surface representations of the underlying idea expressed in
the fourth quoted line.

A depth paradox, on the other hand, aims more directly at
some transcendent truth which is so mysterious and so many-
sided in its suggestions of meaningful possibilities that either
half of the paradox taken alone would be grossly inadequate
and partisan. The great paradoxes of traditional theology are
of this kind: God's justice *and* God's mercy; God's foreknowl-
edge of all things to come *and* man's free will. Eliot's *Four
Quartets* contains a number of expressive paradoxes which
function in free variations of the same manner:

Only through time time is conquered.

So the darkness shall be light, and the stillness the dancing.

In order to arrive at what you do not know
You must go by a way which is the way of ignorance.

Our only health is the disease
If we obey the dying nurse . . .[6]

Some of Eliot's depth paradoxes are aided by a serious playfulness which bears a rough analogy to the examples cited
from Chesterton and Lord Russell. The line, "To be redeemed
from fire by fire," in *Little Gidding* could be prosaically explicated by a distinction between the fire of damnation and

the fire of purgatorial cleansing. Yet the paradoxical expression is necessary, not arbitrary here, for it evokes, as an overtone of allusion, the archetypal idea of the finding of life through voluntary death ("He who will save his life shall lose it . . ."), and more archetypally still, the idea of the transcendent Oneness that is approached through even the most discrepant particulars.

The type of paradox most characteristic of poetry is the third: which occurs when a direct statement—i.e., some part of a poem's scenario meaning—is either mocked or playfully opposed by the suggestions latent in the imagery. The opening lines of Donne's *The Extasie* offer an illustration:

> Where, like a pillow on a bed,
>   A pregnant bank swelled up, to rest
> The violet's reclining head,
>   Sat we two, one another's best.
>
> Our hands were firmly cimented
>   With a fast balm which thence did spring,
> Our eye-beams twisted, and did thread
>   Our eyes, upon one double string;
>
> So to'entergraft our hands, as yet
>   Was all the means to make us one,
> And pictures in our eyes to get
>   Was all our propagation.

The latter stanza asserts plainly that there has been no full carnal union and no propagation of new life as yet—a statement which the wooer's plaint is presently to confirm:

> But O alas, so long, so far
>   Our bodies why do we forbear?

The three opening lines, however, had already imprinted on a responsive and uninhibited reader's mind a set of images suggesting both feminine and (with startling bravado) masculine fulfillment—a sly and delicately ribald qualification of the subsequent chaste avowal. Most of the later paradoxes in the poem, on the other hand, are of the second (the depth) type, such as:

> Might thence a new concoction take,
> And part far purer than he came.

> But as all several souls contain
> Mixtures of things, they know not what,
> Love, these mixed souls, doth mix again,
> And make both one, each this and that.

Such paradoxes as these underline the theme of the inextricable union, in love's mysteries, of oneness and manyness, purity and concoction, spirituality and bodily expression.

8. *Principle of significant mystery:* that the truth or falsity of an expressive statement transcends to some degree the evidence of any possible set of propositions which might stand to it in the relation of ground—whether deductive or inductive—to consequent. Truth is more than a function of logically articulable evidence; the meaning of an expressive question (and all deeply important questions are expressive to some degree, or have an expressive aspect)—is never entirely exhausted by its possible answers. This is another way of saying (subjectively) that intuition is always a factor in the apprehension of truth, and (objectively) that any integral truth—as opposed to either conventional or technical truths—involves irreducible semantic and logical surds.

In the general muddle of slovenly thinking which is so prevalent today there is a tendency to confuse the ideas expressed by the words "mysticism" and "mystery." The foregoing semantic analysis shows their difference. Although both meanings have too much semantic plenitude to allow of adequate definition, their difference is indicated by the difference between Principle 1 and Principle 8. The mystical involves a fusing of this and that, of knower and object known, of symbol and referend. The mysterious—i.e., the radically enigmatic, not the temporarily puzzling—is that character or quality or relationship in things which, however much "explained," always transcends in its essence any totality of explanations given. The two elements are deeply interrelated, but analytically distinguishable.

Thus these eight dialectical escapes from the limiting assumptions of steno-language to the liberating principles of expressive language confirm the conclusions reached in Chapter III. In the present chapter we have found, simply by making those eight assumptions explicit and identifying their exact meaning, that there is a set of meaningful possibilities which they deny, and which therefore a critic is free to explore. In the earlier chapter we had discovered the more general psychological assumption which underlies the eight steno-semantic assumptions—namely, that the semantic function belongs only to the operations of intellect upon the data of outer or inner perception, and that the semantic function of emotional experience as such is zero. Although the steno-semanticist admits that emotions may, and doubtless always do, accompany every actual occasion of semantic reference, he maintains that in themselves they tell us nothing about any reality other than their own bare and transient being. Hence the familiar counsel to disregard the promptings of emotion in the search for truth; and the counsel is both right and valuable in two respects. It is right when the truth in question is a logical, monosignative truth, which calls into play man's abstractive intellect in quest of definite and publicly securable results. It is right, again, when the emotional promptings are crude and immature, or foreign to the matter in hand, and the emotional commentary is an impertinence.

Nevertheless "the heart, too, has its reasons." *All* experience has, to some degree or other, a semantic role: it points, however uncertainly and dimly, to a reality other than itself and other than the subject who enjoys the experience. It is the essence of experience to be vector-like: to transcend in reference what it is in existence, and thereby to enact a more or less cognitive role. Emotional as well as intellectual aspects of mental activity give a kind of knowledge—not merely knowledge of the subject, such as a psychologist might derive by empirio-intellectual analysis, but knowledge about that towards which the emotion is felt. Love of a thing is presumptive evidence of the quality "lovable" in that thing, just as a sensation of green is presumptive evidence of the quality of green being actually present. Some degree of judgment is implicit in all experience, emotive as well as sensory, and this implicit judgment tends to make a claim about the nature of things. Further experience and further activity of judgment may, of course, modify or reverse the original judgment, but this possibility affects sensory experience too, not emotive experience only. The important discrimination is between good emotions and bad: the quest for truth and the larger intelligibility require an abandonment of petty emotions reflecting primitive impulse and ingrown self-love, in favor of those integral and expansive intuitions—neither exclusive of intellect nor identical with it—which enable the knower to transcend his natural limitations and penetrate darkly a little way into the enveloping mystery.

FIVE

Four Ways of Imagination

WHAT MAINLY distinguishes depth-meanings from steno-meanings is the greater vivacity of imagination that goes into their making. Authentic imagining is more than play of fancy. Since Kant's day it has been widely accepted that imagination is neither that mere decay of sensation which Hobbes had supposed it to be nor an irresponsible commentator upon a world already given, but an original contributor to the very nature of that world. Coleridge, employing an independent vocabulary and drawing upon his own ample reserves of poetic insight, renewed and confirmed Kant's doctrine that the mind is more than an onlooker, that it is constituent, or largely so, of the world which it knows.

To look at a tree and recognize it as the thing we humans mean by the word "tree" is possible only because my mind is actively fusing the fleeting impingements of sensation into a meaningful, recognizable whole. A woodpecker, a dog, and myself each has his separate business with the tree; and as each responds differently to it, so each of us perceives and recognizes it in a way largely impervious to the others. The outreaching of the mind, in that primordial, preconscious enterprise of comparison and selective recognition, is what Kant calls the Transcendental Unity of Apperception, and Coleridge the Primary Imagination. What Coleridge calls the Secondary Imagination—the specific forms of imagining employed in the poetic art—is a continuation and reflection of that "living power and prime agent of all human perception" which is "a repetition in the finite mind of the eternal act of creation in the infinite I AM."[1]

Now I want to accept this Coleridgean doctrine of the continuity between man's primary (or constitutive) imagination and his secondary (or poetic) imagination, while rejecting the too limited conception of how imagination works, which Coleridge took over, though I think somewhat uneasily, from Kant. For Kant conceives the original role of imagination in building the world as a synthesizing activity— a synthesizing of the manifold of sensation into intelligible patterns.[2] Coleridge echoes this view of the matter when he speaks of imagination as a "completing power" and as "esemplastic." The imagination, to his view, is (in Walter Jackson Bate's paraphrase) "a process of realization by which the products and insights of two distinct aspects of mind become transmuted and funneled into a single stream of awareness."[3] It is only as philosopher and critic, to be sure, that Coleridge thinks thus; in his poetry, as I shall presently illustrate, a much wider range of imaginative activity is to be found. Nevertheless the overemphasis upon the esemplastic function has been responsible for certain exaggerations in the critical theory and practice of the present day. The "New Criticism" has come to mean a number of things since Dr. Ransom innocently launched the phrase a decade or more ago, and some of them—notably the demand that we concentrate on milking our cow instead of investigating her clinical history and the abstract virtues of milk—are both valid and important. But the thing that has chiefly irritated and estranged the opponents of the New Criticism is precisely this overemphasis on the esemplastic, the synthesizing role of the poetic imagination. And understandably so, because although the synthesizing and fusing activity of imagination is indispensable, it is by no means the only way in which man's imaginative power mingles constitutively with his world. There are, in fact, it seems to me, four main general ways in which the world receives its meaning and significance from the active, responsive, integrative power of the mind. That is to say, there are four main respects in which the imagination functions cognitively and constructively at once. There is the Confrontative Imagination, which acts upon its object by particularizing and intensifying it. There is the Stylistic Imagination, which acts upon its object by stylizing and distancing it. There is the Archetypal Imagination, which sees the particular object as embodying and adumbrating suggestions of universality. And there is the Metaphoric Imagination, which fuses heterogeneous elements into some kind of unity.

CONFRONTATIVE IMAGINING

What we directly confront in experience is always, in the first instance, something individual. When you pass from generalizations about mankind to direct acquaintance with Bill Smith, and with some particular grief or enthusiasm that Bill Smith is undergoing, you pass from concepts to real existence. The great evil encouraged by a technological and bureaucratic way of life is to forget that the individual exists and to treat him as a mere instance of a generality. Granted that generalizations are sometimes a practical necessity: yet when we make them so much a habit that they become substitutes for the bright world itself the result is a travesty of human reason, whether done in the name of business efficiency or political necessity or alleged science. Cassiodorus, the sixth century statesman and monk, declared: "God is really wonderful and extremely wise in having distinguished every one of his creatures by a unique dispensation lest unseemly confusion overwhelm them." The depth words here are "unique" and "confusion." Each one of us is unique; each is a *Gestalt*, an *ousia*, an essence, not quite identical with any other. And every experience, every moment of beauty or of pain, is likewise unique. But the Devil seeks ever to confuse, or (in the potent old word of the prayer book) to confound us, into forgetting that precise and ultimate fact. Commonplace language plays into the Devil's hands by dulling the edges between one experience and another; poetic language undertakes to speak of the concrete particulars with directness and experiential precision. "To particularize is the alone distinction of merit," says Blake.[4]

Accordingly, the first and most indispensable attribute of poetic language is its radical particularity of reference, its presentative immediacy. Poetry's first urgency is, in Richard Hovey's words, to "have business with the grass"; it presents as well as represents, it evokes something of the very quality, tone, and flavor of the concrete qua concrete with a directness and a full experiential relevance that steno-symbols cannot do. Authentic poetry will always have this attribute to some degree, for—to paraphrase Yeats—poetry is love, and only the concrete is loved.

Now the point I especially want to make in this connection is that a lively recognition of the particular and unique in experience is an imaginative achievement, and that when keyed to the highest pitch it may become an imaginative achievement of a very high order.

> Down dropt the breeze, the sails dropt down.

John Livingston Lowes speaks of this powerfully laconic line from *The Ancient Mariner* as descending "with an abruptness like that of the fall of the shot bird off the Cape."[5] But

the simile is explicit only in the critic's account: in the poet's
it is left implicit, an unspoken overtone at most. The power
of imagination here is not exercised to blend and fuse diverse
particulars—at least that is not its main thrust—but to intensify the immediate experience itself, the horror of tropical
seas to men becalmed.

> The fair breeze blew, the white foam flew,
> The furrow followed free;
> We were the first that ever burst
> Into that silent sea.

It may be true, as Lowes plausibly argues, that Coleridge
has here drawn upon two or more accounts of seamen's voyages—notably Marborough's account of Magellan's first passing through the Straits of Cape Horn into the Pacific Ocean
and George Forster's *A Voyage round the World, in his Bri-
tannic Majesty's Sloop, Resolution*. If such be the case, I
would say that the synthesis or fusion of these accounts takes
place prior to the decisive imaginative act that enforms and
moves the poetry. The poetic imagination in this quatrain is
wholly taken up with the perceptual qualities of the breeze
and foam and furrow and with the unique awe of aloneness,
of being the first ever to have entered that watery region.
   Coleridge himself recognized the intensifying function of
imagination. In the *Biographia Epistolaris* he writes: "For
from my very childhood I have been accustomed to abstract,
and as it were, unrealize whatever of more than common interest my eyes dwelt on, and then by a sort of transfusion of
my consciousness to identify myself with the object."[6] But
"identify" is too strong. If there is complete identification,
the self becomes lost in its object and no longer confronts it;
the poetic mode of consciousness becomes submerged in the
mystical. Accordingly I would prefer to describe the confrontative process, in language borrowed from Rosenstock-

Huessy and Martin Buber, somewhat as follows.[7] Where the entire self is given up to a single impression and is in a state of tranquil tension toward it, owing to a fairly equal commingling of love and awe, a balanced sense of beauty and of mystery, then the self finds its object confronting it as a *thou* and becomes in turn a *thou* before the presence of its object.

The positivistic way of thinking stresses the *I-it* relationship, in which all objects of knowledge are regarded as theoretically explicable and manipulable. The poet, on the other hand—and that includes the pure function of poet so far as it exists in every one of us—tends to regard each really significant object in his world as a *thou*. To regard anything honestly as a *thou* means, first, to value it intensely for its own sake, and secondly, to accept a potential interchange of roles with it—to let it speak as an *I* while I myself become a listener. The rhetorical devices of personification and apostrophe are sometimes employed as syntax-symbols expressing this relationship. But they are not indispensable. Wordsworth's explicit apostrophe—

> And O ye Fountains, Meadows, Hills, and Groves
> Forbode not any severing of our loves
> (FROM *Intimations of Immortality*)

does not strike me as evoking the sense of *thou*hood in nature so forcefully as do some of his expressions in the grammatical third person, such as:

> The holy time is quiet as a Nun
> Breathless with adoration

and

> Listen! the mighty Being is awake,
> And doth with his eternal motion make
> A sound like thunder . . .
> (BOTH FROM *Evening on Calais Beach*)

To conclude my first subdivision, then: Imagination is active in the awareness of individual presences in their radical individuality—i.e., in both the grasping and the expressing of them; and this activity is especially pronounced when that which experience presents is confronted with such intensity of insight that an *I-thou* relationship is struck up between us and it.

IMAGINATIVE DISTANCING

But we do not wish to carry our hearts too much on display. An *I-thou* relation is possible without grimaces, sighs, and backslappings; indeed it can often achieve a sounder depth when its expressions are decently restrained. Alan Porter has sung:

> Let him that beds a princess fear
> To show himself too free,
> And ceremoniously draw near:
> There should between two lovers be
> An excellent immodesty.[8]

A sense of right distance is an imaginative achievement and one of the conducements to civilized living. It is the primary factor of style, both in life and in art.

Edward Bullough in his much quoted essay on "Psychical Distance" says some enlightening things about the aesthetic importance of this element.[9] Not merely distance in space, of importance to the painter in the guise of visual perspective; not merely distance in time, of which Aristotle took account in the *Poetics*, when considering why tragedy is most effective when built around events of long ago. There is also a kind of distancing in relation to the whole object of experience, which consists of "putting the phenomenon, so to speak, out of gear with our practical, actual self" and thereby looking at it with a fresh objectivity. Thus there is at once a negative and a positive side to the experience of Distance: a refusal to be concerned with the practical aspect of things, and an elaboration of the experience exhibited within the framework which this inhibitory action establishes. In normal workaday situations our attention is given to those sides of our experiences which float more or less by habit, and to some degree from practical necessity, up to the surface of our consciousness. So much, so very much that we could attend to is ignored. What art contrives to do is give us a "sudden view of things from their reverse unnoticed side." Thus aesthetic distancing has an element of the impersonal, although of a quite different sort from the impersonality of science. Unlike science, art does not rule out or regard as of lesser importance the subjective and personal factors in a situation. "It describes a personal relation, often emotionally colored, but of a peculiar character. Its peculiarity lies in that the personal character of the relation has been, so to speak, filtered. It has been cleared of the practical, concrete nature of its appeal, without, however, thereby losing its original constitution."

How much distancing is desirable for effective art? No easy answer is possible. Over-distancing breaks the circuit between the work of art and one's own prepared field of receptivity; under-distancing destroys the aesthetic character of the experience. The ideal spectator at a performance of *Othello* is neither he who lacks the emotional potentiality of being jealous, nor yet he who is actively harassed by pangs of jealousy at the very time.

The one kind of over-distancing which Bullough analyzes is that of idealistic art, which he explains as "the subordination of Art to some extraneous purpose of an impressive, exceptional character." When art is put to subserve commemorative or hieratic functions, in either a religious or a patriotic context, the object to be honored has to be distin-

guished as markedly as possible from profaner objects in the
environment and has to be invested with an air of sanctity
by a symbolic removal from its ordinary context of occurrence. Certain objects of nature, especially (in a mythopoeic
society) the curious and unusual and the apparently potent,
would meet this tendency halfway by assuming divine rank;
the process then gets completed by the distancing power of
art—through exaggeration and insistence upon special features, or contrariwise by the removal of all features that were
noticeably individualistic and concrete: a process which
achieves loftiest development in Greek sculpture of the classical period.

The kind of over-distancing which confronts us typically
in contemporary art, on the other hand, is not idealistic but
dissociationistic. Much of modern art involves, as Ortega has
remarked, a process of dehumanization. There have been
those who fell in love with La Gioconda; but it would be impossible for anyone, and indeed meaningless, to fall in love
with a Picasso female whose eyes and mouth and breasts
have been transposed in accordance with the painter's ruth-
lessly neo-geometrizing spirit. Whatever aesthetic pleasure
we take from such an un-portrait arises not from anything
human but from the triumph over what is human. Why is
this? What is the motive behind such over-distancing? The
new sensibility, Ortega believes, is dominated by an uneasiness toward the human in art very similar to the uneasiness
which a sensitive person has always felt before wax figures:

In the presence of wax figures we have all felt a peculiar uneasiness. This springs from the ambiguous impression they make on
us, which prevents our adopting a definite attitude toward them.
When we feel them as human beings they mock us; and if we
see them as fictions they seem to quiver in irritation. There is no
way of reducing them to mere objects. Looking at them we are

confused with the suspicion that it is they who are looking at us, and we end by feeling a loathing toward this kind of superior corpse. The wax figure is pure melodrama.[10]

The theatre is an art-form which offers interesting analogies in the matter of distancing. Jean-Louis Barrault observes out of his distinguished experience as actor and director that in a classical drama such as the tragedies of Racine, where the essential virtues are Measure and Design, the actor must make both his utterance and his gesticulation calculated, chosen, and rhythmic. If he fails to do so, "any transition from gesture to speech becomes impossible, for a synthesis of what is seen and what is heard cannot take place. The 'chemical precipitate' of this delicate operation cannot come about, the theatrical phenomenon ceases to exist," and the characters seem to be ordinary men and women speaking in an affected and unnatural way. Consequently, Barrault continues:

When we play the classics we have to abandon naturalism and yet remain *true* when operating within a particular *tone*. The problem is to find the tone and at the same time to remain true. The other day I was observing a newspaper-seller. He didn't have to be as it were *present* in his cries, because he had found the correct tone. If you want to teach someone how to sell papers it is no good telling him to "think carefully about what you're saying." No, he must find the *right tone* and it follows that his cry will produce the *right sound*. The right tone is the key to style.[11]

Style in poetry, as in the other arts, is partly "a playful demonstration of the properties of the medium itself"—an independent dance of the mind along its imagistic and musical patterns. But a dance to have pattern must be disciplined; and the stylization of poetic language is an imaginative emphasizing of certain features and toning down of others in accordance with the rhythmic life of the language itself. "Even in the most imaginative flights," T. E. Hulme has written, "there is always a holding back, a reservation. The classical poet never forgets this finiteness, this limit of man. He remembers always that he is mixed up with earth."[12]

If that were all, however, poetry would be reduced to the condition of music; and by the logic of the diagram with which I concluded Chapter III its language would therein be but a mingling of the phatic and ejaculative. Poetry is typically more than that. Its language is expressive, which implies that there is something to express. Stylization is the medium through which the expression is realized; and most of all this is seen in rhythm, the purpose of which, Yeats has said, is "to prolong the moment of contemplation, the moment when we are both asleep and awake, which is the one moment of creation, by hushing us with an alluring monotony, while it holds us waking by its variety, to keep us in that state of perhaps real trance, in which the mind, liberated from the pressure of the will, is unfolded in symbols."[13] Style involves a hushing of ordinary compulsions, a veiling of ordinary associations, and therein makes its unique semantic contribution, as even somehow a creator and revealer of meanings which only in that style could be uttered at all. The Imagist Manifesto of four decades ago declared: "In poetry a new cadence means a new idea."[14] Imagination, even in its stylizing and distancing aspect, is more than play of fancy; it is subtly but effectively a real contributor to the very nature and significance of "our world."

ARCHETYPAL IMAGINING

The role of universals in a poem, which Aristotle stresses in his famous distinction between poetry and history, is often obscured by wrong emphasis. Few poets, I dare say, would subscribe fully to Brunetière's remark: "What, after all, is poetry but metaphysics made manifest through sensible images?" Dante, Spenser and Traherne, let's say, might have found each some carefully guarded sense in which they could accept and advocate it, but it is hard to think of Homer or Chaucer or Shakespeare or almost any twentieth-century poet as doing so. Naturally it is important to recognize and respond to the universal meanings and implications of a poem so far as they are really present. When a poem exploits the depth-dimension by stirring archetypal associations, we cannot ignore that dimension if we are to understand and adequately respond to the poem. But the depth-dimension is more insistent and relevant in some poems than in others: more so in *Faust* than in *Egmont,* and in *Faust Part II* than in *Faust Part I;* more so in *Measure for Measure* and *The Tempest* than in *Othello,* more so in *The Revolt of Islam* than in *Ode to the West Wind.* In offering such comparisons I do not mean to suggest that the one term of any comparison is poetically superior to the other. The question at present is not of valuation but of interpretation; the inquiry is a semantic one—whether in a given poem the dimension of depth-meaning is or is not prominent, and how it is related to the organic totality of response-inviting elements which *is* the poem.

Moreover, there is the question of the *way* in which a universal enters into a poem. Not preferably as an abstract universal, the same once and for always, unchanged by its temporary commerce with poetic discourse. A poem which handles nothing but abstract universals in their abstract character is didactic and, if it employs a sustained symbolism, allegorical. When a poem succeeds in being didactic and good poetry at once—Lucretius' *De Rerum Natura* and Pope's *Essay on Criticism* come to mind—it is by virtue of fresh insights and sometimes metaphoric imagery in Lucretius' case, chiefly by irony, nuance, and subtlety of framing in Pope's.

Such cases are rather special. More generally the universals that enter into poetry are *concrete* and *radically implicit* universals, which is to say the universal idea cannot be divorced from the given context, cannot be logically explicated, without distorting it. For its universality exists by analogy only, and not by definition. There are significant analogies between *Oedipus Coloneus* and *King Lear,* but how lame are any attempts to formulate them in critical language, compared with the insights we draw from each of them in the reading, when our memories of and responses to the other of them are unconscious, not explicit! Coleridge acknowledges the poetic importance of concrete universality when he praises Shakespeare for effecting a "union and interpenetration of the universal and the particular"; and Professor W. K. Wimsatt has observed that "in one terminology or another this idea of a concrete universal is found in most metaphysical aesthetic of the eighteenth and nineteenth centuries."[15]

Perhaps the most interesting case of a great poet who consciously made concrete universality the governing condition of his poetry is Goethe. "Every character," he declared to Eckermann, "however peculiar it may be, and every representation, from stone all the way up the scale to man, has a certain universality; for everything repeats itself, and there is nothing in the world that has happened only once."[16] All nature, in Goethe's view, is variously and changingly interrelated, but the phenomena which manifest themselves on the surface not only interpenetrate one another but variously reveal the perduring archetypes which they express and symbolize. For Goethe holds that the world is intrinsically "symbolic": by which he means that every quality, character, happening, is at once concrete event *(Phänomenon)* and archetype *(Urphänomen)*. The Goethean archetype, however, is not like the Platonic *eidos* something separate in existence or even in thought from the particular; it exists only in and through the particular, and hence can be known only by opening our eyes and ears and hearts to the sensuous living world. There is an undercurrent of Goethean seriousness in Mephistopheles' chaffing of the closet-scholar:

Grau, theurer Freund, ist aller Theorie,
Und grün des Lebens goldner Baum.

The green and golden archetype, as distinguished from the gray abstract idea, is at once genuinely universal and undivorcibly concrete.

Certain particulars have more of an archetypal content than others: that is to say, they are "Eminent Instances" which stand forth in a characteristic amplitude as representatives of many others; they enclose in themselves a certain totality, arranged in a certain way, stirring in the soul something at once familiar and strange, and thus outwardly as well as inwardly they lay claim to a certain unity and generality. Such Eminent Instances are the keystone of Goethe's conception of art; for he defines beauty, or the beautiful, as "a disclosure of secret natural laws, which would have remained forever hidden if it had not been for just this manifestation." The beautiful, to Goethe, carries a connotation of the symbolic, to greater or less degree. But symbolism ("a living-moment disclosure of the Inscrutable") must not be confused with allegory ("a dream or a shadow"):

It makes a great difference whether the poet starts with a universal idea and then looks for suitable particulars, or beholds the universal *in* the particular. The former method produces allegory, where the particular has status merely as an instance, an example of the universal. The latter, by contrast, is what reveals poetry in its true nature: it speaks forth a particular without independently thinking of or referring to a universal, but in grasping the particular in its living character it implicitly apprehends the universal along with it.[17]

The notion of archetype has come into greater public prominence lately because of the psychological studies of it published by Dr. Carl G. Jung. In order to distinguish my own use of the words "archetype" and "archetypal" from Jung's, let me briefly indicate what I take to be the most relevant points of his doctrine.

Jung differentiates a personal unconscious, which he also speaks of as the subconscious, and the *impersonal* or *superpersonal* or *collective* unconscious. The former contains forgotten memories, suppressed (which is to say purposely forgotten) painful ideas, pre-threshold or subliminal apperceptions which are not yet strong enough or ripe enough to reach consciousness. The collective unconscious consists of *primordial images,* which are the most ancient and most universal thoughts of humanity. They are as much feelings as thoughts, but their strong feeling-tone does not reduce them to the status of the merely subjective. They impress themselves upon our subjectivity as something having a deep kinship with it but at the same time as having an individual life of their own. St. Paul's apperceptive experience of angels and archangels, principalities and powers (for we may suppose that his impassioned language is not just lofty verbiage but reflects some kind of visionary experience), the Gnostics' doctrine of *archontes* and kingdoms of light, the heavenly hierarchies of Dionysius the Areopagite, and the gods and daemons who have activated the various religions of the world, "all come from the perception of the relative independence of archetypes, or dominants of the collective unconscious." Such primordial images are buried deep in man's psyche, way below the suppressed or inchoate memories belonging to the individual, and the libido has recourse to them "when it becomes freed from the personal-infantile form of transference."[18]

What is involved in describing the archetypal images as

trans-individual? Jung's answer involves two steps—the one valid and important, the other dubious and in any case non-essential. The most valuable part of his theory pertains to the rough but sometimes striking parallels between patterns of the unconscious as indicated by clinical evidence and certain great thought-patterns of mythology. On the basis of such parallels—whether discovered, inferred, or postulated—Jung declares the archetypal or primordial image to be a "mnemonic deposit," a precipitate formed by "condensation of innumerable similar processes" which make up "a certain ever-recurring psychic experience." The image, that is to say, is shared; it has a character at once collective and ancestral; and our unconscious experiences today reflect and recapitulate the more persistent of mythological motives. This, I repeat, is the more valid side of Jung's doctrine, despite his unfortunate readiness to select and magnify or minimize anthropological data in ways that make the parallelism seem more continuous and coherent than it probably is.

Jung's other, and more questionable hypothesis, is that the life and vitality of the primordial image is determined phylogenetically—by changes in brain structure, which in turn are produced by the impact of environment upon living matter. Employing Herder's term *mythologem* to signify any great theme of mythology, typical because recurrent in different cultures and in individual psyches, although amenable to reshaping, Dr. Jung argues that typical mythologems have been observed by clinical methods in individuals to whom any previous acquaintance with them, through religious, literary or popular channels, was "absolutely out of the question." Where this negative condition is met—and a layman may be pardoned for wondering whether it is met quite so demonstrably in all of Jung's cases as he supposes—we are forced to the conclusion that we must be dealing with "autochthonous revivals" independent of cultural tradition and historical causation. If this is so, and if such revivals are of too frequent and too striking a character to be attributed to chance, then it would indeed seem to follow, as Jung claims it does, that certain fairly specific myth-forming tendencies exist as structural elements in man's (or at least many a man's) unconscious psyche. How did they come there? Presumably (and here, of course, we have no real evidence at all, only a need of rounding out the theory) by a modification of brain structure. This unverifiable codicil is not essential to Jung's theory of archetypes, and unfortunately its inclusion has prejudiced a number of psychologists against giving the rest of the theory a fair hearing.

Like Jung I take archetypes to be preconsciously rooted symbols inherited (although unlike him I can't say how) from "the dark backward and abysm of time"; equipping our thought and imagination with an ancestral dimension without which true reverence, and therefore the very substance of our conscious life, would go dry and dead. The Divine Father, the Earth Mother, the World Tree, the satyr or centaur or other man-animal monster, the descent into Hell, the Purgatorial stair, the washing away of sin, the castle of attainment, the culture-hero such as Prometheus bringing fire or other basic gift to mankind, the treacherous betrayal of the hero, the sacrificial death of the god, the god in disguise or the prince under an enchantment—these and many other mythologems are persistent patterns of human thought and expression, and have become story-elements in the literature of many distinct races. They are closer to man's natural human vision than are the products of brain-ingenuity, and I agree with Jung that the true philosopher is he who conceptualizes his ideas not at random, and not for the lone sake of consistency, but as transmutations of the "primitive and purely natural vision" which the archetypes express. When it comes to determining just what an archetype is, however,

and how it operates and is transmitted, I fear that either
Freud's or Jung's stubborn insistence upon the exclusive
rights of a single method and a single theory tends to throw
darkness on the path. No method is fool-proof; but at least we
should take care to gather evidences from literature, myth,
and religion on as broad a basis of investigation as possible
and to interpret those evidences so far as we can in their own
terms instead of prejudging them (as Freud and Jung both
do) on the basis of discoveries made, or claimed to be made,
in modern clinics.

METAPHORIC IMAGINING

In both the Archetypal and the Metaphoric Imagination
a certain blending and semantic fusion takes place. In the
one, the Archetypal, the fusion is between image and idea,
between concrete and general, individual and type-form. In
the other, the Metaphoric, the fusion is between two or more
concrete images, each perhaps carrying certain emotive and
ideational associations.

What is metaphor? The familiar textbook definition, descended from Aristotle and Quintilian, is based upon syntactical, not semantic considerations. Both those masters of
rhetorical theory regarded metaphor as little else than ab-
breviated simile. And since this jejune view of the matter
has imposed itself upon many readers' minds, it is important
to understand the reason of its inadequacy.

Aristotle illustrates his view of the relation of metaphor to
simile as follows. "When the poet says of Achilles, 'He sprang
on them like a lion,' this is a simile. When he says, 'The lion
sprang on them,' this is metaphor; for as both animals are
brave, he has transferred the name of 'lion' to Achilles." Elsewhere he calls simile "a metaphor with a preface" and declares it inferior to metaphor on two counts: it is lengthier,
therefore less pleasing; and "since it does not affirm that this

is that, the mind does not inquire into the matter."[19] Now it is true that metaphor is often (not, I think, always) preferable to simile on both these grounds, but the grounds are rhetorical not semantic ones. Terseness is more pleasing and more stimulating to thought than verbosity: that is what it comes to. And by no means let us ignore the canons of good rhetoric, whether in poetry or out of it! Poetry is not less than rhetoric, but something more. Nevertheless the rhetorical distinction, whatever its incidental uses, can hardly be said to open up any important insight. It evinces that great vice of bad classification: overstressing an obvious surface difference and ignoring the differences and resemblances that go to the heart of the matter. By Aristotle's rule it is simile to say, "He dances like a clumsy elephant," and metaphor to say, "That clumsy elephant gets in everyone's way." But there is no semantic difference here—no difference, that is to say, in degree of intensity, or in depth of penetration, or in freshness of recombination, or in anything else that matters much. The difference is merely one of rhetorical strategy.

A far more adequate definition is Herbert Read's: "Metaphor is the synthesis of several units of observation into one commanding image; it is the expression of a complex idea, not by analysis, nor by direct statement, but by a sudden perception of an objective relation."[20] Metaphor, by this criterion, could include some instances of what is traditionally designated simile—given the commanding image and the sudden perception of an objective relation. George Eliot writes: "That sudden clang, that leaping light, fell on Romola like sharp wounds"; and while superficially the sentence contains one metaphor ("leaping light") and one simile ("like sharp wounds"), I would say that we grasp the full resident meaning more nearly if we take the entire sentence as projecting a complex metaphoric fusion or metaphoric tension. The tensive quality of George Eliot's figure is clearly something more than that simple terseness and economy which Quintilian finds admirable in the similes of Cicero, such as: "He fled from court like a man escaping naked from a fire." Cicero's simile rests on a plain logical analogy, and the pleasure which it gives, if any, is simply of intellectual recognition. The same may be said of many tropes which have the grammatical form of metaphor, as when Aeschylus calls a harbor the stepmother of ships. This minor piece of wit is not metaphor in the essential and semantic sense of the word, for it makes its connection by analysis and labored comparison rather than by the "sudden perception of an objective relation." One might perhaps call it a tabloid simile. It lacks what Martin Foss calls the "energy-tension" proper to real metaphor.[21] Compare it with Homer's description of the wrathful Apollo: "His coming was like the night." Grammatically considered Aeschylus' trope is a metaphor and Homer's is a simile; semantically and essentially the distinction stands in reverse. Why so? Because of the great difference of semantic energy-tension. Homer's comparison stirs us emotionally as with a sudden revelation of half-guessed half-hidden mystery, whereas Aeschylus' phrase pleases us superficially as a riddle or a joke might do.

An especially keen and searching contribution to the philosophy of metaphor has been made, in various writings over the past thirty years, by the eminent Mexican philosopher and statesman José Vasconcelos.[22] "Knowledge," he writes in his *Aesthetics*, "consists essentially in a unifying act which integrates instantaneously any given multiplicity into an organic whole that has meaning": so far Vasconcelos is a good Kantian. But the unifying process does not normally take place in the formal way postulated by Kant's doctrine of the categories. If the unification really occurred in so strict a manner, he argues, our world would be as clear and distinct as a geometrical figure. The world by which we actually find ourselves surrounded is by no means completely or even predominantly rational—unless we insist on judging it so by ignoring or belittling all evidence to the contrary. It is a world full of surprises, confusions, subtly blended qualities, dramatic oppositions—generally speaking, *of maximum concretion*. Now if we accept this observed fact on the one hand, and on the other Vasconcelos' Kantian principle that all knowledge takes place through a unifying act of the mind, what may we conclude? In unifying the heterogeneous elements presented to it as raw materials for cognition the mind *may* act as Kant supposes it to do: viz., it may unify in such a way that the radical heterogeneity of the raw materials is virtually nullified in the process. The result then is a conceptual one—we see the world as rationally ordered, in terms of causes and effects, substances and attributes, measurable space and time or space-time, necessities and probabilities, and so on. But the synthesis which expresses our actual living encounter with the world—the "vitalistic" synthesis— "tends to preserve the heterogeneous in its natural character (i.e., in its heterogeneity), thereby giving it a place in a meaningful whole that is not mechanical but vital." Our world thus contains an irrepressible element of paradox, of dramatic tension, and of unresolved ambiguity.

Now this vitalistic synthesis is essential alike to the poetic vision of life and to the strategies of combination involved in the making of an authentic poem. In one of his early writings, *Aesthetic Monism*, Vasconcelos offered the thesis that modern thought at its best tends to nourish itself on elements of meaning which have little to do with logical generalizations, and seeks forms of unification which have more in common with musical structures than with literal language. Recently in an article on Eliot he related this doctrine of "the unification of the heterogeneous" *(la unificación de los heterogéneos)* to Eliot's method of poetic composition both

as partially formulated in "The Music of Poetry" and as exemplified in *Four Quartets*. The full consequence of the doctrine is clarified in Vasconcelos' most recent work, *Todología*.
"The very concept of truth in our time," he declares in his
announcement of the new volume, "has become something
different from formerly. It becomes a function of the unification of disparate elements which are combined without being subjected to logical identification"—i.e., without being
subsumed under a logical class-concept. Vasconcelos' searching analyses thus arrive, by independent ways, at a thesis
which I am arguing in this book and which I believe is essential to a right understanding of man's poetic envisionment
of things—the thesis, namely, of *the ontological status of radical metaphor*. That is to say, metaphor is a medium of fuller,
riper knowing; not merely a prettification of the already
given.

"As a poet," Hart Crane writes, "I may very possibly be
more interested in the so-called illogical impingements of
words on the consciousness (and their combination and interplay in metaphor on this basis) than I am interested in
the preservation of their logically rigid significations at the
cost of limiting my subject matter and perceptions involved
in the poem."[23] The so-called illogical—more accurately, *paralogical*—impingements are not only legitimate instruments of
expressive language, they are a part of its very life. A concrete universal, as I have just observed, fuses a universal idea
with some concrete embodiment. That is one way of transcending the logical distinction between universal and particular, but it is not the only one. What a poem, or a passage
or a symbol within a poem means, need not be a combination
of particular and universal in anything like the logician's understanding of these terms. Poetic meanings can overreach
concrete particulars in quite different ways, along quite different lines, as well as by very different techniques, from

logical literal meanings. An adequate semantics must recognize and make room for what I have called the principle of Paralogical Dimensionality, otherwise it will be incapable of dealing with poetic meanings in one of their most characteristic aspects.

An expressive symbol, as I declared in the last chapter, transcends the dualism of logical singular ("concretion in existence") vs. logical universal ("concretion in discourse"). For besides the two types of mental association which respectively make these two kinds of meaning possible, there is another important type of association, which we may call, slightly modifying a phrase from William James, *association by emotive congruity*.[24] Our reason for associating a certain man with a grasshopper may not be found in any similarity or relation that we can put a finger on: it may be a "reason of the heart" which eludes all rational formulation and yet has great strength. Association of this kind is esemplastic in a fuller than ordinary sense, and tends to involve a strongly, richly, and freshly imaginative energy-tension. It is present in all art that is anything more than purely formal or purely decorative; for an artist's characteristic attempt, in its semantic aspect, is to express and communicate an experience comprising some grouping of perceived and imagined herenows for which there is no publicly accepted word, formula, or other symbol already available.

Drawing an example from poetry, let us consider the two words "stew" and "honey." They can be logically understood and defined when taken as universals, and particular instances of them can be recognized and identified empirically. Both modes of knowing represent conventional ways of grouping elements of experience together for purposes of everyday action and communication. "Stew," on the one hand, is a general concept built up from various experiences of stews which have been grouped and named on the basis of resemblance, to be distinguished from soups, minestrones, casseroles, etc. "This stew" (if I were indicating a particular stew on the table before me) would express a logical particular, a set of data joined by continuity in space and time—all in one dish, or all at one meal. When Hamlet, on the other hand, in the Queen's-closet scene, declares:

> Nay, but to live
> In the rank sweat of an enseamed bed,
> Stew'd in corruption, honeying and making love
> Over the nasty sty . . .
> (*Hamlet,* Act III, Scene iv)

the meaning of the two words is appreciably altered. "Stew" and "honey" lose their isolationist purity here; they are gathered into a single context of moral corruption and disease, wherein their meanings are more or less blended into one another and into the other component meanings that the context establishes as relevant. This fresh contextual establishment of meanings may be called *radical* or *essential* metaphor. When great art is spoken of as having universal significance I think we should keep our fingers crossed. What it really tends to have is an eccentric and adventuring *style* of universality.

The semantic principle which is involved in metaphoric fusion can now be summed up as follows. All meaning has as its subjective condition a certain mental responsiveness—a readiness to make connections and associate this with that, a readiness to *see* this and that in a single perspective and thus as forming a single individuality, a single semantic object, an *ousia*, a Something Meant. Logical meanings, or literal meanings, such as are employed by science and in much everyday intercourse, represent conventional and stereotyped associations, necessary no doubt for carrying on much of the world's work but limited in experiential reference. Fresh associations can generate fresh meanings, and the semantic function of poetry consists largely in this: that poetry quickens and guides man's associative faculty, keeps it in athletic trim, and thus actually generates new meanings—meanings that would lose their identity outside the context of the individual poem, but which are authentically real within that context.

Metaphoric Tension

IT SHOULD be clear by now that metaphor in its radical, which is to say its semantic sense, is much more than a grammatical maneuver or rhetorical stratagem. The essence of metaphor consists in the nature of the tension which is maintained among the heterogeneous elements brought together in one commanding image or expression. The word "tension" has enjoyed some prominence in recent critical discussion as a result of Allen Tate's well known essay on the subject.[1] Subsequently Martin Foss has employed the term "energy-tension," and Cleanth Brooks has put forward the word "paradox" with roughly the same intent. All of these writers are elaborating in their several ways the idea which I expressed toward the end of the last chapter by means of Sr. Vasconcelos' phrase "the unification of the heterogeneous." The point might be summarized by saying that poetic language becomes alive and vibrant largely by reason of its semantic multiplicity-in-unity; or, less technically, because of the precarious balance among various suggested lines of association which it invites the imagination to contemplate. Of course I do not imply that all poetry must be of a highly metaphoric and tensive type. But whatever else poetic language may do, its exploitation of essential metaphor, or metaphoric tension, properly controlled in relation to the poetic context, is one of its most distinctive and sometimes triumphant achievements.

Unfortunately, despite my admiration for Mr. Tate's writing in general and for much that he says in his essay, I find his way of analyzing poetic tension somewhat perverse. His eleven "touchstones" illustrating "not poetry of the extremes, but poetry of the center: poetry of tension, in which the 'strategy' is diffused into the unitary effect" are excellently chosen and offer further proof, if any were needed, of his well attuned poetic taste and judgment. It is not his direct apprehension of the poetic, but his brief raid upon textbook logic for inappropriate tools of analysis at which I cavil. He explains that he uses the word "tension" as a special metaphor "derived from lopping the prefixes off the logical terms *ex*tension and *in*tension." The meaning of poetry, he concludes, is to be found in its tension, which is to say "the full organized body of all the extension and intension that we can find in it."

Such a limitation of what poetry must essentially be has, to my mind, a too dogmatic character, quite at variance with the latitudinarian remarks with which the same essay opened. "There are all kinds of poetry," Mr. Tate had said, "as many as there are good poets, as many even as there are good poems, for poets may be expected to write more than one kind of poetry; and no single critical insight may impute an exclusive validity to any one kind." Yet in the later passage he defines poetry in such a way as to impute an exclusive validity to such as operates by tension, and not merely by tension in general but by tension in a rather special sense. For if we were to take the terms "extension" and "intension" literally, in the sense in which logicians use them, and were to interpret poetic tension as combining them to a maximum degree *in that sense*, what would be the result? Not the tension of metaphor, but the tension of concrete universality—of symbolism in the Goethean mode. It is clear, however, from some of Tate's other critical writings, particularly from "Hardy's Philosophic Metaphors," that he does not find or expect much semantic tension in that direction. He has adopted, then, only the logician's pair of words, without their accepted meanings. And he is using that pair of words, evidently, to designate what Mr. Richards has more appropriately called tenor and vehicle.

Let us examine the test case which is offered—a stanza from Donne's "Valediction: Forbidding Mourning":

> Our two souls therefore, which are one,
>   Though I must go, endure not yet
> A breach, but an expansion,
>   Like gold to airy thinness beat.

The *tenor* here is the unity of the two lovers' souls, indivisible even when physically separated: such is the "logic" of the passage (Ransom), the "scenario meaning" (Richards); Tate calls it "the abstract form of its extensive meaning." The malleable gold is the spatial and visible *vehicle* by which that meaning is poetically represented: Tate calls it "the intensive meaning." And he declares that "the interesting feature here is the logical contradiction of embodying the unitary, non-spatial soul in a spatial image." Well, in the first place the word "contradiction" is out of place. There is no contradiction between a vehicle which is a spatial image and a meaning which is a non-spatial idea. It is just by such relationship between a concrete vehicle and an abstract tenor that symbolic and metaphoric language characteristically works. The relation here is not the logical one between extension and intension (wherein, if they were both maximized, there *would* be a contradiction from the strictly logical standpoint) but between the expressed and the impressed, between tenor and vehicle, meaning and symbolic image. It is

Mr. Tate's confusion of these two relations that has led him to ascribe contradiction where none exists.

Furthermore, his use of that questionable pair of terms has misled him, I think, in his exploration of what the vehicle connotes. "Expansion" in the poem he takes as "a term denoting an abstract property common to many objects, perhaps here one property of a gas." From the logician's standpoint the expansion of a gas is included in the extension (the extensive coverage) of the word; but I cannot read Donne's stanza and feel that gas expansion has anything whatever to do with it. Moreover there are two other poetically relevant connotations which I think Mr. Tate might have mentioned but does not—the beauty, richness, and value of gold, and the associations of "airy," appropriate to the souls unhampered by bodily conditions and tending (from the archetypal background of the Four Elements) to heighten the color aspect of gold to suggest the idea of fire. The details of my interpretation are no doubt challengeable, but they should be challenged or accepted within the context of the poem itself; the implications of "extension" and "intension" can prove nothing, and may start us off on false trails.

The other recent view of metaphor that I want to consider here is that of Martin Foss.[2] His stated intention in *Symbol and Metaphor* is to show the place of metaphor among other forms of thought, indicating both its unique and irreducible role and its interrelations with non-metaphorical forms. Metaphor, he declares, is more than Wundt's *Gesamt-Vorstellung;* it is "a process of tension and energy" which has a unique generality of intension involving a sacrifice of the systematic and conventional meaning of the terms, and "it is their mutual destruction in this process out of which a new and strange insight arises." Professor Foss describes this metaphoric process as "energy-tension," and emphasizes that it is a process running through the texture of expressive language and not confined to single words and phrases.

Now the double idea provoked by the epithet "energy-tension" contributes substantially to the discussion of metaphor, but I have certain reservations about Mr. Foss's handling of it. In the first place, while "sacrifice" is correctly introduced, "destruction" is surely too strong. If the conventional meanings of the terms drawn into the energy-tension were really destroyed, would not the tension cease to exist? Vasconcelos' idea of vital synthesis should be recalled: a unification of heterogeneous elements in which the heterogeneity is yet paradoxically preserved. With this stipulation in mind it is possible, I would think, to accept *"Gesamt-Vorstellung"* without cavil—translating it "representation of a togetherness [of disparate elements]." To oppose, as Foss does, "a process of energy and change" to *Gesamt-Vorstellung* is misleading, for when the radical disparity of the wedded elements is *not* destroyed, an effective energy-tension is the natural result of such togetherness.

The confusion is increased, it seems to me, by Professor Foss's claim to share this promising view of metaphor as energy-tension with Aristotle. Surely if Aristotle had really understood metaphor in such a way it would be a matter of great importance and the only wonder would be that so provocative an interpretation had escaped the notice of his commentators for so many centuries. But has not Foss mistranslated the passage he cites (*Rhetoric*, 1412a)? Aristotle is there discussing a particular employment of metaphor whereby to represent inanimate objects as if animated. His illustrations are such commonplace Homeric ones as "The arrow *yearning* to fly to its mark" and "Down to the valley the boulder *remorselessly* bounded." He is not characterizing all metaphor as *energeia* (which in any case would not quite mean "tension") but is showing how one use of metaphor is to ascribe *energeia* (in the sense of fulfillment of an animate potency, hence quasi-deliberate action) to inanimate things. It is quite certain from Aristotle's treatment of *metaphora*, both in the *Rhetoric* and in the *Poetics*, that he is not thinking in the least of the kind of energy-tension which is generated by a union of heterogeneous elements in one commanding image, but simply of "the transference of a name (from the thing which it properly denotes) to some other thing." Aristotle's metabiological conception of *energeia*, then, cannot help us in analyzing what metaphoric energy-tension means and how it operates.

SIMILE AND PLURISIGNATION

The hypothesis which I should like to put forward is that metaphor at its best tends to achieve fullness of semantic energy-tension by a merging of two complementary elements— *simile* and *plurisignation*.[3] In simile, two verbal expressions each conveying an individual image or idea, are joined; in plurisignation, a single verbal expression carries two or more meanings simultaneously. That is to say, in simile the vehicle is plural, the tenor single; in plurisignation the vehicle is single, the tenor plural. If this contrast appears too simple and gross to describe most actual poetic situations, that is because there is a tendency in poetic language for the two tropes to blend into a metaphoric unity-in-diversity—as the following set of graded examples, starting first from the side of simile and then from the side of plurisignation, is intended to show.

SIMILE

A simple simile without any plurisignative depth is usually not very interesting. Examples come readily to mind: "He ran like a scared rabbit"; "He pecks at his food like a canary"; Aeschylus' designation of dust as "the brother of wind" and of a harbor as "stepmother of ships"; Coleridge's remark that "an author's pen, like children's legs, improves by exercise." Such similes depend in each case upon a single point of resemblance. They offer us no fresh apperception: only, at best, the amiable surprise of a likeness before unnoticed ("The majority of husbands remind me of an orangutang trying to play the violin"—Balzac), or the comedy of one deftly presented ("A simple fellow in gay clothes is like a cinnamon tree: the bark is of more value than the body");[4] at worst a stereotyped mental prop ("as fast as greased lightning").

Consider next the simile, "Shame covered him like a garment." To my sense there is a bit more of poetic expressiveness here (nothing remarkable, to be sure) than in the examples that precede. Why so? There are three reasons, I think. First, the tenor, *shame,* has deeper roots of emotive interest than any of the tenors above except possibly, to some persons, "harbor"—certainly more so than running, pecking, dust (in this context), and pen—and therefore offers more latent possibilities of effective association. Secondly, the vehicle, *garment,* carries unidentified overtones of literary, especially Biblical, association, which most of the other vehicles —scared rabbit, canary, stepmother, and legs—lack. (The vehicle "brother" might evoke a good deal in other contexts; in the one presented, however, it is somewhat prosaically restricted by the general sense.) Finally, the vehicle-idea of a garment covering a man physically and the tenor-idea of shame taking possession of his mind and psyche, are connected by an unmentioned intermediary, which is almost certainly on the verge of presenting itself to the reader's consciousness—namely, the idea of a blush covering the face. The blush is like a garment in being spatial and external, while at the same time it is causally related to and symptomatic of shame. Accordingly the imagination is stirred and enriched by the present simile more than by the earlier ones. The simile has, semantically speaking, a touch of the metaphoric.

There is a more celebrated as well as a more amply poetic use of the garment image in Wordsworth's sonnet, "Upon Westminster Bridge":

> The City now doth like a garment wear
> The beauty of the morning . . .

Here, in addition to the idea of "covering," there are two other characteristics of a garment which were not suggested in the earlier instance. Garments are ornamental, as "beauty" in the next line reminds us; and garments are transient, for the beauty is but the beauty of the morning and will not last. The idea of covering, moreover, would doubtless suggest the physical phenomenon of a morning mist; yet the imagery of the sonnet suggests on the whole a pellucid purity of the early morning scene, so that there is a touch of paradox, never brought to explicit recognition, in the garment image as employed here.

When a simile is stated in very explicit terms there is sometimes danger of overlooking the plurisignative depth which lies beneath it. The following stanza by Emily Brontë appears, on the surface, to depend on a single point of resemblance:

> Love is like the wild rose-briar;
> Friendship like the holly-tree.
> The holly is dark when the rose-briar blooms,
> But which will bloom more constantly?[5]

The analogy, or proportionate equality, which is of the essence of simile, stands out with unusual clarity here. Baldly

we could paraphrase: As the rose-briar's beauty blooms earlier and more strikingly than the holly's but fades sooner, so
it is with love and friendship respectively. And yet the comparison has an unmistakably poetic quality; it is no mere
workaday tool of explication. What produces that quality?
Partly, no doubt, melopoeia, the music of the cadences; but
there is more to it than that. Much can be attributed to the
plurisignative overtones of the component images as well.
The main statement which is made about love (implicitly in
the final question) is reënforced by the connotation of un-
predictability in "wild" and of possible hurt in "briar"; while
friendship, on the other hand, is caught up in the associations
of cool and green (since the holly-tree blooms through the
winter and its green leaves and bright red berries are especially associated with Christmastime) and restfully dark
(over and above the logically restricted scenario meaning
wherein "dark" refers only to the time before the berries
have appeared).

In technical contrast to the foregoing examples let us compare two lines from Shakespeare's Sonnets which have the
grammatical appearance of metaphors:

[A] To thy fair flower add the rank smell of weeds.
(Sonnet 69)
[B] Time's thievish progress to eternity.
(Sonnet 77)

I would judge [A] to be a suppressed, or tabloid simile. Its
expressiveness is limited by the implicit analogy: the beauty
of the youth likened to a fair flower, and his treachery likened
to the rank smell of weeds. On reading [B] I think we feel
at once the greater expressiveness of the figure, and I do not
believe that this comes merely from the melodramatic evocations of the word "thievish" nor from the quasi-mystical and
hyperbolic lift of the word "eternity." The greater interest of

it depends more legitimately upon the way in which the word "thievish" functions in the sentence. As connected with "progress" it suggests the kind of progress that a thief might be supposed to make—a sneaking, furtive sort of gait—and thus reminds us of one aspect of time, how it slips away without our noticing it. But "thievish" also connotes the act of stealing; and one of the main themes of the Sonnets is how time purloins and preys upon the beauty of youth. Let us say, then, that there are two images evoked by the word "thievish" in its given context—the image of seizing something that is supposed to belong to another, and the image of sneaking away clandestinely after the deed. But if that double image is the immediate tenor of the linguistic vehicle it is not the ultimate one. The images are not suggested for their own sake, but because they refer to, and evoke a sentiment about, the concretely complex idea of the pang of loss through time's passage. There are the particular losses, such as the beauty of a fair youth, of which time is the perpetrator; and there is the more pervasive loss of time itself, as the present tumbles into the past, and the blaze of the experienced moment fades first into the twilight glow of memory and then into the coldness of a dying image.

The comically ribald may be allowed to offer its own sort of testimony. Aristotle writes:

And Gorgias' address to the swallow when she dropped her leavings on him as she flew over, is in the best style of tragic diction. "For shame, Philomel," he said. For to a bird it was no disgrace to have done it, but to a young lady (parthenos) it was.[6]

Unfortunately the old master can't forget his vocation as a school-teacher, and feels compelled to add: "His reproach was apt, therefore, in addressing her in her former, not her present character." Ignoring the gloss we may observe that what makes the jolt of absurdity possible is the fact that ve-

hicle and tenor are drawn together not by any natural analogy but by the traditional story of Philomel being changed
into a bird. The idea of a young lady behaving as this particular bird behaved is plurisignative in its incongruity, since
the implications of such behavior for the arrangements of
human living might well be disruptive; our Freudian censor
inhibits our free contemplation of them however, and we
are left with an unexplored sense of the mock-scatological.
Doubtless Aristotle drew a supplementary laugh from his
Lyceum auditors by speaking of the ravished heroine as a
parthenos, with its secondary connotation of "virgin."

Of course there has to be a properly informed and fitly responsive set of readers if the metaphoric tension is to operate
effectively. In *Beowulf,* when one of King Hrethel's sons
compares the old king's desolation to that of a man whose
son is hanging on the gallows, a modern reader is apt to
judge the simile far-fetched; even, perhaps, without point; in
any case containing nothing of the metaphoric. But Dorothy
Whitelock has pointed out[7] that the utterance would have
struck the poet's contemporaries with a very different force
and sense. In feudal times the two terms of the comparison
had a specific connection. A son's death at another's hand
demanded vengeance; only so could the pain of it be as-
suaged. But of course a father could not take vengeance on
one son for the accidental killing of another. Now Anglo-
Saxon law forbade the taking of vengeance for an executed
criminal. Thus King Hrethel was quite as effectively de-
barred from taking vengeance in the one case as he would
have been in the other. The desolation produced by an un-
avenged death was overwhelming, and (semantically speaking) so manifold in its implications and meaning-connec-
tions, that any difference in the circumstances was minor.

"Satan hath desired to have you, that he may sift you as
wheat."[8] Here the vehicle is simple: the image of a miller
sifting meal. In the background, however, lurks the Biblical

warning that the chaff shall be separated out and burned; there is consequently the implication that if Satan gets his desire what *he* will be sifting is not the wheat-grain at all— an undercurrent of paradox; and there is the strong sense of horror, almost of melodrama, attaching to the fate of those (perhaps ourselves!) who fall through the sieve.

PLURISIGNATION

Having observed how simile tends to acquire expressivity and depth through the evocation of multiple meanings, fused and latent for the most part, let us now look more specifically at the technique of multiple reference, or plurisignation, starting with instances where it functions entirely by itself.

The readiness of expressive language to carry a plurality of meanings shows itself in such popular and familiar forms as innuendo, *double entendre,* and the pun. In a pun the multiple reference is potentially quite definite; i.e., it becomes explicit and even logically exact when the point of the pun is discovered: two or more clearly distinguishable denotations being joined together as the referends of a single word or phrase. Ordinary popular puns, however, combine the two meanings mechanically, as a joke, without involving any significant emotion, and have therefore no poetic relevance. But when Lady Macbeth replies to her husband's announcement that King Duncan comes tonight with the question, "And when goes hence?" the double meaning carries an ominous foreboding, functionally related to the movement of the drama.

Marvell's couplet which concludes the second stanza of *To His Coy Mistress* contains two interrelated instances, one of triple reference, the other of double:

> The grave's a fine and private place,
> But none, I think, do there embrace.

On the surface the word "fine" expresses approval of a place so "private" (also in the most obvious sense) where lovers might embrace without interruption, if only they were any longer capable of embracing at all. But the grave is "fine" also in marking the *finis,* the end of all earthly joys, the end of all embracing: an attentive reader thus gets a preview of the counteractive idea even before the second line of the couplet makes it explicit. And thirdly, "fine" carries the added meaning of narrow, constricted: as when we say "a fine line." Meanings 2 and 3 of "fine" stir up a second meaning of "private," from the Latin *privatus,* "deprived." Marvell is saying, then, with striking poetical economy, that in one of its aspects, its privacy, the grave would be a welcome refuge for lovers; that the grave marks an end, in that it deprives lovers of the joy of mutual embrace; and that the grave is very cramping.

What strikes us most impressively in the couplet just cited is Marvell's wit. Such is the case in general where a plurisignative expression is effective without any help from simile. Compare the lines in *Romeo and Juliet* where the old nurse promises Juliet

> To fetch a ladder, by the which your love
> Must climb a bird's nest soon when it is dark.

"Bird's nest" is a simile-vehicle here, for which there is no counterpart, in the Marvell couplet, which makes its *main* statement without indirection. But the Shakespeare passage carries plurisignation also. When we ask what is signified by climbing a bird's nest, the uninhibited reader may discover two principal referends, both of them prognosticative of later events. Romeo will use the ladder to climb to Juliet's balcony: that, of course, is the most obvious meaning. But since we have learnt to expect ribald innuendos when the nurse gabbles, and since what she actually says is not "climb up to" but "climb"—i.e., climb the bird's nest itself—we have, evidently, a witty advance notice of love's consummation. The ribaldry is inoffensive, however, not only because of its wit, but also because a profounder idea invites the attentive reader's imagination. As I shall show in Chapter X, climbing to the balcony of light ("It is the east, and Juliet is the sun") and its antithesis, descent into the tomb's darkness, furnish the main structure of the play's imagery, as well as evoking the archetypal life-and-death, light-and-darkness pattern which runs through all experience.

Not all cases of plurisignation are as plainly expoundable. Frequently only a single meaning is denotative and capable of literal translation, while the remaining meanings are purely connotative—felt rather than thought—and although controlled to a high degree by the context, do not have the kind of precision that would enable them to be satisfactorily explicated in analytical language. "Pray you, undo this button"; the request is plain, the denotation single; but the connotative overtones, generated by the context of King Lear's final tragic predicament and vision, have a strange power of suggesting more than can possibly be articulated—not excluding, perhaps, a hushed archetypal reference to some undefined ceremony of preparing for the soul's release from the body.

In most of the greater instances of depth metaphor the elements of plurisignation and simile-analogy are so firmly and naturally harmonized that a reader has no disposition to inquire whether the one or the other predominates.

> DUNCAN: Whence cam'st thou, worthy thane?
> ROSS: From Fife, great king;
> Where the Norweyan banners flout the sky
> And fan our people cold.
>
> (*Macbeth*, Act I, Scene ii)

The power of this metaphor comes in part from the tension between the two implicit similes: (1) the Norweyan banners are visually like great fans in the air; and (2) as fans cool our outward parts, so the banners chill our inward parts with fear. But the effect is ambivalent, for the psychological antithesis strikes us more forcibly than the resemblance. Moreover, there is a tension between the fear so indicated and induced by the present metaphor and the fear-*motif* which is dominant throughout the play and which has already been announced by the haggard appearance and ominous words of the Weird Sisters in Scene i. This fear, in turn, moves along in dramatic tension with Macbeth's (and his Lady's) *hybris,* their over-vaulting ambition, their eventual usurpation and tyranny. The image of banners flouting the sky is perhaps a kind of visual foreshadowing of that sequent rage. These are but clues; the power of the metaphor outruns every expository maneuver.

Homer's "His coming was like the night" shows a similar intransigeance. To explain conscientiously that as the darkness of night brings dangers and terrors to men, so Apollo in his anger brings dangers and terrors to the offending Greeks, is beside the mark—as perhaps every attempted explication must be. For night does not invariably bring evil; it may also bring peace and soothing rest. There are different ways in which we can conceive night, and the particular way here appropriate is pointed by the metaphor itself. Thus not only does the simile of night explain the manner of Apollo's coming, but simultaneously Apollo's manner of coming explains the relevant characteristic of night. What we have here is a kind of *floating* plurisignation.

Consider now Dante's description of Hell as "there where the sun is silent" *(dove il sole tace)* and the "Blind mouths!" of Milton's *Lycidas*. In these two instances a further technique is involved: synaesthesia—the fusing of imagery drawn from two different sense-channels. "The darkness caused by the sun's absence is analogous to the silence caused by the stoppage of its voice if it could speak." "Mouths which cannot speak the word [sub-metaphor: "have not learned to hold a sheep-hook"—hence, by implication, cannot call to Christ's lost and wandering sheep] are analogous to eyes which have lost their faculty of sight." These logical similitudes are probably about as close as we can approximate to the poetic meanings analytically, but they still leave us far away.

It might be instructive to cite, by way of contrast, a case of poetic synaesthesia where logical explication is much more nearly relevant (if never quite completely so), and has indeed been sanctioned by the poet. The case I have in mind is the synaesthetic metaphor in the line from Edith Sitwell's *Aubade:*

The morning light creaks down again . . .

In her *Poetry and Criticism* Miss Sitwell has written a lively defence both of synaesthesia in general and of the particular case of it here quoted.[9] In general: "The modernist poet's . . . senses have become broadened and cosmopolitanised; they are no longer little islands, speaking only their own narrow language, living their sleepy life alone. When the speech of one sense is insufficient to convey his entire meaning, he uses the language of another." Commenting on the metaphor of "light creaking" she observes that "in a very early dawn, after rain, the light has a curious uncertain quality, as though it does not run quite smoothly. Also, it falls in hard cubes, squares, and triangles, which, again, give one the impression of a creaking sound, because of the associations with wood." This strikes me as an apt enough exposition, as expositions go. But it would be misleading to take the instance as altogether typical. The peculiar brand of *translatio,* the quality of quasi-neurosis and extrapolated nausea, with which Miss Sitwell so frequently invests her verbs, establishes, after one has read a good bit of it, a sort of aesthetic stereotype of its own; which, however, her spurts of real poetic dedication, as in *Still Falls the Rain*, are sometimes able to overcome. More to the point, her reasons for metaphoric fusion are likely to be intellectually expoundable ones, so that the fusion tends to crumble, I mean the poetic quality of it does, under examination. The splendor of Dante's great synaesthetic metaphor is perduring; once uttered it shows not the least tendency to crumble; it affirms itself with the authenticity of an age-old archetype, drawn from correspondences that lie deep within the heart of nature herself.

LATENT METAPHOR

It has often been remarked that essential, or functional, or radical metaphor, is a chief contributor to the growth and enrichment of language. Friedrich Max Müller, who brought the phrase "radical metaphor" into general use, was especially concerned with just that power of it.[10] Sanskrit, the oldest known member of our Indo-European language group, shows many examples of the process, as Müller demonstrates. The Sanskrit word *arka,* from a root meaning "to shine," comes to signify both the sun and a hymn of praise. The splitting seems to have occurred not by deliberate comparison and transference, but through a mode of experience in which the visible shining and the bursting forth of joy from the heart appeared as two manifestations of one and the same effulgent reality.

Again, as the record of language demonstrates, early Aryan man, in developing the distinct arts of weaving and of setting lines to catch birds, saw enough similarity between the two manual procedures to warrant calling them by a single name. Weaving, says Müller, would thus take the sense of putting snares, and when a new word was wanted for setting snares in a figurative sense—that is, for tricking, cheating, luring, inveigling a person by false words—nothing, again, would have been more natural than to take a word signifying "to weave" and use it in that sense. Thus when Homer speaks of "weaving a plot" he may not have been putting two distinct ideas together, as he was evidently doing in many of his similes; he may have been perpetuating a very old metaphoric fusion of ideas which became intermittently distinct only as practical conditions might require, but which remained more or less fused in the traditional poetic phraseology that was part of the ancient bard's heritage. This particular metaphoric fusion has left its trace in our word "subtle," from the Latin *subtilis,* which in turn (if Müller's view is correct) comes from *subtextere,* "to weave beneath."

The last example is a reminder of the fate that eventually overtakes radical metaphors. They grow old and moribund, losing the vital tension of opposed meanings, dramatic antithesis, paradox, which was theirs at their inception. They become fossilized and enter into our everyday speech as steno-symbols which have lost their one-time color and allusiveness and power to stir. Sometimes the metaphoric origin of a word is obvious if we stop to think. Familiar words like *skyscraper, arm* of a chair, *leg* of table, *leaf* of book, and countless others that will readily suggest themselves are plain enough cases. Other ex-metaphoric words reveal their ancestry only if one recognizes their Latin or Anglo-Saxon, more rarely their French or Greek roots. *Compose, propose, depose, dispose, repose, impose, oppose*—such a group as this illustrates the metaphoric branching out from an original Latin root which has made possible so many useful and sometimes expressive discriminations in English. In the case of still other words the metaphoric origin cannot be traced directly but can sometimes be inferred circumstantially on the basis of comparative philology. This is a task for scholars in that field: the rest of us can only accept their results and apply them to the elucidation of semantic principles. All in all, it becomes evident that the extension, amplification, or transference of an original plain meaning through metaphor is a major factor, perhaps the most important of any, in the making of language. "Three-fourths of our language may be said to consist of worn-out metaphors," declares A. H. Sayce.[11]

Some writers, at the opposite extreme from Aristotle and Quintilian, are so impressed by the semantic power of metaphor that they regard *all* meaning as metaphoric. Thus I. A. Richards has argued that all language is "radically metaphoric, inasmuch as all language, and even all wordless thinking, depends on our sorting *this* from *that*," classifying *this* along with other entities similar to it and differentiating them as a group from what does not share their qualities or functions.[12] Accordingly Professor Richards distinguishes between metaphor as equivalent to language in general and metaphor more narrowly defined. In the latter, more restricted sense of the term, "we cross sorts to make occasional new sorts, but the sorting process is fundamental." In short, all language is metaphorical in the broad sense because to speak referentially at all involves a "sorting"; certain specimens of language are called metaphoric in the narrower and more familiar sense because they involve a *new* kind of sorting.

But surely Mr. Richards has driven an important half-truth too far. Metaphor is doubtless the most important single factor in the evolution of language, but it cannot be the explanation of language unreservedly. The metaphoric extension of language presupposes that language of a sort already exists. Some words have originated by imitation of natural sounds or animal cries; others as simple ejaculations, growl-and-purr words—either laryngeal reflexes which a situation calls forth we know not how, or (at a more conscious level) sounds that just seem fitting to designate a certain thing or quality entertained in a certain mood. Children frequently make up words in such a fashion, and men in the childhood of history probably did so pretty freely. The associative law of emotional congruity is at work in such behavior: a sound and a situation are coupled because at a given moment they strike the speaker as having the same emotional tone. The mood passes, but the wedlock has been joined.

A milder form of the error in question seems to be contained in Martin Foss's view, in the volume already cited, that the word "being" is metaphorical. Now etymologically it is a fact that the several forms of the verb "to be" are ex-metaphors, as Müller (among others) has demonstrated.[13] Our word "be" is derived, by Müller's hypothesis, from the same root as the Sanskrit *bhu*, "to grow, or make grow." The English forms "am" and "is" have divergently evolved from the same root as Sanskrit *asmi*, "to breathe." The irregular conjugation of our most nondescript verb is thus a surprising record of a time when man had no independent word for "existence" and could express the idea only by choosing whether to say that something "grows" or that it "breathes." Mr. Foss, however, does not confine himself to acknowledging the verb's history. He maintains that the word *as we now use it* is in some sense metaphorical. As I see the matter there is one sense in which his ascription is both true and important, another in which it is both false and trivial, and it may throw some further light upon the nature of metaphor to understand just what these two senses are.

In the one, the trivial sense, Foss asserts that the copula "is" functions metaphorically in the very process of bringing together two distinct concepts, a subject and a predicate.

Now surely the idea of metaphor becomes unusably flattened out when it is broadened to such a degree. Are we to allege that "The moon is round" and "The moon is a pancake" are equally metaphorical on the ground that in both cases a meaning other than "moon" is predicated of the moon? But partial otherness is predicated of a subject in *any* significant predication, it does not specifically establish the presence of metaphor. (Let us keep our terms as tidy as the general crepuscule allows.) There is a plainly understood sense in which it is metaphorical to describe the moon as a pancake and not metaphorical to describe it as round. Foss's term "energy-tension," which I adopted earlier, might (although he does not himself use it in this way) help to explain the difference. There is more energy-tension, I would say, in the idea of a pancake moon than in the idea of a round moon, because there are more disparate groups of qualities huddled together and thus an element of paradox, of ambivalence, of tension between astronomical and breakfast-table associations, is introduced.

The other and more valid sense in which "being" is intrinsically metaphorical could be put somewhat like this. When I say "There is (exists) a God" and "There is (exists) an Empire State Building," does the word "is" have the same meaning in the two cases or two different meanings? Operationally the meanings are different, since different procedures of validation would be called for. Shall we say, then, that the word "is"—or better, the phrase "there is," which is roughly equivalent to "exists"—is used metaphorically in both or either of these instances? The answer, again, can be stated with the help of that good term "energy-tension." In our technosophic age the most literal meaning of "exist"—i.e., the most familiar, natural, unreservedly acceptable—is the naturalistic one: a thing exists so far as it has place in the publicly shared space-time continuum which Foss designates "environment," and thus so far as it can be verified by experimental techniques. On this basis it is meaningful and true to say that there is an Empire State Building and it is largely meaningless to say that there is a God—at least some of the indispensable elements of God's meaning are canceled out. From this standpoint, then, the word "exist" is used metaphorically in the statement "God exists"—either as a dead, perfunctory metaphor (which is doubtless how most of us use it most of the time) or as a living paradox, a vibrant, highly charged tension between more or less incompatible meanings—between "being" in the sense of plain empirical existence and "being" in some incompletely defined sense that ploughs up our ordered reality-perspective in struggling for birth. The statement "God exists" is thus inescapably metaphorical and paradoxical in an age like ours where the notion of existence is straitjacketed by experimental and statistical techniques. But it is an inexpungeable expression of what Foss calls our "world," in contradistinction to our "environment"; of the flowing wholeness of things, which we know through the total response of our personhood, and which generates the central divine myth around which our being revolves. The metaphor and the myth are necessary expressions of the human psyche's most central energy-tension; without it and the other expressive energy-tensions that it has engendered during several millenia of cultural history mankind would succumb to the fate that the Forgotten Enemy holds ever in store for us, of falling from the ambiguous grace of being human into the unisignative security of the reacting mechanism

SEVEN

Emblem and Archetype

As man desires not only novelty but also a security of connection with the stable and unchanging, so the imagination operates not only creatively but interpretively—not only by fusing or recontextualizing old ideas in such a way as to generate new ones but also by grasping the particular idea and the transient image in relation to something more universal and perduring. The former is the metaphoric way of imagining, to which the preceding chapter was devoted. The latter may be called archetypal, or (where picture-thinking is stressed) emblematic. The two strategies are natural complementaries in poetic discourse, the one giving liveliness and freshness, the other depth and significance. The expressive imagination is thus, in one aspect, a kind of melting-pot, fusing together diverse elements into a highly individual brew; while in another aspect it is a kind of threshold—a "gateless gateway," as a Chinese philosopher has said[1]—drawing the attention toward truths greater than ordinary.

THE SUN, THE WHEEL, AND THE SVASTIKA

There is one daily phenomenon in particular that impresses men repeatedly, and in the most diverse ages and countries, as symbolizing certain attributes of godhead. That is the sun. The solar effulgence arouses men's minds to a sense of power and majesty, while the light of it, in making vision possible, becomes a ready symbol for the spiritual vision which is synonymous with the highest wisdom. A further attribute of the sun, its orderly course through the sky, is symbolically suggestive of the element of law in nature. The stars, to be sure, as distinct from the planets, show equal evidence of order, but the size and radiance of the sun tend to give him clear priority as its cause or guardian. These are the most general of the transcendental associations of the sun, supplemented by other more special ones in various localities according to the conditions of living or the accidents of tribal experience. An example of such transcendental particularity is the ancient Egyptian identification of the sun with the scarab, or dung-beetle, which protects its eggs by rolling them up in a ball of dung, which it then pushes along the ground to a proper hatching place. By an obvious step the sun's movement becomes attributed to an invisible cosmic scarab which pushes it slowly each day across the blue sky. Moreover, since the dung-ball contains fertilized eggs, the sun is analogously conceived to possess the germs of life and growth. The Egyptian solar journey falls with equal ease into other imagistic patterns too: notably that of Amon-Ra navigating a boat with the sun as its cargo. In Greece it is not a boat but a chariot that Apollo harnesses up and drives across the vault each morning; and so, with changes of detail, in many other countries.

As an introduction to certain other solar symbols and associations let me cite a more particular and more recent piece of evidence. In Gloucestershire and Herefordshire, England, according to the testimony of Mrs. Murray-Aynsley,[2] it was a not uncommon circumstance half a century ago to see on the external walls of some of the older houses one or two pieces of hoop iron moulded into characteristic S-like forms, of which the following are typical:

According to local legend these insignia had the double virtue of protecting the house both from fire and from collapse.
How can this curious combination of ideas be explained?

As a preliminary to explanation let us examine another
piece of evidence, which I take from the same authority. The
coat of arms of the Macleod family of the Isle of Man contains in its second quarter the three-legged Manx man, or
trinacria, described in heraldic terms as "the three legs of a
man proper, conjoined in the center at the upper part of the
thighs, placed in a triangle, garnished and spurred, *or.*"

The motto belonging to this fugitive figure is: *Quocunque
jeceris stabit,* "However you throw him, he will stand." Another ancient family of the Isle of Man, the Stanleys, use
the same three-legged armorial emblem but with a different
motto: *Luceo non uro,* "I give light, but I do not burn." Observe how the two ideas associated with the Manxman figure
are virtually the same as those associated with the English
hoop-iron patterns: the idea of security from collapse, which
on the positive side is self-sufficiency and self-sustension; and
the idea of security from fire, which now turns out to be connected with the positive idea of light. We seem to be on some
kind of a trail.

The *trinacria* and associated forms, grouped under the
general term *triskelion,* have been widespread throughout

Europe. To mention only a few of many examples, the coat
of arms of Sicily includes a *trinacria* fitted out with a face, a
beard, and what might be large ears:

And the following figures are found on old coins—the first
Lycian, the second Celtiberian, the third from Megara:

Their iconographical connection with the three-legged Manxman is not hard to see, and the Megarian figure appears to
be also a symbol of the sun. But the most telling evidence
of all is furnished by sun and fire symbols from ancient
Denmark:

Here we find one of the hoop-iron figures and can see its relation to the svastika, while both in turn are related to the
circular figure containing a cross. What is the significance
of this latter? Does it represent the Sun or a Wheel? The answer, based on the evidence of ancient Aryan symbols preserved in India, must be—both!

The symbolic significance of the Wheel is well known. A

perfect wheel has the property that the circumference moves
uniformly while the center, the mathematical axis, stays unmoved. The Wheel thus symbolizes the blessed state of attainment which the great teachers of India— Krishna and
Buddha in particular—have taught as man's true goal; to
find the pure center, the *atman* or absolute self, at the heart
of every action and choice, and thereby to act in perfect
harmony and serenity. As Krishna tells Arjuna the troubled
warrior, "Act for the sake of good action only, and not for
the fruits of action." Circular movement is the one perfect
form of movement, both to Hindu thinkers and to Greek, because of its geometrical self-sufficiency. Purity of motive,
riddance of all desire for fruits, which is the one secure
ground of human self-sufficiency, is symbolized in some Buddhist emblems by a lotus flower at the wheel's hub.

Clearly the Wheel has an iconic connection with the Sun.
The spokes of the one are the rays of the other, and in either
case they stood to the Hindu for the lines of influence streaming out from the divine center of things to all created beings.
The number of rays, or spokes, varies: sometimes sixteen,
sometimes eight, sometimes four, and more rarely some other
number. The reduction of the outgoing lines to four is hardly a matter of economy; they probably represent the four
cardinal directions, as the following ancient Buddhist figure
strongly suggests:

Here we can see the process of transition of the Sun-Wheel
figure to the Svastika. If you take the figure as a wheel, the
broken circumference can be (and has been) taken to represent rotary motion. If you take it as the sun, they probably

represent the four winds. For our ancestors were less inclined than we to think of directions abstractly: concretely
experienced they are not directions on a map, but directions
from which the different types of wind were likely to arise,
bringing weal or bane to men. But the motionless sun lives
serenely above the moving winds, even as the mathematical
axis of the wheel remains unmoved by the circling spokes.
Since the wheel, then, symbolizes perfect and self-sufficient
motion and since the sun is the primal source and representative of light and fire, we discover in this ancient Aryan
symbol-connection the likeliest explanation both of the Herefordshire legend and of the seemingly inconsistent inscriptions on the Manx coats of arms.

Now if we were to think of the svastika as actually having evolved into the *trinacria,* or into other forms of the
triskelion, we would have to agree with the theory which
has been advanced that these are but forms of the svastika
as a sun and fire symbol which in process of time has lost
one of its arms. There does not appear to be any actual evidence for such a development however; the theory can hardly be anything more than an admission of ignorance. Granted
that any theory of the matter must fall far short of certainty,
I think that a comparative study of the symbols makes it
probable that the threefold (triskelion) figures and the fourfold (svastika) figures represent independent paths of development from a common source.

For in general it may be said that Three is associated
with heavenly, Four with earthly attributes. Stated so baldly
the principle is oversimplified and exceptions can be found.
Nevertheless the distinction is valid in a broad way, and it
has its reasons. Those relating to the mundane character
of Four are the more obvious: the importance of the four
cardinal directions is sufficient to account for it. The ancient prominence of the svastika confirms this explanation—

if the curved form of the segments attached to the points of the cross really did, as some think, represent the winds. For the winds, as I have said, were likely to be associated with the four cardinal directions, or, as we would say, the four points of the compass. The directions themselves were more concretely envisaged then than now. There was the place of the rising sun and there was the opposed place where the sun at the end of his quotidian journey dropped into the caverns of night or dissolved in the circumambient sea of fire. Then there was the direction of the pole star, from which, in the northern hemisphere the wintry blasts come; and there was the contrary direction, where the sun retires in winter ("to escape the cold," as Herodotus reports), bringing the zephyrs back with him when he returns. In Egypt the north-south axis is marked by the Nile River, which notwithstanding its sinuosities, flows generally northward. Anatomically, moreover, it is natural for a man to think in terms of front, back, and both sides—what he sees ahead, what lurks behind, and what moves along in equal-going companionship. The winds, to be sure, do not observe the geometrical requirements of such a conception, but the stylizing imagination supplies that formal pattern which the natural phenomena themselves lack. Fourness is primarily associated with earth, particularly with earth in its geographical rather than in its reproductive and nutritive character.

In Western tradition there are certain more special meanings attached to the number four, by virtue of such influential though culturally restricted doctrines as the Four Elements and the Four Humors. These conceptions would have no archetypal validity to an Easterner, unless affected by Western indoctrination. But that the idea of the Four Elements has achieved archetypal status in the literary consciousness of the West is proved by Shakespeare's symbolic exploitation of it: the immersion of Ariel and Caliban in air-and-fire imagery and earth-and-water imagery respectively, and the contrast between Cleopatra's earth-and-water imagery, concretized also in the crocodile and Nilus' slime—

> Rather a ditch in Egypt
> Be gentle grave unto me! rather on Nilus' mud
> Lay me stark naked, and let the water-flies
> Blow me into abhorring!
> (*Antony and Cleopatra*, Act V, Scene ii)

with her air-and-fire imagery, as the spirit is about to find release—

> Husband, I come:
> Now to that name my courage prove my title!
> I am fire and air; my other elements
> I give to baser life.
> *(ibid.)*

Outside of the West and its sphere of influence, however, the Four Elements doctrine has little or no standing. In the Hindu intellectual tradition its place is supplied by the doctrine of the three *gunas;* in the Taoist by the dyad, *yang* and *yin.* And so far as I can discover, every concrete manifestation of Fourness other than those associated with the cardinal directions is analogously limited.

THE PRIMAL TRIAD

The number Three tends to be symbolically associated with the religious perspective as Four does with the mundane. But there is no simple factor that will explain the former of these associations as readily as earth's four windways seem to explain the latter. Any phenomenon of a religious sort that may be appealed to, such as the Christian or the Egyptian or the Hindu Trinity, is more plausibly understood as a manifestation or effect of the triadic archetype than as its cause. Of natural phenomena there is one that undoubtedly contributes to the triadic idea in some cultures, and that is the basic family structure of Father, Mother, Child. In Egypt the resultant divine archetype—Osiris, Isis, Horus—was the supreme manifestation of Three-ness to the popular religious consciousness. An analogous family archetype is prominent in Christian iconography, displayed usually in one of two settings—the Manger (or Cave) and the Flight into Egypt. Had the popular elements of primitive Christianity been allowed to follow their natural bent I dare say this family triad might have become a dominant one, moulding the structure of Christian thinking—although the ambiguous role of Joseph in the family relationship might have proved a stumbling-block. Historically the Christian Trinity took a different form. Father and Son are present in it, but the place of the Mother is taken by the sexless Holy Pneuma. In ancient Greece, in the Eleusinian Mysteries, the two aspects of womanhood—the fruition of maternity and the desirable femininity ripe for first ploughing—are symbolized by Demeter and Persephone respectively, the father figure remaining in the shadowy background, from which the ancient mythologizers would draw him forth for purposes not of worship but of rationalization. Zeus was needed simply as stud. In that other most prominent of the early Greek chthonic cults, the Dionysian, it is the father-son axis that was emphasized. Dionysus, the divine bull-man child, is the object of worship. Zeus, not involved in the worship, serves as his mythic begetter. In both these cults the family pattern is incomplete and ill-balanced; reflecting no doubt the deficiency (from our point of view) of the actual family relationship in Greek life. It is not through the family pattern but in a religiously deeper and culturally more pervasive way, as will be evident from Chapter X, that the Triad mani-

fests itself in Greek religious thought. In Hinduism and Buddhism, too, the most influential forms of triadicity are not
those drawn from the pattern of family life.

When we turn from the biological model to the fundamental structure of human thought itself, it seems that there
are two primary ways in which the idea of Threeness tends
to impress itself upon man's awareness and enter into his
interpretation of situations and events. Geometrizing them
for clearer consideration, I will call them the linear and the
triangular. The linear triad may take the temporal forms,
Beginning-Middle-End and Past-Present-Future. Its chief
spatial form, archetypally, consists of the three elements:
Down-here (Earth), Up-there (Sky), and In-between (Atmosphere). The religious importance of the Linear Triad
shows itself in the search for, and mythic imagining of, a
meeting-ground between Earth and Heaven. Spirits of the
middle air, the *asuras* of Hinduism, the *daevas* of Zoroas-
trianism, the *daimones* of ancient Greece, and in a more special way the angels of the Lord in Christianity, are among
the special forms of intermediary between man and God—
between the vicissitudes of Earth and the blessedness of
Heaven. A cosmographic form of the idea is represented in
ancient Egypt by the combined figures of Nut, the sky-god-
dess encompassing both Shu, god of the atmosphere, who
seems to be holding her up, and Geb, recumbent on the
ground:

The triangular form of triadic thinking, on the other hand, is the one by which Hegel has endeavored to systematize all thought and all existence, structuralized as Thesis—Antithesis—Synthesis. There is a firm core of truth in his basic insight, despite the extravagances into which his zeal for system betrayed him. The dialectical movement of thought is fundamental to human living. A says "Yes," B says "No." If they stop there, the outcome must be either indifference or capitulation or war. Can they, however, find a reasonable way of resolving their dispute? In making the characteristically human, because rational, search for a common meeting ground we are declaring in effect that Antithesis, the Dyad, is insufficient as a terminus of thought, and are accepting the triangular Triad as our schematic guide. We are postulating that there shall always be, ideally, a reconciling principle.

Aristotle, in analyzing the principles by which, most basically, nature is to be explained, is insistent on the need of a reconciling principle in all understanding of nature. We cannot simply follow Heraclitus, he argues, and explain the world as a passage from opposite to opposite. If we did so we could apprehend the world kaleidoscopically, but we would have no ground for thinking and speaking of a thing (an *ousia*, in his vocabulary) as changing its qualities while still remaining itself. Yet we obviously cannot get along without this kind of thought-pattern. Hence, he concludes, "the subject of any change is numerically one, but with a duality of form." When wood burns up there is the old form which is destroyed (the wood), there is the new form which is created (the ash), and there is the substance *(ousia)* which persists through the change, enabling us to say not merely that some wood has vanished and some ash has come into existence, but that this ash is the product of that wood.[3]

Aristotle's triadic way of envisioning all natural process is a kind of skeletal reflection of a religious archetype of funda-

mental importance: the triad of Destruction, Creation, Preservation. In many of the sacraments connected with seasonal
worship it is the first two terms that are stressed—the dying
and resurrected god. But the third term is usually implicit,
for it is the same Tammuz or Attis or Osiris who is born to
new life in the new year. The sacred *uraeus* of Egypt, consisting of winged globe and serpent,[4] is a symbol of this
triadic relationship:

The dark disc represents the unknown God as the creative
source of all things. The wings represent "the brooding and
flying and protecting care and goodness of the Spirit." The
serpent is symbolically ambivalent. To complete the triad
neatly we would have to suppose that the serpent, by reason
of its lurking deadliness symbolizes death. Actually, however, all three archetypal elements are recapitulated in the
serpent itself. Death it signifies, for familiar reasons. But
stretched out straight, the serpent becomes a phallus symbolizing the reproductive power of Godhead—an idea which
is reinforced by the serpent's periodic shedding of its skin
and thus being born, as it were, to new life. Finally, when
coiled into a circle, it symbolizes the self-sufficiency and oneness which are associated with God's preservative power.
Thus both the serpent figure itself and the winged figure
which includes it represent the divine triad of Creation—
Destruction—Preservation.

In India an analogous form of the Triad has attained even

greater prominence. The three great gods—Brahma the Creator, Shiva the Destroyer, and Vishnu the Preserver—are, according to the *Mahabharata,* emanations or manifestations
(trimurti) of the impersonal Atma-Brahman,[5] the supreme
principle and World-Ground. In actual worship, however,
the three gods receive unequal treatment. Brahma evidently
keeps his place in the triad in order to fill out the logical
structure—the logic of process, which Aristotle's independent
analysis has laid bare—and he has enjoyed a certain emblematic development, as when he is portrayed as a four-
headed king riding a white goose; but he has only a minor
place in the devotional life of India. Shiva and Vishnu are
the gods principally worshipped, and for reasons which appear different on the surface but have an underlying bond
of connection. Shiva, like the Egyptian *uraeus*-serpent, is
ambivalent in nature. Out of his destructive aspect, classi-
cally emphasized in the *Mahabharata,* there has arisen a
belief in his reproductive power. His principal emblems are
the *linga* and the *yoni,* representing the male and female organs of generation. He is worshiped, therefore, as symbolizing the mystery of reproduction (with its allusive overtone
of death passing into new life), and more broadly of creative
force in whatever form. The twin ideas of death and new
birth, appealing so strongly to our fears and our hopes, carry
a strong potential of emotional experience, as every deeply
ambivalent idea tends to do.

If Shiva represents the paradox of two-in-one, Vishnu represents the paradox of many-in-one. The difference is not a
numerical but a qualitative one. For Vishnu is the god who
incarnates himself, who comes repeatedly to earth in one
or another heroic or saintly guise *(avatar)*—notably as Rama,
the legendary hero of the epic *Ramayana,* and as Krishna,
the godlike transfigured charioteer of the devotional *Bhagavad-Gita.*[6] Thus the proliferation of interests and problems

breaks up the symmetry of the original triad, without however altogether destroying the sense of triadicity as somehow
basic.

In a more intellectualized way the Hindu urge to think
triadically shows itself in the doctrine of the *gunas*—the
three kinds of quality-substance-action (the three categories
are fused here) of which the manifested world is composed.[7]
The manifested world *(prakriti)* is not simply the world
around us; it includes our psychic states too. Both outwardly and inwardly (unless by disciplined renunciation of the
manifested we penetrate to the innermost core of Selfhood,
the *Atman*) we find these three tendencies at work, or (from
a passive standpoint) these three qualities apparent. They
are *sattva*—the bright, serene; *rajas*—the active, intense;
tamas—the dark, inert. Every human disposition, as every
substance and event of nature, contains the three elements
in one proportion or another. Members of the Brahmin caste
approximate pure *sattva,* it is said; the Kshatriyas (warriors)
are a mixture of *sattva* and *rajas;* the Vaisyas (farmers and
artisans) a mixture of *rajas* and *tamas;* while the lowly Shu-
dra caste is explained as unleavened *tamas.* By this ingenious
set of interlocking correspondences the Hindu thinker has
succeeded in harmonizing the triadic principle, whose origin
is religious, with the quartic principle, which manifests itself
in the differentiation of men in society.

The Platonic triad of mind, energy, and appetite stands in
such striking analogy with the Hindu triad of *gunas* as to
prompt the question whether they may possibly have had a
common Indo-European root. There is no historical evidence
for the proposition, although additional analogical evidence
may be found in the fact that Plato's symbol of the charioteer
driving the spirited and the sluggish horse has a loose analogue in the *Upanishads.* At all events Plato, as most readers
know, used that psychologically oriented triad as a basis for

The Tree

The Tomb

The Wheel

EMBLEMS FROM MAHAYANA BUDDHISM.
BAS-RELIEF PANELS ON A GATE OF THE
BUDDHIST STUPA AT SANCHI.

understanding not only man but society. Mind *(nous, noesis)* must be the ruler of the energies (which, properly disciplined, support it) and the appetites (which are naturally recalcitrant); in the commonwealth it is those with harmoniously functioning minds, the effective lovers of wisdom, who should similarly have authority over both the energetic citizens (their potential allies) and the sluggishly appetitive (who have mainly to be kept in check).[8]

How does the Christian Trinity relate to these other trinities and triads? An attempt to answer this difficult question can be facilitated by appealing not directly to the theological dogma, which is an intellectual abstraction, but to a triad of Scriptural images which draws us closer to the primitively Christian way of thinking. In the Gospel according to John, Christ is declared to be the Word (John, 1:1), the true Light (John, 1:9), and, in a later chapter, the true Vine (John, 15:1). Of these three symbols it was the Word that became, in Christian history, specifically identified with Christ, the second Persona of the Trinity. What then of the other two? Since our aim cannot be certain proof; but must be content with probabilities or even plausibilities based upon relevant archetypal analogies, I would like to introduce by way of suggestive comparison a triad of emblems from Mahayana Buddhism—the Tree, the Tomb, and the Wheel.[9]

The Tree, in one aspect, represents the *bo* tree under which Siddhartha Gotoma sat when he experienced the great revelation wherein he knew himself to be a Buddha. But it has developed also a broader significance, as the Tree of Life. The Tomb represents, of course, Death. But neither death nor life is final; they are complementaries, ceaselessly conjoined in the world of *maya*, the illusionistic world of manifold phenomena. Living and dying are, as it were, convex and concave of the same arc. Behind them both (or above, or beneath, or at the center of them) is the Self-Subsistent, the ultimate Ground of all things. How shall it be represented unless by the most perfect figure of all, the circle? Its emblem, then, is the Wheel, which (as I have shown) is often iconographically interchangeable with the Sun, and the Wheel's spokes with the Sun's rays. The Wheel symbolizes the self-created and self-preservative, the primal and ultimate form of being, unmoved at the pure center, thereby causing perfect harmonious movement throughout its parts. A formalized version of the three emblems is found on ancient Indian-Buddhist coins:

In Christian iconography the Cross takes the place of the Tomb as death symbol. As an article of faith the death is followed by a resurrection, but it is the Crucifixion itself that looms most prominently among the emblems of Christianity. Moreover, if we take the statements in John 14:25-26 in their most natural signification, it would appear that Christ is about to depart, and that after he shall have done so the Holy Spirit will take his place. That such an interpretation is one of the classical heresies I am well aware, but I am discussing symbolic analogies, not the truth or falsity of doctrines. There does seem to be a symbolic affinity between Christ and the Tomb, as there is also between the Holy Spirit and the flourishing Vine of the Invisible Church. And somehow ontologically prior to them is the ultimate Godhead—at once the self-sustaining Cause (the Wheel) and the Light that gives meaning to all things (the Sun).

That the Cross symbolizes not only death but new life, would be admitted and indeed proclaimed by most Christians. It was the early Christians of Egypt, however, who found a visible emblem uniting the two conceptions. In place of the familiar form of the Cross they substituted the *tau*— T—which they called "the sacred sign" and "the sign of life." The Egyptologist Wilkinson writes that "the early Christians of Egypt adopted it in lieu of the Cross, which was afterward substituted for it; prefixing it to inscriptions in the same manner as the Cross in later times, and numerous inscriptions headed by the *tau* are preserved to the present day in early Christian sepulchres at the great Oasis."[10] Why was there this substitution of an emblem which to a Christian of the West might appear to be only a mutilated Cross? The *tau* had already been a potent symbol of renewed life in pre-Christian Egypt. When a new Pharaoh assumed the reins of government, the gods presented him with a *tau*—the presentation being enacted by human representatives in a sumptuous ceremony. The ceremony was regarded as quickening the life of the kingdom and ensuring health and power during the new king's reign.

But what lay back of the sacramental importance of the *tau?* The likeliest theory is that the emblem developed as an icon representing the key or plug with which the Egyptians closed and opened the dykes along the Nile—a device for spreading the periodic inundations more equitably among cultivators. When the river rose to a fixed height the appointed guardians made a T-shaped cut in the dam, releasing the waters. The gift of the *tau* to the Pharoah at his coronation, Mrs. Murray-Aynsley writes in the work already cited, "may have been intended to signify the bestowal on him by the gods of a typical key of the waters of the Nile, i.e., that it was a token of supreme power; thus it would not unnaturally be regarded as a sign of life, for without it the land could not yield its increase." Thus the *tau* is strongly ambivalent: symbolizing on the one hand Death (by its association with the Cross) and on the other hand more abundant Life (through release of the waters)—an ambivalence altogether appropriate to the Christian archetype, the second Person of the Trinity, which it was designed to express.

DIVINE CREATION

God made the cosmos. Why? It was a very odd thing to do.
                                                        DOM JOHN CHAPMAN

In the Shiva-Christ-Logos persona we see death and life, creation and destruction, as complementary sides of the same coin. But man's religious imagination refuses to stop there. What, it asks, are creation and destruction in the ultimate, not a relative sense? And since the idea of absolute destruction, sheer annihilation, scarcely bears thinking of, we find little attempt to express it emblematically (damnation being quite another matter). The creation symbols, on the other hand, are many and various. Three analogies for the idea of cosmic creation have been especially appealing: the Love Union, the Craftsman, and the King's Nod.

The Maori aborigines of New Zealand tell that Father Sky and Mother Earth had lain in close-locked embrace for countless years, until in the course of time Mother Earth became pregnant and bore him children—the brood of men and animals. At first the offspring lived in darkness and semi-suffocation between the embracing parents, until at length they revolted, thrust Father Sky far up overhead and thereby let in light and air and room for themselves to grow. But the loving parents weep in endless sorrow over their separation—the tears of Father Sky falling down again and again as rain and those of Mother Earth mounting upward as mists.[11]

In this legend the primal Father and Mother appear to have been distinct beings from the very first. Often, however, the speculative imagination is unwilling to accept an original duality. There is a type of mind to which Unity seems a more final explanation than Duality, and where this type of mind prevails, the myth of an original love consummation presumes a mythic prologue in which one of the partners emerged out of the other, or in which the original being was androgynous and split up into male and female. Aristophanes' quaint fantasy in Plato's *Symposium* transfers the myth of the Androgyne from the original to a secondary order of creation, but it was probably suggested by some older and more radically mythic tale.

In Hesiod's *Theogony* the account of origins is somewhat confused; but after the first stage in which wide-bosomed Earth, snowy Olympus, dim Tartarus, and fair Eros come-to-be out of Chaos in an unexplained manner, the story begins to fall into the archetypal pattern of the Androgyne. For "Earth *(Gaia)* first bare starry Sky *(Ouranos)*, equal to herself, to cover her on all sides, and to be a sure dwelling for the blessed gods for ever."[12] Having then brought forth the hills and the sea "without sweet union of love," she lay with Sky, and one after another she bore him sons and daughters. Earth, then, is both mother and wife to Father Sky: he begets by the same womb from which he emerged, so that the total creative process has a kind of androgynous unity.

A more abstract version of the Love Union is found in the Scandinavian poem *Völuspa*,[13] which describes the phantom-germ of the universe as having lain originally in *Ginnunga-gap*—the great Cup, or Abyss, or Womb—a region of night and mist *(Nebelheim)*. Into this world matrix a ray of cold light from the blue vault shot down and froze itself into the Cup. When a scorching wind at length dissolved the icy substance and cleared the mist, the streams of living waters gushed forth, creating a new male principle in the giant Ymir, and a new female principle in the cow Audhumla, from whose udder flowed four streams of milk, marking the four directions of space.

The Craftsman. A second analogy for the primal act of creation is *homo faber,* man the maker. Perhaps the universe did not come into existence by biological generation, perhaps a divine artist moulded it. If so, it must be that the artist had to work with materials. If we deny this implication we are discarding the craftsman analogy, for an artist works by shaping a preëxistent material into a form, and in doing so he is limited to some degree by the nature of the material. The craftsman analogy thus has the advantage of absolving the Creator from the stain of the world's evil. We can suppose, if we will, that God did the best he could with the materials at hand. Thus Plato writes that the Divine Artificer, the *Demiourgos,* created the world by *persuading* Necessity —evidently with incomplete success.

In that oldest surviving epic of the Americas, the *Popul Vuh,* of the Quiché Mayan Indians of Guatemala, instead of a single divine Craftsman we find a Committee of gods experimentally trying to fashion a race of beings that will be able to honor them with proper worship. The author of the document was a native convert to Christianity, and an apparent mingling of Mayan and Christian ideas is suggested by the opening drama of creation:

This is the account of how all was in suspense, all calm, in silence; all motionless, still, and the expanse of the sky was empty.

This is the first account, the first narrative. There was neither man, nor animal, birds, fishes, crabs, trees, stones, caves, ravines, grasses, nor forests; there was only the sky.

The surface of the earth had not yet appeared. There was only the calm sea and the great expanse of sky.[14]

In the midst of the silence "only the Creator, the Maker, Tepeu, Gucumatz, the Forefathers, were in the water surrounded with light." As a seeming afterthought it is declared that there existed "also the Heart of Heaven, which is the name of God and thus He is called." Tepeu and Gucumatz were great sages and thinkers. They came together in the darkness and united their words and thoughts. They planned the creation of earth and dawn, and mountains and valleys, and thickets and groves of cypress, perceiving too that in the end, when the dawn appeared, they would have to create man, as ruler of all the creation. Again as a seeming afterthought: "Thus it was arranged in the darkness and in the night by the Heart of Heaven who is called Huracan."

The second chapter tells how "the Creator, the Maker, and the Forefathers" (this being one of several ways of speaking of the primordial creative alliance) brought the various animals into existence, assigned them their respective homes, and commanded them to speak. But alas, the animals could only hiss or scream or cackle according to their several natures, they could not say the names of their Creators and Makers, hence could not properly adore them. "This is not well," said the Forefathers to each other, and they condemned the animals which were on earth to the fate that ever after they should be killed and eaten. Again the Forefathers deliberated: "Let us try again! Already dawn draws near. Let us make him who shall nourish and sustain us! What shall we do to be invoked, in order to be remembered on earth? We have already tried with our first creations, our first creatures; but we could not make them praise and venerate us. So then, let us try to make obedient, respectful beings who will nourish and sustain us." Thus they spoke. This time they made men's flesh out of mud. But unlike their august Hebraic Anatype they found mud to be poorly suited to the purpose: the resulting creature was limp and had no motive power, its face sagged and its sight was blurred. Although it spoke it had no mind. Presently it soaked away in the water. The Proto-Experimenters had to try again. On the next attempt they made creatures out of *tzité*-wood. The wooden figures looked like men, talked like men, and populated the surface of the earth; but "they did not have souls, nor minds, they had no thought of their Creator, their Maker, and they walked on all fours aimlessly." So the Heart of Heaven sent a great flood, by which the wooden figures were all annihilated.

After a digression into folk-tales concerning the exploits and adventures of Mayan culture-heroes, the narrative resumes the account of the faltering creation of man. Before the dawn appeared, before the sun and moon arose, man was made, with white and yellow maize thoughtfully provided for his nourishment. The first men were able to reason and speak, and as no limits had been set to their sight they knew all things at once. Although they were devout and offered prayers of thanks for the gift of existence, the gods were frightened at the prospect of such admirably endowed beings, and breathed a cloud over the mortals' eyes in order that they might see only a little way and not preen themselves on being divine. Somewhat later moreover, when the race of men had become populous, the gods deprived them of their original language, and gave to each geographic group a language of its own—presumably a further precaution against human cockiness.

At all events, so far as the matter of creation is concerned, there is doubtless a good deal to be said for the Mayan *mythos*. If man, with his conspicuous failings, could be understood as the product not of a single fiat by the Alone Omnipotent One, but of trial-and-error methods by a genially bungling group of Cosmic Powers who admittedly were

not sure what the outcome was going to be, the most scandal-
ous of Christian paradoxes would have found its solution.

The King's Nod. But neither the Conjugal nor the Craftsman analogy satisfies all worshipers as being sufficiently ex-
alted to symbolize the primal act of Divine Creation. The
one seems too much akin to purely natural process to reflect
any credit on Deity as its real author; the other seems too
effortful and incomplete. How else can the process of original creation be conceived? The classical answer in philosophical terms is given by Aristotle. God causes cosmic
process *(kinesis)* not by propagating and not by operating,
but simply and completely *through being loved.*[15] That is to
say, God is not an Efficient (i.e., propelling) but a Final
(i.e., telic) Cause. He does not push things into their changes
of state, but draws them toward their highest perfection *simply by virtue of being what he is.* He is "that for the sake of
which" in the most radical and purest sense; he thus causes
process in all things without undergoing process himself in
any respect. He is like, but transcendently more than, a wise
father who sets an example for his child instead of continually prodding the child into action.

To most ancient peoples the Father archetype finds its
highest mundane expression in the King. Now the more
powerful a king, the less effort he has to make in order that
his will shall be effective. The perfect king trains his ministers to be so alert to his hidden wishes that the merest nod
or frown is a sufficient signal of command. At a nod from
the Homeric Zeus a tremor ran through all the universe. The
Hebrew Jahveh said, "Let there be light," and there was
light. As a limiting ideal the Monarch would not even have
to speak or nod; his will, even his implicit will, his being-
what-he-is, produces the full effect.

Although the visual form is so different, the King's Nod
has close archetypal affinity with the already discussed sym-

bol of the Wheel. The King who makes his will effective without utterance or gesture and the perfectly rotating Wheel with an immovable axis are both limiting conceptions; they employ our empirical acquaintance with kings and wheels to construct two different threshold symbols pointing to the idea of the Unmoved Mover. Aristotle's main argument for an Unmoved Mover, as given in the *Metaphysics,* shows that the images are implicitly associated in his mind; for immediately after his declaration that God causes movement or process through being loved, he adds: "The primary kind of process *(kinesis)* is spatial movement, and the primary kind of spatial movement is circular; this, then, is the kind of process that the Divine Whatness directly produces." The pure unmoved Center of the Wheel is to the motion of the spokes and rim as the sheer *being* of God is to the activity of the entire universe.

THE THRESHOLD AND THE MELTING-POT

How do archetypes enter into the living discourse of poetry? In a great diversity of ways to be sure. But one general principle needs to be reëmphasized: that so far as the poetry is poetically alive, the ingredient universals are somehow concrete, which is to say freshly envisioned and therefore somehow metaphoric, not the static and preëxistent universals which a logical conception involves. Philosophers, trained to think in logical categories (which is not always synonymous with thinking logically) are sometimes prone to ignore this qualification. Filmer S. Northrop, for example, is a philosopher renowned in both the scientific and the legal field, but his published views on poetry err by taking the archetypal element too simply. When poetry goes beyond sheer concrete immediacy, when it does anything more than describe the intuited surface-qualities of experi-

ence, Professor Northrop holds that it must then serve "as
the instrument or handmaid for metaphorically and analogi-
cally conveying a theoretical doctrine"[16]—where the criteria
of the poem's truth and even (if I understand him correctly)
of its meaning, reside in some other science or system of
thought, independent of the poem. And so he interprets the
Divine Comedy as taking the philosophic concepts that constitute the *Summa Theologica* ("concepts by postulation," he
calls them) and conveying their analogue in terms of what
is concretely sensed and imaginable ("concepts by intuition"): because the general public "must have bells rung for
them while they salivate, and have vivid images instead of
postulationally-prescribed scientific concepts." A prescrip-
tion more appropriate to advertising than to poetry! What
Professor Northrop's view amounts to (despite his undeveloped use of the word "metaphorically") is that all poetry
must be either presentationally descriptive or else allegorical.

A modified form of the error, more cautiously qualified,
confuses the discussions of poetic meaning in Wilbur M.
Urban's *Language and Reality*.[17] A good deal hinges, I grant,
upon just what Professor Urban means when he describes
poetry as "covert metaphysics." He is wise enough, indeed,
to make an important reservation. Although the transition
from poetry to metaphysics is "inevitable," he concedes that
"the poet, as poet, is not the one to make it." The poet should
not depart from his figurative and symbolic way of speaking,
"for precisely in that symbolic form an aspect of reality is
given which cannot be expressed otherwise." So far I am in
full agreement. But Urban unfortunately cannot let a poem
stand ontologically on its own. "It remains true," he insists,
"that poetry is covert metaphysics, and it is only when its
implications, critically interpreted and adequately expressed,
become part of philosophy that an adequate view of the

world can be achieved." Poetic meanings, so far as they are really meaningful, in Urban's view, must enjoy ultimate membership in the great Philosophical Tradition of the West, as it has received successive expression and formulation at the hands of such master-dialecticians as Plato, Aristotle, Spinoza, Kant, and Hegel.

Naturally, such a theory of poetry influences one's evaluation of particular poems. Mr. Urban ignores Shakespeare but praises Ibsen as "an outstanding example of the use of the poetic symbol in order to give insight into 'spiritual reality,'" and thus to embody an ideal content not otherwise expressible. In Ibsen's poetic plays "we have symbolism at its highest." And indeed, so long as you confine your attention to examples drawn from classical German literature and from Ibsen, the theory of poetry as covert metaphysics looks plausible. The reader of *Peer Gynt* catches pretty adequately the universal significance of the button moulder, the onion, the Great Boyg, and the balls of wool; a literal explication of their meaning, while never quite a perfect fit, would perhaps not be too far off. The Peer Gynt type of personality, which goes through life asserting itself irresponsibly *as* a personality, is brought at length to self-recognition; to lay up one's treasure on earth is finally to lose it; and the ultimate damnation is to know oneself light and fluffy as a ball of wool, empty as an onion of which layer after layer is peeled off, an evader always yielding to the Great Boyg's slogan "Go roundabout!"—and consequently fit for nothing but to be thrown back into the melting pot like a defective button and lose all traces of selfhood in order to be moulded into a new button that is more serviceable; yet always with some hope still, because of the constant love of Solveig, the saving grace of the Eternal Feminine. Granted, however, that some such approximate meanings—and they are no more than that—can reasonably be assigned to Ibsen's symbols, it does not follow that a similar kind or degree of analysis is appropriate for all styles and species of poetry. And it is dangerously easy for the academically oriented critic to deprecate certain poets on finding that the propositional distillate of their poetry is either trivial or ridiculous or hopelessly obscure.

Now without wishing to claim universal validity for any pronouncement about so fluid and diversified a thing as poetry, I would like to propose the guiding idea that in many of the most heightened passages of poetic utterance the effect comes from a combination of the metaphoric and archetypal modes of envisagement—where what I may call the Melting-pot and the Threshold activities of imagination are in a serene but quickening state of tension. A few illustrative examples follow.

> Golden lads and girls all must,
> As chimney-sweepers, come to dust.

The most obvious expression of the radically metaphoric in these lines from the dirge in *Cymbeline* is the amusing little pun, "come to dust." Taken merely as a pun, however, it becomes, on reflection, distastefully snobbish; for chimney sweeps come to dust in a sordid, plebeian, literal way (which we cannot feel very humorous about after reading Blake, for instance), golden lads and girls in a cultivatedly tragic, A. E. Housman, *lacrima rerum* sort of way. The pun, under Shakespeare's hand, passes beyond the antithesis of amusing vs. snobbishly unpleasant; it becomes a serious metaphoric pun, a poetic plurisign, by reason of the deeper meaning which, instead of separating, connects the golden youths and the chimney sweeps. Three main devices give the pun its wider range of reference. The two preceding lines have prepared for it:

Thou thy worldly task hast done,
Home art gone, and ta'en thy wages

—where there is a shrewd balance between the universal and
the particular; for while the primary reference is to the human life-cycle, a simple deletion of the word "worldly" will
make the lines perfectly applicable to the daily life of a chimney sweep: "You have finished your task, taken your wages,
and gone home." The word "worldly" is thus the fulcrum on
which the archetypal and presentational elements are delicately balanced. Secondly, there is the ambivalent contrast
between *golden* and *dust:* connoting on the one hand life vs.
death, on the other (more lightly) the happy estate of more
fortunate children vs. the murky life of the chimney sweep.
Finally, in Shakespeare's day there appears to have been a
third basis of connection; for, as a contributor to *The Explicator* has recently pointed out,[18] it was the practice in
parts of rural England for the leader of May Day revels
(which celebrated the cyclic return of summer and abundant life) to be dressed as a chimney sweep. The mythic
connection here goes pretty deep, for there is a widespread
tendency, in rural England as in ancient Eleusis, for spring
and summer festivals to develop beyond the stage of agricultural magic, and to symbolize and promote spiritual rebirth, of which the first step is purification. And who, after
all, can more aptly symbolize the ritual of periodic cleansing
than the chimney sweep? Thus, hidden within Shakespeare's
radical metaphor, there is a light suggestion (no more!) of
one of mankind's most persistent and indispensable archetypal ideas. We are on a threshold almost without knowing
it.

Take now another Shakespearean metaphor, which approaches the threshold of universality somewhat differently.

When Cleopatra is dying and Charmian exclaims "O eastern star!" the Queen replies:

> Peace, peace!
> Dost thou not see my baby at my breast,
> That sucks the nurse asleep?
>
> (*Antony and Cleopatra*, Act V, Scene ii)

The remarkable power with which this utterance affects us seems to derive largely from such elements as the following. There is the idea of quietude connoted by the words "peace" and "asleep," which contrasts satisfyingly with the tumult of environing events. Then there is the reversal of normal order, suggested by the baby's putting the nurse to sleep—a reversal which, like Shakespeare's various tempests and tumblings of nature's germens, furnishes a symbolic parallel to the tumbling of empire. At the same time the abnormal idea is counterpointed by a normal one, for the baby is at its usual place on the nurse's breast and seems to perform its usual action of sucking; only the result is opposite, for it is the nurse instead of the baby who is put to sleep in the process. And contrapuntive again is the paradox of life and death: for the very action of nursing which normally furthers life in the baby now brings death to the nurse. Finally, over and above such justifications by immediate context there is the above-mentioned archetypal significance of the serpent as at once the sharp tooth of death and the symbol of new life. This ancient and widespread piece of symbolism appears to have been suggested and perpetuated by the several impressive characteristics of the serpent discussed in connection with the sacred *uraeus* of Egypt: its casting off of old skin, its mysterious arising out of the ground, that is to say out of the womb of Mother Earth; its phallic shape, its electric quickness, its hypnotic stare, and its aptitude of coiling itself into a circle (for, as Heraclitus remarked, "In the circle the beginning and end are one")—all these aspects standing in effective tension with the idea of lurking deadliness. It is impossible to be sure how much of the archetypal meaning Shakespeare and the audience for whom he wrote were aware of, but I should think a good deal.

For contrast of symbolic style I offer finally an example from Hafiz. The poem has no title so far as I know, and the translation is that of Peter Avery and John Heath-Stubbs.

> I saw the green meadow of the sky and the sickle moon,
> And remembered my own tillage and the time of harvest.
>
> I said, "Oh my fate, while you slept the sun has risen."
> The answer came: "In spite of what's past, do not de-
> spair."
>
> Go pure and naked like the Messiah to Heaven,
> From your lamp a hundred beams shall reach the sun.
>
> Don't trust your star, that sneak-thief of the night,
> The trickster who stole the crown of Kaus, and the belt
> of Kaikhosrou.
>
> Though gold and ruby bangles pierce your ears,
> Attend the voice which tells how beauty fades.
>
> And good luck to the mole which makes your face more
> lovely:
> That little pawn can check the sun and moon.
>
> And say to the sky: "Don't lay this trumpery out:
> Love buys the moon for a barley-corn, and the clustered
> Pleiads for two."
>
> The hypocrite's zeal makes religion a burnt harvest:
> So burn your woollen cassock, Hafiz, and go![19]

In the first stanza I think we must take not only "sickle moon" and "meadow of the sky" but also "green" as functioning metaphorically. I do not know what the precise color of the sky may have been in Iran during the fourteenth century of our era, nor how much of the spectrum the Iranian word for "green" may have covered. At any rate I doubt that the sky could have been green as the meadows are green, and suspect that the poet is extending the normal meaning of the adjective in pursuance of his general metaphor, which presumably had its origin not in a color resemblance but in seeing the new moon as a sickle. The second line is direct, and explains the point of the first line. Or rather, a part of the point. For not only is Hafiz alluding to the physical tillage and harvest; these in turn become symbols of the tilling and reaping of his, and perhaps man's, spiritual life. The third level of meaning is made more explicit in the second stanza. With reference to the surrounding imagery it might be paraphrased: "Till your own life's field now, while there is still time, for death (the sickle) will come all too soon." This moral archetype is confirmed in the fifth stanza, on which the translators offer the comment: "The harvest theme, this time not imagining the reaping of souls, but of the transient objects of this life, bursts out in splendour with the gold and ruby that weighs down the ear (as the ripe grains weigh down the cornstalk) and which must pass; while this passing, this ripening and falling serves also the purpose of allegory for the major theme of the poem, the harvest of souls."

Observe now a further element, the Light symbolism, which plays counterpoint to that of Harvest. The idea of death, first represented by the sickle, becomes transformed in stanza three: in accordance with Sufi mystical theology the death of one who is purified of bodily dross becomes a merging of the individual soul with the Supreme Spirit. The

Sun in this passage has a paradoxically different tenor, almost contrary to the sun image in stanzas two and six. The purity and nakedness of the prepared soul stand in contrast to the soul weighed down by egoism, trusting his own star. The mole in stanza six was considered a mark of beauty; here it symbolizes the spiritual beauty as distinguished from the mundane and transient beauty of the gold and ruby bangles. That small unostentatious pawn of true beauty, by the analogy of the chessboard, can checkmate both king and queen, those measures of time mentioned in stanzas one and two. Virtually the same thing is said in the seventh stanza: those jewels up there in the night sky are of tiny worth compared with the power of devoted love of him who can "go pure and naked like the Messiah of Heaven." So the Harvest imagery returns triumphantly in the concluding couplet, where it introduces the ambivalent employment of the image of burning. Burn the woollen garb of conventional religion and seek the salvation that can only be won by devotion to the single-pointed beauty of the mole.

In poetry at its most heightened moments, then, there is apt to be some fusion of the two imaginative procedures which I have called the archetypal and the metaphoric, the Threshold and the Melting Pot. The way of the Melting Pot is to create a fresh relationship between two or more images (with attendant ideas or adumbrations of idea) which outside of just that poetic context would be somewhat disparate and irrelevant, but from whose present unexpected combination a nuance emerges which has not hitherto existed. The way of the Threshold is to see a general idea in and through the particular images drawn from the real world, heightened but not radically distorted by the poet's creative imagination. To combine these two ways in a single living act of being, thought, and utterance is to accept the challenge of Wannemunne and sing the full human song.

EIGHT

The Mythic World-View

All is prepared in darkness. Enormous light
is but the foetus of big-bellied night.
The image hatches in the darkened room:
the cave, the camera, the skull, the womb.
Future and past are shut. The present leaps:
a bright calf dropped between two infinite sleeps.

DILYS BENNETT LAING, "The Apparition"[1]

HOW FAR can we divest ourselves of paleface preconceptions and enter imaginatively into that more primeval world-view from which even our most familiar meanings and most plausible beliefs have lumberingly evolved? The divestment will be partial and uncertain at best; for when once the virus of civilization has thoroughly infected us—for better *and* for worse—our tribal habits of conceptualization stubbornly assert themselves as of universal validity. The result is an ingrained partisanship, which renders myopic the backward look, and encourages a collective snobbery toward earlier peoples in proportion as their ways of thinking, feeling, and behaving differ radically from our own. The proliferation of technical researches into primitive cultures during the last seventy-five years is no guarantee that our understanding of the primitive condition has been commensurately deepened.

What is meant by "primitive?" Do we prejudge important issues by playing fast and loose with the word? Is it simply a verbal stopgap of ignorance, an omnibus-symbol for societal types on which it pleases our pride to look with condescension? Admittedly there are real obstacles to an objective study of cultural primitivity. If we collect data from

among the non-civilized peoples of the present day, there is
first the difficulty of finding tribal specimens any longer un-
contaminated by civilizing influences; second, the difficulty
of overcoming radical language barriers and sly native re-
ticence to achieve real communication regarding perennial
matters; and third, the unanswerable doubt whether these
contemporary so-called primitives—even where we can find
them and understand them—are truly primitive in the sense
of preserving custom and belief intact since before the beginning of recorded history. If, on the other hand, our data
are taken from the earliest literary remains of ancient peoples, there are, besides interpretative difficulties of another
kind, haunting indications of long prior ages, of which even
the most venerable writings are late after-products and therefore imperfect records.

Such obstacles, faced candidly, would be formidable if the
object of search were the primitive in a strictly chronological
sense. There is no real knowledge of how men thought, felt,
and acted ten thousand or fifty thousand years ago. Fortunately, however, there does not need to be. Any such time-
spans are arbitrary. Mankind's primitive condition had no
assignable beginning and end. Besides, an interest in what
the *earliest* men were like, even if it could be satisfied, is
more antiquarian than philosophical. Primitivity in its most
relevant sense is a character to be recognized not by its
when but by its *what*. Out of both of the two great systems
of evidence conjoined—those furnished by uncivilized peoples of today, or rather of two or three generations ago before their molestation had proceeded to such destructive
lengths, and those furnished by ancient documents and supplemented by archeological exhumations—there emerges a
picture of the human condition which, regardless of how
far back into prehistory it may or may not refer, is nevertheless significant both because, with abundant deviations, it is

so widespread, and because it stirs even in our minds today some dim response of recognition.

The primitive world-view has so many facets—magic and legend, totem and taboo, initiation ceremonies and death chants, worship of gods and ghosts, and many others—that anything like full treatment in a single chapter is out of the question. A simplification is required, and it must be one that without distorting the main data and main emphases which anthropological science discloses as typically primitive, will be sufficiently relevant to our present semantic inquiry to throw light upon the nature of expressive language. Such a simplication is found in the fundamental pair of cultural phenomena: *ritual* and *myth*. Ritual connotes a way of doing, and myth a way of envisaging; but the doing and the envisaging are of a special not of an everyday sort, and imply in their turn the existence of a penumbral reality, something extending beyond yet interpenetrating with the affairs of mortal men.

Now doing and envisaging bring into play the two most basic types of imagery we have—the kinaesthetic and the visual. By these the substance of our world is presented. Discovery and interpretation play back and forth through them both, particularly in combination, as the case of an infant, exploratively exercising its muscular reflexes to reach toward an object which it sees, will confirm. Kinaesthesis and vision —the Dionysus and Apollo of Nietzsche's *Birth of Tragedy*— are the two most indispensable and typical ingredients of the human situation at whatever level of advancement. If Hindu seer or Christian saint can sometimes virtually subdue his motor-impulses to emancipate the beatific vision in its purity, that is a brilliant exception which does not invalidate the general rule. Again, if an occasional creative musical genius experiences tones—i.e., contrasts and patterns of musical timbre and pitch, purely auditory—as the main area of reference in his world (analogously, perhaps, to a dog's radical reliance upon odors), still for most persons musical sounds are adjectival appendages of "the real world" rather than its very substance. The eye and the muscle normally come first. And when they function on the human as distinguished from the merely animal level they tend to assume (as Susanne K. Langer has persuasively argued)[2] a *symbolic* role in addition to their practical one. In man qua animal, sight and behavior are little more than phases of a predictable reflex-circuit: they simply *are*. But in man qua man, vision and action become enjoyed, furthered, and controlled for their own sake; developed into visual imaginings, story-telling, legend and myth on the one hand, and into gesture and ritual on the other.

MYTH AS PERSPECTIVE

What is myth? In defining it, or at least using it in a manner that will fruitfully advance our study of depth-meanings we had better avoid the popular imputation of "fictional" and "false." For if we let the word carry that pejorative sense (as many writers and speakers do), we shall find ourselves using it to express our own prejudices about the nature of things rather than as descriptive of a certain type of cultural phenomenon. Since it is chiefly the adjective "mythical" that people employ in the prejudicial sense, I will avoid this adjective altogether (except in rare instances when I may wish to express that implication), and will employ instead the adjective *"mythic."*[3] The noun "myth" seems to be used more flexibly in contemporary writing than the adjective, but wherever there is likely to be much doubt in the matter I will substitute the Greek word *"mythos."* Thus if I should speak of Adam and Eve's ejection from the Garden of Eden as a Christian mythos (or myth), or of Krishna's incarnation as Arjuna's charioteer as a Hindu mythos, or of the mythic content or tone of either of these stories, I do so without any implication that they are "mythical." Whether the narrated events actually occurred or not I do not know and do not see how anyone can know conclusively. Our judgment of the probabilities, being based on evidences drawn from a non-mythic way of life, is beside the point. The important thing is that a significant mythic (or mythopoeic) vision finds symbolical expression in both cases, and the symbolic patterns, taken in their respective religious, literary, and cultural contexts, are the really interesting and the only really discoverable thing. Hence, bracketing off all questions as to their literal truth or falsity, we may characterize both stories as mythic because, although accepted as literally true by large respective circles of believers, they convey also, to the more religiously sensitive and the more intellectually acute of those believers, something more than appears at first glance. Each embodies an archetypal idea—a set of depth-meanings of perduring significance within a widely shared perspective, and transcending the limits of what can be said via ordinary literal speech.

Myth, then, is not in the first instance a fiction imposed on one's already given world, but is a way of apprehending that world. Genuine myth is a matter of perspective first, invention second. This radically cognitive function of myth, as a kind of primitive epistemic, is stressed particularly by Ernst Cassirer in his study of "Mythic Thinking," which forms the second part of his three-volume work, *The Philosophy of Symbolic Forms.*[4] Cassirer starts out from the Kantian principle that all knowledge involves a synthesizing activity of the mind; that in the very act of knowing an object the mind contributes those lines of connection whereby the particulars of sense are combined into an intelligible unity. Certain colors and shapes impinge upon our visual awareness and we recognize unhesitatingly, "A tree!" What

is involved in such recognition? Something more than the
visual data themselves, evidently, for they might equally
well be given in dream or delirium. In themselves they are
but pictures on the mind's portable movie screen: separate
them from mental interpretative response and one's awareness of them would resemble that of the idiot Benjy in Faulk-
ner's *The Sound and the Fury,* whose world consists of bright
shapes and uninterpretable fragments of conversation flash-
ing on and off the screen. We are superior to idiots because
for us a bright shape is an index of something more permanent and more contextual than the moving kaleidoscope of
bare uninterpreted sensations. "It is not merely a bright
shape, it is a tree": if the distinction means anything it means
at least that the bright shape is connected with other shapes
and colors, such as we could espy by circling around the tree,
and with possibilities of tactile sensation which we could
realize by approaching the tree and touching it. To identify
a certain visual configuration as a tree involves at very least
a psychic activity—instinctive, immediate, and implicit, not
consciously controlled—of combining the present shape-and-
color sensations with appropriate subconscious memories and
expectancies to form a significant whole object. The expectancies include a confidence that if one continues to look at
the tree it will not unaccountably vanish away, Cheshire-cat
fashion.

Cassirer, "transposing [as he says] the Kantian principle
into the key of myth," inquires how the mind's primary activity of integration—what Coleridge called "the primary
imagination"—operates in the condition of pre-civilized living. Such basic categories of thought as space, time, number,
quality, cause, and law, he maintains, are conceived in a
more flexible, more organic and, one might say, more hos-
pitable manner than would be acceptable to the science-ori-
ented mind. The mythic consciousness "finds its being and

its life in the immediate impression, to which it surrenders itself without attempting to 'measure' it by something else." A Navaho Indian *sees* the clouds in the tobacco pipe smoke, and sees them in a context that includes their desired and expected effect, the rain. The rain is not, to him, something entirely other than the puff of smoke; there is an indefinable coalescence between them.

This coalescence of things is connected with the primitive view that existence is vaguely alive and indeterminately fluid. Its fluidity involves a flowing-into-one-another and disappearing-into-one-another of distinctions that to our way of looking at the matter are clear and definite. One of the most important forms that such coalescence takes, and one particularly significant for the development of religious and poetic language, is that *concrete universality* which I have defined in the third section of Chapter V and have illustrated in Chapter VII. Envisaging the phenomenon in anthropological context, Cassirer declares, "In mythic thinking the species is immediately present in the particular; in the particular it lives and works." The sacrificed totemic black bear is a representative of its entire species: not a merely numerical instance of it, but a real participant in it, as evidenced by the usual primitive belief that a noble specimen of black bear has *more* of blackbearhood in it than a puny one. The Christian doctrine that every individual man falls from grace through Adam's sin and receives new life through Christ's death and resurrection exemplifies the sense of effective concrete universality on a higher level. The doctrine becomes intelligible when Adam, and when Christ, are understood not as atomically distinct beings but as truly participating in the essence of all mankind and as epitomizing that essence in themselves.

What of the mythic conception of space? Primitive man knows nothing of the geometrically rigid three-dimensional

box-like space which is our own accustomed background of
physical reference; his idea of space is not precisioned by
ruler and compass, plumb line and surveying instruments;
it does not possess, therefore, the Euclidean-Newtonian characteristics of constancy and homogeneity. What he perceives
and understands is not space but *place,* and one place is distinguished from another by its qualities and potencies quite
as much as by position. Concrete place, unlike abstract space,
is not homogeneous. Space exists by postulation; place is
known experientially and responsively. Consequently, each
place—so far as it is known and accepted as a place—comes
laden with intimations of universality. A boyhood scene re-
visited will unfold something of this character, although the
what of it can hardly be spoken without breaking the spell.
The primitive sense of place-qualities, which is to say place-
universals, is sometimes more forthright.

Consider, for example, the African Joruba tribe, for whom
each of the main regions of the known world is thought of
and spoken of in terms of a particular color. Its members
appear to be incapable of forming a concept of region or
place in the abstract; a color property must accompany it.
More highly formalized still is the topography found among
the Zuni Indians, for whom the four cardinal directions are
correlated with the four elements, the four seasons, the four
main types of occupation, and other fourfold groups. The
north, for them, is more essentially of the nature of air, the
south of fire, the west of earth, the east of water. North also
means winter, south summer, west spring, and east fall.
Again, north means war, south agriculture, west hunting, and
east magic. In addition to the four directions on the earth's
surface there are the directions of above and below, carrying
various overtones of religious and mythological suggestion,
and there is also the central point from which all six directions start—the "here." These seven spatial directions of ref-

erence, constituting as they do a natural mode of orienting oneself spatially in the world, may possibly, Cassirer suggests, have contributed originally to the sacred character which the number 7 acquired in so many widely separated localities.

Sacred mountains like Olympus, Zion, Fujiyama, and Nakauvadra, sacred cities like Jerusalem and Mecca, a sacred river like the Ganges, and a sacred grotto like that at Delphi, have served for their respective worshipers as spatial foci of reference around which all mundane existence seemed to flow. Mediaeval maps of the world appear quaint and laughable by modern standards of cartography; but their misinformation as to what might lie beyond the Scythian plains, the great African desert, and the Pillars of Hercules was of small consequence to men before the age of global exploration, and the pious stylization of such maps into a geometry more symbolic than descriptive recorded and promoted a vast corporate security, a sense of knowing where one stood in relation to the visible and navigable world of one's own age.

Time is subtly different for the mythopoeic consciousness as compared with the empirio-scientific. Myth knows nothing of the Newtonian mathematico-physical conception of absolute time which "flows along as something utterly itself [*an und für sich*] and without dependence on anything other than itself"; although, of course, it likewise knows nothing of post-Newtonian refinements which make time interdependent with technologically conceived space. Mythic differs likewise from historical time, which, as envisaged quasi-scientifically, "rests upon a firm chronology, upon a clear-cut difference between what is earlier and what is later, and upon the postulation of a distinct, single-ordered, serial ordering of its particular moments, so close-locked that there is one and only one place for every occurrence."

To begin with, mythic time is at once vaguer and more humanly oriented than ours. In the life of the Quiche Maya of Guatamala even today time is not reckoned by the Gregorian calendar (dates of induction into civil offices excepted) but by the simple agricultural year. "When the corn is green" and "during the early days when there is no rain" are deemed sufficiently informative for the dating of a fiesta.[5] Moreover, mythic time is felt to be cyclical and therefore, in a way, recurrent. Each thing, or what may pass for it, has happened before and will happen again. Time spirals rather than marches. As distinguished both from the mathematico-physical and the linear-historical conceptions, the mythic idea of time sets up a relationship that is not serial but exemplifies what Cassirer calls the Law of Concrescence: the tendency of events, perhaps remote if measured by historical standards, to coalesce on the basis of some similarity or felt congruity or recurrent tribal ritual. Although such a time-ordering may seem uncomfortably close to idiot Benjy's befuddlement of past and present, yet when its cultural roots and justification go deep into the tribal Unconscious it becomes creative of a certain kind of experienced world, as Thomas Mann's Joseph novels majestically exhibit. Past, present, and future coalesce, and in place of the, to us, familiar lines of distinction between them the mythic attitude substitutes the ideas of Creation, Sacrament, and Prophecy. "The true nature of mythic perspective reveals itself in its concern for origins; the Holy, in mythic perspective, finds its ulterior reference in an original act of creation." Creation-myths are therefore an inexpungeable part of mythic perspective. At the same time many such myths, or elements of them, or analogies to them, become re-enacted in sacrament; or where that is not the case, there is at least likely to be a felt connection between the power that created the universe and the power or powers that are worshipped in sacramental (i.e., non-magical) ritual. Prophecy becomes naturally associated with the creation-element and the sacrament-element of primitive time-consciousness; indeed, Cassirer speaks of prophecy as "revealing the interrelationship of all time-moments" and as "an integrating principle of the mythic consciousness in its time-dimension."

A third category wherein the mythopoeic envisagement differs notably from our own is *law*. In the ancient Babylonian myth of Marduk's victory over Tiamat (victory of the culture-hero over the monster of daemonic unbridled power) Cassirer traces the emergence of mythic law-consciousness out of the proto-mythic perception of particulars. Early Babylonian thought had been animistic, with survivals of an earlier totemism; it involved belief in friendly and baneful powers, daemons of sky and storm, field and forest, mountain and rivulet, confusedly overlapping one another's territory and operating mostly by sheer caprice. As Babylonian wonder and inquiry concentrated more and more on the starry sky, their form gradually changed. The primitive daemon-mythology was retained in popular superstition, but the religion of priests and sages began to emphasize holy times and holy numbers, specifically with reference to celestial movements. Out of contemplation of the plain orderly course of the sun and stars, and the more complex but still orderly courses of the moon and planets, the idea of Godhood (so Cassirer's theory runs) began to emerge. For it was no longer the particular star as such, but the particular star as exemplifying universal rhythms, that was coming to be the object of attention and to be reverenced as divine. After vanquishing Tiamat, Marduk established the stars in their courses as abodes of the high gods; he divided the year into twelve months, represented by the zodiacal signs, and he set limits beyond which the days were prohibited from wandering. Thereby he established orderly motion and the possibility of life: much as Maui, the racial progenitor and cul-ture-hero of the New Zealand Maori, long ago seized the sun in its falling and gave to it, which had theretofore moved capriciously about the sky, laws governing its motion.

Like most other culture-heroes, Marduk established laws not only for nature but also for man; he was the protector of justice. Such linkage of cosmic and ethical ordering finds lordly expression in the great symbols connoting the Way, Justice, Right, and related ideas in nearly all of the more advanced mythopoeic cultures: as, for instance, *Tao* in his-toric China and especially in the *Tao Teh Ching*, *Rta* in the *Vedas*, and *Asha* in the *Zend-Avesta*. These, says Cassirer, "are expressions of the orderly connection and dispensation of occurrences grasped simultaneously from the standpoint of *being* and *ought*." Nature and right action are seen as two sides of the same mythic reality.

MYTH AS STORY

Cassirer's emphasis upon myth as a basic way of envision-ing reality has contributed valuably to a more objective un-derstanding of primitive thought; nevertheless it is one-sided. For myth is more than simple envisionment; it is a way of envisionment that *tends toward story form*.[6] Without some narrative or dramatic element it is not proper (according to a long tradition of usage) that the word "myth" should be employed. Some phrase such as "mythic perspective" suits better. As a matter of fact, however, such manifestations of the mythic outlook as Cassirer has cited tend of themselves, by a kind of inherent spur to the collective imagination, to develop into stories. Olympus, from being a sacred and prob-ably tabooed mountain, suggested itself to the imaginative pre-Homeric Greeks as the natural dwelling place of the gods; and to imagine the gods as living there is to open the gates of fancy to any number of story-possibilities. The mythic apprehension of Time as a cycle of living and dying seasons suggests myths of the birth and death of a vegetation god. The mythic idea of Law (as Cassirer's own illustration shows) tends to generate stories about either a divine creator or a culture-hero who establishes and sustains the laws, both cosmic and human.

How does the evolution of mythic stories out of the mythic perspective take place? One answer, and a plausible one at first glance, is that the stories were invented and spun out somewhat deliberately by prehistoric poets. Richard Chase's *Quest for Myth*[7] is the most recent defender of this view, with its declaration that "myth is literature and must be considered as an aesthetic creation of the human imagination." The earliest mythologizers are said to have been individual poets, more sensitively imaginative than their fellows, weaving the mythic stories out of the resources of their individual genius. At the same time, although stressing the narrative character of myth, Chase warns against identifying myth with *mere* story as it might be told to a modern child. When it is so emasculated, a myth no longer furnishes "that peculiar mythical [I would prefer to say "mythic"] complication of brilliant excitement, of the terrific play of the forces natural and human," and of that reassurance and reconciliation that are the deeply desired upshot of such interplay. The emasculate myth—the philosophical concept, moral allegory, or bare narrative cut off from the living whole—Chase calls by Herder's name *paramyth*. The distinction is worth while, but unfortunately its momentum has driven Mr. Chase to the dubious counter-assertion that myth is "only" art.

The explanation of myth as the artistic creation of individual poets is interrelated with Chase's curious view that the mythopoeic age never really existed. He is against overstressing the differences between primitive and civilized culture, and his opposition stems from a fear that myth is likely

to become either sterile or socially dangerous if it is reintroduced bodily into modern thought as socially stabilizing
dogma, or into modern literature as an alleged source of
poetic vitality. So far, good. He admits that there are large
differences in environment, education, custom, and sensibility among different cultures, and that "we have invented
numberless surrogates to take the place of primitive ritual."
Nevertheless, he claims, "we live in the same world as the
savages. Our deepest experience, needs, and aspirations are
the same, as surely as the crucial biological and psychic transitions occur in the life of every human being and force culture to take account of them in aesthetic forms." By such
emphasis Professor Chase does a service in inviting our attention to evidences of mythic activity, or the undeveloped
germs of it, in the human psyche today and at all times.
There is as much need now as ever, he believes, for the sort
of story which by reaffirming the "brilliancy and drama of
life," keeps us in contact with the mythic (he says "magical")
view of things—with the preternatural forces, divine or daemonic, which, though perhaps largely imaginative projections of our wishes and fears, are nevertheless potent for
blessing or bane. And he invokes to his support Eliot's remark that the artist should be "more primitive, as well as
more civilized, than his contemporaries."

With the view that there is a contemporary need for some
restoration of a more mythopoeic outlook I cordially agree.
But it does not in the least follow, either in logic or in fact,
that the savage culture persisting in our own "is here *as much
as anywhere else*" (italics mine), or that "the needs which
call forth magic, ritual, and myth are *as much* with us now
when we turn from science to poetry or to the crucial problems of life as they are with the Maori and the Bushmen."
To say that we live in the same world as the savages is rhetoric, not reasoning. The rational procedure would be to dis-

tinguish between elements of sameness and elements of difference where they exist, and then to evaluate the total
relevance and effect of each. Chase does do this to an extent,
but not, I should judge, with a scientist's impartiality. There
is a somewhat too partisan effort to magnify the resemblances
and soften the differences between those earlier ages when
myth was alive, fresh and effective, and our own.

Although the development of myths, particularly the later
development, may have had a good deal of help from individual poets long since forgotten, there has been another,
more impersonal force at work in the development of mythic
ideas of nature. For in mythic perspective nature is not only
known, it is enacted. "Nature yields nothing without ceremonies," Cassirer observes; he might almost have ventured
the more radical judgment that to the primitive mind Nature
virtually *is* nothing without ceremonies, for in order to know
nature truly in a mythopoeic way one must engage in the
gestures and ritual acts which bring oneself into the desired
communion. Nor can such strategies be private. Primitive
mysticism is an affair of the forum. If we ignore the special
status of magicians, shamans, primitive priests, who in any
case play a representative role, we may say that primitive
acts of participation in nature must be undertaken tribally,
or by a cult or totem group within the tribe. Mythos, then,
is not self-intelligible; it has to be studied in the context of
rite and ceremony which have engendered it or which at
any rate have moulded its distinctive form. We must turn
next, therefore, to the other side of the mythopoeic picture—
from the mythic forms of consciousness to the process of
their formation in ritualized response.

NINE

The Semantics of Ritual

CASSIRER'S REMARK that nature, as mythopoeically conceived, yields nothing without ceremonies, can be supplemented by the observation that ceremonies, if entered into wholeheartedly and accepted as the natural way of living, tend to mould a certain view of nature and of existence generally. Some scholars have even thought that all myth could be explained as an extrapolation of ceremonies. They have argued, for instance, that men probably began the practice of burying their dead in the earth as the most convenient means of disposal, and then as a result began to imagine the buried ghosts as congregating in a subterranean Hades. There are many myths which can doubtless be thus explained as rationalizations of preëxisting ceremonies, but the generalization should not be pushed to the extreme. For, on the other hand, there are many ceremonies which would appear to have arisen as expressions of preëxisting mythic beliefs. Mythic belief and ceremonial practice affect each other interactively, and no single explanation can do justice to the wide diversity of rituo-mythic phenomena.

Ritual is in the broadest sense mimetic, even where the object of mimesis is vague and undifferentiated. There is always some reference to a fit occasion that is socially shared or at least socially recognized. A child carefully stepping on all the cracks in a sidewalk takes a kind of formalized pleasure in its action; two or more children who walk together in such a manner are engaging in an elementary act of ritual. Even the lone child's action may be called ritualistic in so far as he feels it to be a kind of demand imposed, a kind of homage paid; for he is then on the verge of imagining himself related somehow socially to the object.

Ritualized action tends to be rhythmic in some manner or other: not only because rhythm is pleasant *per se* (unless carried too far or expressed too grossly), but also because it is only through rhythm that two or more individuals can effectively act in unison. Men usually like to keep step when walking together, two wood-cutters swinging their axes from opposite sides at the same notch in a tree find a steady rhythm necessary to their safety and efficiency, and friends or lovers have often cared to express and consolidate their fellowship by singing in harmony or in antiphonal response— an impromptu art which hyper-sophistication has all but destroyed. The dance, in its old-fashioned community forms, was secular ritual at its best; contemporary ballroom dancing, however, reduces the scope of togetherness from a group to a couple, and substitutes an arbitrary "leading" by the male and submissive "following" by the female for the older dance ideal of mutual acceptance of a choreographic pattern that somehow reflected, or seemed to reflect, nature's own rhythms.

RITUAL AND THE MYTHIC REFERENCE

As contrasted with even the best forms of social ceremony found in a secular culture—square-dancing, singing while you work, and such—where the action is not much complicated by ulterior significance, the corresponding instances in mythopoeic societies are more than pure kinaesthesis; socially sanctioned action among them tends to have, however vaguely, an ideational aspect which serves as its justification. In simplest form this is a sense of "wehood" that extends indefinitely beyond the community of actual persons, including totemic beasts, ghosts, ancestral gods, and friendly aspects of nature. Gradually, we may suppose, the simple vague primordial sense of "wehood" became articulated and expanded into narrative. Ungraspable elements of the *we-hood*, felt nevertheless to be potently real, received names, and the names suggested stories about them. Thus, perhaps, myths were born.

A death chant from the islands of Fiji will serve to illustrate this natural interrelation of the ceremonial and the mythic. On the largest island of the Fijian group, some three-quarters of a century ago a British surveying party discovered a road, overgrown and evidently no longer in active use, leading through the wilderness. Further exploration revealed that it ran straight on for fifty miles, often through difficult terrain, from the principal village to the sacred mountain, Nakauvadra, which faces the western sea, and on which is a high ledge, Nai-thombo-thombo, "the jumping-off-place" of ghosts departing for their submarine after-life abode. The road's great length was all the more surprising because at the time when it must have been built the Fijians had possessed no tools to work with other than crudely sharpened stones. What fears or hopes or strange inner compulsions could have urged these savages to so formidable an undertaking?

Because both the road and the mountain were strongly taboo the explorers' inquiries were nearly always met with silence and evasion. At length, however, after much patient research the following account was pieced together. Some two or three generations ago, the tribal saga ran, the inhabitants of the village were bothered by loitering ghosts, who played such pranks as putting snakes in the cooking-pots, making young women unaccountably pregnant, and turning yams rotten in the ground. The elders took counsel and diagnosed the situation as caused by the ghosts' losing their way to Mt. Nakauvadra. Hence the path was built—laboriously, and with the periodic spur of cannibal feasts—in order to ease and direct their journey.

Formerly when a Fijian died, the funeral rites lasted three days. These three days of sacrament on the part of the survivors were correlated step by step with the events of the three-day journey which the departed one must take along the path to the sacred mountain. Particular chants and ritual acts symbolize particular adventures which the ghost must encounter, and magically aid him as well, for the ghostly path is full of terrors, each in its apportioned place. When the three days have expired the ghost reaches the mountain, and before it comes time for him to dive into the sea he is hospitably received into the mountain cavern, where the spirits of ancient hero-ancestors dwell, guardians of the tribe's morality and well-being. Here, after joining with them in a feast and the singing of tribal lays (enacted also in the actual ritual of the funeral ceremony, where portions of food are laid aside and magically treated in order that their *mana*, or vital essence, may be transported to the sacred cave) the newcomer breaks the last tie with his physical body, and now for the first time clearly realizing his condition, he is overwhelmed with grief. To the accompaniment of native instruments, addressing the ancestors he chants these words:

My Lords! In evil fashion are we buried,
Buried staring up into heaven,
We see the scud flying over the sky,
We are worn out with the feet tramping on us.

Our ribs, the rafters of our house, are torn asunder,
The eyes with which we gazed on one another are destroyed,
The nose with which we kissed has fallen in,

The breast with which we embraced is ruined,
The mouth with which we laughed has decayed,
The teeth with which we bit have showered down.
Gone is the hand that threw the tinka stick
The testes have rolled away.

Hark to the lament of the mosquito!
It is well that *he* should die and pass onward.
But alas for my ear that he has devoured.

Hark to the lament of the fly!
It is well that *he* should die and pass onward.
But alas! he has stolen the eye from which I drank.

Hark to the lament of the black ant!
It is well that *he* should die and pass onward.
But alas for my whale's-tooth that he has devoured.[1]

The whale's tooth is a peculiarly expressive symbol, carrying the double significance of economic wealth (ivory whales'
teeth having been used in Fiji as a standard of exchange)
and vital potency (the whale's tooth being also phallic, iconically representing the male organ). The realism of the black
ant becomes almost agonizingly clear when it is recalled that
Fijian men used to squat or sit on ant-infested ground clad
only in a loin-cloth. The ending of the lament is thus dramatically and metaphorically apt; and it marks the climax
of the entire mortuary drama—both actually among the survivors and suppositionally in the mountain-cave. When it is
over, the ghost ascends to Nai-thombo-thombo and plunges
into the sea, while his survivors bring their festivities to a
close and bury his now ripe body in the earth.

How are the ritualistic and mythic factors related in the
foregoing situation? From a sociological standpoint the festivities and the burial will be taken as the real aspect of the
matter, the ghostly adventures as a fictional projection de-

signed to explain and justify them. To the Fijian mourners, on the other hand, the ritual is but an adjunct to a perfectly real supernatural set of occurrences, being designed partly to celebrate and partly by imitative magic to assist the dead man's spectral journey. Probably, to be sure, the mourners do not rationalize in any such distinct way; what they mythopoeically enact in ritual and envision in story being as inseparable as convex and concave in a curve. In any event the dirge I have just quoted serves by its strongly marked rhythms—both the vocal rhythm (so I am assured, although it is lost in translation) and the ideational rhythm which the individuality of the lines preserves—to establish a sense of widened community, whereby, for the duration of the ceremony at least, the chanting survivors, the recently deceased, and the ancient ancestor-spirits are brought into a strongly felt and tersely articulated togetherness. Such reaffirmations of communal participation in the Something Beyond, paced in the tribal calendar according to the occurrence of emotively significant events like births and deaths, puberty, marriage, and war, are the most vitalizing forces in primitive cultural life. And the periodic expression of tribal fellowship tends to find oblique expression in the stories and shapes, the myths and proto-artistic forms, that become, despite their ready inclusion of the fantastic and the grotesque, the treasury of inherited wisdom and cultural cohesion.

RITUAL, MAGIC AND PARTICIPATION

A sharply different view of the nature of ritual has received currency from the admirable but too often seductively partisan writings of Sir James G. Frazer, especially in *The Magic Art*, which occupies the first two volumes of *The Golden Bough*. Frazer's theory is that all ritual and all religion have their origin in magic—i.e., in action intended to work coercively upon nature and bring about specific desired effects by exploiting the "sym-pathetic" connection that subsists between things that have once been joined or that are significantly similar. The coercive motive preceded, he thinks, both the petitionary and the celebrative. Men shifted to petitionary tactics only when their evolving intelligence discovered that coercion too often did not work. Ostensibly celebrative ceremonies, like those of the marriage of Zeus and Demeter at Eleusis, of the marriage of Zeus and Hera at Plataea, and the Midsummer Eve festivals of later Europe, he thinks were originally magical rites intended to produce or aid the effects which they dramatically set forth. "If the revival of vegetation in spring," he writes, "is mimicked by the awakening of a sleeper, the mimicry is intended actually to quicken the growth of leaves and blossoms; if the marriage of the powers of vegetation is simulated by a King and Queen of May, the idea is that the powers thus impersonated will really be rendered more productive by the ceremony. In short, all these spring and midsummer festivals fall under the head of homoeopathic or imitative magic. The thing which people wish to bring about they represent dramatically, and the very representation is believed to effect, or at least to contribute to, the production of the desired result."[2] Similarly, since Demeter's anger and self-seclusion after the loss of Persephone is described in myth as causing the failure of the crops, Frazer infers that the ritual connected with her worship is essentially magical in intent, aimed at preventing a recurrence of crop-failure.

Frazer's vast erudition has not guarded him, unfortunately, from an elementary logical mistake. His evidence establishes a strong case for the presence of a magical element in the Eleusinian worship of Demeter; it does not in the least prove that her worship was entirely or even primarily magical. Celebration, veneration, and praise on the one hand, magical incantation and petitionary prayer on the other—

who can assign precisely, after this span of centuries, the relative importance of such complementary motives in the Eleusinian Mysteries? Inasmuch as the Mysteries were kept hidden from the profane view and not committed to writing, the known details are sparse. Among other things a sheaf of grain was displayed as a kind of blessed sacrament by the hierophant to the neophytes, and the prominence of that symbol may appear to support the view that we are dealing with a survival of vegetation magic. (Freudians, on the other hand, are more likely to see a phallus in any object so shaped.) But Frazer pays too little heed to the religious tone of the ceremonies. The Eleusinian worship was conducted, according to available testimony, with deep reverence, and the worshiper underwent a genuine purgation of soul, a *katharsis* or *katharmos*, casting off the old self even as Nature discards last year's raiment to be reborn in the new year. Magic is imperious, worship is acquiescent. The magician's aim is to manipulate nature, the worshiper seeks to know her and to become attuned to her pulsations. There may well be magical elements in the Eleusinian as in other religious ceremonies—whether as survivals or as degenerative novelties—and their importance is much greater in some cults and in some ceremonies than in others, but they probably do not lie nearly so close to the heart of the matter as Frazer, with his strong positivistic bias, is disposed to believe.

For although all magic employs ritual as its instrument, it is by no means true that all ritual is primarily or even appreciably magical in intent or in origin. The problem can be understood more objectively if we distinguish ceremonies, from the standpoint of the idea that governs and justifies them, into four main types: the coercive, the contractual, the assimilative, and the confrontative. The first two may be called, in a broad way, magical; the latter two are at least embryonically religious. I ignore such ceremonies as are merely imitative, habitual, and perfunctory, for in them the governing idea has been lost.

Coercive ritual (the adjective connotes the intent and does not prejudge the results) is magical in the most commonly accepted sense of the word. Its magic may work, or be expected to work, either negatively or positively; in the exorcism of troublesome ghosts or in the transformation of natural objects or events at the magician's bidding. In either case such magic is set to work by tapping certain magical potencies, quasi-natural forces which the Melanesians call *mana*, and which the magician can control and exploit by virtue of the superior degree of *mana* in himself or in his magical words or magical instruments.[3]

I will not attempt to estimate, and do not believe that anyone today can possibly do so without bias, how much truth and how much illusion there may have been in the primitive magical belief. At any rate it seems likely that ceremonial magic would have been mixed, even quite early in human evolution, with elements of empirical method, trial-and-error, primitive experiment. Great fundamental inventions, such as the rude necessities of clothing, shelter, and weapons, the discovery of fire and of making food more palatable by cooking it, the first use of the wedge and the wheel, the first sowing of seed and waiting for the harvest: such monumental steps from savage to proto-civilized ways of living, however much attended by magic and ritual, were essentially a kind of infant technology, and thus, despite their aberrations, point at long range to the scientific view of things and to the semantic which is its instrument. In primitive times, however, the earliest technology can hardly have developed much of a semantic of its own: it evolved within a predominantly mythopoeic framework.

Attempts to coerce nature sometimes alternate with, sometimes combine with, attempts to propitiate and persuade her.

In its simplest forms propitiation may involve no more than the fear-inspired or awe-inspired sacrifice of some valued possession, to appease either the greed or vengeance or the sheer unexplainable cussedness of the alien forces. At a more sophisticated and consciously deliberate stage it begins to embrace the idea of covenant—the ancient *Do ut des,* "I give in order that you shall give in return."[4] Such an attitude shows an incipient transcendence of the mana-taboo type of consciousness, involving as it evidently does a belief in spirits who can be trusted to uphold their side of the agreement and correspondingly an acceptance of a moral obligation by oneself.

Coercive and propitiatory types of ritual may both be described as magical—the former in the basic and accepted sense, the latter by derivation and analogy. They are alike in two ways. First, they maintain an already developed distinction between self and not-self, between the magician and the natural or supernatural force with which he is concerned; and secondly, the magician's interest in that outer force is utilitarian, he wants to exploit it, turn it to his own uses. The two remaining ceremonial types, the assimilative and the religious, differ respectively on just these two points.

Assimilative ritual consists in reaffirming and attempting to intensify man's continuity and partial oneness with nature, or with the mysterious creative force behind nature. The omnipresent mana-power is conceived not as something separate from oneself and manipulable by one's independent will, but as (so to speak) the womb of reality to which it is a joy to return. Mana tends to be a borderland idea, a mode of existence somehow between and combining the personal and impersonal, the natural and supernatural, the self and not-self. That is not to say that primitive man first thought these antitheses and then blurred them (as our own differently oriented intelligences perhaps oblige us to do) but simply that he did *not* make the distinctions which to us appear logically and experimentally self-evident. His relation to nature was largely one of participation, much in the same way as was his relation to fellow-beings within the tribe.

Accordingly Lévy-Bruhl has declared the Law of Participation to be a governing condition of all primitive thought.[5] "In the collective representations of primitive morality," he writes, "objects and phenomena can be, though in a manner incomprehensible to us, at once themselves and not themselves." Thus when the Bororo tribe of northern Brazil declare that they are red parakeets, they are not merely taking a name or claiming a relationship; they are asserting positive identity with the species of red parakeet. On the basis of our accustomed logic—the logic of Literal Discourse—it is paradoxical to regard them as human beings and as birds of scarlet plumage at the same time, but "to the mentality that is governed by the law of participation there is no difficulty in the matter." Lévy-Bruhl characterizes such mentality as "pre-logical": not implying that it is necessarily antecedent in time to the birth of logical thought, but merely "that it does not bind itself down, as logical thought does, to avoiding contradiction." In practical situations, he observes, like seeking shelter in a storm or capturing a wild beast, where it is necessary to think and act as an individual, the primitive man reasons in much the same way as a civilized one, although with a different fund of information and memories to draw on. Typically primitive "pre-logical" ideas do not depend on the individual but on the group: "they present themselves in aspects which cannot be accounted for by considering individuals merely as such; they cannot be deduced from the laws of a psychology based upon the analysis of the individual subject." Lévy-Bruhl calls them "collective representations."

The law of participation governs not only the logic of primitive man but his semantic as well. That is to say, it operates not only in the use and combination of concepts but in their very formation. Our familiar and logically distinguishable concepts—man, animal, organism, and the like—involve mental operations of which we are scarcely aware: the memory of similar instances, the judgment of what similarities are relevant, and the grouping of instances into classes on the basis of those similarities. Pre-logical collective representations also involve mental selection and synthesis, but along different lines from those concepts which we call logical. The collective representations "contain, as integral parts, affective and motor elements, and above all they imply, in the place of our conceptual inclusions or exclusions, participations which are more or less clearly defined, but as a general rule very vividly sensed."

Thus for instance the Navaho language, which seems from our paleface standpoint to be full of confusions and contradictions, becomes somewhat more intelligible when certain distinctive principles of semantic grouping are recognized.[6] Things and qualities are grouped under a single name and perhaps even thought of as constituting a single or continuous entity, not so much because of observable similarities as because they carry similar emotive associations, such as are not likely to be evident to an outsider. Thus, to break an incest rule by looking at one's mother-in-law, to see a ghost, and to desecrate a sacred object are regarded as forming a single generalization, since they all have the effect of making a man go crazy, the Navahos say, and "acting like a moth at the fire." Other concepts may be bipolar: a single word may, in different contexts, mean either up or down; another, off or on; another from or toward. Still others fall into what I dare say might be called a flowing synecdoche: the word *djic* may denote either a medicine bundle with all its contents, or the container alone, or the contents alone, or any particular item of the contents. These are but samples of the many idiosyncratic (as they look to us) symbolic usages of the Navahos, which not only characterize their language but also influence (and perhaps are influenced by) their way of envisioning their world.

Again, a portrait to the primitive mind is different from what it is to ours: it participates in the very nature, life, and properties of the man whose image it is. The chieftains of the Sioux Indians refused to let Catlin make pictures of them, since by the law of participation whatever might happen to their likenesses, delivered over into strange hands, would happen identically to themselves. And the other tribal members were as much disturbed over the idea as the chieftains, because by virtue of the same law the tribe's welfare and very existence depend upon the sound condition of its chieftains, living or dead. Participation implies real identity, at least in significant respects, a transcendence of either-or, an ontological overlapping by which emotionally congruent things, qualities and events blend into oneness.

The potency of assimilative ritual is backed up by the fact that nature, to the mythopoeic vision, is vitally rhythmical. The primitive idea of nature, to a degree that we find hard to imagine, is time-oriented, as distinguished from the techno-scientific idea of it which is space-oriented. In all physics, even post-Einsteinian, the unassailable evidence of the Instrument proves that space and not time is the ultimate fulcrum of reference. For the time-hypotheses of physics can be objectively tested only by "readings" on some kind of chronometer, and the readings are visual—which is to say, what they immediately report are discriminations of space, which can be seen, and not of time, which cannot be seen. The primitive starting-point, on the contrary, is time as experienced: in the succession of day and night and the cycle of the seasons, in the progress from childhood to maturity and from maturity to old age and death, and in the tribal calendar of ceremonies of planting, reaping, feasting, war, the hunt, adolescent initiation, marriage, totemic sacrifice, and the like. Nature, in rituo-mythic perspective, is cyclical; its pulsations are not conceived mechanistically—they are alive, organic, and roughly harmonious with the pulsations of man's own psyche.

THE SENSE OF PRESENCE

Now the element of participation and sympathy, of kinship between society and nature, is not the entire story. It is complemented by a lurking sense of nature's otherness, strangeness, and lurking possible hostility. Man is not only immersed in, he also confronts his world. The typically primitive attitude toward nature is a sort of tension between naïve trust and watchfulness. The former gives men a feeling of membership, of at-homeness, of being comfortably rooted in Mother Earth. The security of the cave, of the family, and subconsciously perhaps of the womb, supplies the primordial ground-plan of human living. Familiar localities, persons, objects, and events confirm the basic sense of belonging; as do the patterned festivities of seasonal and tribal occurrence. But the familiar is not the whole of life, and to bask in it exclusively is to approach the condition of vegetable. Man encounters also, and develops a readiness to encounter, the strange; and this readiness in turn has a double aspect. For the strange can alarm and it can fascinate; it is likely to do both at once, although in different degrees; and the two emotions in combination—terror subdued by wonder—produce awe. Where the effect is more intriguing than frightening, men see fetishes in pebbles, spirits in rocks and rivers, totem-brothers in beasts, and gods in the sun and mountaintops. Where the note of alarm predominates, and where it is not definite enough to arouse the self-preservative instincts by suggesting particular measures of defense—as in the unguessable menace of hurricane and jungle fire, in black night and bottomless pool, in the tiger's sinewy power and the snake's beady stare—men fall into a primal terror of the Wholly Other, of the sheer ruthless mystery of things. The intensity of awe that arises from the simultaneous operation of these two contrary attitudes toward nature's otherness is a fertile breeding-ground of both religion and art.

An instructive instance, if properly understood, is found in the Cro-Magnon peoples who somehow dispossessed the ape-like Neanderthal men in Europe, roughly perhaps some twenty or fifteen thousand years before the Christian era. The Neanderthal savages had reached the ceremonial stage of burying stone weapons with the dead and painting corpses and grave-slabs with red ochre. But their caves appear to have been used only for shelter. Their Cro-Magnon successors, especially in the Aurignacian period, used the caves not only for domestic but also for ceremonial purposes, as the extensive remains of wall-paintings and insignia left in France and Spain bear witness. According to Frazer's theory we would have to suppose that the wall-paintings had originally served a magical intent, and that any purely decorative or purely ceremonial properties therefore represented a later development. Certain particular wall-figures, to be sure, such as the well-known bison pierced with arrows in the cave at Niaux, give strong though limited support to the magical hypothesis. But does magic sufficiently account for the most characteristic types of drawing in the Aurignacian caves?

In *The Gate of Horn*, a recent study of the religious conceptions of the European stone age as suggested by its cave records, Gertrude Rachel Levy gives attention to the problem.[7] She acknowledges that magic has had a large influence; not only paintings of arrow-pierced bison and sculptures of exaggeratedly pregnant females show magical intent, but even the ground-plans drawn on the cave walls at Niaux, La Pileta, La Pariega, and elsewhere she thinks may have served as magical entry permits rather than as mere guides to the actual route. Magical intent does not, on the other hand, explain the remarkable artistry of many of the paintings—the representation of great strength and force in the bison's body together with exquisite grace in the preternaturally thin legs. Dr. Levy concludes that what Aurignacian man wanted even more than magical effects was a condition of reciprocity with living nature, "a participation in the splendor of the beasts which was of the nature of religion itself, and so required this elaborate separation from normal activities." Why did the Aurignacian artist contrive his drawings with such exactitude that the brown bear is still distinguishable from the cave bear and that three distinct breeds of horses can be recognized? She suggests that exactitude may have been desired for the sake of closer attunement with the objects; for to the mythopoeic vision, then as now, there is more of reality in what is more concrete. Consequently, "the perfected forms which flowered in the pitch-dark solitudes were types by which ritual called up the species." And when a drawing is quite explicitly magical, like the one in the cave of Les Trois Frères of two hybrid beasts being commanded by a masked horned magician, she characterizes it as "over-ripe"—a composition in which "the integrity of the animal idea is broken by the intrusion of magic into the domain of religious art."

A further interesting question is raised by the practice of utilizing natural formations of rock and stalagmite deposit, as in the ribs and legs of the horse at Font-de-Gaume and of some of the bison at Altamira, and in the stag's horns affixed to a natural skull-shaped depression at Niaux. Was such practice a mere clever contrivance, a utilization of necessity by the craftsman, analogous to Orozco's ingenuity, when creating the Baker Library Murals at Dartmouth College, in fitting his pattern gracefully around the radiators and his darkest pigments over discolorations of the plaster? But Orozco, like every genuine artist, did more than merely yield to necessity; he turned necessity to effectively expressive purposes, so that the iron gratings of the radiators seem —after repeated acquaintance, at least—to be a part of the total New World pageant, a part of the caustic metallic commentary which the artist is making on the conquest of America. In much the same way that Orozco could enter into such intuitive sympathy with his medium as to see unrealized expressive possibilities in radiators and blotches, so the Aurignacian artist must have felt toward the fissures and depressions and stalagmite protuberances on the wall-surface of the cave. Unlike Orozco he was not obliged to accept them: there was plenty of bare wall-space to utilize if he had preferred. Gertrude Levy (whose area of survey does not include Orozco) concludes that the practice was considerably more than a matter of utilization, that the cave was "a repository of mystic influence," in which nature's markings on the rock appeared as indications of animal souls dwelling there.

May we not see, then, in those early artistic completions of what nature had barely hinted at, a record of the stage at which the human vision was passing from animatism to animism—from a sense of undefined mana-presence to an articulate, figured belief in definite animal souls; and even, at a crude level, in semi-divine presences? The impulse to give visible form to those souls by impressing their shapes upon durable rock would seem to illustrate what Cassirer has called the great revolution of early man—the first necessity of distinguishing the permanent from the transient. Such urgencies are more subtle, more deeply human, and more pregnant with unborn possibilities of meaning than the mere power-drive that impels men to the practice of magic.

These two types of ceremonial attitude toward nature, the assimilative and the confrontational, evolve, in religious context, into mysticism and theism respectively. God can be shadowed forth as that Infinite in which all things find their dwelling, and again as that Presence before whose majesty one's selfhood is at once humbled and reaffirmed. These are complementary aspects of a full-bodied religion. In art the two attitudes find expression in what Nietzsche has identified as the Dionysian and Apollian components—a self-yielding to the magical power of the musical beat and an aesthetic perception of the balance and bright clarity of plastic form. In poetry the cadences allure us into kinaesthetic identification, while the patterns of image and metaphor confront us quasi-visually. Some such vitalizing tension, between the beholder's intuition of oneness with an object and his intuition of that object's otherness, is what distinguishes genuinely expressive thinking from mere fancy on the one hand and the stereotypes of everyday usage on the other.

TEN

Dramatic Action and Mythic Imagery

THAT ACTION is of first importance to drama, the indispensable condition of its being, probably needs no argument. Aristotle elevated the truism to the dignity of a philosophical principle, particularly in the following two passages from the *Poetics:*

Tragedy is a representation *(mimesis)* essentially not of men but of human action *(praxis)*—of human life, its happiness and misery; for these must find expression in action, and the end for which we live is to be active in a certain kind of way, not just a certain passive quality of experience. . . . Consequently the plot and the incidents which constitute it are the real end and justification of tragedy. (Chap. 6.)

From all this it is evident that the poet *(poietes)* must be a maker *(poietes)* of plots rather than of verses, for he is a poet by virtue of the representing *(mimesis)* which he does, and what he represents are actions. (Chap. 9.)

Although Aristotle nowhere defines action, it is clear from his mention of plot and incidents that he is employing the concept in the usual sense, as involving conduct, gesture, overt response. Action is more than mere behavior, to be sure, as a study of the ethical writings confirms. Both inten-

tion and effect are involved. An action originates in a purposive choice *(proairesis)*, or else in a habit which has been
formed as a result of earlier purposive choices; and it finds
outlet in overt behavior which is followed by consequences
of weal or woe. The entire cycle of intention, act, and consequences is connoted when Aristotle uses the word *praxis,*
"action." In the *Poetics* the action under discussion is of
course *dramatic* action, and something more than the ethical
definition is involved in the conception. What is that something more?[1]

Dramatic action may be differentiated from action in the
broader sense with respect both to form and content. For-
mally, an action to be dramatic must have what Aristotle
stenographically describes as "a beginning, a middle, and an
end" (Chap. 7). What he means, of course, is a *dramatically
significant* beginning, middle, and end: otherwise the ascription would be no more than a tautology. "That is to say, a
well-constructed plot must neither begin nor end at random,
but must observe these distinctions"; and plot, he adds, is a
mimesis—an imitation or representation—of dramatic action.
His one other generalization about the form of a dramatic
action has to do with its proper length: "In general a sufficient length will mean one which allows of a development,
by steps whose connection appears inevitable, or at any rate
plausible, from misfortune to happiness or from happiness
to misfortune." The rules have at least the negative virtue
of being free from hampering dogmas about "the unities,"
which have vitiated so much subsequent dramatic theory;
and they apply with notable aptitude to the tragic single
plays which Aristotle most admired, such as the *Oedipus
Tyrannus.* They have the tolerant air of leaving a good many
possibilities open. Unfortunately, one possibility which they
do not leave clearly open is that of treating an entire trilogy,
such as the *Oresteia,* as a single dramatic whole. Agamemnon

moves from prosperity to misfortune in the single play that bears his name; Aegisthus, Clytemnestra, and finally Orestes move in the same direction in the *Choëphori;* while in the *Eumenides* Orestes moves from adversity to prosperity, and the Furies (if it is fair to consider them) move first one way and then the other. Each of the three component plays could be interpreted without over-much violence so as to meet the general requirements of Aristotle's rules. But the action of each component play, although it *can* be regarded by itself, is primarily interesting as a phase of the total action of the trilogy. And the action of the trilogy involves complementary movements—from prosperity to misfortune *and* from misfortune to prosperity. What is to be made of a complex form of action such as this?

Aristotle might have discovered the reason for it if he had pursued farther his investigation into the origin of tragedy. It arose, he informs us, "from improvisation, as practiced by choral leaders of the dithyramb" (Chap. 4). Now dithyrambs—as Aristotle must have known, or at any rate could have ascertained—originated in the worship of Dionysus, the deity of wild vegetation, fruits, and especially the vine. They were sung or chanted by dancing priests as a part of vegetation ritual, and consequently they tended to follow the general pattern marked by the death and rebirth of a vegetation god—whether Dionysus, Iacchos, Demeter, Pan, or some other.[2] The action of the *Oresteia* reflects the entire cycle of such vegetation rituals in a way that the action of a component play does not. Aristotle was hindered by his obdurately naturalistic cast of mind from perceiving anything of positive value and significance in the mystery cults of his day. His only serious contact with religion is intellectual— through his conception of God as the Unmoved Mover of the universe. Rational theology interests him, the superstitions and ceremonies of unenlightened peoples and cults do not.

Thus his philosophical vision, although broad, has a blind spot which incapacitates him from understanding the nature of Aeschylus' achievement.

The second way of distinguishing dramatic action from action in general is with respect to content. Dramatic action—unless artificially delimited by the theatrical conventions of a secular society—has a mythic dimension. It draws in various ways upon notions of good and evil as they are concretely set forth in the religious perspectives of a given culture. In this respect it may be broadly stated that dramatic action has stronger affinities with the chthonic than with the uranian side of religious interest. The *with*ness of earth is richer in dramatic potencies than the remoteness of an Olympian heaven. The gods of the bright sky invite mimesis in other media—in the clear delineations of sculptured forms, in the open geometry of temples and shrines, and, where literature is concerned, in the epic. When they step down into the drama it is, so to speak, *ex machina;* and the actual *machinae,* or pulley contraptions, which lowered them on the ancient stage in Euripidean and Senecan tragedy were symbolic of their really alien status. But the spirits of grain and grape, the Dionysian half-animal creatures who roam the forest, and the mysterious figure of a seasonal god who is slain and reborn annually, have a character which the Olympians lack and which excellently fits them for dramatic representation. Emerging as they do from the passage of the seasons, they are embedded in a natural time cycle, and this provides both the movement and the pattern which drama requires. Dance, too, even more directly and intimately, is made up of movement and pattern, and lends a sacramental character to ancient tragedy.

> The holy blessed Delphian Land,
> throbbing with hymns, begins to dance

when Thou thy holy shape revealest:
poised upon Parnassus' slope,
with reverent maidens attending.

And even:

The whole earth bursts into joyous dance
when Bromios leads his troop toward the hills,
where the bands of women await him, drawn
from loom and shuttle in reverent ecstasy.[3]

There is one maxim laid down in the *Poetics* which, had
Aristotle perceived its full implications, would have pointed
to the mythic depths of tragedy which he ignores. The remark in question occurs in Chapter 13, just after Aristotle
has been specifying types of plot to be avoided. The protagonist should not, he warns, be either a thoroughly good
or a thoroughly wicked man: the fate of such a one would
not produce tragic *katharsis* in the beholders, for tragic *katharsis* is compounded of pity and fear, and while pity can
be aroused by any undeserved misfortune, "fear is aroused
only by the misfortune of someone like ourselves." Accordingly, he concludes, let the tragic protagonist be a man "who
is a mean between the extremes of perfectly good and perfectly bad: who, though not outstandingly virtuous and just,
yet falls into misfortune not through vice or depravity but
through some "tragic flaw" *(hamartia)*.

The word *hamartia* outside of the dramatic context was
applied to human faults quite generally, just as the word
praxis outside of the dramatic context was applied to actions quite generally. In that more general context, however,
"fault" is not only an ethical, it is also a religious notion;
and this is especially true of those faults which are grave
enough to furnish material for tragedy. Taken religiously a
fault wears the look of *guilt*, or, so far as the religious sanc-

tion is inward rather than outward, of *sin*. In life as in drama a familiar pattern is that of a man neither wholly perfect nor wholly depraved—"like ourselves"—moving from happiness to misfortune and misery because of *hamartia*. Fortunately, the cycle does not stop there. Although guilt (or sin) brings requital sooner or later, outwardly or inwardly, upon the evil-doer, what religion offers is a way of eventually escaping from the bondage of such sin. Ancient Greek religion shows four main ways of interpreting *hamartia*, requital, and redemption; and our understanding of the depth-meaning of dramatic action will be improved if we see what these are.

GREEK IDEAS OF HAMARTIA

Any attempt to schematize Greek religion is bound to fall short of the complex reality. Recognizing this, I nevertheless offer the schema on the following page for whatever it may be worth as a clarifying instrument. In it are distinguished four main religious types. The *Olympian* type, the religion having to do with Zeus, Hera, Apollo, Artemis, Aphrodite, and other majestic presences inhabiting the bright vault overhead, is the one most commonly associated with the Greeks, for the simple reason that these skyey figures, being clearly delineated in the mythopoeic imagination, most readily entered into the ancient myths and eventually into the two Homeric epics. But in Greece, as in nearly all mythopoeic cultures, there was a religion of the soil, a *chthonic* religion, as well.[4] And this for two reasons. Man dies and is buried in the ground; his ghost therefore inhabits the tomb, or, it may be, a subterranean region, a *hades*, where all ghosts (except those of specially favored heroes) congregate. One part of chthonic religion is thus connected with the tendance, placation, and sometimes exorcism of these shadow people whose life is half-death but who can still make their influence felt, usually in unpleasant ways. The other part of chthonic reli-

ASPECTS OF ANCIENT GREEK RELIGION

Aspect	Typical Divinities	Hamartia	Penalty	Solution
I. Chthonic: A. Mortuary	Ghosts of the dead	Breaking of taboo or tribal mores	Troubled by restless ghosts, or by the Furies	Exorcism: "Do ut abeas"
II. Olympian	Zeus, Apollo	Hybris	Nemesis	Sometimes none; sometimes sacrifice: "Do ut des"
III. Chthonic: B. Vegetative	Demeter, Dionysus	Pollution	Sickness and blight	Ritual cleansing; banishment
IV. Mystical	Orpheus, "The Unknown God"	Individuation	Separation; blindness	Mystical union; new vision

gion rests upon the fact that vegetation grows out of earth's womb, and that this happens periodically, so that the vegetation ceremonies punctuate, or perhaps even constitute, the annual calendar. Let us designate these two elements of chthonic religions the *mortuary* and the *vegetative*. Finally there is a fourth type of ancient Greek religion, which can best be described (in the most exact sense of that abused word) as *mystical*. In the diagram I have listed the Olympian type second, between the two species of chthonic religion. This apparent disordering is done because whereas the mortuary type represents, on the whole, the most primitive mode of feeling, thinking and behaving, vegetation ritual is normally less in bondage than mortuary to the Primitive Terror, and shows a readier tendency, as it evolves, to develop something of a mystical character.

(1) The mortuary component by itself is not so much religious as proto-religious. Its emotional tone is determined predominantly by fear; it may occasionally rise to awe, but almost never to the essentially religious emotion of reverence. Its corresponding ethical conception is a respect for taboo, backed by a terror of breaking it. Its mythic symbols are likely to be such figures as Dis, lord of the dead, or Death itself personified, or his ministers, or Hermes conductor of souls to the nether world, or ghostly agents of retribution— either the angry ghosts of those who have suffered injury, such as that of Clytemnestra in the *Eumenides*, or generalized ghost-avengers such as the Furies. Such ghostly antagonists are not easy to placate. Clytemnestra appears to have succeeded in winning the Furies over to her side by rituals of libation, but that is because they are in a vague way mother-archetypes, less insistently concerned therefore with the murder of a husband. She has more difficulty in placating Agamemnon's individual ghost, as the opening of the *Choëphori* makes evident. Orestes when plagued by the Furies

has no chance at all, until at the end he is saved by Athena's divine act of grace.

(2) The Olympian religion, and consequently the Olympian ethic, is an affair of bright space and clear boundaries. Homer tells that when Zeus, Poseidon and Dis drew lots for the world and Zeus won the sky, Poseidon the sea, and Dis the underworld, they swore by the River Styx, the most dreadful of oaths, to respect the fall of chance and *not overstep the boundary*. The broad earth, inhabited by men, remained a common territory, unassigned to one god more than another. The late Francis M. Cornford has remarked that this cosmic legend appears to reflect what must have been an earthly situation during the years when the Dorian invaders of Greece were consolidating their victory and settling down to the unaccustomed arts of agriculture. A nomadic people, which depends mainly on the luck of the hunt for its food, is likely to regard the food thus obtained as common property, to be distributed according to some accepted principle or other of rank or need. When such a people becomes stationary and begins to live by planting and reaping, the principle of universal sharing becomes unwieldy and encourages sloth. Boundaries must be set up, and as Hesiod's *Works and Days* records, a new ethical idea must now be insisted on: "Respect your neighbor's boundary!" or, more generally, "Do not overstep the boundary!"[5]

The topographical division on earth and the Olympian myth of the division of the cosmos combine to give great force to that most characteristic of Greek moral principles, the Golden Mean. For the injunction not to overstep the Boundary grows into the more general and humanistic principle of following the Middle Way—"Nothing too much!" "Do not overstep the boundary between courage and cowardice, nor yet the opposing boundary between courage and recklessness": such, in effect, is the intellectualized form which the principle assumes in the ethics of Aristotle. But meanwhile there is an application which has great importance in Greek epic and dramatic literature—the idea of respecting the boundary between man's estate and that of the Olympian immortals. Failure to do this, a wish to emulate the gods by being something more than man, whether in wealth or power or even (like Hippolytus) in virtue, is the hamartia of *hybris,* arrogance. The arrogant man errs by overstepping, yes, but in terms of another metaphorical figure he upsets the natural balance of things, which must then be restored. The divine judgment which tends to overtake such a man becomes half-personified, never wholly so, as Nemesis. The Erinyes, too, are operative in this connection—only secondarily as "Furies," primarily as restorers of the order of nature. Thus Heraclitus declares: "The sun will not overstep his measures [*metra*—i.e., the boundaries of his course]; if he does, the Erinyes, attendants of Justice, will hunt him out."[6]

(3) The vegetative type of religion can be better understood if we stop to reflect upon the nature of good and evil from a radically organic standpoint. Good is life, vitality, propagation, health; evil is death, impotence, disease. Of these several terms *health* and *disease* are the most important and most comprehensive. Death is but an interim evil; it occurs periodically, but there is the assurance of new life ever springing up to take its place. The normal cycle of life and death is a healthy cycle, and the purpose of the major seasonal festivals was at least as much to celebrate joyfully the turning wheel of great creative Nature as to achieve magical effects. Disease and blight, however, interrupt the cycle; they are the real destroyers; and health is the good most highly to be prized.

What is health? This is a question upon which all schools of medicine in ancient Greece seem to have been essentially agreed.

Health is a right proportion of parts and functions in an organism, disease is a corresponding disproportion. Medical schools differed, to be sure, in their identification of the elements to be ordered. But whether the parts were conceived in terms of opposites (as by the Pythagoreans), in terms of the four natural substances: fire, air, water, and earth (as by the doctors of that "ancient medicine" which Hippocrates criticizes), or in terms of "bodily juices" (as by Hippocrates himself), the opinion was general that health consisted in a right relationship among the organic parts, enabling the organism to function well as a whole, and that disease was the lack or loss of such right relationship.[7] How, when lost, was a right relationship to be restored? The logic seemed clear. The simplest way of changing a disproportion into a true proportion is by ridding the body of the superfluous elements, thereby allowing (as the Empedocleans put it) the elements that remain to unite in health-giving love. If the unwanted element was such that it could be cut away, then cautery was indicated; if not—if it was, for instance, an excess of heat as in fever, or an excess of cold as in rheum— then the cure was to be found in purging (*katharsis* or *katharmos*) or, symbolically, in ceremonial ablution (expressed by the same pair of Greek words).

Murder, from the standpoint here entertained, does violence to the natural order of things. It destroys the right relationship of the social organism. Symbolically, therefore, the murderer is diseased. When his victim is someone in his own family, the disease is the more virulent, for the family is even more compactly an organism than the *polis*. When his method of murder is as unnatural as that of Atreus in serving up Thyestes' children to him baked for dinner, the disease is again the more virulent. The soul of the perpetrator is rendered vulnerable to hostile influences, such as to the curse which Thyestes invoked against Atreus. Moral disease, like physical, spreads by contagion, and the vulnerability was shared therefore by all Atreus' descendants.

Symbolically, murder is a spilling of the victim's blood upon the ground. Since the act is a diseased act, the flowing blood receives the contagion and transmits it to the soil where it is spilt.

> When blood is shed and drunk by Mother Earth
> The vengeful gore congeals immoveable.[8]

The disease spreads through the land, sometimes (as in *Oedipus Tyrannus*) causing a general blight, and eventually its evil effects return upon the murderer or his descendents. Orestes' pursuit by the Furies after he has spilt his mother's blood can also be understood in this manner, and Aeschylus offers imagistic clues that would have enabled the more alert and responsive members of the audience in the City Dionysia to carry an overtone of such interpretation in their minds. The punishment of the murderer is not merely an act of retribution; it is also, from the present standpoint, a means and a symbol of saving the city. Ablution, which may be effective in removing the stain of ordinary murders, will not serve for the extraordinary ones.

> Though stream on stream should pour
> Their swift-cleansing waters on the hand of blood,
> The old stain shall not be washed away.[8]

Sometimes cautery is the only answer, and as a diseased limb must be lopped off from the parent stem to prevent further contamination, so a murderer must be sent into exile. Such is the situation at the end of *Oedipus Tyrannus*. Orestes, too, suffers a self-imposed exile; and in the third play of the trilogy it turns out that his crime of matricide has contaminated him to the very bone, so that even Apollo, god of healing, is helpless against it. The solution has to await the bestowal of Athena's divine aid.

(4) The relation between the third and fourth types of Greek religion, the vegetative and the mystical, is partly indicated by the password of the Eleusinian mysteries which Clement of Alexandria has preserved for Christian readers: "I have fasted, I have drunk the barley drink, I have taken the things from the sacred chest, having tasted thereof I have placed them into the basket and again from the basket into the chest."[8] The ceremonial fasting of the worshipers corresponds to the mythic fasting of the grain goddess Demeter when, sorrowing for the abducted Persephone, she tasted neither meat nor drink. The drinking of barley-water corresponds to the goddess' eventual breaking of her fast with a drink composed of "meal and water and tender herb of mint." Accordingly, as Harold R. Willoughby writes, "in drinking a similar potation the *mystae* shared the cup from which the great Goddess drank in her sorrow. It was a direct and sympathetic participation in the experiences of the goddess, an action expressive of attained fellowship with the deity."[9] The sacrament of communion with the goddess is continued by the taking of barley cakes (for that is what the "things in the sacred chest" probably were) out of the chest and tasting them. Here too the worshiper receives an incorporation of divine substance into himself, symbolized by the assimilation of the sacred food into his body.

As the highest good, from the mystical standpoint, is union with the godhead, however conceived and symbolized, so the worst of evils is separation. To sin is to separate oneself from the divine fellowship—a fellowship which hovers on the verge of mystical union. How is the union to be restored?

From the most ancient times among the Indo-European peoples it was taught that as separation from Godhead comes only through ignorance (for why should anyone willingly separate himself from what he knows to be the source of all good?) so restoration of the vitalizing relationship is made possible only by right knowledge. The deadly ignorance consists in the illusion of individuation, the belief that one can decide one's purposes and way of life entirely by and for oneself, and that the greatest felicity is attained by so doing. It is not my intention here to argue the point one way or the other. The philosophy of mysticism holds as its cardinal truth that individuation is error and illusion, and that *we know the truth about anything only so far as we enter into union with it.*[10] Especially can the truth about divine matters be known only in this way. But although union is necessary to adequate knowledge, the blessedness which is to come (as a state both of being and of knowing) may be foreshadowed by a symbol. The sacramental eating of barley bread symbolizes the blessedness of mystical union with Demeter; in neighboring cults the sacramental drinking of wine symbolized the blessedness of mystical union with Iacchos. Of course mystical cults, since they teach the blessing of union, naturally tend to unite with one another; and the twin sacraments of bread and wine, offering so lively an appeal to the religious imagination, have tended to merge and to spread widely.

A more important and more philosophical symbol of mystical religion is Light. The analogy between the action of physical light upon the eye and the dawning of wisdom upon the mind and soul is familiar, in one form or another, to virtually all nations and races. The idea of Spiritual Light vs. Spiritual Darkness is one of the hardiest of archetypes: partly because it expresses the most essentially human (as distinct from animal) of man's characteristics—the desire to know; and partly because it also reflects iconically the cycle of day and night and symbolically the cycle of winter (Persephone in Hades) and summer (Persephone restored). The passage from a dark chamber, where often certain ordeals must be endured, into a Hall of Light, is a usual stage in the initiation which neophytes to any of the Greek mystery religions must undergo. As I shall show in the next chapter, the darkness-light imagery in the *Oresteia* is a powerful symbolic means of reinforcing the depth-meaning of that great cyclical drama.

DRAMATIC IMAGERY

The role of imagery in revealing and accentuating the depth-meaning of a tragic drama may be approached by way of a passage from Claude-Edmonde Magny's incisive little study, *Les sandales d'Empédocle.*[11] "There are two parts in every book, as in every work of art," Mlle. Magny writes; "on the one hand, the author's conscious and expressly intended message, the effect for which he has purposely fitted out his machine . . . ; on the other, the truth which he reveals without realizing it, the aspect of the world which he has discovered almost in spite of himself, in the course of the actual experience of composition; which is doubtless more or less what Gide, in the preface to *Paludes,* refers to as 'God's share.'" And Mlle. Magny draws two corollaries from this. The first she offers as a law of literary creation: "To the extent that an author is over-successful in communicating his conscious message, the jealous gods refuse him their collaboration." From this there follows the other corollary—a principle which we as readers, critics and interpreters of literature should keep in mind: "The greatest writers are just those who have found themselves thinking at odds with themselves."

Now there is more than one way of thinking at odds with

oneself; and some of the ways—schizophrenia, for example—
are destructive, not creative. Poetic self-division, as distinguished from schizophrenic, is never a breakdown, but a
pleasurably vibrant tension between meanings which are antithetical yet surreptitiously related, or related yet surreptitiously antithetical. One of the most powerfully expressive
kinds of poetic tension is that which exists between the story
or scenario of a poem and the suggestions thrown off by its
imagery. Such tensions are dramatic by their very nature,
and give a certain dramatic character, an inherent dialectic,
to the poem in which they occur. In a poetic drama enacted
on the stage they tend to be ignored by the casual playgoer,
whose mind is given to spectacle and plot, but they will reward whatever attention is bestowed upon them by offering
important indications of the integral meaning of the presented drama. They are an organic but semi-independent
part of that total movement which Francis Fergusson has
called the "tragic rhythm of action,"[12] and to which the joy
of a serious reader or auditor consists in responding as adequately and integrally as he is able.

Such thematic imagery may be derived from the overt action itself, as with most of the blood imagery in *Macbeth;* or
it may be imported into the action by means of metaphor
and simile, as is the case with Shakespeare's tempest imagery
in plays where no tempest is represented as actually occurring. Generally speaking, Aeschylus relies more on imagery
produced by metaphor, and Sophocles on imagery derived
from overt action and situation. One of Shakespeare's most
engaging peculiarities is the way in which a set of images
which he has originally employed as metaphor, relating them
to the plot only by airy imaginative indirection, may gradually take so firm a grip on the poet's stage-conscious mind
that at length in some later play he will project the imaged
idea into the actual frame of the theatre. Tempest and gar-

den imagery, first employed as early as *Henry VI* to meta-
phorize the antithesis of struggle and attainment, war and
peace, doubt and security, etc., become actual parts of the
stage machinery in many subsequent plays. The tempests
which crack and deracinate in *Julius Caesar, Macbeth, King
Lear, Pericles,* and more sportfully, in the play to which
they finally give their name, and the garden scene of *Richard
II* (so superfluous by ordinary standards of dramatic con-
struction) are familiar illustrations of Shakespeare's disposition to crown the life of an image that has done him service
by bestowing a playwright's badge of honor on it.

The twofold distinction just drawn becomes threefold
when not only the source but more relevantly the function
of dramatic imagery is considered. Imagery may confirm
plot, or amplify it, or contradict it. That is to say, a set of
images may give emphasis and concreteness to situations
and ideas already present in the overt action. Or it may pro-
vide another imaginative dimension, a set of significances
and possible interpretations, which the plain sense of the
drama, taken literally, neither affirms nor denies. Or finally,
the suggestions that it makes may stand in such sharp antithesis to the overt action that they virtually contradict it,
producing thereby a heightened dramatic tension and an air
of challenging paradox. In practice, of course, these lines of
division may be blurred: a given use of dramatic imagery
may be confirmatory and amplificative at once, or it may
amplify in a way that suggests contradiction, or its precise
mode of functioning may be difficult to determine. But let
us take some well-known examples.

A confirmatory image-pattern of tremendous effectiveness
is found in the blood and darkness symbolism of *Macbeth*.
I am not denying that the imagery of that wonderful play
is often put to realistic, denotative use as well. Generally
speaking, confirmatory imagery is apt to be realistic in its

immediate intent, and the symbolic overplay becomes evident mainly from the cumulative effect and the contextualization. Thus it is plausible enough from a realistic standpoint that the idea of blood should permeate Macbeth's thoughts:

> Blood hath been shed ere now.

> Thy bones are marrowless, thy blood is cold.

> It will have blood, they say; blood will have blood.

> For the blood-bolter'd Banquo smiles upon me.

And psychological plausibility would likewise explain the sleep-walking utterances of Lady Macbeth:

> Yet who would have thought the old man to have
> had so much blood in him?

> Here's the smell of blood still—

joined with the kinaesthetic imagery of a compulsive and (as Judith Anderson interpreted it) a convulsive washing of the hands. Naturalism of a more outward, objectively descriptive sort is present when Lennox says, "Their hands and faces were all badg'd with blood," when Banquo speaks of "this most bloody piece of work," and Ross of "this more than bloody deed." A literalist might take such references as simply elements of the plot, and see no justification for interpreting them symbolically. Nevertheless the cumulative effect of *blood, bleeding,* and *bloody,* occurring so many times during the play, goes well beyond the requirements of naturalistic drama; it works semantically by giving an iconic emphasis to one of the dramatic themes. Macbeth as a tragic figure, as a *persona,* is steeped in blood; his slayer had been ripp'd untimely from his mother's womb, and in the witches' cave the apparition of a bloody child commands him to "be bloody, bold and resolute." This injunction is symbolically important, because throughout the play the blood imagery acts as a symbol of boldness and resolution, of violence and crime, and finally of the horror that is their effect, even as the contrasting darkness and tempest imagery symbolizes the deceptiveness and confusion that eventually prove Macbeth's undoing. The result is a two-color symbolism, announced at the outset in the cinematic transition from Scene i to Scene ii:

> Fair is foul, and foul is fair:
> Hover through the fog and filthy air.

—of the Weird Sisters, followed by an instantaneous shift of scene and King Duncan's exclamation, "What bloody man is that?" The sergeant in his excited report to the King, unwittingly combines the two themes into one:

> Which *smok'd* with *bloody* execution.

The combination is exactly suited to the plot; for the kingdom which Macbeth wins through bloody boldness he will finally lose through trusting the half-true half-lying promises of the Weird Sisters ("these juggling fiends . . . That palter with us in a double sense"). Accordingly Shakespeare surrounds the Sisters not only with visual imagery of darkness, fog and filth, but with what I'll venture to call *intellectual images of contradiction:*

> Fair is foul and foul is fair.

> So foul and fair a day I have not seen.

> This supernatural soliciting
> Cannot be ill, cannot be good.

> When the hurly-burly's done,
> When the battle's lost and won.

Such contradiction has moral and dramatic importance in *Macbeth* as leading to man's spiritual confusion. Elizabethan theology was precise on this point: agents of evil cannot seize man's soul directly, for his power of free will remains his own; they can, however, confuse or "confound" him with false hopes, so that he is seduced, not coerced, into wrong choices.

> Though his bark cannot be lost,
> Yet it shall be tempest tost.
> (Act II, Scene iii)

The Witches' Brew, which the hellish sisters are preparing when Macbeth approaches them for the last time (IV. i) is a thing of monstrously unnatural combinations—fragments of things all "poured together" *(confundere, confusus)* so that their distinctive characters are lost. "Make the gruel thick, and slab." From this imagistic standpoint the climax of the play—the climax of the symbolic action—would seem to lie in Macbeth's great speech of conjuration to the Weirds:

> Though you untie the winds and let them fight
> Against the churches; though the yesty waves
> Confound and swallow navigation up;
> Though bladed corn be lodg'd and trees blown down;
> Though castles topple on their warders' heads;
> Though palaces and pyramids do slope
> Their heads to their foundations; though the treasure
> Of nature's germens tumble all together,
> Even till destruction sicken: answer me
> To what I ask you.
> (Act IV, Scene i)

When the germs of nature, the seeds of things (*semina rerum*), the spermatic principles (*logoi spermatikoi*),[13] visually represented by the salt spume of the yeasty waves, are confounded, then things no longer (in words from elsewhere) "observe degree, priority and place." Raging of the sea and shaking of the spheres are outward correspondences to the mutiny at the heart of man. And in *Macbeth* Shakespeare has produced the supreme tragedy of a man who gives that mutiny free rein.

Although *Richard II* contains as many instances of the word "blood" as *Macbeth* does, its symbolic role there is milder. At the outset of the play it is repeatedly employed to symbolize high lineage. Henry Hereford (successively to be known by the titles Lancaster, Bolingbroke, and King Henry IV) and Thomas Mowbray, Duke of Norfolk, confront each other with opposing charges of treason. One of them must be lying, and later events make it probable that the liar is Hereford, at least in great part. During the dispute each of the antagonists violently protests his loyalty, and argues it by appealing to his "blood." Thus "blood" becomes a focal symbol of the twin ideas (twin according to the play's dominant *mythos*) of lineage and loyalty. In the opening scene Bolingbroke offers to "lay aside my high blood's royalty," Mowbray denounces Bolingbroke as "this slander of his blood," the King declares "Such neighbour nearness to our sacred blood/Should nothing privilege him," and Mowbray wants to fight "To prove myself a loyal gentleman/Even in the best blood chamber'd in his bosom." The slight transitional Scene ii echoes the theme: Gaunt opens it by speaking of his oneness in blood with the murdered Woodstock, Duke of Gloucester; while the bereaved Duchess of Gloucester, trying to egg him on to vengeance, asks, "Hath love in thy old blood no living fire?" and reminds him that "his blood was thine" and that Edward's seven sons, which included

Gaunt and Woodstock, "Were as seven vials of his sacred blood." At once, however, a supplementary image is introduced: that of "seven fair branches springing from one root." The importance of this juxtaposition, blood and branches, is suggested by the peculiar chequered way in which the Duchess alternates them in successive lines:

> One vial full of Edward's sacred blood,
> One flourishing branch of his most royal root,
> Is crack'd, and all the precious liquor spilt,
> Is hack'd down, and his summer leaves all faded,
> By Envy's hand and Murder's bloody axe.

Lines 1 and 3 of the passage and the word "hand" in line 5 carry out the logic of the "blood" image; lines 2 and 4 and the word "axe" in line 5 carry out the logic of the "branch" image; while the description of the axe as "Murder's bloody axe" allows the blood image to impenetrate the other. Echoes of blood continue throughout the play. As the tournament is about to begin (Scene iii) Richard addresses Bolingbroke as "my blood," and Bolingbroke in turn addresses old Gaunt his father as "the earthly author of my blood," to which Gaunt replies by urging his son, "Rouse up thy youthful blood."

A more literal, or more nearly literal, mention of blood is also found with some frequency in the play. In Act I, Scene i, in fact, the symbolic instances are interspersed and patterned with such literal ones as the following: "Sluic'd out his innocent soul through streams of blood"; and "Let's purge this choler without letting blood"; and (semi-literally) "The blood is hot that must be cool'd for this."

But there is one aspect of the literal meaning of blood that deserves special attention, since it becomes the basis of another symbolic development. Froissart records that the historical Richard had a physical weakness which caused the blood to rush readily from his cheek. Shakespeare's Richard refers to this trait when angered against the dying Gaunt, who has dared to

> Make pale our cheek, chasing the royal blood
> With fury from his native residence.
> (Act II, Scene i)

Here the meaning is fairly literal. But later when Salisbury has announced the defection of Richard's Welsh followers to Bolingbroke, the King, on Aumerle's asking, "Why looks your Grace so pale?" replies:

> But now the blood of twenty thousand men
> Did triumph in my face, and they are fled;
> And, till so much blood thither come again,
> Have I not reason to look pale and dead?
> (Act III, Scene ii)

Here we see another dimension of the magical and symbolic connectedness that blood connotes. There is not only the backward connection by heritage, lineage, descent. There is also the outward connection, political in the most fundamental sense; for the blood of the king's subjects is both magically and mystically one with the king's blood—i.e., both the support and the participating symbol of his life and strength.

The magical relationship extends beyond the human sphere to the earth and all that grows in it. When Richard, returning from the Irish campaign, arrives in Wales he salutes his earth, wounded by rebels with their horses' hoofs, and adjures it:

> Feed not thy sovereign's foe, my gentle earth,
> Nor with thy sweets comfort his ravenous sense;
> But let thy spiders, that suck up thy venom,

And heavy-gaited toads lie in their way,
Doing annoyance to the treacherous feet
Which with usurping steps do trample thee. . . .
Mock not my senseless conjuration, lords.
This earth shall have a feeling, and these stones
Prove armed soldiers, ere her native king
Shall falter under foul rebellion's arms.
                              (Act III, Scene ii)

The rhetoric may be heavy for some tastes, but the important thing is the strong sense of that magical connectedness.
Shakespeare has not brought it in at random, as a bit of royal
décor; the common people, too, are at one with English soil,
and Richard can declare that the spilling of English blood

Shall ill become the flower of England's face,
Change the complexion of her maid-pale peace
To scarlet indignation . . .
                              (Act III, Scene iii)

Such mythic connections in the background do much to
heighten the power of Richard's dying words:

Exton, thy fierce hand
Hath with the king's blood stained the king's own land.
                              (Act V, Scene v)

Such imagery as I have been citing combines with the
plot-situations of the play to produce a *total dramatic meaning.* Although that meaning cannot be given authentically
in other language than that of the entire drama itself, I might
roughly indicate its nature by quoting two prose extracts
from William Tyndale's *Obedience of the Christian Man,* a
work widely read and admired in Shakespeare's day. On the
one hand Tyndale declares:

God hath made the King in every realm to judge over all, and over him is there no judge. He that judgeth the King judgeth God, and he that layeth hands on the King layeth hands on God, and he that resisteth the King resisteth God. . . . The King is in this world without law, and he may at his lust do right or wrong and shall give accounts but to God only.

But then comes a counter-theme. Tyndale continues:

Yea, and it is better to have a tyrant unto thy King than a shadow, a passive King that doth nought himself but suffereth others to do him what they will, and to lead him whither they list. . . . A King that is soft as silk and effeminate, that is to say, turned into the nature of a woman, shall be much more grievous unto the realm than a right tyrant.[15]

Here is a royal antinomy, which in another writing Tyndale applies explicitly to the case of King Richard II. Richard is a weak and unjust king, a shadow, "soft as silk and effemi-nate." Nevertheless his insufficiencies did not, to the Tudor mind, justify deposition. Richard has gathered about him worthless parasites, robbed the exchequer, borrowed money from a faithful subject and then banished him, put his uncle the Duke of Gloucester to death. Ignoring the venerable John of Gaunt's sage and patriotic counsel, he unlawfully con-fiscates his estates. These are wrong acts, but they are not for the king's subjects to avenge. As Shakespeare's Gaunt declares:

> God's is the quarrel . . .
> Let heaven revenge, for I may never lift
> An angry arm against His minister.
> (Act I, Scene ii)

The total statement of the play *Richard II* is somewhat of a poetic equivalent of the compound literal statement quoted from Tyndale. "Divine sanction of the King *but* human frailty of earthly kings, and particularly of this one" would express approximately, in steno-terms, the theme which Shakespeare has reformulated in the language of dramatic poetry. The first phase of the theme receives poetic formulation not only in the blood symbol but also in the abundant religious imagery and scriptural allusion in which King Richard's character is embedded. Richard denounces his supposedly false friends as *Judases* damned without redemption; those who show an outward pity are *Pilates* who have delivered him to his sour *Cross;* the Bishop of Carlisle sees England as "the field of *Golgotha* and dead men's skulls"; Bolingbroke tells Exton to wander with *Cain* through shades of night; there are references to the camel and the needle's eye, to "Come, little ones," to baptismal usurpation, and so on. Besides the allusions to Scripture there are numerous metaphoric connections of the king with God, with the sun, and with the firm sanctity of earth: "Down, down I come, like blist'ring Phaethon" (III. ii. 178); "Not all the water in the rough rude sea/Can wash the balm off from an anointed king" (III. ii. 54); and the like. But kings are not only divine, they are human too. The human frailty of Richard is indicated in a variety of ways, chiefly through the plurisignative ideas, *earth, time,* and *unweeded garden.* In earlier passages the earth is mentioned as a royal possession, as a symbol of the sanctity, the power, and the stability of kingship. Later, after Scroop has announced the disastrous rebellion of most of Richard's followers, and the execution of three of his favorites, the earth-tune changes. The talk is now "of graves, of worms, and epitaphs," leading to the nostalgic loveliness of

> For God's sake, let us sit upon the ground
> And tell sad stories of the death of kings.

Here is the second symbolic phase of the plurisign *earth-ground,* associated this time with the man-king, not with the king-god. The earth, or ground, is now simply the place where the man-king's bones and hollow skull are to be buried; it is a symbol of the later, descending movement of the play.

The third functional type of dramatic imagery, the contradictive, is more often found as a momentary or intermittent phase of imagery that amplifies, than in pure form. Consider *Macbeth* again. The play is built, as I have remarked, upon the Christian assumption of free will; and in particular the dialectic of Act I, Scene vii is predicated upon Macbeth's belief that the future is still open, and that a choice is still to be made. Without that belief the soliloquy with which he begins the scene would be mere vaporizing. And the belief is implicit in his opening words, "If it were done when 'tis done, then 'twere well/It were done quickly"—which in their literal sense evidently presuppose some measure of freedom, power, and real agency in the protagonist. Yet, as I remarked in Chapter Four under the heading "Paradox," the auditory imagery produced by that repeated word "done" conveys an opposite and ominous hint that the knell of fate has sounded and that the choice (although Macbeth's conscious mind does not yet know it) is already an accomplished fact within him.

In a gentler way the religious imagery of *Romeo and Juliet* functions somewhat analogously. The plot of the play may be taken as roughly epitomized in the second quatrain of the Prologue:

> From forth the fatal loins of these two foes
>   A pair of star-cross'd lovers take their life;
> Whose misadventur'd piteous overthrows
>   Doth with their death bury their parents' strife.

The dramatic movement on the literal level is thus a single-tracked descent from happiness to adversity; the *hamartia* resides not in the lovers but in their families, and in the star-crossed situation which the family feud has produced. But side by side with the literal story, setting limits to its finality, runs another, an almost contrary dramatic development—*a para-plot of religious redemption*. Such a descriptive phrase is too heavy, as any attempt to mark a poetic direction by means of steno-language must be. Nor would anything valuable be gained by a meticulous inventory of the play's imagery. I would not wish to spoil the greatest of all love-tragedies for any reader by over-analysis, but a few indications may encourage a more alert re-reading.

Observe how the triviality and emotional confusion of Romeo's early love for Rosalind is suggested by the facile paradoxes of his "Why, such is love's transgression" speech (I. i) and by the cumulative effect in it of such words as *anything, nothing, lightness, vanity, misshapen, chaos, feather, smoke, sick, sleep*, and *not what it is*. Such gossamer love, though innocent at first, can end by confounding "the single state of man" unless it is redeemed by grace. The first announcement of a higher form of love—love as a state of grace—is made by the imagery with which Romeo and Juliet exchange their first unspoken vows—*profane, holy shrine, pilgrims, saints, prayers, sin is purged*. And in the Balcony scene (II. ii) love is no longer "smoke"; it has begun to be, in some manner, a god. Juliet asks Romeo to "swear by thy gracious self,/Which is the god of my idolatry"; her bounty and love for him are boundless and deep as the sea, and "infinite"; and she would call him back to her with "a falconer's voice," which in Renaissance symbolism might sometimes stand for Christ's word drawing back the errant soul.

The Balcony itself is a symbol, as is shown not only by

Shakespeare's unforgettable use of it in the play, but by the imagistic prominence of the up-down, light-dark, balcony-tomb antithesis in the play as a whole, signifying not only the life-death, love-hate pattern that forms the plot, but also (without heaviness) the religious antithesis salvation-vs.-damnation. The negative, downward movement is expressed in such remarks as Romeo's despairing cry, "More light and light; more dark and dark our woes" (III. v), followed by Juliet's vision of him "As one dead in the bottom of a tomb." It is expressed, too, in the doom of Romeo's banishment (the *poena damni* of Scholastic eschatology) and in the ritual-like repetition of the words *doom, death,* and *banishment* when the sentence is announced (III. iii), climaxed by Romeo's cry:

> Banished?
> O friar, the damned use that word in hell;
> Howlings attend it.

But Friar Lawrence has already declared the identity of womb and tomb, and that there is no evil without an emergent good. The friar's optimism is reflected symbolically by the redemptive imagery in the play, which becomes more intense as the course of outward action darkens. The Prince's phrase,

> My blood for your rude brawls doth lie a-bleeding

would not go unnoticed by a Christian audience schooled in the doctrine that the blood of a yet greater Prince has redeemed the rude brawls of all mankind. And the play's final scene offers repeated imagistic suggestions of light conquering darkness and (more particularly) of Christ opening the tomb:

A grave? O, no! a lantern, slaughtered youth.
                    (line 84)

Here is a friar, and slaught'red Romeo's man,
With instruments upon them, fit to open
These dead men's tombs.
                    (lines 199-201)

Anon comes one with light to ope the tomb.
                    (line 283)

Thus our inquiry into the nature of dramatic action, with which the chapter opened, has split into two separate inquiries—one concerning the directions of mythic reference which tend to make a tragic action plurisignatively meaningful, the other concerning the role which imagery may play in complementing what takes place overtly on the stage. The convergence of the two lines of inquiry is especially marked in the tragic dramas of Greece, particularly those of Aeschylus and to a lesser degree those of Sophocles, for in them the basic thematic imagery-patterns are still closely tied to the mythic traditions of their quasi-primitive heritage. Accordingly I shall devote the next two chapters to a reconsideration of the two greatest of ancient drama sequences (virtually, indeed, the only surviving examples), with particular attention to the mytho-imagistic devices by which their overt stage-exhibited meaning is amplified or qualified and in either case enriched.

ELEVEN

The Guilt of Oedipus

IF WE COMPARE the best Hellenic studies of the last two or three decades with those of the half-century preceding, three new emphases become apparent: anthropological, psychological, and semantic. The change has been gradual, of course; and it might be objected that anthropology, in particular, is no new arrival, having been a factor in the critical consciousness of western Europe almost since the founding of the Royal Anthropological Institute in the early 1870's. But although that is true, and although scattered anthropological references can be found in the books and textual annotations of the older classicists, there are two reasons, I think, why the influence of anthropology did not become a substantial factor in classical scholarship until somewhat recently. One reason was the natural intellectual lag between any large discovery and the full realization of its pertinence. Partly the ingrained conservatism of many (by no means all) classical scholars, and partly the magnitude of the field newly opened up, made the process of reinterpretation a gradual one. The other reason lay in the uncertainty and lively disagreement among anthropologists themselves regarding the theoretical substructure of their researches. Until the turn of the century the animism of Tylor and Spencer exercised strong influence, especially in

England; and such theories offered little to classical scholars
that would change the tenor of their thinking or the direction of their researches. Belief in ghosts, in dreams, and in
magic had always been a popular disposition, exploited by
every teller of tales, without need of gloss.

But another anthropological theory began to find expression in the first decade of our century, which was to affect
classical procedures a great deal. This was the theory variously called animatism, pre-animatism, and theory of mana—
protopsychism might denote it best—associated particularly
with the names of T. K. Preuss in Germany, R. R. Marett in
England, and (as has been mentioned in another context),
Lucien Lévy-Bruhl in France:[1] that the primary religious
phenomenon, the primordial stage in religious evolution (if
we choose to think chronologically), is something vaguer
and more fluid than either gods or human or ancestral souls;
that it is an undefined sense of *presence*, stirring awe and
perhaps dread in the beholder, capable on the one hand of
developing at length into an object of reverence, and on the
other of inviting attempts at magical control. Such is declared to have been the primitive belief-matrix from which
religion, myth, and magic gradually, and sometimes divergently, evolved. The clearest indication of the power of the
new theory to affect classical scholarship appears in Gilbert
Murray's emphasis on the "error of treating Homer as primitive, and more generally in our unconscious insistence on
starting with the notion of 'gods.'" Although Murray's specific evidences were drawn from within his own field of
study, the new anthropological emphasis on intangibles was
creating a climate of opinion and an openness of intellectual
sensibility most favorable to his view.

The psychological element in classical modernism owes
most, I suspect, to Nietzsche. The Nietzschean symbols of
Apollo and Dionysus, although they oversimplified the many-

sided phenomena of the Greek mind, provided a schema of interpretation which, so far as it went, was relevant. Moreover it set limits to the over-intellectualization of the Greek achievement of which traditional scholarship has often been guilty; and in doing so it invited attention to a rich field of evidence and allusion which the older scholars had not adequately explored. The effective presence of dark, vague chthonic forces, lacking the clear bright outlines and specious personality of the Olympian gods, was an aspect of the Greek thinkers' world which in the heyday of classical scholarship could be, if not quite neglected, at least explained away as atavisms. The Nietzschean rehabilitation of Dionysus, backed by such related German theories as Schopenhauer's philosophy of the will and von Hartmann's of the unconscious, and subsequently by the experimental approach to unconscious phenomena associated largely with the name of Freud, encouraged a disposition to look for non-rational mental factors in the interpretation of human phenomena. When this trend of psychological voluntarism (largely German, since the analogous work of de Biran, Ravaisson, and Fouillée in France exercised no comparable influence) began to unite early in the present century with the new protopsychic anthropology emanating largely from England, the result was to provoke the more forward-looking classicists—Jane Harrison and Gilbert Murray, for instance[2]—to reëxamine their postulates of method and interpretation. Sometimes enthusiasm pushed them too far, as in Miss Harrison's celebrated cry, "There, I *knew* Zeus was only that old snake!" But a revised equilibrium was sought, and, in such admirable scholars as Werner Jaeger, Georges Méautis, and the late Francis M. Cornford, eventually found.[3]

Of course the outstanding, or at any rate the most vociferated example of psychological method applied to classical problems has been Freud's Oedipus theory.[4] Whatever the clinical uses of that provocative idea (and I suspect they have been overplayed) its interpretive value for an understanding either of the ancient legend or of Sophocles' two plays is sharply limited. For it is a commonplace among classical scholars that Oedipus himself never exhibits the well-known complex that bears his name. His marriage to Jocasta was a matter of civic duty: having rid the Thebans of the baleful Sphinx by answering her riddle correctly, he received the throne of Thebes and the widowed queen to wife as his due reward. There is no indication in Sophocles' play or in any of the surviving records of the ancient myth, that Oedipus and Jocasta were drawn to each other erotically. But clearly Freud's interpretation of the Oedipus pattern could hold good of the ancient story only if there were an erotic attraction, whether conscious or repressed, between Oedipus and Jocasta, and moreover only if they felt, or if at least one of them felt, some conflict, however dimly, between the two relationships of son-mother and husband-wife.

Freud, to be sure, foresaw and met the objection after a fashion. The fact that Oedipus performed both acts, the slaying of his father and the bedding of his mother, without suspecting the true relationships, is in Freud's view "a deviation from the analytical subject matter which is easily intelligible and indeed inevitable." Inevitable, he explains, because of the need for "a poetic handling of the material"; for Freud's idea of poetry and the poetic seems to be pretty much limited to its alleged psychic function as a ritualized substitution for ideas which in their native form are suppressed. Intelligible, he goes on to explain, because "the ignorance of Oedipus is a legitimate representation of the unconsciousness into which, for adults, the whole experience has fallen; and the doom of the oracle, which makes or should make the hero innocent, is a recognition of the inevitability of the fate which has condemned every son to live

through the Oedipus complex." Thus in interpreting the
Greek myth of Oedipus as an embodiment of that psychotic
pattern which he has named the Oedipus complex Freud is
not insisting on the motivations of the characters in Sophocles' play but on the general unconscious acceptance of that
pattern, by reason of which the myth took strong hold of the
Greek popular imagination, finally causing Sophocles to recognize its unparalleled dramatic possibilities.

The first palpable expression of incestuous and patricidal
elements in Oedipus' own psyche occurs, so far as I know, in
Dryden and Lee's late seventeenth century version of the
tragedy.[5] In the opening scene of their *Oedipus,* Jocasta addresses her husband as though haunted by some dark intuition of her true relationship with him:

> When you chid, methought
> A mother's love start [*sic*] up in your defence,
> And bad me not be angry. Be not you;
> For I love Laius still, as wives should love,
> But you more tenderly, as part of me.

So much was Dryden's work. Nathaniel Lee, who wrote the
second act, becomes tediously explicit:

> . . . This horrid sleep
> Dash'd my sick fancy with an act of incest:
> I dreamt, Jocasta, that thou wert my mother;
> Which, though impossible, so damps my spirits,
> That I could do a mischief on myself,
> Lest I should sleep, and dream the like again.

And Dryden, back on the job again in Act III, has Oedipus
tell of an omen which struck him like "a pestilential blast":

> A young stork
> That bore his aged parent on his back;

Till weary with the weight, he shook him off,
And peck'd out both his eyes.

It would seem to have been Dryden and his collaborator then, not Sophocles, who introduced the Oedipus complex into literature. But the Dryden-Lee *Oedipus* is an inferior play, and the Oedipus story as they develop it is a hothouse growth, so artificial as to have lost most of its properly *mythic* character. Let us therefore look back to Sophocles' great play, the *Oedipus Tyrannus,* and inquire what its depth-meaning really is. For if we are to understand an archetype rightly, we must study it in its mature and artistically finished expressions even more painstakingly than in its cruder psychological and anthropological embodiments.

Erich Fromm, in *The Forgotten Language,*[6] raises just this question of the depth-meaning of the play. Rejecting Freud's interpretation as inconsistent with the play's premises, he offers an alternative hypothesis of his own: namely that the Oedipus myth is "a symbol not of the incestuous love between mother and son but of the rebellion of the son against the authority of the father in the patriarchal family; that the marriage of Oedipus and Jocasta is only a secondary element, only one of the symbols of the victory of the son, who takes his father's place and with it all his privileges." The dramatic conflict presented by Sophocles recapitulates, in Fromm's view, the prehistoric struggle between the matriarchal and the patriarchal forms of social organization. To substantiate this interpretation he appeals to Bachofen's theory that the earliest human sexual relations were promiscuous, and therefore, since only the mother's parenthood could be known, the inheritance of blood and hence of authority had to descend through her. Woman, therefore, Bachofen deduces, must have been the earliest lawgiver, and since the character of divinity in any period tends to reflect

certain basic characteristics of human society, he draws the
corollary that the religion of the Olympian gods was pre-
dated by a religion in which mother archetypes, dire and
awful goddesses of which the Furies are the best known
classical survival, were the supreme powers. Then in subsequent history (so the theory runs) man revolted against his
servile role, and gradually succeeded in subduing woman, in
establishing a patriarchal order on earth and the dynasty of
the Olympian gods in heaven.

On the basis of Bachofen's provocative but tenuous theory
Fromm amplifies his hypothesis, suggesting "that the hostility between father and son, which is the theme running
through Sophocles' trilogy, is to be understood as an attack
against the victorious patriarchal order by the representatives of the defeated matriarchal system." Notice his word
"attack." Fromm interprets Sophocles as taking sides, as presenting a thesis. He sees the Theban dramas as intended to
put across an idea—"the idea that the patriarchal world was
triumphant, but that it would be defeated unless it adopted
the humanistic principles of the older matriarchal order."
The dramas, in short, (if we accept this interpretation) are
didactic in intent; they are not primarily dramas, but dramatic vehicles for Sophocles' attack on the too brittle and
too authoritarian principles of patriarchal rule, dramatic ex-
trapolations of his nostalgia for the good old days of matriarchy.

In all interpretations let's keep our focus clear. The primary evidence of what a work of art means is always the
work itself. Hints and clues may legitimately be sought outside, but their relevance and validity must always be ap-
praised internally. Even if the theory of a primitive matriarchy should happen to be true, it does not follow that every
ancient play must serve as a record of the prehistoric struggle. The *Oresteia* may indeed do so; the conflict between

Apollo's command to Orestes to slay his mother and the wrath of the Furies as avengers of Clytemnestra's maternal rights lends a good deal of color to that view. But if we make any such judgment of the depth-meaning of the *Oresteia*, or for that matter if we dispute such a judgment, it must be primarily on the basis of evidence found within the play, rather than by undue reliance on sociological or psychological hypotheses. Can we find, then, in the *Oedipus Tyrannus*, any internal evidence of a conflict between the matriarchal and patriarchal principles?

The answer is plainly no, as any reader can see for himself; and even Mr. Fromm does not claim otherwise. He bases his interpretation of *Oedipus Tyrannus* partly upon the sociological theory just cited and partly upon an incident in each of Sophocles' other two Theban plays. In *Oedipus at Colonus* the now aged Oedipus expresses hatred and resentment against his two sons Polyneices and Eteocles. In the *Antigone*, where the dramatic action takes place after Oedipus' death, there is a violent flare-up of antipathy between Creon and his son Haemon. Fromm concludes: "If we interpret *King Oedipus* in the light of the whole trilogy, the assumption seems plausible that the real issue in *King Oedipus*, too, is the conflict between father and son . . ." Note the three main assumptions of his argument: (1) that the father-son antagonism in the other two Theban plays is of primary, not incidental, dramatic importance; (2) that the three Theban plays are closely enough related to justify a deduction of the meaning of one of them from the supposed meaning of the others; (3) that granted the legitimacy of such a deduction in general, it is reasonable to argue a father-son antagonism between Laius and Oedipus (for which there is no independent evidence) from the acknowledged father-son antagonism between Oedipus and *his* sons, and even from the existence of such a relationship between Creon and

Haemon. The last assumption is so inherently weak as a principle of dramatic interpretation, and moreover is so logically dependent upon the validity of Assumption 2, that I shall not do more than cite it as a curious sample of circumambulatory reasoning. What, then, of the two remaining assumptions?

The *Antigone* is the one Theban play to which Fromm's theory of a patriarchal-vs.-matriarchal conflict might conceivably apply. Creon and Antigone in that play do seem to stand, as Fromm maintains, for the principle of order and authority, obedience and hierarchy on the one side, and on the other for the principle of blood relationship as the fundamental and indestructible tie. But this is only one aspect of their relationship to each other and to the total dramatic pattern. To overstress the dramatic conflict in these terms is to convert the *Antigone* into a sociological tract. Robert F. Goheen in his recent study of the play's dominant imagery[7] adopts a more promising approach, examining (as Fromm never bothers to do) the specific language and imagery that constitute the play's symbolic action. "The imagery employed by Sophocles," Goheen writes, "is a functional means of communication in his dramas. It is aesthetic not simply in the sense of the decorative, but in the true sense of being a means of perception *(aisthêsis)* offered to the reader by the poet to take him into the meaning of the work." The recurrence of sight imagery, especially in the Haemon scene, throws the Creon-Antigone conflict into another perspective than the sociological. The drama becomes internalized: the emphasis is not merely on the question of domination by one sex or the other, nor even on the preferability of one or the other way of life; it is also, and far more subtly, upon the nature of human awareness. The conflict is primarily between two ways of grasping truth: Antigone's, the way of direct intuition, vs. Creon's, the way of sound sense and reason, or reliance on "right thinking" (*phronêsis*), on the linear, the measured, the plainly ordered. Each way of knowing has both its special reward and its special limitation of partial blindness. Fromm, to be sure, admits this spiritual antithesis as an aspect and derivative of the matriarchal-patriarchal conflict. But he errs, I believe, in two respects. He underrates Sophocles' artistic objectivity by assuming him to be taking sides. And he ignores the rich pattern of associated imagery —Goheen stresses in particular the images drawn from money and merchandising, from warfare, from animal life, and from seafaring—in which the characters of the two protagonists are caught up and given both fullness and concretion of meaning.

In any case, whatever our interpretation of the *Antigone,* there is no ground for drawing deductions from its supposed meaning to the meaning of the *Oedipus Tyrannus.* Fromm distorts the evidence by speaking repeatedly of the three Theban plays as a "trilogy"—despite his footnoted acknowledgment that they were not composed in the same order as the dramatic action represents. As a matter of fact they were written long intervals apart. The *Antigone* is generally accepted as having been written in or about 441 B.C., the *Oedipus Tyrannus* in 430 or later, and the *Oedipus at Colonus* shortly before Sophocles' death in 406. Moreover, each play was originally produced with two other Sophoclean tragedies, of which no record remains. Not in any sense, then, do the three extant Theban plays constitute a trilogy, and it is by no means permissible to deduce the purpose of the *Oedipus Tyrannus* from the purpose (if we know it) of the *Antigone.*

In the *Antigone* Creon is something of a melodramatic villain. In the plays written later his character becomes more ambivalent. Fromm, since he mistakenly treats the *Antigone* as if it had been written after the two other plays, misses the significance of the character change. He describes the figure of Creon as "indistinct" in the two Oedipus plays and as "becoming" colorful and definite in the *Antigone*. Since the *Antigone* was actually written first of the three, our critical problem is the reverse of the one he raises. Why does Sophocles blur the moral outlines of his Creon figure in the later plays? The likeliest answer surely is that with advancing maturity he no longer saw the moral issue in the relatively simple black-and-white terms of the *Antigone;* he had come to accept his characters as irresolvably ambivalent—no plain heroes and villains but multi-dimensional men steeped, like all of us, in moral ambiguities, which, though we see them in shifting perspectives, we must carry with us to the grave.

How, then, may a critical reader discover proper clues to the depth-meaning of *Oedipus Tyrannus?*

The first evidence is found in the title. You cannot perfectly rely on a writer to give you a major clue in the title of his work, but it is likely enough that he may want to do so, and the possibility should be explored. What is the meaning of the title *Oedipus Tyrannus?* Not, as in so many translations, "Oedipus Rex" or "King Oedipus." And of course not "Oedipus the Tyrant" either. Liddell and Scott's unabridged Greek lexicon declares that in classical Greek the word *tyrannos* was never applied to a hereditary monarch, for whom the word was *basileus;* it was restricted to those who had received the royal power by some means other than direct succession.[8] Not even force or trickery was necessarily involved. Oedipus used none; he was offered the throne by the grateful Theban people. No matter: he was still a *tyrannos,* or usurper, within the accepted meaning of the word. The closest translation we can give for the play's title, then, is *Oedipus the Usurper*. And we must try to see a little further what *tyrannia* or "usurpation" connoted, and especially what its moral involvements were, to the mind of a fifth-century Greek.

To usurp is to overstep the measure, to erupt the proper limits of one's station in life, or of what is morally fitting, or (it may be) of the area of human as distinguished from divine prerogative. It is the vice or guilt or "tragic flaw" *(hamartia)* of arrogance *(hybris)*. Cornford's alluring hypothesis that the rise of the idea may have been connected with the agricultural arrangements in prehistoric Greece has been mentioned in Chapter X. At all events, whatever its early history the idea of overstepping the boundary soon developed cosmic, moral, and political analogies. Just as (in the fragment quoted from Heraclitus) the sun dare not overstep his appointed path, lest the Furies, in their role of the handmaidens of Justice, find him out and punish him, so likewise a man dare not step beyond the path which Destiny has appointed him. Specifically he dare not emulate the gods, for divine indignation and vengeance *(nemesis)* will crash down upon him if he does. The primary hamartia, from this standpoint, is usurpation.

Oedipus was a usurper not only with respect to his father's throne and his mother's bed. That aspect is present in the play to be sure, and to a Greek audience Oedipus' ignorance of the relationships would not absolve him of guilt, nor does Oedipus ever expect that it will do so. Usurpation is still a half-physical, half-mythical thing; it happens and produces its terrible consequences regardless of motive. In this respect, therefore, so far as it goes, Freud would seem to have made a valid point after all. But there is another respect in which Oedipus was a usurper more consciously. His victory over the Sphinx was almost godlike, and for man to become too nearly godlike in any way at all (recall Hippolytus' tragic excess of chastity) is a display of *hybris*, arrogance, which by the inherent laws of destiny must be stricken down. The half-articulate usurpation imagery, then, together with the accusations of usurpation which the characters directly or obliquely hurl at one another, represents one depth-theme of the drama.

Next, there is the blight, afflicting the Theban countryside as the play opens. And here we meet with a quite different conception of moral law from the one involved in usurpation. The earlier idea is primarily an Olympian conception—an affair of clear boundary lines marked off in the bright vault of space. Blight and sickness, together with their opposite, which is health, are elements in the chthonic conception, appropriate to Mother Earth and the flora and fauna that grow out of her womb. Evil doing, from this standpoint, is felt as a kind of sickness, a malady in the individual, the commonwealth, and environing nature alike, and with terrible powers of contagion. When the blood of a murdered man seeps into the earth all vegetation sickens. And the same infection creeps into the human commonwealth, the *polis,* the city. What to do save lop off the offending member as one would lop off the diseased branch of a tree? The penalty of sin is at once a withering away in some sense of the individual and his exile from the commonwealth—not by arbitrary decree but by the sheer logic of the chthonic idea.

It is worth noting with what thematic effectiveness Sophocles introduces the word *polis* again and again at the beginnings and ends of lines, where it will have greatest prominence. Finally, after numerous such echoings Oedipus caps his emotional attack on Creon with the cry, *"O polis polis!"* ("O city city!") The contrasting word *xenos* (alien) is first used by Oedipus with unconscious irony when, in explaining why he did not know the details of King Laius' murder, he says, "I'm just an alien here." The irony is a double one: he is not an alien in the way he thinks, since he is actually a son of the Theban royal house; but he is presently to be an alien in a more terrible sense, namely an exile.

The third and most central set of thematic images has to

do with the blindness-vs.-vision antithesis and the solving of riddles. As the usurpation theme epitomizes Olympian morality and as the blight theme epitomizes chthonic morality, so I might venture the proposition that the blindness-riddle-vision theme epitomizes the morality of the mystery cults of Greece, and in a broader way one aspect of mystical religion generally. In the higher forms of the Greek mystery cults, such as the worship of Demeter at Eleusis, the rebirth cycle of crops and seasons develops into the idea of spiritual rebirth.[9] And when that happens the agency of rebirth is no longer magic, nor is it mere orgiastic ecstasy; it involves both inward purification and the imparting of a secret. The initiates at Eleusis performed a symbolic act of entering into darkness; in the inner shrine of the Eleusinian temple a new light was lit, and the sacred mysteries were revealed through such symbols as the sacred ear of grain. Oedipus, who solved the Sphinx's riddle and now would open up the dark mystery of his own origin, is inwardly blind, as the blind visionary Tiresias tries to tell him; and in putting out his eyes after his dreadful self-discovery he completes the symbolic pattern.

What can be concluded, then, as to the depth-meaning of *Oedipus Tyrannus?* Nothing in plain expository terms; of that I am sure. Sophocles was not at all the didactic and partisan writer that Fromm would have him. Francis Fergusson remarks in *The Idea of a Theatre* that "the peculiar virtue of Sophocles' presentation of the myth is that it preserves the ultimate mystery by focusing upon the tragic human at a level beneath, or prior to any rationalization whatever."[10] I fully concur, and at the same time I think we can penetrate a little farther into the mystery—never to its heart—by awareness of the "concrete universals" that reside in the most characteristic uses of imagery. Our analyses are at best propaedeutics. They explain nothing essential, but do their work if they steer us to a fresh reading of the play with our visual and auditory imagination newly alerted.

TWELVE

Thematic Patterns in the *Oresteia*

IT IS A SURPRISING lacuna in what is loosely called the New Criticism that so little study has been made of the imagistic and symbolic patterns in the dramas of Aeschylus. The methods of verbal, metaphoric, and archetypal analysis which have been applied so effectively in our time to Shakespeare, Dante, Donne, Eliot, and many others are especially pertinent to one with whom Pindar alone among ancient writers can compare as a master of expressive metaphor. For Homer prefers simile to metaphor, and Sophocles achieves his noblest effects by other means. Aeschylus, whose metaphoric patterns in the *Oresteia* are the more telling because of the scope and grandeur of that masterwork, has received little critical attention in this respect, despite the endless books and articles and footnotes that deal with other aspects of him.[1]

Aristotle was clearly more interested in Sophocles and Euripides than in Aeschylus, and his misunderstanding of the older dramatist's aims gave many later readers a false lead. The only references in the *Poetics* to the *Oresteia* are obtuse and trifling. In Chapter 16 Aristotle caricatures the opening of the *Choëphori* by formulating the recognition scene as a logical syllogism; in Chapter 17 he praises Orestes' madness, purification, and salvation as "appropriate episodes." Nowhere in Aristotle is there any recognition of the supreme importance of the religious sentiment in Aeschylus' tragic vision, nor of the expressive function of his imagistic patterns. Had he understood the role of either of these elements he would not have considered "appropriate episode" a suitable way of describing the central theme of the trilogy. Presumably he is uncomfortable because neither the plot nor the characters of the *Oresteia* fit at all smoothly into the system of prescriptions and valuations laid down in the *Poetics*.

Aristophanes, in the previous century, had set the fashion of praising Aeschylus for secondary or partial or obscure reasons. In *The Frogs* he explains Aeschylus' style by his temperament—a half-truth but no more. He describes the style by epithets that parody it—*horse-crested, horse-prancing, bolt-fitting*—and the man himself as proud, stubborn-mouthed, bombastic, laboring forth his verses with grim frown, vast puffings, and heavy labor of lungs. The "Euripides" of that comedy declares that in good poetic diction "one should speak like an ordinary human being"; to which "Aeschylus" retorts that "great thoughts and great imaginings need words commensurate." One likes to believe that the historical Aeschylus would not have retorted in quite those terms. The history of literature has shown that there are many kinds of expressive style, and that the relatively plain speech of Homer, Chaucer, the early Wordsworth, and the later Yeats is by no means incompatible with "great thoughts and great imaginings." It is revealing, and doubtless a part of Aristophanes' comic intent, that Dionysus, acting in *The Frogs* as judge of the contesting playwrights, and probably representing the average fickle Athenian playgoer of the day, seems to accept Euripides' warning that Aeschylus' style gains its effects by imposture, but nevertheless praises Aeschylus for his "towering tragic diction" and concludes by awarding him the prize. The moral, reduced to lowest terms, seems to be that poetic greatness must combine bombast with illusion.

At worst the bombast is only occasional, and it probably went over better with a word-loving Greek audience than it would today. In any case, Aeschylus' best poetic effects, the expression of his most essential insights, triumphs over minor defects of word-play. It is those insights, particularly as expressed through thematically developed imagery, that I am going to speak of. What the Choral Leader in the *Agamemnon* says of Clytemnestra's boast of wifely loyalty—"a specious tale to shrewd interpreters"—might apply more generally to the entire trilogy. Behind the surface-story a shrewd interpreter will discover potent depth-meanings. E. T. Owen does not overstate the case when he writes: "The subject of the *Oresteia* is the creation of a new moral order; Aeschylus depicts the vast chain of events which the death of Agamemnon started in heaven and earth, how it and its results shook the universe to its foundations and altered the spiritual history of the world; he presents the legend as a turning-point in the destinies of mankind."[2] Professor Owen's view is not novel, to be sure, but it is worth reëmphasizing. And the important thing, for an alert reader, is that the indications of this vast theme show forth in several ways at once: through the story, both as dramatically represented and as narrated, through the dark brooding reflections of the Choruses, and, most subtly and most richly of all, through the metaphoric and archetypal associations evoked by the imagery. It is the last aspect, the overtones of meaning which are thrown off by the main images and image-patterns of the play, that will be my subject in the present chapter.

We may begin, in fact, with the very speech to which the "shrewd interpreters" remark is a reply. Clytemnestra had previously foretold King Agamemnon's homecoming from the conquest of Troy, announced to her by the system of island fire-beacons telegraphically connecting the mainlands of Troy and Argos. Her words had been met with suppressed doubts and suspicions. Now that the news has been confirmed by the Messenger's arrival, she triumphantly reminds the Chorus of Elders how right she was, and then proceeds to boast of her loyalty, her watchdog faithfulness, during her husband's ten-year absence.

> Take this message to my husband:
> that he come with all speed, beloved by his city,
> and may he find a wife within his house as loyal
> as on the day he left her, watchdog of the house,
> good to *him* but fierce to his enemies,
> and in all else as before,
> keeping her pledge throughout that length of time.
> I know no more of adulterous pleasure or scandal
> than I understand the art of dyeing bronze.
>   (*Agam.*, 609–617)[3]

Most commentators have been aware of an ominous irony in the speech, and have identified at least some of its elements. But the full power and dark threat of Clytemnestra's words become evident only as we bring the various ironic and ambivalent elements into one focus of attention. "Beloved of his city" (*sotto voce:* but not by me!); "As loyal as when he left her" (but how loyal was that?); "Good to *him*" (the force of *ekeinos* must be rendered either by italics or by "that man"—and which one is meant, Agamemnon or Aegisthus?) The next two phrases, "In all else as before" and "Never having broken her pledge," repeat and reinforce the "loyal wife" ambiguity. Two subtler points of irony call for further analysis: the metal-dyeing and watchdog images. I shall take them as points of departure for the next two sections respectively.

THE BLOOD BATH

The dyeing of metal, in the usual meaning of the phrase, is a man's work, one of the arts subsidiary to preparing for war, and obviously outside a woman's range of competence. But the hidden meaning is the important one, which the re-iteration of the *blood* theme makes sufficiently unmistakable to the audience. It would be wearisome to enumerate all the many references to blood in the *Agamemnon,* direct and oblique; the crimson thread runs through that play much as it does through *Macbeth.* I will confine my observations to some of the most trenchant instances. The most important of them, around which the others may be conceived to re-volve, is presented not only in language but also as an iconic symbol upon the stage: the crimson or purple tapestry which Clytemnestra orders spread out for her returning husband to walk on, as a token of his victory. Colors were not classified along the same lines in ancient Greece as they are today. Purple and any of the darker shades of red were joined by a common name, inasmuch as the dye for them had its source in the *murex* or purple-fish (πορφύρα). The sight of the pur-ple-crimson tapestry therefore carries two trains of thought at once: on the one hand it is a sacred color, reserved for certain religious ceremonies, and on which no mortal, not even a king, dare walk in the ordinary manner without com-mitting *hybris;* while on the other it is an iconic symbol of blood and therefore carries some of the potency of blood—the blood in which Agamemnon is to be bathed. Agamemnon at first angrily rejects the over-zealous attentions of his wife (of whose faithlessness his manner suggests that he may have received some report) and twice describes the carpet-tapestry as ποικίλος (*Agam.* 914 and 927), which can mean *elaborately colored* but can also mean *artful, riddling, am-biguous.* At length he yields, although with open misgivings, praying that no god may cast baneful eyes upon his act, and twice mentioning the deadly crimson thing that fascinates him and draws him on (lines 937, 948).

While Agamemnon moves into the palace in the stylized

manner of a sacrificial procession—"Treading the crimson I pass into my house"—Clytemnestra speaks again in double meanings:

> There is the sea, and who shall drain it dry?
> It breeds in inexhaustible plenty
> the crimson ooze which men exchange for silver,
> the wherewithal for dyeing of our garments.
> In these matters, my lord, the gods have well endowed us,
> a royal house that knows no penury.
> (Agam., 949–954)

The literal sense is plain enough: "Don't worry about the costliness of the carpet you trample on. There is abundance of crimson coloring matter in the sea, and we are rich enough to buy all we may want of it." But the sinister tone of the opening question puts us on guard. It appears, at one level of meaning, as a cynical echo of the Chorus' repeated plaint, "When will there be an end to all the blood-spilling?"—as an answer, too, appropriate to the dark chthonic powers with which Clytemnestra becomes increasingly allied, that there will never be an end to it, and thus as a denial of the redemptive theme which is central to the trilogy. The House of Atreus, burdened by its evil past and the power of a curse, surely "knows no penury" in the bloody dyeing of garments.

The more furtive meaning of the crimson ooze becomes explicit finally after the murder, when Clytemnestra comes forward to justify her deed before the Elders:

> Then he lay prostrate, coughing up his soul,
> and pouring forth his blood he sprinkled me
> with murky drizzle of the deadly dew;
> while I rejoiced no less than the sown field
> when in the God-given rain the cup
> gives birth to the ear of wheat.
> (Agam., 1387–1391)

Clytemnestra here emerges briefly as the hierophant of some bloody sacrificial rite—even, indeed, of two rites merged into one. The image of the priestly sacrificer spattered with the victim's blood is probably derived from the *taurobolium*, the ritual slaughter of the bull-calf sacred to and representing Dionysus. The images of rain (the sperm of Zeus) dropping upon the sown field and of the sacred ear of wheat budding forth from the cup or sheath that enfolds it are probably derived from the mystery cult of the grain-goddess Demeter, which was centered at Aeschylus' birthplace Eleusis. Moreover, while the cup and the ear of wheat by their shapes carry a hint of feminine and masculine symbolism, the Greek word for "cup" (καλυξ) stems from the verb καλύπτω, "hide," and thus sounds an undertone of religious mystery, as though we should say: "Out of the hidden place, out of the dark womb, is born the sacred bud." And although my botanical friends assure me that the description does not quite accurately apply to the birth of grain, it probably did, by symbolic association, to the mind of the Eleusinian worshiper; for the ear of corn or the sheaf of wheat (no one seems quite sure just what species of grain it was) served him as a symbol of life potency, and, in its deeper meaning, of spiritually restored life. The passage is thus one of concentrated irony, with Clytemnestra blasphemously perverting the religious meaning of the Eleusinian symbols by relating them to her private lust for evil vengeance.

THE HOUNDS ON THE TRACES

Let us look now at an earlier image in the original quotation—Clytemnestra's boast of having been "watchdog of the house" (*Agam.* 612). The Greek word is simply "dog" or "bitch," the genders of κύων not being distinguished; but the added phrase "good to him but fierce to his enemies" leaves

no doubt that a watchdog here is meant. The Greek word
has, however, three other interwoven meanings.

There is the pejorative feminine sense of the word, as in
our slang use of "bitch." When Helen, in the *Iliad,* walks
with King Priam along the walls of Troy and is stirred by
the old man's goodness to feel compunction at the slaughter
which her adultery has caused, she reviles herself as a "bitch."
In the *Agamemnon* the prophetess Cassandra hurls the epithet against Clytemnestra with a bit of descriptive elaboration:

> Little does he know what that foul bitch,
> with ears laid back and panting tongue,
> will bring to pass with vicious snap
> of treacherous destruction.
>   (*Agam.*, 1227–1230)

Still another use of the word is to connote lowliness of
condition, though without any ascription of blame. In this
sense Electra complains to Orestes that after her father's
death she was "kenneled in her chamber like a dog" (*Choe.*
445); and partly in this sense the Watchman at the opening
of the *Agamemnon* complains of having been "couched like
a dog on the roof of the House of Atreus." The Watchman
functions as a dog also in the first sense I have noted, since
he is on the watch for the beacon signal to be flashed from
Troy.

But most important of all in the *Oresteia,* and especially
in the final play of it, is a fourth connotation of "dog": that
of hunting dog or *hound on the scent*.[4] This meaning has
more affinity with the first of the meanings enumerated (that
of "watchdog") than with the second and third; but it calls
for separate examination, not only because of its important
symbolic role in the trilogy, but also because of its affinity,

through the idea of avenging ghosts, with one of the main elements of Greek religious thought.

Although the greater use of hound-imagery occurs with reference to the Furies, who do not appear until the end of the second play, a preparation has been made in the *Agamemnon*. The Chorus of Elders, half in awe, half in compassion, describe Cassandra as "a hound on scent of blood" (*Agam.* 1078), and Cassandra afterward applies less explicitly the same metaphor to herself: "I track down the scent of ancient crimes" (*Agam.* 1184). A like image is applied by the Chorus of Elders to the Achaian warriors following the traces of Helen and Paris over the sea. "Huntsmen down the oarblades' fading footprint" is Richmond Lattimore's translation. Edith Hamilton puts it:

> And a host,
> shield-bearing huntsmen, followed hot,
> tracking the oar blades' unseen footprints.
> (*Agam.*, 696–698)

Both versions indicate the main metaphoric fusion involved, but neither one brings out the full force of κυναγοί. "Huntsmen" is the virtual meaning to be sure, but what the compounded Greek word connotes is *leaders of dogs*, and that connotation helps to build up the gathering momentum of the idea of hounds in pursuit.

The real significance of the hound imagery becomes evident at the end of the *Choëphori*. The Greeks tracking down the fleeing lovers and Cassandra prophetically tracking down the crimes of the palace have been preliminary to the main imagistic movement. Orestes' vision of the Erinyes, the Furies, who begin to pursue him for his deed of matricide, involves both snake-imagery and hound-imagery. The one is pictorially specific, since the creatures have snakes for hair; the other is non-visually symbolic. Orestes cries out:

> What women are those—see!—Gorgon-like,
> dark-robed, their hanging hair entwined
> with many snakes? I dare not stay.
> > (*Choe.*, 1046–1048)

And when the Chorus of Bondswomen, not sharing the vision, seek to comfort him, he cries again:

> These are no phantom terrors that I see.
> Full plain they are my mother's hounds of vengeance.
> > (*Choe.*, 1051–1052)

And a moment later:

> You do not see them, but I see them.
> They drive me on, and I can stay no more.
> > (*Choe.*, 1059–1060)

Let us avoid the oversimplification of assuming that because Orestes alone sees the Furies they are therefore unreal—that is to say, hallucinatory or "merely subjective." The line between subjective and objective is less rigidly drawn in a mythopoeic than in a technosophic culture, and Aeschylus' audience would, on the whole, have accepted the reality of his supernatural figures to whatever degree the dramatic context required. No special "suspension of disbelief" was needed—at least not to anything like the same degree as with a modern reader. The Greeks could be genially sceptical on occasion, but it was not until the age of the Sophists and the iconoclastic dramas of Euripides that scepticism toward the entire supernatural apparatus began to spread. Even then the beliefs of the large majority were comparatively untouched. And back when the *Oresteia* was first performed (458 B.C.) there was small disposition to doubt that the Furies were effectively and dangerously real. How, then, account for the bondswomen's failure to perceive them? The most natural answer, to the mind of a critical Athenian playgoer who might ask himself the question, was not that Orestes was deluded but that the bondswomen were obtuse.

Even Shakespeare's supernatural figures, it would appear, must often be interpreted in an analogous way. In the first act of *Hamlet* the murdered king's ghost is visible not only to Prince Hamlet but also to Horatio, Bernardo, and Marcellus; in the Queen's closet scene of Act III Hamlet sees it and Queen Gertrude does not. To the Elizabethans there was no inconsistency. Spirits that walk by night, although not grossly corporeal as our living bodies are, yet do affect the air, coagulating it into a vaporous semblance of their sometime physical selves. Such shadow figures, real enough to be sure, are yet not visible to everybody, but only to such as, for one reason or another, are more sensitively responsive to their subtle influence. The royal ghost no doubt stirred the air more cautiously on his second appearance than on his first, mindful of the still loved queen—"But, look, amazement on thy mother sits. /O, step between her and her fighting soul." Nor is it surprising that Hamlet was keyed up to a hyper-perceptiveness in the matter.

Similarly in Orestes' case it is plausible enough that the crime of matricide backed by the ancestral curse should have rendered him vulnerable to supernatural influences, and particularly to those atavisms of matriarchy and jealous defenders of maternal rights, the Erinyes. Their shadow-substance is real and dreadful to him, even though the bondswomen, whose psyches are pitched in a milder key, do not share the perception. Dramatically considered, Orestes' vision is not wholly private. Aeschylus has skillfully prepared for the Erinyes' appearance in the *Choëphori* by at least two occasions in the *Agamemnon* which testify to visionary experience: Cassandra's vision of fiends dancing on the roof of the

palace and Clytemnestra's admission that in murdering her
husband she was possessed by an evil spirit. But on those
occasions the audience sees nothing out of the ordinary; the
world of the *Agamemnon* transcends nature by allusion and
imagery alone, not yet by direct action. In the *Choëphori*
several related forces contribute to breaking through the
walls of the natural world and quickening the sensibilities
of actors and of audience to the impact of the ghostly: the
murdered Agamemnon's unquiet spirit, the command of
Apollo by which Orestes is driven, the mounting intensity of
the lengthy ritual in which Orestes, Electra, and the bondswomen engage, and at length the power of maternal vengeance which Orestes' deed sets in motion. These forces act
magnetically, so to speak, drawing the Erinyes from mythopoeic semi-obscurity into clear dramatic and theatrical focus.
In the *Eumenides* their ontological emergence is complete,
and they are projected into the action of the play no less
realistically than the other characters.

In *The Eumenides* the Furies are first shown in sleep, and
as Clytemnestra's impatient ghost prods them out of it their
first utterances are a muttering and a whining sound, described in the stage directions by the words μυγμός and
ὠγμός. A student whom I asked what he took these sounds
to mean replied, "Well, I guess that's the way Furies talk
when they're off by themselves." Maybe it is unwise to go
much beyond that modest conjecture; yet it is worth re-
marking that Diodorus Siculus uses the first word of the
pair to describe sounds emitted by dogs. In view of the unmistakable hound imagery that follows I would guess that
Aeschylus intended his two problematical words to suggest
onomatopoeically the two familiar kinds of sound which dogs
awaking from uneasy sleep might make: a muttering suppressed bark, something like *grfff!* and an incipient whine.
Doubtless the ancient actors understood what was intended

and the simple directions *mugmos* and *ogmos* were all the prompting that was required. Our English word *bow-wow* is surely no model of mimetic realism!

Evidently the Furies have been dreaming of pursuing their quarry, for after three such barkings and two such whinings they mutter half in sleep: "Seize him, seize, seize, seize! Don't lose track!" In contemptuous rejoinder the dead Clytemnestra brings the metaphor into the open: "You hunt your prey in a dream, giving tongue like a hound that never rests from his task" (*Eum.* 131–132). The verb which I have translated "give tongue," is regularly used of hounds, according to the lexicon. And later the Furies, who compose the Chorus of *The Eumenides,* take the comparison upon themselves:

> Ha! Here are the clearest traces of the man.
> Follow the trail which the silent witness indicates.
> For as the hound pursues the wounded fawn,
> so do I follow the smell of dripping blood.
> (Eum., 244–247)

The imagery of the hunt is further elaborated by the many references to nets and snares, which were habitually employed by ancient Greek hunters. The primary reference of the net imagery is to the manner in which Clytemnestra murdered Agamemnon by entangling him in a crimson-purple robe:

> I so contrived the deed, I'll not deny,
> that he could not avert his doom nor flee.
> Inextricable like a net for fishes
> I cast an evil wealth of robe about him.
> (Agam., 1379–1382)

The relevance of the symbol goes far beyond either the visual or functional similarity between a net and the encircling robe. Cassandra in a prophetic vision sees "some net of Hell"

appear (*Agam.* 1102) and then applies a synonymous word
to Clytemnestra: she is a "snare of slaughter" (*Agam.* 1103).
Since beasts caught in a net were sometimes killed by a ceremony of stoning, the lines immediately following, wherein
Clytemnestra invokes the Erinyes, are also germane to the
thematic pattern:

> Now let the hellish company, ever insatiate,
> raise a long howl *(ulululu)* over the ritual stoning.

Two earlier occasions of the net imagery are noteworthy,
as preparing the audience's visual imagination for what is to
come, and as indicating the force with which the image persists in Aeschylus' own far-ranging mind. After Clytemnestra
has announced the fall of Troy to the Elders, they at one
point describe its destruction as entanglement in a net:

> O Zeus our Lord! O Night beloved,
> housekeeper of Heaven's bright jewels!
> You have cast on the Trojan towers an enclosing net,
> so that none, adults or children, could overleap
> the trap of capture and bondage.
>   (*Agam.*, 367–372)

The image of a snare strung so high that the victim cannot
overleap it is repeated by Clytemnestra in *Agam.* 1374–1375,
and evidently alludes to the futile leaps attempted by des-
perate beasts whom a net or other sort of trap has captured.
Again there is Clytemnestra's use of the image when she is
hypocritically, but with an innuendo of deadly truth, pro-
testing how she has worried about the rumors of Agamemnon's wounds:

> If he had as many wounds as rumor said,
> his limbs would have been perforated like a net.
>   (*Agam.*, 858–860)

Variations of the net imagery continue to be developed in the `Choëphori,` as when, during the invocation of Agamemnon's ghost, Orestes cries, "They snared you in bronzeless fetters"—a metaphor within a metaphor, the bronzeless fetters meaning of course a net; and Electra echoes the idea in a more feminine sort of metaphor: "Ignobly trapped in cunning veils." But these instances are transitional. For in the *Eumenides* the net image is transferred from the slaying of Agamemnon to the Furies' pursuit of Orestes as its new focus of reference, and thus it serves as one of the major poetic devices by which Aeschylus moulds the entire trilogy into an aesthetically satisfying unity.

THE SNAKE AND THE OMPHALOS

The action of the *Choëphori,* the middle tragedy of the *Oresteia,* hinges upon an ambiguity. Clytemnestra's supernatural solicitings, like Macbeth's, have brought her a dark prophecy which, though true in one sense, is false in another; and like Macbeth also, her failure to perceive its real import and to guard against the impending ill, leads to her doom. After murdering her royal husband Clytemnestra has been careful to placate the Furies regularly with solemn midnight offerings, and thus for a time has made good her boast on which the *Agamemnon* closed: "You and I (to Aegisthus), now masters of the house, henceforth shall govern it well." But at length, as the exiled Orestes secretly returns to his native land, she is visited by an eerie dream, which is announced by the Chorus of Bondswomen:

Clear-piercing indeed, causing the hair to rise, was the Phoibos who divines for the house in dreams, when, breathing forth wrath, he caused a shriek from the inner chamber, and terror fell heavily about the women's quarters.

(*Choe.,* 31–36)

The description (which I have translated as literally as possible) is ingeniously duosignative. To a Greek acquainted
with the manner of divination at the shrine of Apollo at
Delphi such epithets as *clear-piercing, hair-on-end, Phoibos,*
and *inner chamber* would carry in addition to their literal
meanings a coherent allusion to the sacred Delphic mysteries. On the literal level, *phoibos* can be translated "a spectral
vision," the inner chamber is a synonym for the women's
quarters, and the other terms are simply descriptive. But
Phoibos is also an epithet of Apollo; "inner chamber" alludes
to the Inner Sanctum, the Holy of Holies, where the clair-
voyant priestess received the dread disclosures; "clear-piercing" alludes to the unearthly tones of the priestess speaking
in a trance; and "hair on end" to the atmosphere of awe and
supernatural terror which surrounded the seance. But these
poetic innuendoes, although they enrich the essential drama,
do not affect the overt plot. They are followed by an ambiguity which does so.

> Seers, wise in the lore of dreams,
> bound to speak true, do say
> the dead beneath the ground
> are angered sore, and wroth
> at them that slew them.
> (*Choe.,* 37–40)

Clytemnestra, taking the seers' reading of the drama in the
likeliest sense, has sent Electra and the bondswomen with
offerings to pour on Agamemnon's grave, in hope of placating his angry ghost. Later, however, in the *kommos* between
Orestes and the Chorus of Bondswomen, the audience is ap-
prised not only of the dream's content but of its real meaning.

ORESTES: From what motive did she send the libations? Why
did she show such tardy regard with so paltry an offering? . . .
Tell me if you know, for I am eager to learn.

CHORUS: I know, my good youth, for I was there. Because her heart quaked at dreams and night-wandering alarms the impious woman sent these libations.

OR.: And did you learn what the dream was, so that you can describe it truly?

CHO.: She thought she gave birth to a serpent. We have it on her own word.

OR.: And what followed? What is the story's upshot?

CHO.: She dressed the creature in swaddling clothes and laid it to rest, as one would do to a child.

OR.: How did she nourish the new-born monster?

CHO.: She dreamt that she put it to her breast.

OR.: How could the teat have been unscathed by so deadly a thing?

CHO.: Scathed it was, for the creature drew curds of blood with the milk.

OR.: Ah, this looks like no empty apparition!

(*Choe.*, 520–532)

In telling what the apparition signifies Orestes makes explicit one of the major symbols of the play:

OR.: So then I pray to Earth and to my father's tomb, that this dream may be a surety of my accomplishment. It plainly fits my case, as I interpret it. For if the snake issued forth from the same place as I had done, if it was wrapped in infant swaddling bands and opened its mouth to the same teat that once suckled me, if it mingled the kindly milk with curd of blood so that the pain and fear of it made her cry out,—why surely it follows that even as she nourished that monster into life, so now she must die a violent death. 'Tis I, made over into the serpent of her dream, that shall murder her.

(*Choe.*, 538–549)

Clytemnestra, whatever her vices, did not lack intelligence, but she was prevented from reading the dream aright since she still believed Orestes to be alive. On the other hand it might be remarked that Orestes was in exile, which to the ancients bore an analogy to death, and the figure of a snake issuing from the womb and taking nourishment at the breast should not have been so very obscure to a people skilled at dream interpretation. However, we need not overstress a small implausibility which the plot required; and in any case Clytemnestra grasps the situation quickly enough when events begin to move and Aegisthus is slain.

CLYT.: What is happening? Why are you filling the house with such outcries?
SERVANT: It means that the dead are slaying the living.
CLYT.: Oho! I take the meaning of your riddle. By craft we perish even as by craft we slew.
(*Choe.*, 884–887)

And Clytemnestra completes her version of the symbolic pattern when on finding herself powerless to soften Orestes' purpose she cries:

CLYT.: Ah me! so this is that serpent which I brought forth and nourished.
(*Choe.*, 927)

In one set of connections, then, the serpent symbolizes Orestes. But in another it symbolizes Clytemnestra and the dark maternal forces that brood about her. When Orestes first sees the Furies, it is in the guise of wingless Gorgons with coils of writhing snakes, and they retain this character in the *Eumenides*, presumably up to the point of their persuasion and conversion by Athena. Aeschylus makes an effective passage to the feminine phase of serpent symbolism, by introducing it just after the Chorus has been praising Orestes for liberating the land of Argos by "deftly severing the heads of the serpents"—i.e., of Clytemnestra and Aegisthus. It is the same word—*drakon*—with which Orestes immediately after describes his horrid vision. The snake is not directly or primarily a feminine symbol—indeed, its phallic shape tends to give it an iconically masculine imputation wherever the aspect of sex is involved; but as the snake-form is a usual one for *chthonioi,* earth-spirits, to take, it enters into many associations with earth-mother symbolism—especially where, as at the end of the *Choëphori* and the beginning of the *Eumenides,* the mother-figure is also an embodiment of vengeance.

A deeper meaning of the snake-symbolism can be seen in its relation to Delphi. The action of the *Eumenides* opens in front of the temple of Apollo at Delphi, and it is there that the priestess, after praying to representative divinities of both sky and earth, discovers the snake-wreathed monsters. In the pre-classical age it would appear that the worship at Delphi was purely chthonic, and that a snake was the guardian of the ancient oracle-spirit of the place. The legend of Apollo killing the Delphic snake evidently reflects the actual event of an Apollonian cult succeeding the older chthonic one in that place. Chthonian religion had grown up most naturally there, from the physical character of the grotto, within which a deep cleft gave forth vaporous exhalations that seemed to arise from the nether world. At some early period the grotto had come to be conceived as the Omphalos, the world's navel, the umbilical cord by which the children of Mother Earth retain a pristine connection with the older world of vague dark forces which affect human life with blessing or bane. At the coming of Apollonian worship the earlier notion did not disappear; it merely merged, a bit incongruously at first, with the cult of the bright Olympian sun-god, who was also, especially at Delphi, the god of prophecy and healing.

Accordingly the Pythian Priestess' description of Orestes at the Omphalos seeking expiation for his crime acquires an added dimension of significance when it is remembered that Orestes stands as suppliant at the door to the womb of mundane creation.

> PRIESTESS: O horror to behold, horror even to say! . . . As I was passing into the laurelled shrine I saw at the Omphalos a man in suppliant posture, god-accursed for some deed of guilt, his hands all dripping with blood, holding a sword newly unsheathed, and the topmost branch of an olive tree decently filleted with large white tufts of spotless wool.
>
> (*Eum.*, 34, 39–45)

The primary blood-reference is of course to Orestes' deed of matricide, for the Furies, as maternal avengers, lie sleeping about him, presently to be spurred to action by Clytemnestra's restless ghost. But the blood can also represent the bloody state of a new-born babe—which the newly unsheathed sword and the purity of spotless wool might differently indicate. If this interpretation seems lightly allowable, we have here a momentary, iconically suggested prognostic-symbol of Orestes' coming reversal of role. He has cut himself off from the mother-image by murderous violence, thus becoming an exile in more senses than one—not only geographically from the city of Argos, whence the Furies have pursued him, but psychically from all the warmth and naturalness of life which the mother-image properly connotes. The excision was needful because his own particular mother-image had become an embodiment of evil: that was part of the curse upon the royal house. But he cannot find salvation until he has placated the maternal forces of earth which are now taking vengeance upon him. The snakes with which the Furies are semi-identified represent those chthonic powers, potentially both dreadful and beneficent, with which Orestes must eventually make his spiritual peace.

THE COMING OF LIGHT

CHORUS: Now is the test. Either the murderous blade-points will leave their stain and cause the ruin of Agamemnon's house forever, or else the son, kindling fire and light for freedom, shall reëstablish the duly-ordered rule in his city and the prosperity of his fathers.

(*Choe.*, 858–864)

These words, uttered by the Chorus of Bondswomen in the *Choëphori* just before Orestes' slaying of Aegisthus and Clytemnestra, can be taken in two senses. Paley's paraphrase indicates the surface meaning: "Orestes will either lose all or gain all by the present stake; either he himself will be killed, or he will recover the sovereignty, and offer sacrifices for the release of the Argives from an unjust usurpation."[5] The personal interpretation—what Orestes himself will lose or gain by the immediately forthcoming contest—is borne out by the athletic metaphor of the next four lines: "In such a wrestling match the noble Orestes, the extra contestant, is about to cope with his two adversaries." The word *ephedros,* which I have translated "extra contestant," was applied technically to the third fighter who sat by in a contest between two athletes, prepared to challenge the victor to a fresh encounter. In terms of this figure Clytemnestra has won the first bout by slaying Agamemnon, and Orestes the *ephedros* is accordingly ready to take her on, with Aegisthus as a preliminary. Paley carries out the logic of the interpretation by taking "fire" and "light" to signify the sacrificial flames which would be lighted in celebration if Orestes should prove victorious.

Now there is a deeper meaning as well—continuous with the surface meaning and even reinforcing it, but yet something more, adumbrating a tragic judgment about the nature and destiny of man in his universal condition. The state of unredeemed nature is a state of war: of ego against ego, group against group. Life on such terms is a denial of man's high destiny. Parallel to the Christian mythos of Adam's disobedience and loss of Eden stands the mythos around which Aeschylus has built the *Oresteia:* the crime of *hybris,* the curse upon the House, the malign working out of that curse even to the third generation, and the salvation which comes down from above by divine grace in the person of Athena. Forefather Atreus' crime of serving up Thyestes' children to him as baked meats was *hybris* of so extraordinary a degree, doing such dreadful violence to the balanced course of nature (there is balance even in the natural state of war, as Heraclitus keenly perceived), that the entire family of him who committed it became more than usually vulnerable to the curse which the bereaved and outraged father invoked against it. A morality of vendetta follows, a morality of the hunter and the hunted, in which Aegisthus seeks to avenge the cannibalism practised upon his brothers, Orestes to avenge his father by slaying his slayers, and the Furies to avenge Clytemnestra by continuing the deadly pursuit against Orestes. How shall it all end, the Chorus of Bondswomen asks?

> Here, then, upon this royal House
> a third storm has blown and swept along to its end.
> First came the wretched meal of children's flesh;
> next the sad fate of our lord and king,—
> slain in the bath he perished who had led all Greece to war.
> And now a third has come—we know not whence—
> a savior? or shall I say a doom?
> O where shall fulfillment be found?
> How shall the power of guilt be lulled to rest?
> (*Choe.,* 1063–1074)

The tone of these words, with which the *Choëphori* closes, transcends a concern for the fate of Orestes as an individual.

It points, although still darkly, toward the fundamental motif of the trilogy: the passage from a morality of vengeance and vendetta to a morality of law.

Aeschylus prepares us for his gradual development of this central theme at the very outset of the *Oresteia*. The *Agamemnon* opens with the great overture which is the Watchman's speech, wherein several of the dominant motifs of the trilogy are announced. I here offer it in as literal a version as English idiom and Aeschylean depth-ambiguity allow, italicizing certain words of symbolic importance:

Of the *gods* I ask *deliverance from these labors,* watching a year's length now, bedded like a dog on the roof of the house of Atreus. Here I have come to know the assembly of the *nightly stars*—the *shining potentates* which, by their rising and setting, bring *winter tempest and summer harvest* to mortal men.

And now I *keep watch* for the *beacon signal,* the *flame of fire* that bears a tale from Troy, news of its capture. Such is the task commanded me by her whose hopeful woman's heart is joined with a man's strong purpose.

Night after night I keep my dew-drenched couch, never looked upon by dreams, for fear stands at my side in place of sleep, and I cannot close my eyelids in restful sleep. Then when I think to sing or hum a tune, as counter-charm for sleep, I fall to weeping for the fortunes of the house, no longer well labored and administered as of old. But now would that a stroke of luck might bring *deliverance from labors*—*a fiery flash of good news appearing out of the darkness.*

(A distant light flares up.)

Welcome, O torch of the night, who givest us *token of the light of day!* inaugurator of many dances which in Argos will celebrate the *happy outcome!* Eeya! Eeya! I *give the sign* to Agamemnon's sleeping queen, that she rise quickly from her bed and raise a joyful *ololugmos* throughout the palace in response to this beacon-fire;—if the city of Troy be really taken, as the torch seems to *announce*.

I myself will dance the prelude. For I shall share in my lord's good fortune, now that this beacon torch has thrown me a triple six. And may it be that I with this hand of mine may grasp my master's beloved hand again when he returns! For the rest I am silent. *A great ox stands upon my tongue.* The House, if it had a voice, could tell a tale all too plainly. *My speech is meant for those who know.* For those who know not—I have forgotten.

(Agam., 1–39)

The opening word of the Watchman's speech is "gods"— *theous,* the accusative plural. The context of star-imagery shows that the invocation is to the gods above—the gods of Olympus, yes, but through and beyond them to a vaguely conceived providential order of things. Such interpenetration of the personal and impersonal elements in religion keeps appearing variously throughout Aeschylus' writings. The Watchman has, of course, no strong or definite theological beliefs, for he makes no further mention of the gods, and in repeating his hope of release some lines later he finds it enough to invoke good fortune. But the watchman moves in symbolic depths of which his limited consciousness has no knowledge. Whereas the *Agamemnon* opens with this brief mention of the upper gods, the *Choëphori* opens with Orestes' more substantial prayer to Hermes, divine attendant of souls on their way to the world of shades below; and finally the *Eumenides* opens with a long formal prayer by the Pythian priestess of Delphi addressed to a number of gods, some of sky and some of earth. The prayer for deliverance from evil times is, in its larger context, not polytheistic but *henotheistic*—an expression of that outreaching of man's heart toward the divine unity which may take the form now of one god now of another, but which transcends every such mythic particularity. The sentiment of henotheism is perhaps more active among early peoples than might be guessed from the multiplicity of their god-names, and the Chorus of

Elders in the *Agamemnon* strikes the note of it more than once—as when invoking "Zeus, by whatever name thou art called!" and prophesying, "There is One above, whether called Zeus or Pan or Apollo, who hears the cry of the birds" —i.e., the victims of tyranny—the eagle-chicks molested by the dragon.

Another religious allusion, more oblique but still no less contributory to the undercurrent of religious meaning which gradually widens and deepens as the action proceeds, is the phrase "deliverance from labors" *(apallagê ponôn)*. It occurs twice, and the second occurrence is anticipated by the sound and meaning of *pon-* in the verb which I have translated (to keep the full connotation) "labored and administered." The phrase was probably one employed in certain of the mystery religions, although we cannot be sure; in any case it expresses an idea which was central to them, as is evident from Chapter X. Aeschylus employs the word "deliverance" or "release" *(apallagê)* and its related forms with great care. In the *Agamemnon* they carry dramatic irony. The Watchman speaks of "deliverance from labors" without consciously intending any more than his own hope for release from his irksome vigil. Toward the end of the *Agamemnon* (1288), when Cassandra is prophesying Agamemnon's and her own murder, she charges the word with a more sombre meaning: those who laid waste to Troy are now, in the person of their king, to be "released" from life by the gods' righteous judgment. Then in the *Choëphori*, while Orestes is murdering his mother off-stage, the Chorus of Bondwomen chant a triumphant hymn:

> Raise a joyful ololugmos for the release from evils, from waste of wealth by the two polluters [of the home], and from the rough path.
>
> *(Choe.,* 941–944)

There are religious overtones to virtually all the main words of this little passage. The ololugmos (found also in the Watchman's Prologue) was the ceremonial outcry of joy and triumph, sometimes combined with agony, on the successful completion of a sacrifice; the rough path could readily symbolize the evils and difficulties of this life from which a release is craved; and the significance of pollution I have discussed in Chapter X. Here the irony is differently oriented but equally strong: the Bondswomen think that the act of matricide will release the House from the curse; but as the audience well knows and as Orestes' pursuit by the Furies will presently confirm, release is not yet possible. Finally, however, in the *Eumenides* the prayer for release becomes intense and direct. Orestes is told by Apollo to make a pilgrimage to Athena's citadel, "and there we shall find means at last to *deliver* you from your trials." (78–83). Apollo's particular expedients *(mechanai)* do not work, to be sure; but Orestes, after making the journey, can declare that having been "taught by suffering" he has learnt the first requirement of a religious initiate, "the occasions when it is right to speak and when to be silent" (276–278). The release is effected in a way that suggests the rites of initiation at Eleusis or Crotona or one of the other religious centers.

The mention of "when to speak and when to be silent" takes us back to another religious symbol in the Watchman's speech. The phrase "A great ox stands (or has trod) upon my tongue" was, to be sure, a colloquialism for "I must be silent." But how did so curious an idiom arise? Generally speaking when the ox *(bous)* or bull *(tauros)* enters into ancient Greek symbolism it is a fair indication that the god Dionysus, whose icons display a bull's or ox's head, lurks in the background. Probably, then, the Watchman's casual phrase (or *was* it so casual?) would remind the Greek audi-

ence of the ritual silence imposed upon candidates for purification in the Dionysian and other mystery religions.

The imposition of silence is not a mere negation, either in
the *Oresteia* or in the mystery cults to which its imagery so
often alludes. Silence is part of the preparation of that essential wisdom which comes through silent suffering—a wisdom
that is represented symbolically as a secret imparted only to
those who have become ready for it. The idea of a secret fits
in very well with Aeschylus' manner of writing upon two
levels at once—a public meaning for the "pro-fane" (literally,
"those outside the temple") and an esoteric one for the initiates. Such religious ambivalence was practiced universally
in the ancient schools of wisdom. Thus the Pythagoreans
were taught, "Do not touch beans": which seems to have
signified both "Do not violate the organ of generation"—
beans symbolizing the testicles, and "Do not participate in
politics"—which involves dropping the white and black beans
into the ballot-urn. The symbolic meanings were of course
the important ones for the followers of Pythagoras; nevertheless, in order that the vulgarly inquisitive might not be
led to pry into the secret, the literal meanings were the ones
emphasized publicly, and Jamblichus tells of two Pythagoreans, a man and his pregnant wife, who let themselves be
tortured and killed rather than eat some beans at a tyrant's
orders, *or even tell why they would not do so.*[6] The Watchman (the first of many "watchers" in the drama) reflects
this characteristic of the Mysteries in the closing words of
his speech, and the Chorus of Elders conveys its forebodings
in dark hints and surmises. Particularly after Clytemnestra's
lying but double-edged speech to the Herald, the Chorus
tries vainly to warn the unimaginative fellow, in language
that might be taken to epitomize the dramatic ambivalence
found everywhere: "Thus she has spoken to you, a neophyte,
a goodly tale for shrewd interpreters."

Such religious phrases, allusions, and attitudes become important dramatically just so far as they form part of the inner dramatic action, leading to a dramatic consummation. The idea of consummation is itself a religious idea as well as a dramatic one. A most popular way of invoking Zeus for the success of an undertaking was as *Zeus Teleios,* which connoted at once "Zeus the Perfect One" and "Zeus the Perfecter, the Ripener, the Fulfiller." The word and its cognates occur frequently in Aeschylus' writings. But consummation is of different kinds. Often it means no more than fulfillment of the terms of blood feud, as for instance in the *kommos* between Orestes and the Chorus of Bondswomen.

CHO.: Ye mighty Fates, grant that Zeus send this consummation, in which justice is on our side. "For word of hate let word of hate be consummated," Justice loudly cries as she gathers in the debt; "and for murderous blow let him pay murderous blow." *Suffering to the doer,*—so speaks an age-old saw.

(*Choe.*, 305–314)

That last maxim represents consummation on the low level. Paradoxically it calls to mind the complementary maxim already met with—*Wisdom through suffering*—which represents the consummatory process in what Aeschylus regards as its highest human form.

We are now prepared to understand the full import of Clytemnestra's irony in her final words to Agamemnon as he retires into the palace just before the murder:

CLYT.: Your coming signifies (*semainein*) summery warmth in wintry storm. When Zeus draws wine from the sour grape, then coolness is already present in the house, with the perfect (*teleios*) master in residence.

(*Agam.*, 959–963)

Look at the second sentence first. Its first two clauses, taken literally, might be simply a way of describing the season, and the last clause might seem just an overstuffed compliment likening Agamemnon to Zeus—a verbal equivalent of making him walk on the sacred crimson carpet. But "coolness" ($\psi\acute{v}\chi$os) can also mean "chill," "already" ($\tau o\tau$' $\mathring{\eta}\delta\eta$) can also mean "then straightway," and with these shifts of interpretation the sentence becomes:

> When Zeus draws wine from the unripe grape (*symbolically:* when divine justice spills blood before the victim's normal span of years has ripened), then straightway a chill settles down upon the house, and the resident master is "ripe."

On this level the adjective *teleios,* applied to Agamemnon, is no longer a vapid compliment but a sinister threat. Its related grammatical forms appear three times within the next two lines as Clytemnestra concludes:

> Zeus, Zeus the Ripener, ripen thou my prayers (i.e., bring them to fulfillment) and have a care for all that thou intend'st to ripen.

The ripening-fulfillment-consummatory motif that runs through the *Oresteia* is associated with several characteristic sorts of imagery. The ripening of hunters' and hounds' pursuit of game I have already spoken of. The political metaphor of a successful lawsuit occurs, as does the economic one of profitable exchange. The consummation of childbirth is suggested several times, and in the *Choëphori* it becomes complicated with the idea already discussed of Orestes' symbolical rebirth from the dead. The childbirth idea becomes naturally connected with that of ripening of crops and summer harvest, as in the first sentence quoted from Clytemnestra's words to Agamemnon: "Your coming signifies summery warmth in wintry storm." The surface meaning is an expression of courteous hyperbole, as though the queen were to say, "You have brought summery warmth into my winter";

or, as Conington translates, "Thy coming shows like heat in winter cold." But the statement could also suggest that the summery warmth which the king's return represents is caught up in the wintry blast of violence and evil that overwhelms the house. Similarly, when the Watchman (as quoted earlier) says that the stars by their rising and setting bring winter storm and summer harvest to men, he is expressing more than a fragment of naïve science. The Chorus in the *Choëphori,* it will be recalled, uses the word χειμών (which combines the meanings "storm" and "winter") to refer to the misfortunes of the house: "Upon this royal house a third storm has blown." And Clytemnestra uses the word θέρος (which combines the meanings "harvest" and "summer") in a symbolical sense that is also ironical: "the unhappy harvest of our ills" (*Agam.* 1655). The cycle of winter storms and summer harvest becomes a threshold symbol for the cycle of bane and blessing, deprivation and fulfillment, in the human lot.

A more awful theme of consummative symbolism is that of the priestess consummating the sacrifice—illustrated by the ritual blood-bath passage already quoted and by Clytemnestra's earlier double-dealing announcement:

Go within, Cassandra, you too; since Zeus has auspiciously made it your privilege to stand among the slaves by the altar and share the consecrated pouring of our household sacrifice . . .
I have no time to idle here outside the door. The sheep stand before the central altar by the hearth awaiting the knife.
(*Agam.,* 1019–1022, 1039–1041)

But the most important consummative image of all, I would say, is the emergence of light out of darkness. Observe that in the Watchman's speech the light-imagery has three phases: the stars, the expectation of the beacon flame, and finally (as consummation of his hopes) the visible appearance of the flame itself. The Watchman speaks of the flame as a *symbolon;* and while it is not certain that the word had acquired in the fifth century B.C. the religious significance it was to carry in the time of Plutarch, one of the meanings which it indubitably did have in the earlier century was "watchword," and thence it could easily have come to mean "watchword for initiates" and therefore "symbol of experiences which only initiates have shared." In any case the contextualization of the light imagery in the Watchman's speech leaves no doubt that it has a symbolic meaning as well as a literal one.

To particularize all the light and darkness images in the *Oresteia* would be tedious for writer and reader alike. But two are especially noteworthy—where Clytemnestra fuses the images of childbirth (with so complex an Oresteian significance of its own) and dawning day:

CLYT.: Bringing good news, as the proverb says, may dawn come to birth auspiciously out of Mother Night.
(*Agam.*, 276–277)

CLYT.: In the night that gave birth to this dawning day.
(*Agam.*, 291)

These two utterances are followed by the tremendous light-imagery of the Queen's description of the fire-god winging from island pyre to island pyre the news of Troy's fall. Even Aegisthus is caught up in the power of such imagery. When he comes on the scene at the end of the *Agamemnon,* after letting Clytemnestra do the bloody deed whose fruits he will enjoy, he reveals something of his hypocritical character in the cry:

O kindly light of a day of just reward!
(*Agam.*, 1577)

With admirable art Aeschylus withdraws light imagery almost entirely in the *Choëphori* and through the early part of the *Eumenides*, and stresses instead the darkness imagery appropriate both to the invocation of Agamemnon's ghost and the appearance of the Furies. For the Furies are children of Mother Night, and until their transformation they must exhibit only sombre associations. As their ancient prerogative of unrestricted vengeance is being stripped away they howl:

> Black Night, my mother! dost thou look on this?
> (*Eum.*, 748)

> Hear my vehement wrath, O Mother Night!
> (*Eum.*, 847)

But under the new dispensation which Athena establishes by setting up the Court of the Areopagus, wherein the rights and wrongs of murder cases will be adjudicated by legal deliberation instead of determined by blind vengeance, the Furies will receive new honors and functions in return for the old "natural rights" of which they are deprived:

> CHORUS OF FURIES: O Queen Athena, what seat dost thou assign me?
> ATH.: One free of all bane: accept it!
> CHO.: Suppose I accept, what honor then is mine?
> ATH.: That no house shall prosper apart from thee.
> (*Eum.*, 893–897)

The Furies, although ceasing to be *mere* agents of vengeance, are to retain enough of their old character so that the well-being of men is unattainable without their good-will.

In political terms the issue might be stated: On what grounds is law enforcement justified? Now law enforcement implies a disposition to punish certain kinds of wrongdoing if and when committed. On what grounds, then, may we punish? The lowest ground, to which a certain bestial instinct sometimes prompts us, is retaliation: "You injured me, so I will injure you." As the concept of retaliation advances, it undergoes two changes. It becomes codified—"An eye for an eye, a tooth for a tooth"—declaring in effect that the punishment should be commensurate with and appropriate to the crime. And it becomes impersonal and at least relatively impartial: the "eye for an eye" formula is meant to apply equally to all persons of a given community—or, it may be, to all of a certain rank within the community. Both of these developments involve some appeal to a principle of justice, but the justice is purely retributive, which is to say backward-looking.

To pass from the retributive to a higher conception of justice requires the raising of two questions: *with what authority,* and *for what purpose.* In a healthily evolving society the two questions will develop in mutual relationship. If every individual pursues his own purposes, or even the common purpose as he privately conceives it, without any respect for the authority of existing rulers and laws, the result is anarchy. On the other hand an authority which issues decrees by rule and rote without any demonstration of its purpose is too brittle to satisfy the human craving for justice; the authorities to which we look up with fervor and willing devotion are those who are concerned for some large common good and who (so we believe) know better than other men how it is to be attained. The one type is authoritarian, the other authoritative. A most important step in the evolution of moral notions can be discovered in the transition from authoritarian codes to authoritative laws—from rules to principles. Ideally speaking, we follow a rule because we are told to; we observe a law because we regard its purpose, or that of the authority that issues it, as good.

The situation, however, is not always ideal. To achieve any purpose, and especially a social purpose, adequate means must be taken, and the means do not usually wear the same look of authenticity as the end. The means, therefore, may have to be enforced if the end is to be achieved. And that is precisely to be the role of the Furies under the new dispensation that Athena establishes. Athena was the Olympian goddess of wisdom; she was also, as her name indicates, the patron goddess of the city of Athens; therefore she was *par excellence* the goddess and symbol of *civic wisdom.* Her great act of civic wisdom, which the *Oresteia* celebrates, was to found the law court of the Areopagus with its institution of trial by jury. Certainly it represents a great advance in public weal that murder cases should be tried so. But public weal cannot be the only consideration. To put men to death simply in the name of public weal is an act of gross and dangerous tyranny. In a state of justice a man may be put to death only if he has done something to forfeit his civic right: thus in the very conception of penal justice there must be an element of implicit retribution *as well as* of civic purpose. The Furies, then, who represent the retributive force in human relationships, must still be retained under the new conception of justice by law. They are to be the "teeth in the law." They will still pursue evil-doers, but now as agents of legally constituted authority. They represent the negative, primitive side of man's social conscience, as Athena represents the positive and constructive.

Thus the Furies, the Erinyes, are transformed into the Eumenides. Aeschylus here gives symbolic depth to what had otherwise been merely a quirk of Greek idiom. The name *Erinyes* had become so dreadful, and its utterance invited

such baneful effects, that people largely refrained from pro-
nouncing it and referred to the dread sisters by a euphemism
—as the Eumenides, the Well-Minded Ones. In the *Oresteia*
the transformation is not merely verbal but real. They become the *Semnai,* the Holy Ones—beneficent yet still commanding awe. In religious perspective they are thus recon-
cilers of the light above and the darkness of earth below:

That so the glorious sun and bounteous earth may unite to
yield thick burgeoning growth.

(Eum., 925–926)

Thus light imagery is reintroduced at the end, and with
great expressive power. When the ex-Furies put on crimson
robes and march in the torchlight procession, the symbolism
is political and transcendental at once. The ceremony is that
of the annual Festival of *Panathenaia,* in which eminent al-
iens residing in Athens were given honorary citizenship—
"the keys to the city," as we would say. Thus in stately analogy the Awful Goddesses, who formerly were alien to men's
purposes, shall henceforth enjoy the highest honors among
the citizenry. The light and song that mark the procession
symbolize the new wisdom and the new harmony which
the great transformation has brought into the world. As the
Eumenides pass onward to their sacred abodes the Chorus
of Citizens chants responsively the verses with which the
Oresteia closes:

> *Strophe*
> Go to your home, ye powers fond of worship,
> Daughters of Night, in auspicious procession.
> Speak only fair words, O countrymen.

> *Antistrophe*
> There in the gloomy caverns of earth
> To be worshiped with honors and sacrifices.
> Speak only fair words, O populace.

Strophe

> With benign heart and propitious for the land,
> Come, O holy ones, in gladness,
> Follow the torches that light up the way.
>> O sing *ololugmos* now to our songs.

Antistrophe

> Let the drink-offerings flow,
> There shall be living in peace for Pallas' children.
> Zeus the All-Seeing is thus with Destiny reconciled.
>> O sing *ololugmos* now to our songs.

THIRTEEN

Expressive Statement and Truth

ONE OF THE logical stunts attributed in ancient times to Gorgias the Sophist, after whom Plato named one of his most engaging Dialogues, was to prove that nothing exists, that if anything did exist it could not be known, and that if by any chance a person could know anything he could not communicate it to anyone else. An impressive example of defense in depth! Ignoring Gorgias' particular demonstrations, which appear to have been no better and no worse than most such displays of precocity, I suggest that his three conclusions can offer, although in ways that he did not intend, a clue to possible starting-points for philosophical reëxamination. As they stand, of course, they are plainly inconsistent. If nothing can be known, then how can we say with such assurance that nothing exists? And if nothing can be communicated, then we shall have to reckon with the possibility (unverifiable but still a possibility) that other persons may have knowledge in which we do not share. In short, philosophical nihilism is, in strict logic, a private possession; any attempt to impose it on others by reasoned argument becomes ludicrous. A genuine scepticism must be quite as sceptical toward negative conclusions as toward positive.

And yet in a rough and blundering way Gorgias was on

the scent. For the three questions, *What is? How can we know it?* and *How can we say it?* are the ones that most inevitably impose themselves when the itch of philosophic wonder assails us. How shall we indicate the ultimate *what*, the X toward which any philosophical inquiry is, in the last resort, directed? Laotze called it *Tao*, the Way, even while warning that "the Tao which can be tao-ed (named? thought? trodden?) is not the real Tao"; Vedanta philosophers named it *Atmabrahman*, although they met all attempts at closer definition with *neti neti* ("Not quite that, not quite that"); others have called it God, or Being, or the Word, or the Divine Fire. But the meaning of such symbols comes to us distorted by the lenses of alien speech, alien culture, and in any case alien mentality and intent. Our problem becomes not only that of trying to know, but of trying to say; and, more fundamentally than either of them, of studying to ask the right questions.

If being and knowing demand utterance, so utterance in turn, when authentic, is motivated by a demand for reality. To speak is more than to talk; it is to speak *about* something, to make a cognitive claim, and therein to imply a judgment about the nature of reality in some respect or other. That expressive language is speech in this firm sense, and not just chatter and tinkle, has been one of the main propositions espoused in the foregoing chapters. The word "expressive," as I have been using it, connotes an exploitation of linguistic resources to a larger than usual degree in order to say something, however tentatively and obliquely, about the nature of what *is*. Poetry has its deepest roots in metaphysics.

But if this affirmative role of expressive language is to be accepted, how are the truth-claims which it carries as an implicit part of its expressiveness to be tested and validated? On what grounds can an expressive statement be declared true—or false? Restating the question in a more personal perspective we might ask: On what grounds may I, and should I, assent to an expressive utterance with intellectual conviction? For the problem of valid assenting or affirming, and the problem of what is true as distinguished from what is false, are the complementary aspects—subjective and objective respectively—of one identical problem.

Our first step must be to delimit the semantic area to which questions of truth and falsity are relevant. In formal logic, both old and new varieties, it is generally postulated that "true" and "false" may apply only to propositions; and conversely from that standpoint propositions are frequently defined as those linguistic complexes, or those types of signification, to which "true" and "false" can meaningfully apply. As an escape from the circularity of this procedure many contemporary logicians have agreed to define "true" and "false" by reference to the conditions of their verifiability. And since verifiability is usually taken to mean empirical and public verifiability, implying the possibility (under ideal conditions) of being checked by that wonderful abstraction the Normal Observer, the end result of that line of reasoning is a positivistic conception of the nature and apriori limits of truth. In Chapter III a jaundiced eye was cast toward the general positivistic conception of meaning; here the question has to do with *affirmable* meaning, and the conditions under which, outside of either a strictly empirical or a strictly logical context, the act of affirming may be justified.

In order to investigate the question of justifiable affirmation, and hence of truth, without limiting ourselves to the specialized scientific applications of these words (which would involve a begging of the question as to what truth in broadest scope *is*), it is necessary to distinguish between affirmable meanings in general and that special form of affirmable meanings which is the proposition. For the broader of these categories I shall use the word "statement." That is to say, by "statement" I shall mean anything so far as it can be meaningfully affirmed or denied in any way whatever—whether strongly or weakly, firmly or lightly, whether with full reference to the public world or as a testimony of private insight, and whether in the broad general context of a shared cultural milieu or in the more adroitly delimited context of a particular work of art. By "proposition," on the other hand, is meant a special kind of statement, a limiting type. Whereas a statement expresses any affirmable relationship between meanings of whatever kind, a proposition consists of a logically formalized relation between terms which have logically identifiable denotations. Consider, for instance, the total statement made by the opening three verses of the sixty-ninth Psalm:

Save me, O God; for the waters are come in unto my soul.

I sink in deep mire, where there is no standing; I am come into deep waters, where the floods overflow me.

I am weary of my crying; my throat is dried; mine eyes fail while I wait for my God.

Doubtless several propositions can be extracted here—i.e., several plain common-sensical meanings which can be understood, and (except for incidental barriers of time and place) verified, by virtually anyone, religious or irreligious, sensitive or emotionally obtuse, who understands the component terms and relations. The Psalmist feels some kind of danger to the integral character of his selfhood, he seeks some means of averting that danger, he is near to despair, and yet he is sustained by a hope that help will come from a higher than human source—these or some similar group of propositions might be agreed on as the "scenario meaning" of the passage. For anyone, however, to whom the original utterance spoke directly and memorably in the first place (which would exclude, I should think, both the stubbornly irreligious and the casually unreligious, to whom "God" and "soul" are vacuous pseudo-concepts and "deep mire" suggests only the sort of predicament for which human ingenuity might furnish an extrication) the main thrust of the Biblical utterance is lost in the analytic paraphrase. The Psalmist is saying something which invites assent in its totality; and a religiously oriented reader, especially if he has had some personal involvement with the deep mire and the engulfing floods, feels disposed to assent to the whole of it in its integral character, not just to the parts that can be held up to scrutiny piecemeal. The idea of "the whole" is a shifting one, to be sure. It is not confined to these three verses. It is also the entire Psalm, ultimately perhaps even the entire Bible. For in expressive writing, wholes are not strictly unitary, but merge into one another without sharp division. A given expressive statement elides with its neighbor statements, and all of them tend to be sublated (*erhoben*), in something like the Hegelian sense) into some fuller statement which gradually strikes upon a reader's understanding as he reads further and as he meditates upon what he has read already.

In order, then, to avoid prejudging the question of truth in such a way that non-logical or trans-logical kinds of truth are ruled out in advance, we must avoid defining "true" and "false" in such a way that they pertain only to propositions. The main object of our inquiry is not the proposition but the expressive statement. We must first ask, *"What is the nature of expressive statement?"* and then ask, *"In what sense can an expressive statement be judged true or false?"* These seemingly remote and abstract questions are actually among the most important we can ask when trying to think philosophically, as becomes evident when we consider their four main impingements upon man's perennial depth interests. (1) When we make a *religious* statement—more particularly when we make the most basic of all religious statements, "God exists"—are we really affirming anything, or are we just beating the air with vocal noises? (2) What does even the positivist mean when he makes the *metaphysical* statement that positivism is a truer philosophy than, let's say, Hegelian idealism? (3) Has an *ethical* statement such as "Neighborly good-will is intrinsically better than hatred, suspicion and revenge," any objective validity? Can it mean something more than either the autobiographical observation that I happen to prefer the one state of affairs to the other and would be happier if everyone agreed with me, or the statistical observation that a majority of persons probably do prefer that state of affairs? (4) Is there any reasonable sense in which we can speak of the total *poetic* statement of *King Lear* or the *Ode to a Nightingale* or the *Four Quartets* as something more than, and somewhat other than, any and every literal exposition of what they mean? The semantic positivist, as I defined him in Chapter III, is inclined to answer Questions 1, 3, and 4 negatively; and he either sidesteps Question 2 or develops ingenious arguments to make its status appear different from that of the other three questions. At all events, when he carries out his positivistic principles consistently he has to deny *a priori* the possibility of there being any such thing as religious, metaphysical, ethical, or poetic truth; and by the second of these denials he destroys (without admitting it) the very basis of his own position. When a positivist affirms the possibility of truth in any of these four senses he manages to do so only by using the words "true" and "truth" homonymously—by using, as a courtesy to the general practice, the same set of English words to express two or more distinct sets of meanings.

Now the conviction that lies behind my argument is that we should keep the truth-possibilities of religion, of metaphysics, of ethics, and of poetry linguistically open. It is bad strategy—methodologically inept and philosophically obfuscating—to set up our definitions of "statement" and of "truth" in such a way that what appears to be a religious, or a metaphysical, or an ethical, or a poetic statement, always turns out to be no real statement at all, but only an emotionally satisfying collocation of words. To rule out in advance, by definition or by deduction from arbitrary postulates, the possibility of there being any real truth of other than a scientific and logical kind, is not a reasonable procedure. It is the old trick of stacking the cards before the hands are dealt.

In the first two sections of the chapter, then, I shall deal with the two following questions respectively. First, what is an expressive statement and how is it distinguished from that strictly logical kind of statement which is a proposition? Secondly, how far can one ascribe truth or falsity to an expressive (trans-propositional) statement without talking nonsense? These general inquiries will be followed by some attempts at application to the more particular fields of religion and poetry.

THE NATURE OF EXPRESSIVE STATEMENT

A starting-point for an understanding of expressive statement (beyond what has already been offered in the chapters on expressive language in general) may be found in the grammarians' well-known classification of sentences into four kinds: declarative, interrogative, imperative, and exclamatory. Since our present interest is not grammatical and rhetorical, but semantic, we must regard such a classification not from the standpoint of verbal form, but as representing differences of meaning. From this more basic standpoint two modifications of the standard classification seem called for. These may be put in the form of two hypotheses regarding the nature and semantic functioning of sentences: (1) that there are five sentential functions, not four; and (2) that in an expressive sentence several of them, possibly all, tend to be co-present to some degree or other.

(1) The first point, that there are five basic sentential functions, becomes clear when we consider how the several sentence-types can be paired. Interrogative and declarative obviously go together, since a question invites a reply, and conversely a statement, if significant, may be regarded as a reply to some real though perhaps unspoken question. The third type of sentence, the exclamatory, is self-sufficient; it can stand by itself without requiring any further sentence to complete it. But what of the fourth type, the imperative or hortatory? To command or urge is a significant act only in the presence of someone who is commanded or urged (in special cases that someone may be oneself) and who may possibly acquiesce. The words "may possibly" are of course important. Just as significant interrogation implies the possibility that there may be an answer even though on particular occasions no answer is forthcoming, so in a parallel manner significant hortation implies the possibility that there may be acquiescence, although on particular hortatory occasions it may be that no acquiescence follows. Asking and declaring are semantically paired; commanding (or urging) and acquiescing are also semantically paired; while exclaiming needs no mate, but is complete in itself. These, then, are the five sentential functions: exclamation, interrogation, declaration, hortation, and acquiescence.

But there is a difficulty. If acquiescence is a semantic function on a par with the four others, why (it may be asked) have grammarians taken no account of it? The answer is that although the acquiescent function enters into a great deal of language *as a semantic component*, there are not many verbal expressions which stand out as having a predominantly acquiescent character and therefore it has not seemed worth while, from the grammarian's standpoint, to think of them as forming a separate class. A few locutions, such as "All right," "O.K.," etc. serve most of our needs in communicating an acquiescent attitude. Usually it is in the commands that the discriminations of meaning are made explicit—"Go!" "Come!" "Hurry!" "Listen!" etc.—while the yielding in each case can be expressed by a single acquiescent expression or even by a gesture. That is to say, when one acquiescent expression stands alone there is often little or nothing to differentiate it from other acquiescent expressions; the differentiation is furnished by the context.

Nevertheless, even isolated acquiescent expressions may be semantically differentiated from one another to some degree, although not so determinately as in the other types of sentence. There are differences of acquiescent tone, most marked perhaps as between secular and sacred modes of envisagement. The difference between "O.K., Joe!" and "Thy will be done!" is more than a matter of linguistic convention. Where the latter phrase is employed honestly and meaningfully its tone is reverent, and to speak with reverence is to ascribe some character of holiness to the object addressed. No such ascription is involved in a flippant or perfunctory or utilitarian colloquialism like "O.K."

The principal difference of acquiescent tone is found in the demarcation between sacred and secular. The Hebrew word *hineni,* usually translated "Here am I," is a Biblical expression of acquiescent reverence, addressed most frequently by man to God. Abraham, addressed twice by God—once to command the slaying of Isaac, and again to remit the command—replies both times *"Hineni"* (*Gen.* 22:1, 11). The boy Samuel hearing God's voice in the temple and mistaking it for Eli's, runs to the priest three times saying *"Hineni,"* and finally when he knows himself to be addressed by the Lord he amplifies his acquiescence into the full sentence, "Speak, for thy servant heareth" (*I Sam.,* 3:4–10). The Deutero-

Isaiah teaches the comforting doctrine that God, too, may say *Hineni* to his devout worshiper:

> Then shalt thou call, and the Lord shall answer; thou shalt cry, and he shall say *Hineni*.
>
> (*Isaiah*, 58:9)

The word *Amen*, taken over unchanged from Hebrew into English, functions similarly in one of its several uses. Although when used at the end of a petitionary prayer it becomes little more than a devout equivalent of "Please!" its sturdier meaning, found frequently in the Bible, is "So be it," "So let it be!"

(2) In expressive language, as distinguished from the artificial conventions of steno-language, the five sentential functions do not exist in perfect isolation: a given sentence, when examined, semantically, is likely to combine several of the functions at once. Sometimes one of them is sufficiently dominant to establish the sentence as of one type or another; but occasionally two or more functions are so nearly in balance, or let us say so thoroughly blended and interpenetrating, that we cannot be sure just how the sentence should be classified. A hybrid mixture of the exclamatory and interrogative functions is recognized in Spanish by the allowability of using an inverted exclamation mark at the beginning of a sentence and a question mark at the end: e.g., "*¡Después?*" (combining "Well, then!" and "What, then?"). In English we would have to indicate the secondary function either by tone of voice or twist of phrase. Rubén Darío's sentence, "*¡Conque aquel andariego había llegado tan lejos?*" might be rendered, "So the wanderer had got as far as that, had he?"[1]

Observe the different shades of meaning-tone in the following sentences, caused by the different degrees to which the interrogative and exclamatory functions are emphasized:

A. Have you hurt yourself?
B. Good God, are you hurt?!
C. Good God, you're hurt!

Sentence A, if uttered in a neutral tone of voice, might be taken simply as a request for information. Or less than that, it might be a phatic way of disposing of the situation ("This is what I am expected to say, so let's get it over with!") But assuming it to be a real question, its sentential function predominantly interrogative, one could plausibly argue that there are faint traces of each of the other four functions as well: of the imperative-hortatory, insofar as the speaker demands or invites an answer; of the declarative, insofar as he states by implication that he has received enough evidence to justify his question (a question which he would not have asked if there had been no ground whatever for it); of the acquiescent, insofar as his words represent a yielding up of sympathetic attention to the other person's predicament; and of the exclamatory, so far as the speaker's tone of voice may indicate an implicit attitude of shocked or dismayed beholding. Sentence C makes the shocked beholding explicit; it is predominantly exclamatory, although an analogous set of qualifications would have to be made. Sentence B, on the other hand, represents a more or less equal blend of the two functions. Here a conservative grammarian might try to preserve the grammatical amenities by breaking the sentence into two parts and labeling "Good God!" an exclamation and "Are you hurt?" a question. From a semantic standpoint, however, such *ex post facto* maneuvering conceals the real unity of the utterance, whose purport is not first to invoke the Deity and then as a distinct act of thought to pose a question, but to engage in one unified semantic act which is question and exclamation in one. The sentence is virtually the same whether we write it, "Good God, are you hurt?" or "Good God, are you hurt!" or "Good God! are you hurt?"

Whichever punctuative convention is chosen, the sentence would normally be taken to express a demand for information and an ejaculation of shocked concern all in one single mental thrust.

Another prominent borderland type of sentence is that which combines the exclamatory and declarative functions. Margaret Schlauch, whose philological writings have done much to liberalize contemporary grammatical theory, uses the term "presentative sentence" for a phrasal locution which, although it lacks a subject and predicate, strikes us as being virtually a complete and self-contained statement.[2] She offers an example from contemporary narrative prose:

He entered the room quietly. A moment of silence. "Surprise," he said.

No particular verb is understood, and yet we may vaguely feel something to be stated as well as exclaimed. Such presentative sentences, she insists, "cannot be classified according to traditional doctrines about subjects and predicates."

The French words *voilà* and *voici* offer corroborative evidence. "*Me voici*" is usually translated "Here I am!" and may be regarded as mainly declarative (e.g., when spoken in answer to the question, "Where are you?") or as mainly exclamatory, according to context. In a good many cases the French idiom seems to hold the two functions in fairly even balance. In Old French, however, the sentential functions were combined differently. Older forms of the phrase "*me voici*" combined the exclamatory and imperative functions instead of the exclamatory and declarative; while the declarative element found expression in the phrase, "*Es mi.*" The *voi-* of *voici* still retained much of its original character as an imperative of the verb "to see." When Ronsard writes,

"Approchez, voy me-cy," it would seem that the imperative element is still present to some degree, although either or both of the other two elements may be detected also.[3]

The fusion of these same three elements—the declarative, imperative, and exclamatory—is found again in Jesus' words to Mary from the Cross. It is told in the Gospel according to St. John (19:26) that when Jesus looked down and saw his mother and his favorite disciple standing side by side he said: Γύναι, ἴδε ὁ υἱός σου. Here the dominant emphasis is imperative, determined by ἴδε, imperative form of the verb meaning "to see," "to look at," "to behold." The King James Version retains that emphasis by translating the sentence, "Woman, behold thy son." It is inaccurate, however, insofar as it treats ὁ υἱός, which is nominative, as though it were the object of the verb. The use of the nominative indicates an element of exclamation in the sentence; and no doubt ἴδε in the period of the Gospel writers was employed idiomatically in much the same way as "Behold!" in traditional English and "Look!" in modern English. St. Jerome in his Latin Vulgate version went so far as to throw the main emphasis upon the exclamatory element by translating: *"Mulier, ecce filius tuus."* Then rather oddly, two recent English translators, a Protestant and a Catholic, Dr. Moffatt using the Greek text as his primary source and Mgr. Knox the Vulgate, both stress the lurking declarative element: "Woman, there is your son" (Moffatt); "Woman, this is thy son" (Knox). Martin Luther scrupulously managed to make two of the elements explicit at once: *"Weib, siehe, das ist dein Sohn";* but his very scrupulosity seems to have destroyed the exclamatory element almost entirely. The classical French translation, *"Mère, voici ton fils,"* would appear, in view of what was said in the last paragraph, to keep some flavor of the original Greek imperative meaning. Probably none of it survives for the modern French reader, however, to whom the French idiom has lost its connotation of command; and when Louis Segond made a new French version in 1880, his *"Femme, voilà ton fils,"* was no doubt written with the Latin *ecce* in mind and the Greek ἴδε forgotten.

The foregoing analysis provides a better understanding, I hope, of that character of expressive discourse which I introduced in Chapter IV under the name of *assertorial lightness*. A statement, as I conceive the matter, is *the declarative element in a semantic situation;* and only when a declarative element is present can there be significant assent. But we are prone to think of the declarative function crudely, as something you can turn completely on and off, as operating either in full force or not at all. This conception may be a useful fiction in technical thinking, but at best it represents a limiting case which I do not believe is ever quite attained in any real semantic situation into which a living person enters. An expressive statement tends to assert more lightly than a literal one (i.e., than a proposition) for the reason that it is never quite exclusively a statement, never quite purely declarative, but exercises declarative and other sentential functions in one fused togetherness.

In short, it is the full living situations, not the technical and abstract ones, that are of deepest concern to us; it is in and through them that a serious search for truth must be pursued. But how, in such situations, can we hope to find truth, if truth pertains to the declarative element, and if the declarative element is only a part, and sometimes a minor part, of the total meaning involved? The question is of utmost importance in several major fields. It concerns the very possibility of any religious, ethical, or metaphysical truth, as well as of a truth-function in art. In order to seek and be concerned with truth in these trans-literal fields we shall have to reëxamine, on a broader base than is usual, what truth and falsity most essentially mean.

WHAT IS TRUTH?

The age-old question, "What is truth?" can have either of two meanings. It may be an enquiry as to how truth is to be found, and by what criterion or criteria it is to be recognized. That is to say, it may be a shorthand form of the question: *By what test can a true statement be distinguished from a false one?* This question is of the utmost practical importance, to be sure, and men's attempts to answer it in broad terms have given rise to one of the perennial controversies of philosophy. But a controversy is meaningless unless the disputants are agreed as to what the controversy is *about*. We cannot either agree or disagree as to how truth is to be arrived at unless we can somehow agree on what the word "truth" means. The first question, therefore, implies a second, which is more fundamental: *What is the meaning of the words "true" and "false"?*

It is an axiom of sound definition that the *definiens* (the defining characteristic) should be neither too broad nor too narrow for the *definiendum* (the term to be defined). The trouble with most of the proposed definitions of truth is that they are too narrow. Instead of comprehending all the truth-possibilities inherent in different types of situation, they mask some particular theory about truth which the definer wishes to espouse. A naïve materialist, if challenged as to what he means by declaring his views of things to be "true," is almost sure to appeal to the criterion of *correspondence*. A belief, or statement, or theory is true, he will explain, when it corresponds with reality—with the facts—with what is actually the case. And no doubt his rough-and-ready faith serves him well enough in simple everyday situations. He hears a pattering noise on the roof and suspects that it must be raining: if on looking out the window he sees that it *is* raining, his notion is proved true; if he sees clear sky and dry pavement, it is proved false. The original judgment turns out to be true or false according as it tallies or does not tally with the existing situation.

Even in so simple a case, however, it becomes clear on reflection, that the correspondence theory of truth looks plausible only because it rests on certain unexamined assumptions which most people habitually share. In particular it implies that whereas evidence from hearing is fallible, evidence from sight is the final determinant of what does or does not exist. "Seeing is believing," the popular adage runs. And it is undoubtedly true that for most people the sense of sight is *more* reliable than the sense of hearing. But sight and touch in combination are more reliable still: in many cases we are disposed to verify the testimony of our eyes by stretching forth a hand. And what of blind persons who have no eyesight to rely on, but whose touch and hearing, along perhaps with certain ill-defined extra-sensory powers of perception, are made more acute in compensation for their lack? A blind man would probably have listened more attentively to the pattering sound on the roof, and have discovered from its auditory quality alone the truth or falsity of his initial judgment that rain was falling. Or he might have confirmed his discovery by stepping out-of-doors and *feeling* the presence or absence of raindrops. Surely it becomes increasingly clear, as such possibilities are considered, that the problem of verification, even in a day-by-day situation, is not simply that of discovering a correspondence between one's idea of what is occurring and the occurrence itself. For what we call "the occurrence itself" is not the same for a blind man as for a man with eyesight; the experiential difference is glossed over by the use of an identical vocabulary. Nor is "the occurrence itself" experientially the same for an observer with artistically heightened sensibilities as for a dolt. That is to say, in a depth-situation the notion of truth as correspondence with reality begs the question; for he who is spiritually awake and he who is spiritually asleep, he who is whole and he who is defective, may apperceive reality in such divergent ways that a common yardstick for measuring the correspondence does not exist.

The demonstrable inadequacy of correspondence, then, as a test of truth is one of the reasons which have forced thinkers who are materialist by disposition and conviction to resort to the more carefully defined notions of meaning and truth which constitute the doctrine of semantic positivism, already discussed in Chapters III and IV and in the opening pages of the present chapter. I shall consider it now for the last time, in order to discover dialectically, by comparing positivistic with non-positivistic notions of truth, what the underlying meaning of truth is that they share. For significant disagreement is impossible unless the disputants are agreed as to what it is that they disagree about. An important clue to the meaning of "truth" in its broadest, most comprehensive sense can be discovered in just that area of common reference which the positivist and the anti-positivist share when they most actively disagree.

The positivist's idea of truth is, in effect, a streamlined version of the correspondence theory. Instead of appealing as the naïve materialist does to "reality" as something completely given and knowable in itself, the positivist appeals to the ultimate validity of a certain *method:* i.e., he asserts that certain ways of *conceiving* the world and certain ways of *verifying* statements about it are intrinsically better than other ways of conceiving and verifying. Without delving into the intricacies of positivist logic, still less into the minutiae of disagreement among various positivists, I am content to stand by the rough identification of positivism which I have

already made. The concepts which it employs are steno-con-
cepts; the statements which it undertakes to validate are
propositions, which is to say steno-statements, not depth
statements; and the method of validation is by *public verification*—which is to say, tentatively, verification by the
sharable experience of "normal observers," repeatable under
specifiable conditions, and capable of being discriminated
with an accuracy which approaches the mathematical as a
given type of investigation becomes increasingly "scientific."
In practice, at a more advanced stage of any science, the
appeal to normal observers is less emphasized, and the concept of verification becomes more and more determined by
the nature of the instruments employed, and by the special
kind of observations which those instruments make possible.
Of course there is still the latent assumption that normal observers, if trained to look accurately through a telescope or
spectroscope for instance, could see there the same immediate datum that an astro-physicist would see. The same blob
of light, the same spectrum of colors would be there for all
who properly look. But the important question for astronomical science is what the light or the colors indicate as to the
nature of the physical universe, and the full verification of
any hypothesis requires not only trained observation but
highly trained technical computation and understanding as
well. All of this is involved in the positivist's criterion of what
is "true" as opposed to what is "false." His is a techno-empirical criterion of truth; a philosophy of the laboratory.

But suppose now that the techno-empirical criterion is
challenged. Suppose an anti-positivist were to argue: "Yes,
I believe in God and in Satan as objectively real forces in the
total nature of things. And when I say I believe in them I
mean, of course, that I believe my belief to be *true*. The
reason why I believe it to be true is that the evidences of
repeated depth-experiences testify (to me) strongly in its

favor. I am quite aware (I am not a complete fool, if you please) that to verify the existence of these ultimate Entities by your laboratory techniques is forever impossible. I say 'forever' with perfect confidence: the impossibility is a semantic one; for the *kind* of experience on which I base my belief in God and in Satan and the *kind* of experience which is implied by the term 'scientific verification' are radically different. They are not incompatible, and since depth experience is as flexible as the power of imaginative self-renewal can make it, there may be interesting areas of overlapping. But the main foci of attention are very different, and the validation of a religious truth must be by other procedures, and through the medium of other concepts, than those which you rightly insist on as demanded by science."

What is a positivist to reply when challenged by such an argument as this? He cannot appeal to "correspondence with reality," for the question what reality is, is one guise of the very problem at issue. He cannot appeal to any test of scientific verification, for the question whether that test is adequate to the findings of depth-experience is another aspect of the problem at issue. So he may try (as many positivists do) to excommunicate his opponent by declaring that a belief is "meaningless" unless its truth or falsity can be tested (under specifiable if not actual conditions) by scientific techniques. But how shall he counter-reply to one who refuses to accept such a limiting definition of "meaning" and of "truth"? Presumably he is reduced to saying, "Well, that is what I mean by 'meaning' and 'truth'—and moreover it is what everyone *ought* to mean by them." In the last analysis the positivist, like everyone else, is forced to declare his basic principles as fundamental intellectual loyalties. His conception of truth and falsity rests at bottom on a postulate as to *the conditions under which it is right or wrong to give assent.* Every positivist, pushed to the extreme, must declare:

"We *ought to assent* only to such statements as agree with the facts of potentially public experience, so far as verifiable by methods of controlled experiment." Every anti-positivist, pushed to the extreme, must declare: "There are some statements, to which we *ought to assent,* in whole or in part, on some other basis than this." Positivist and anti-positivist agree, then, on the underlying definition of a true statement as one that ought to be assented to, and a false statement as one that ought not.

By the same type of dialectical analysis it can be shown that *any* intelligible theory of truth must rest at bottom upon a fundamental belief as to the basis on which it is right or wrong to give assent. The coherence theory of truth, which has occupied so prominent a place in post-Hegelian idealism, is sometimes taken as a theory of what truth *means.* Such an interpretation is inaccurate, or at any rate ambiguous. If the question were merely as to what the word "truth" means, there would be no ground other than custom and convenience for stipulating one meaning in preference to another. Most advocates of the coherence theory, when they speak of "the meaning of truth," employ the term "meaning" in a looser and more organic sense than that of stipulative definition. But it is better to keep a clear distinction between what the word "truth" means, and what a given school of philosophers accepts as the criterion for determining what is true and what is false. What the coherence theory affirms, roughly stated, is that a belief is true to just the extent that it is consistent with the entire body of other beliefs which are likewise held to be true. But when that criterion of truth is challenged, what is its sponsor to do? He usually begins by offering arguments to show that his theory of truth is more rational than any alternative theory, and that it makes possible a more rational view of the world. Suppose, however, a pragmatist to retort: "But that's just the trouble! Your theory is over-rational. You distort the real nature of the world by interpreting it in such rational terms as that. I say rather that a belief is true so far as it can successfully integrate *all* human interests and needs in the long run, not just the rational ones." How is the coherence philosopher to reply now? The two opponents cannot appeal to the evidence of "the real world" for a final settlement of their conflicting claims, because in disagreeing about the nature of truth they disagree also, to an extent, about what the nature of the real world truly is. What is left for each of them, then, but to fall back upon a declaration of primary intellectual loyalties? The coherence advocate may say: "I believe that we *ought to assent* only to such statements as are consistent with the entire body of statements to which we likewise assent." The pragmatist may rejoin: "I believe that we *ought to assent* only to those statements the acceptance of which will, in the long run, most successfully integrate *all* human interests and needs—the need for rational explanation included among them, but not given absolute priority." Again, as in the former case, they differ as to the acceptable criterion by which truth is to be distinguished from falsity, but they tacitly agree on the implicit definition that truth is that which ought, by one criterion or another, to be assented to.

One remaining criterion of truth should be considered in this connection—the intuitive: the principle that a belief is true so far as the believer, with his whole mind awake, receives an illumined conviction that it must be so. I am not now concerned with the question of where such illumined convictions come from. Whatever their source, there can be no doubt that human beings do receive them from time to time, and act upon them, sometimes with apparent success, sometimes not. There is, of course, the qualification, "with the whole mind awake," and we can never be sure how far this condition is fulfilled. Nor is the meaning of "success" always agreed on. Moreover, it could be maintained that an intuitive element is present in applying *any* criterion of truth: for, unless we proceed by mere rote and habit, we are to some degree guided by an illumined conviction that we must assent to just that kind of evidence. The intuitive assurance that our criterion and method are the right ones, and that we are rightly applying them to the present instance, is independent of the particular criterion and method which we use. Intuition is a silent partner in every intellectual enterprise. In this general and collaborative sense, as a *part* of the total criterion actually appealed to on any occasion, it is more fundamental than any of the rival ways of knowing; for whereas you can employ the intuitive criterion without employing any of the others—a risky yet a possible procedure—you cannot employ *them* without at the same time employing *it*. The philosophy known as intuitionism, however, makes a stronger claim than this: declaring that the deliverances of intuition should take precedence (in certain depth-areas at least, such as the religious and the moral) over the deliverances of other mental faculties and methods. And such a claim can be translated in the same way as those of the rival claimants. By the same dialectical analysis as has been pursued in the case of the other theories of truth, we discover that what the intuitionist declares, when pushed to the extreme, is: "We *ought to assent* only, or primarily, to those statements toward which, with our whole mind awake, we respond with an illumined conviction of their rightness."[4]

Thus we have discovered, I think, our answer to the problem posed earlier in the chapter: What can truth and falsity mean when applied not to propositions but to expressive statements, where not only the declarative but also, in close fusion with it, one or more of the other sentential functions are operative? The answer is only a beginning, of course; no formula will suffice; but the direction which a semantics of expressive statement must take is clear. In such depth-interests as those of religion, philosophy, and art, the question of truth and falsity is neither as precise and definite as in matters amenable to scientific treatment, nor yet is it entirely subjective. To affirm the truth of God's existence, or the truth of the Golden Rule, is not to affirm a scientific fact, but neither is it simply to exude an emotion, nor is it simply to report that I happen to like the ideas involved. It is to affirm that I *ought* to assent to them—and by implication that others ought to assent to them—regardless of how actively any of us happens to be assenting at the present moment. A judgment of truth is not simply a description of what I think and feel; it involves, as William James has said, a "moral risk"; it dares to speak of what transcends the here and now. Different philosophies represent different characteristic policies of here-and-now transcendence, and the manner of them is an expression of certain fundamental intellectual loyalties that the individual philosopher adopts. Any real consideration of truth, especially in a depth-situation, is inseparable from an expression and development of such loyalties.

Let us now see what light the foregoing analysis may perhaps throw upon the vexed questions of religious and poetic truth. Our method will continue to be semantical; which is to say, our attention will be directed primarily to the nature of religious and of poetical *statement*, as a potential vehicle for truth of an appropriate kind.

STATEMENT AND TRUTH IN RELIGION

The most fundamental and comprehensive statement within the religious domain is naturally the statement, "God exists." What are the principal kinds of sentential functioning here? To begin with, a declarative element is present—some kind of declaration that the universe is of one sort rather than of another. A religious man unversed in theological formulation may be unable to specify in much detail what sort of a universe his belief implies. His belief will doubtless be in soft rather than sharp focus, and such definiteness as it achieves may proceed partly from the ceremonial acts in which he takes part, partly from the definiteness of his ethical attitudes so far as they are religiously grounded, and partly from the familiar traditional language in which his belief is likely to be dressed. Notwithstanding these qualifications, however, a religious man assents to one general kind of universe rather than another; and such assent represents the declarative element in his belief.

What, more specifically, is this general kind of universe to which a religious as distinguished from a non-religious man assents? In view of the wide diversity of beliefs that have sometimes gone under the name of religion any definite answer to that question might appear arbitrary. Nevertheless an answer is necessary if we want to talk about religion without getting lost in vapors. A word that can mean anything means nothing. To speak of the religion of materialism, or the religion of money-getting, or (as a publicized cult in western America has lately done) of "the sexual orgasm as a religious experience" is an irresponsible misuse of language. Other instances lie in the borderland of doubt: may we properly speak of "the religion of marxism"—"of fascism"—"of capitalism"—"of democracy"? I think we should avoid such latitudinarian ascription, although it can be more seriously defended in these than in the previous cases. If individual marxists, or fascists, or capitalists, or democrats are religious, it is not by reason of their political or economic beliefs but because of the nature of their belief about, and their appropriate response to, the kind of universe in which they and their fellows find themselves. To be religious is to believe in and respond to a spiritually responsive universe—of whatever sort. He who ignores the spiritually responsive aspects of himself and his world is non-religious; and he who opposes their recognition by any exercise of power or mockery is irreligious.

Such a definition presupposes a common understanding of the term "spiritually responsive." How shall that in turn be defined? Although no possible definition can be adequate to the largeness of the subject, there is one indispensable aspect which I believe should be emphasized. To borrow the language of Martin Buber: the religious man is he who enters at some point or other into an *I-thou* relationship with the universe.[5] A significant *I-thou* relationship is never unilateral. Even on the human scale, in man-to-man relationships this is true. A unilateral relationship, where one merely speaks and not listens, reduces him on the receiving end from the status of a person to the status of a thing: the use of the second person singular becomes either an empty grammatical convention or a refined technique of control. An *I-thou* relationship implies confrontational mutuality. To honestly address another as "thou" I must be ready to let him be an "I" in his own right; which is to say, I become a "thou" in his presence. The religious attitude involves, most essentially of all, a readiness to become a "thou," a responsive listener in the presence of That which transcends man.

To become a "thou" is to function acquiescently; to speak "thou" is to use language in its acquiescent aspect. The statement, "God exists," when it is a depth-statement and not merely the conclusion of a metaphysical syllogism, can be translated "Thou art God"; and therein it functions acquiescently to the highest degree of any statement that can be made. The statement "God exists" is therefore necessarily true when experienced as a depth-statement, for the fullness of acquiescence which the worshiper gives to it is at the same time a fullness of assent to the declarative element in the situation. The basic definition of truth, arrived at earlier, as "that which ought to be assented to," is here transcended: in the fullness of a religious depth-experience the justification of the assenting is self-evident; the "ought" is transcended in the "is." And the "is" is not an abstract copula; not the neuter "is" of "There is an Empire State Building." It is an unqualified synthesis of "I am" and "Thou art": I am *because* Thou art: because Thou art the primordial "I am" in whose presence I accept the role of a "thou."

And such acceptance is prayer. Essential prayer is not a requesting but a communing, and above all a listening and a readiness to respond. It is a carrying of the I-thou relation beyond the everyday sphere of man-to-man. Every occurrence has the power of "speaking" to me, of penetrating the armor of familiarity, and stirring the soul to new sensibility and response. Professor Buber (to whom of course any such metagrammar as this is fundamentally indebted) has called such occurrences "signs of address." They are not to be thought of as supernatural, i.e., as violating the natural order of physical events; they represent another *dimension* of reality—constantly there, but ordinarily (in our workaday world) ignored. "The waves of the aether roar on always, but for most of the time we have turned off our receivers." The actuality of the "speaking" depends upon the degree to which the power of inward listening is developed.

Who, then, speaks? For if we take seriously the metaphor of being spoken to—and Buber uses his metaphors not as pleasant fictions but as sharp unexpected perspectives upon reality—then we can hardly avoid the question, Who? And a reader sympathetic to religious tradition may be tempted to think that here is a riddle to which the familiar magician's rabbit of an answer is about to be brought forth; that the word "God" can surely be introduced here if anywhere. But easy platitudes are easy evasions, and Buber warns repeatedly against yielding to them. What can we know of that-which-or-him-who gives us the signs? "Only what we ex-perientially discover from time to time from the signs them-selves. If we name the speaker of this speech God, then it is always the God of a moment, a moment God." The situation is loosely analogous to that of understanding a poem: where all we know of the poet, the *I* who speaks to us, is the actual speaking that is the poem. No external biographical facts can be substituted for this pure understanding. The utter-ances that profoundly address us in *King Lear* are unaffected by theories about their author's habitat, condition, and name. Nevertheless when we read other poems by the same poet with the same confrontational integrity, "their subjects com-bine in all their multiplicity, completing and confirming one another, to form one polyphony of the person's existence." In the same way the various *I-thou* relations into which we enter at the heightened moments of experience bear testi-mony to the Other *I* which is always there ready to speak, inviting us to listen. Thus "out of the moment gods there arises for us with a single identity the Lord of the voice, the One."

But there is a difficulty. Depth experiences are not perma-nent. The actual experience of an *I-thou* relationship be-tween myself and That in Whose Presence I am most fully I when I am most yieldingly a "thou," is an experience which comes intermittently, perhaps rarely, perhaps only weakly and doubtfully, and in some persons perhaps not at all. What is the status of God at times when his *I-Thouhood* eludes the concretion of experience? What is his status for persons who believe in him without having known-by-acquaintance the transcendental *I-Thou* relationship? If God is God, he must be permanent and universal. Yes, but so far as finite man's experience is the testing-ground, God's permanence and uni-versality are potential, not actual. God is (let us say) the

permanent possibility of each creature's entering into a transcendental *I-thou* relationship. To declare that God exists is
to declare that there *is* such a permanent possibility, and
that there is no higher standard of true-vs.-false by which
that transcendental *I-thou* experience, when it comes, may
be declared illusory.

So much is the declarative element in the depth-statement
"God exists," or "There is a God." But the depth-statement
has depth-truth only if it functions acquiescently too: i.e.,
only if it represents the speaker's putting himself into a better state of readiness to become the "thou" in such a relationship. Unless the acquiescent element is present along
with the declarative—the sacrament along with the faith—
the statement lacks a specifically religious character; it is
then no more than an important metaphysical hypothesis.

The other three sentential functions also play certain roles.
The acquiescence which a religious judgment involves and
invites is a *reverent* acquiescence; and reverence comprises
both awe and devotion as its components. Now awe, in the
most adequate sense of the word, is a feeling appropriate to
the presence of Mystery; and Mystery is no puzzling riddle
with a solution to be published in next Sunday's supplement,
it is a That which intrinsically and majestically transcends
the possibility of finite comprehension. We can feel awe without the addition of devotion which makes reverence: as
when confronted by an extraordinary cataclysm of nature,
or when witnessing a profound human tragedy. We exclaim,
and our exclamation sounds the note of deep questioning—
to which, however, we do not expect any reply. Perhaps
every serious statement is thus framed in the irony of its own
finitude; in any case a religious statement displays such ambivalence most of all. When we try to represent with a finite
utterance the infinitude of depth-experiences, actual and potential, which constitute God's nature so far as our under-

standings can grasp it, we are sinking a pebble of declaration into an ocean of unanswered and even unaskable query.

In such an ambience of the unknowable it takes sturdiness to maintain a depth-position. "It is evidently so" and "I yield to its being so" require "It shall be so" as their ally. Thus there is an imperative element, too, in a religious judgment. William James was essentially right, although his word "pragmatism" has given rise to misconceptions.[6] There is a pragmatic element in religious truth, but it is only one element among others, and has nothing to do with utility or rewards. It might be better described as *voluntaristic* (as James has sometimes done)—implying not that we may believe whatever we wish to, but that when the note of authentic conviction is rung in the mind and conscience, or for that matter when we are preparing for the possibility of its being rung—a firm response is required, not a lackadaisical one. To declare a religious statement true is at once to declare something about the ultimate character of the universe, to declare that certain ways of responding to such a universe are more appropriate than other ways, and (if it is an honest declaration) to take a step or two toward making or preparing for such a response.

STATEMENT AND TRUTH IN POETRY

A semantics of poetry must allow for the double fact that poems do say something, do make statements of a sort, and yet that they do not make statements in the same way, nor of quite the same kind, as a literal use of language does. Mr. I. A. Richards, for all his excellence as a practical critic, has been so active in stressing the second of these propositions that he has inadvertently maneuvered himself into denying the truth of the first. His doctrine of the "pseudo-statement," announced over a quarter of a century ago in *Science and Poetry*,[7] was the outcome of his denial. The wide influence which that clever and perverse little book has had upon subsequent critical theory makes it a fair target, even though I suspect that if Dr. Richards were to rewrite it today, he would choose his vocabulary and formulate his argument more guardedly.

Richards rightly perceives that "statement" and "truth" are interrelated concepts: that a question of true-vs.-false can be made only where a statement is involved. His error lies in the over-sharpness of his distinction between what is a statement and what is not; hence a corresponding over-sharpness between types of situation where questions of true-or-false can be raised and types of situation where they cannot. By *statement* he means plainly "scientific statement, where truth is ultimately a matter of verification as this is understood in the laboratory"; by *pseudo-statement* he means an apparent statement where "truth" (his use of quotation marks might be translated *pseudo-truth*) is "entirely governed by its effects upon our feelings and attitudes." Note the absolutism of that adverb! A pseudo-statement is "true," he continues, again placing his derogatory quotation marks, "if it suits and serves some attitude or links together attitudes which on other grounds are desirable." And he appends a note of regret that the same word "truth" should be so widely used for two such opposed meanings.

The grounds on which I disagree with Mr. Richards' view are presumably clear from what has been said in the foregoing pages. The position which I have been defending is that the steno-language of science should be regarded as a *limiting case* of expressive language with its manifold possibilities; and that steno-statements, therefore, which is to say propositions (what Richards misleadingly calls simply "statements") are limiting cases of expressive statements (Richards' name for which, or for the expressive element in which, is "pseudo-statement"); and that scientific truth ("verification as this is understood in the laboratory") is a limiting case of truth in general—a special type of what ought to be intellectually assented to. Let us examine some poetic specimens in the light of this disagreement.

First example. To follow Richards in calling Blake's line, "O Rose, thou art sick!" a pseudo-statement on which the question of truth or falsity has no bearing whatever, is to do scant justice to the depth and seriousness, along with the indispensable concreteness, of Blake's metaphysics. Here, epitomized in the rose, is an implicit judgment about the sickness of the created world. Yet the line does not represent a statement in the full sense, as a double test will demonstrate. If we try a literal translation—"That rose is in poor health"—the absurdity is manifest. If we undertake a prose explication of the symbolism we can hardly stop short of trying to expound Blake's entire philosophy. Such an exposition always sidesteps the single direct task of facing up to the meaning of the utterance itself. No two critical expositions of Blake's philosophy are in anything like full agreement; the differences, however, concern strategies of analysis, and do not preclude a substantial consensus regarding an exemplary line such as the one here in question. For the utterance, "O Rose, thou art sick!" appeals to our intellectual and emotive responsiveness at once; and as the two forms of response are not operating separately but are involved together in a single experiential fusion, so (semantically considered) the declarative and exclamatory elements in the sentence are likewise inseparable, scarcely even distinguishable.

Second example. Byron's cry, "The isles of Greece! the isles of Greece!" is grammatically not a statement at all. In its full poetic impact, however, the line has—not a fully assertorial character, to be sure, yet a something implicit that invites assent. In soft focus the exclamation lightly adumbrates a value: we know, at least in a vague way, that the poet finds beauty and a compelling significance in the idea of the Isles of Greece; and this is confirmed by the next line—"Where burning Sappho loved and sung"—which strengthens and further articulates the meaning foreshadowed by the exclamation. Of course the poetic statement in this second line is not merely a historical fact about Sappho; that fact is caught up and transmuted by the special idiom of the second line and by the juxtaposition of the second line with the first. (For simplicity's sake I am ignoring the rest of the poem.) What the resultant poetic statement *is* cannot be translated into a literal statement without gross distortion; but a reader can feel its unobtrusive presence.

Third example. A simpler explanation for the assertorial lightness of poetic statements is the element of playfulness that enters into them. Such might be said, with reason, about the "canary" illustration from Carl Rakosi in Chapter IV. Let us look at a case where the playfulness is extreme—a nonsense verse from the Carolyn Wells anthology:

> We're all in the dumps
> And diamonds are trumps;
> The kittens are gone to St. Paul's.
> The babies are bit,
> The moon's in a fit,
> And the houses are built without walls.

Here are six lines, each of which makes a syntactical statement. Every individual statement, except possibly the first, is sheer fantasy; their crazy-quilt juxtaposition is evidence that the writer does not intend really to assert them but merely to present them for playful momentary contemplation. The assertive weight of "The kittens are gone to St. Paul's" and of "The moon's in a fit" is zero. They are pure examples of what Richards calls pseudo-statement. Each of these component sentences is in clear focus, however: we know pretty unmistakably what it is saying, and we recognize that what it says is indubitably fantastic. Each single statement is clear-cut but carries no assertorial weight whatever.[8]

Does the verse as a whole say anything? Is there a total statement? I think there is. Something is vaguely adumbrated, of which a rough paraphrase might be: "Everything's gone plumb crazy," or "Everything's shot to hell." The total statement is in soft focus, as contrasted with the clear focus of the component statements; but its assertive weight is not, like theirs, zero. The component statements, or rather pseudo-statements, are purely presentative: they offer ideas for contemplation but their look of crisp assertion is illusory. What the total statement expresses is not so much an idea as a vague mood, but it affirms the perspectival relevance and truth of that mood with a certain amount—not very much—of assertive strength.

Fourth example. Getting back to something more serious, reconsider the much discussed pair of lines that terminates Keats' *Ode to a Grecian Urn:*

> Beauty is truth, truth beauty,—that is all
> Ye know on earth, and all ye need to know.

Here the situation is more complex. The statement which the couplet affirms is one of many component statements which make up the *Ode,* but its role is a special one, for its logical appearance combined with its position at the end of the poem gives it an air of authority, as though epitomizing the total statement which the poem as a whole is making. Many readers have in fact taken it as Keats' summary of what he meant to say. But Keats said what he meant to say in the poem as a whole, not in an isolable two lines of it. No doubt these two lines come somewhat closer to epitomizing the poem's total statement than any of the other component statements do, but an epitome is an abstraction at best, and the meaning of the poem is concrete, declared in and through the plenitude of images and cadences, and in no other way.

Another thing to note is that Keats puts the couplet in quotation marks: the Grecian urn is their speaker. Momentarily, then, Keats is a dramatist; he is letting his protagonist —the urn—speak for itself. The statement that beauty and truth are identical will not hold up under logical scrutiny; still less will the statement that follows it. But taken as a half-declarative half-exclamatory utterance which the urn might be imagined to make, the disputed statements seem apt enough. Their truth is a truth in context. And so when Coleridge speaks of "the willing suspension of disbelief" as prerequisite to the proper reading of poetry, he is saying, in effect, that we should be willing to take up residence lightly in whatever poetic situation is offered—willing to accept the partial truth of the insights which are crystallized by a given poetic mood without insisting that their truth must extend indefinitely into all other moods and contexts.

Fifth example. My last specimen illustrating assertorial lightness in poetry is drawn from Eliot's *Ash Wednesday:*

> Redeem
> The unread vision in the higher dream
> While jewelled unicorns draw by the gilded hearse.

In his essay on Dante Mr. Eliot says of the pageantry of the *Paradiso* that it "belongs to the world of what I call the *high dream,* and the modern world seems capable only of the *low dream.*" We dream whether we like it or not, and all knowledge, whether in poetry or out of it, involves suspension of disbelief. In our low dreams, our everyday states of conscious-

ness, it is simple credulity. To combat simple credulity by
logical examination and appeal to public evidence is an act
of intellectual virtue, but we do not thereby leave off dreaming; we are merely credulous on a new level of sophistication,
credulously ready to accept sophistication as truth. In the
low dream we wear a mask without realizing it, in the high
dream we put on a mask with stylized grace. The virtue of a
poem consists in expressing, promoting, and communicating
some phase of the high dream.

Since truth, as I have argued, is "that which ought, by
one criterion or another, to be assented to," we can now see,
I think, the meaning that can be attached to "poetic truth."
A poetic utterance invites our imaginative assent, which is
to say our depth assent, to some degree or other and in some
context or other. So far as we yield such assent joyfully and
gain insight in so doing, there is a real and valid sense in
which we can speak of "poetic truth." Even though an individual statement in a poem would be false if taken out of
context (as is surely the case with Eliot's "jewelled unicorn"
line and with Keats' "all ye need to know"), the relevant
question is, How true is it within that context? And let us
not delude ourselves with the hope that there are truths independent of any context whatever. When we think that,
and act on it, we merely become blind to the contextual
limitations that condition every judgment and every insight;
we fall, so to speak, into a dream within a dream. The poet
stakes out his context, the "world" of his poem, with his
imagination audaciously alive and responsive; that is the way
toward the regaining of Terrestrial Paradise. Most of us most
of the time, with imaginations either stale or running riot,
slip into some form of the lower dream, thereby constantly
reënacting Adam's fall. The ground-bass of poetic truth is
the truth, contextual but real, of man's possible redemption
through the fullest imaginative response.

FOURTEEN

The Cosmic Fire

For in that hour, for on that day
The Universe shall burn like hay,
As Sibyl and St. David say.

ALAN PORTER, "The Transit of Joy"[1]

FIRE IS AN archetypal symbol of wide-ranging importance, owing no doubt to its peculiar combination of properties. Several of those properties, and their
tendencies toward symbolism, are indicated in the opening
lines of a Vedic hymn addressed to Agni, Hindu divinity of
fire:

> By Agni is Agni kindled,
> The sage, house-master, youthful god,
> Oblation-bearing, spoon-mouthed one.[2]

Because fire is the most active, most rapidly changing of
any of nature's elements, it naturally becomes conceived as
something perpetually youthful, ever springing into existence anew, ever being extinguished and rekindled. Thus, by
mythopoeic logic, it is a principle of life; and the conclusion
appears to be confirmed by the vitalizing effect of warmth
upon the bodily functions. The sun sends his fire through the
sparkling air to cause germination and growth; the sun therefore, and the fire that is in him, may plausibly be regarded
as the cause and ground of natural existence. Fire's causal
powers become even more evident as the art of cooking is
discovered.

303

Complementary to the phenomenon of constant change is the permanence of fire as represented in nature by the ever reliable sun, and in ceremony by the hearth-fire, the center and symbol of family life, and the altar-fire, the center and symbol of cult life. Frazer explains such ceremonies as survivals from a time when the art of making fire was unknown and its preservation, when a flame had been captured, was of the greatest practical utility. Any such theory of origins is largely speculative, however, and the anthropological evidence cuts both ways. If in some tribes it is the custom to distribute fire from the central altar to individual homes (which might seem to favor Frazer's view), in others, such as the Thonga tribe of South Africa, it is taboo to take embers from the perpetual fire that burns in the hut of the top chieftain, and moreover the hut itself and the chieftain's wife are taboo.[3] Although the presence of taboo does not disprove a utilitarian origin (since the taboo might have arisen after the invention of the fire-drill had made the utility no longer important), yet on the other hand the custom of distribution is not sufficient to prove it. In any case a theory of origins rarely does much toward explaining the later ceremonial character of an action. If now we attend to the ideal of fire in its character as a threshold symbol, *at once pointing to and partaking of* the cosmic force that flows through all things, the ceremonial phenomena become understandable. Fire is life: there must be continuity of tribal life both in time and in space: perpetuation of the sacred flame symbolizes and promotes the one, distribution of it to the households of the community symbolizes and promotes the other. I say "symbolize *and* promote" to recall the paradox, reasonable to the mythopoeic mind, that fire is ontologically one (particular fires being portions of the all-pervading fire) and that the ceremonies somehow ensure its being so.

Agni, kindled in many places, is but fire;
One the all-pervading Sun;
One the Dawn, spreading her light over the earth.
All that exists is One, whence is produced the whole world.

The problem of One-or-Many was destined to become the central philosophical problem in India, and a very important one in Greece; in both countries fire and water, because of their fluid natures, were variously used as symbols of the inevitable paradox.

In pre-Soviet Russia a peasant when marrying would carry fire to his new abode and deposit it, saying: "Welcome, grandfather, to the new home!"[4] In India, too, fire is the hearth-god ("housemaster") as well as the sky-god; and the Hindu scriptures speak of Fire's three dwellings—in the sun, in the lightning of the middle air, and on the sacred hearth. The fire, like the altar, is customarily a place of sacrifice, and fire becomes "spoon-mouthed" by adaptation to the ladle from which the Brahmin priest would pour the *ghee,* the specially clarified butter used as an offering. Butter makes the flames sizzle and soar: manifestly they are bearing the oblation upward to the gods for whom it is intended. Thus Hindu Agni was not only a god in his own right; he was also a messenger to the other gods.

> Through thee, who art their mouth, the holy deathless gods
> Devour the offering which we sacrifice to them.

It is a short step from the idea of messenger to the idea of intercessor, and in such a verse as the following we see a spiritual and penitential attitude emerging out of the magical:

O Agni, find mercy for us with Varuna.
Thou who knowest Varuna, O Agni,
Appease us from the god's fierce indignation.

Why, in the verse originally quoted, is Agni called "sage"?
The reason is not obscure when we consider that fire, especially in the shape of the sun or a torch, illumines the world
and puts darkness to flight. Light stands for wisdom, darkness for ignorance: the symbolism is familiar and the implicit
analogy is apt. The action of light is to make known visually;
and this is taken, both in East and West, as a threshold symbol for that inward illumination which transcends visual discrimination.

Finally, there are many indications in the *Veda* that Agni
has an ethical character. Some ethical interest, to be sure, is
involved in certain of the attributes already mentioned. As
god of the hearth, as man's intercessor with the watchful
gods of the sky, and as the light which chases away darkness
(including the spiritual darkness of a confused and sluggish
soul) Agni arouses feelings of gratitude and loyalty: he becomes, however haltingly, a god of what should be, not only
of what is. Two other aspects of fire contribute to an ethical
idea of it. Fire can cause burning pain and destruction; it
can also refine and purify. That is to say, it can be infernal or
purgatorial. In its infernal character fire's action is retributive:

May Agni, rich in wealth with flame most scorching,
Agni the sharp-toothed one, consume those people
Who break the laws which Varuna has established,
The holy laws of ever-watchful Mitra.

In its role as cleanser and refiner, on the other hand, fire's
action is redemptive. By burning away the dross it releases
what is pure for new life. A passage from Hebrew prophetic

literature yields a comparison—where Malachi, prophesying the Messiah, combines the fire image with a homelier one which conduces to the same tenor:

But who can endure the day of his coming, and who can stand when he appears?
For he is like a refiner's fire and like fuller's soap; he will sit as a refiner and purifier of silver, and he will purify the sons of Levi and refine them like gold and silver, till they present right offerings to the Lord.

(Malachi, 3:2–3)[5]

The Baptism "in the Holy Spirit and in fire" which John the Baptist announces as an attribute of Christ is a further development of the Christian idea that man can be regenerated only when his sin has been burned away.

The purpose of these introductory paragraphs has been to review the physical characteristics of fire on which its symbolic roles chiefly depend. Of course the full religious depth-meaning which the fire symbol has when operating with maximum semantic intensity transcends the particular implications of the various natural attributes. The meanings of a symbol grow as it is wrenched to new uses. The miracle of Pentecost, when the tongues of fire (literally, "tongues like flames") descended upon the heads of the eleven apostles, filling them with the Holy Spirit, "so that they began to say in foreign languages whatever the Spirit prompted them to utter,"[6] offers an instance of fire as a cleansing, redemptive agent no doubt, but a receptive reader cannot help feeling that its meaning and its mystery recede into distances that our one-two-three intelligences cannot fathom. We cannot dispense with symbols altogether, but we can lessen their hold on us, and release our attention for the larger meanings which they liminally represent, by learning the art of exchanging one depth-symbol for another as the context and

the symbolic traditions in a given case may demand. This is
no mere stipulative and pragmatic exchange, as in substitut-
ing "k" for "a certain constant number" in algebra; the initia-
tive does not lie with us, but is given by the context. We
cannot say that God, Diós, Jahveh, Zeus, Brahma, the Cosmic
Fire, Tao, Om, and other parallel symbols all "mean the same
thing"; for each of them carries a wealth of probed and inherited associations that give it an organic independence of
each other one. To make easy identifications is to destroy the
symbol's concrete, living meaning, and to leave only an abstract question-mark for agnostics to brandish in triumph.
No, the exchanging of which I speak must be done cautiously
and reverently; we are guided by analogies, not identities;
and we must have an eye for cultural boundaries. That ultimate Cosmic Ground which the fire symbol expresses in one
set of perspectives, is expressed in others by symbols drawn
from the experience of air, breath, water, earth, the vineyard,
magical power, music, dance, a revolving wheel, and so on.

ATMA-BRAHMA

In the *Upanishads* the personified fire-god of the Vedas is
no longer emphasized; a cosmological concept of fire has
taken its place. Fire is declared to be the first-born of the
elements:

In the beginning, my son, there was only That Which Is, one
only, without a second . . . It thought: "May I be many, may I
grow forth!" It sent forth fire.

That the order of birth is insisted on in a symbolic not a literal sense becomes clear when the first passage is taken
together with a second from the same Upanishad:

The root of the body is in food, the root of food is in water, the
root of water is in fire, the root of fire is in the True.

What both passages evidently mean can perhaps be formulated best in the language of Neoplatonism: that fire is the first emanation of the Uncreated.

Not only is fire conceived in Hinduism as the primary substance—i.e., as the indispensable precondition of all other substances; it is also commingled with all others to different degrees. It is especially present, so one passage declares, in gold, in the sparkling upper air, in the right hand of a holy Brahmin, in pure water, and in the sacred *kusa* grass. Its action makes possible the digestive as well as the reproductive powers. And its most subtle component develops into speech. What are we to make of this curious idea? I would suppose that the ancient *guru* who taught the doctrine probably intended by "speech" very nearly what Heraclitus intends by "logos"; not simply words, but more importantly the meanings which words and speech carry. A people without yet a developed philosophical language is trying to express the mystery that a thing, and more especially a person, can not only *be* but also *mean*. What better symbol for the purpose than fire, whose tongues lick all other substances, commingle with them, and (in the form of heat) give them life and so make them what they are—even as their meanings also and more essentially do?

But most characteristic of all in the *Upanishads* is the use of fire imagery as a way of approaching the central doctrine and mystery of Brahman:

> This is the truth. As from a blazing fire there fly forth thousands of sparks, like unto fire in substance, so are the various beings brought forth from the Imperishable, my friend, and return thither also.
>
> (*Mundaka-Upanishad*, 2. 1. 1)

> As a spider comes out of its thread, or as small sparks come forth from fire, thus do all senses, all worlds, all gods, all beings,

come forth from that Self. The real name and teaching of the Self [its "upanishad"] is *the True of the True.*

(*Brihad-Aranyaka Upanishad,* 2. 1. 20)

I shall have something further to say about this symbolism of the sparks in relation to the central fire when I come in a few paragraphs to the concept "atman." First, however, let us examine, with such semantic care as an alien standpoint allows, the concept of *brahma* or *brahman.*

It would appear (although certainty in the matter is beyond our reach) that brahma originally meant something like what the Melanesians call *mana,* the magical potency in things—felt on the one hand as an awful presence, susceptible on the other of magical control and exploitation provided only that the proper words and ceremonies could be found. Indeed, it may have been that *brahma* itself was in origin such a magical word. This is the theory of the Vedic scholar Hillebrandt, who believes that the word grew from the same Indo-European root as the Irish *bricht* ("magical spell") and the Norwegian *bragr* ("the art of runic poetry"); and that it was therefore originally a ceremonial word, with a coercive as well as a semantic function, not only denoting a power in the world but also imbued with that same power and requiring to be uttered for the success of a magical act.[7] Another Vedic scholar, Haug, declares further of *brahma* that "in the *Rigveda* it denotes a mysterious power which can be called forth by various ceremonies," and that it may be defined for the Vedic age as "the magical force which is derived from the orderly coöperation of the hymns, the chants, and the sacrificial gifts." Friedrich Max Müller is in virtual agreement, declaring that *brahman* (the neuter, impersonal form of the word) meant originally "mysterious power of creation in things," perhaps with an added connotation of will. Some holdover from that early idea of magical power is doubtless retained in the classical descriptions of Brahma as red in color (suggestive of blood), as having four arms (symbolizing multiple potencies), and as having created the other gods.

However, many traditional representations of Brahma give him not only four arms but four eyes and eight ears as well. He represents not only power but knowledge. And this aspect of him is the germ from which the high metaphysical concept in the Vedanta philosophy evolves. Brahman in the *Upanishads* is Pure Consciousness, free from attributes and actions, because free from attachments. He is no longer merely the magical power of the other gods and lesser beings, but their very selfhood. He or It (the pronoun is misleading in either case) is the sole reality; all finite phenomena and all definable concepts are but appearances, fragmentary manifestations of That which is beyond appearance. All attempts to say what Brahman is—"It is like a flash of lightning; It is like a wink of the eye"—are inadequate; at best they are stages in the learner's gradual realization that Brahman must ever be sought but cannot be spoken. The Hindu *guru* would invite his pupil to say what Brahman is like, then would counter each proposal with a gentle *"neti neti"*—"not just that, not just that."

The situation would be hopeless and frustrating if the *neti neti* doctrine were the last word. Actually it is rather a warning against trying to grasp Brahman in wrong ways. You cannot grasp the selfhood of Brahman by outward assault, but only by inward rediscovery. Knowing without illusion or desire one's own deepest self, one's *atman,* is the way to a knowledge of Brahman, for fundamentally Atman and Brahman are one. The formula of identification, *"Atman is Brahman,"* is the keystone of Hindu metaphysics. Like all formulas it offers the danger of specious intelligibility through mere familiarity of repetition. A declaration that Atman and Brahman are the same is an empty tautology unless we start out with some initial reason to suppose they might be different. Perhaps in the end a point of view may be attained from which the difference is overcome, but at that point there will no longer be any need of words. The situation at the beginning requires proper discrimination. We can say, to be sure, that the *atman* is in the first instance the individual soul, and that *brahman* is the world soul, and that it is the identification of these, the particular with the universal, that is insisted on. That is probably the best way of formulating the matter; the meaning of such a formulation is enriched, however, when we understand the ampler connotations of both the conjoined terms. Let us, then, trace the semantic ancestry of *atman*, as we have already done with *brahman*.

A clue to the ancestral meaning of *atman* is found in the German word for breath, *der Atem*. Evidently that prehistoric people from which the various Indo-European nations branched off, employed (as other peoples have done) the same word for breath and for soul. It would be jumping beyond the evidence, however, to conclude glibly that they took soul to be nothing more than the physical breath. The same glib logic, reversed, would allow the conclusion that they took breath to be not something physical but something spiritual, the soul. Both arguments are invalidated by the probability that our physical-spiritual dualism, whether in its Platonic or its Cartesian form, is a thought-pattern that did not develop till later. As a first hypothesis (to be modified presently) we may suppose that the Indo-European root of *atman* originally meant breath; that as the ancient protothinkers felt the need of a word to express the sense of life within a man they seized upon the familiar fact of breathing (a concrete enough image, although kinaesthetic, not visual) as the most obvious candidate for such metaphoric extension; and that as the moral and metaphysical consciousness deepened and the self came to be regarded not simply as the bare fact of being alive but as the very core of knowable existence, the eye through which the world is known, the judge and interpreter of that world and thus an entity capable of winning some independence over it,—the word *atman* came to mean not so much life as *spirit*. Such, I say, might be our preliminary, although somewhat over-simplified, hypothesis.

Actually the growth of the word's meaning from "breath" to "life" to "essential self" cannot be established beyond the reach of doubt. The latter phase of semantic advance, from "life" to "selfhood," is plainly traceable when we compare the rather free use of *atman* in the *Vedas* (roughly assignable to the second millennium B.C.) with its carefully defined, or at any rate carefully guarded, spiritual meaning in the *Upanishads* (probably between 800 and 500 B.C.). But the earlier phase, from "breath" to "life," although probable on the philological ground just mentioned, lacks clear literary confirmation. Of course the proper translation of the word in the *Vedas* is often problematical in any case. Here are two passages, in the first of which the meaning appears to stand somewhere between "breath" and "life," and in the second somewhere between "life" and "self." The singer of the hymn from which the first group of verses is quoted is invoking Plants or Herbs, presumably medicinal ones, as divine, and describing them as mothers and goddesses.

Steed, cow, and garment may I win, by winning back thy *atma*, O man.

The healing virtues of the herbs stream forth like cattle from the stall,—herbs that shall win me store of wealth by rescuing thy *atma*, O man.

When I restore the vanished strength by holding these herbs in my hand, out goes the disease unable to seize upon the *atma*.

(*Rig-Veda*, X, 97, verses 4, 8, 11.)

The singer was evidently a priest-physician ambitious of success, and would have had no need to distinguish between his patient's breathing and his patient's life. The symptom and the condition were, to the practical mind, virtually identical. Compare now the second passage, from one of the more philosophical hymns of the *Veda:*

> Who has seen how the firstborn, which was the Bone-Possessing [i.e., the shaped world], was formed out of the Boneless [i.e., the Shapeless, the original Chaos]? Where was the vital breath, the blood, the soul [*atman*] of the world?
>
> (*Rig-Veda*, I. 164. 4.)

Here *atman* evidently means something more than breath or even life, since it is contrasted with another word with the same root, which Griffith has thought best to translate "vital breath." There seems to be a semantic stretching process going on here—a reaching out toward a metaphysical meaning not yet fully formed. Juxtaposing other Vedic hymns—where a singer declares that Soma (the ceremonial fermented drink, half-personified) is the *atma* of sacrifice, that Indu (apparently an incarnation, or *avatar,* of the god Indra) is the primeval *atma* of sacrifice, that "rainment is body, food is *atma,* and healing ointment gives strength," that Vayu, the Wind, which also becomes conceived as world-soul, is "germ of the world, the Deities' *atma,* and so moves ever as his will inclines him"; that the Divine Horse (which also symbolizes the sun galloping across the sky) has as his *atma* "a bird flying from below the horizon up into the zenith of heaven"—we recognize the inextricable mingling of the literal and the figurative in all these varied instances.

When we pass from the roughly inspired *Vedas* to the philosophically disciplined *Upanishads* we find the meaning of *atman* to have undergone two further steps of development—one semantic, the other metaphysical and doctrinal. Semantically, *atman* is now clearly distinguished from the senses and sensory modes of awareness; it is declared to be the essence of *dharma,* the voice of conscience, the sense of duty; in particular it is distinguished from the vital breath, which now goes by the name of *prana.*

The mortal who has heard this and comprehended it well, who has separated that Atman, the very core of conscience, from all physical objects and has realized its subtle essence, rejoices, because he has obtained that which is the cause of rejoicing.

> (*Katha Upanishad,* I. ii. 13.)

Beyond the senses is the mind, beyond the mind is the intuitive intelligence, higher than the intuitive intelligence is the Great Atman, higher than the Great Atman is the Unmanifest.

> (*Katha Upanishad,* II. iii, 6.)

The meaning of *atman* has at length been metaphorically graduated to a new height and consolidated there.

Simultaneously with the attainment of a radically spiritual concept of *atman,* conditioning and conditioned by it, the Hindu thinkers of about the eighth century B.C. defined and amplified their central metaphysical insight, "*Atman is Brahman.*" This formula, which runs as major theme through the *Upanishads* and the *Bhagavad-Gita,* has both a practical and a contemplative side: it is a declaration of the one state of affairs (so to speak) that is ultimately true, and it is a guide to right action. Action can be right only when it is in accordance with reality; wrong action is based upon an illusory view of things. Now the fundamental illusion, of which all lesser illusions are the offspring, is to think of oneself as an individual. To think and act on that supposition is to cut oneself off more and more from the highest Reality, which cannot be known either by the senses or by the discriminative mind, but only by concentration upon what *I* most truly am. The simile of sparks from the fire is propaedeutically helpful here. A spark may be considered in two ways. Visually it is a moving entity, separated in space from the fire which gave it birth. In substance, however,—*as fire*—it is identical with its parent. Now which of these ways of consideration is the truer? If we imagine the spark as being conscious, it will feel itself growing cold as it continues to insist on being an individual; its fire-substance can be maintained only as it remembers its substantial identity with its source and lets itself be drawn back into unity with that source. Both the fire symbol and the formula "Atman is Brahman" are existential metaphors, indicating the direction which the soul's quest for truth and reality must take. They declare, in paraphrase: "You will not find Ultimate Reality by splitting the atom, or by tracing the course of the moving world, or by looking abroad among men, or by spinning ingenious theories. You will find It only within yourself; only in the quietude of communing wordlessly with yourself, and thereby of discovering what you most inwardly and self-recognizably are. In that uncompromising perspective you will find the distinction between self and not-self beginning to drop away as unimportant; you will gradually awaken to the primordial identity of all beings with one another and with the World-Ground."

BUDDHA'S FIRE SERMON

A popular subject of Buddhist art is the tale of how Buddha aided a Brahmin whose sacred fire-chamber was haunted by a fire-breathing serpent. The Buddha engaged the beast in an all-night encounter and, breathing forth flames himself, finally vanquished it. In Buddhist literature the incident is sometimes presented as an iconographical preface to the

Fire Sermon, which Buddha is supposed to have delivered soon thereafter on a hill near Gaya. His audience consisted of Brahmin monks, from whose ranks a great number of converts to the new teaching were being won. Sir Charles Eliot reports having seen grass fires spreading rapidly over the slopes of that district in the dry season, and thinks that such a night-time spectacle may have occasioned the discourse.[8] Be that as it may, the Buddha's use of the fire symbol is too characteristic of his teaching to require explanation. Shorn of the ceremonial repetitions, which give it the form of a musical canon, the famous sermon declares in essence:

Everything, brethren, is burning. The eye is burning; what the eye sees is burning; thoughts based on the eye are burning; the contact of eye with object is burning; the sensation produced by that contact, whether pleasant, painful or indifferent, is also burning. With what fire is it burning? It is burning with the fire of lust, with the fire of anger, with the fire of ignorance; it is burning with the sorrows of birth, decay, death, grief, lamentation, suffering, dejection and despair.[9]

The same sequence is then repeated for the ear, the tongue, and the other organs of outward and inward perception; but the eye may stand as type and representative of the rest.

The same doctrine finds a more standardized version in the Four Noble Truths.

The first of them, the Noble Truth of Suffering, declares that all things endure constantly the pang of coming-to-be and passing-away. This is not a happening that comes once only, at the time which we call death. The personality may survive death, for a limited time; but the accident of survival does not change its essential state. Both in this life and in any next one that we may have yet to endure, existence entails radical suffering—which is to say, continual dying, continual passing into otherness, and hence ever-present frustration and loss. Nothing can heal or remove the tragic condition, for it is intrinsic to the very nature of existence. To exist is to be in time, and time is heteromorphous. A homomorphous time is a conceptual abstraction—a confused idea masked by the clarity of a visualized line running from a backward length called the past through a point called the present into a forward length called the future. Nothing in our actual experience corresponds to so sterilized a graph. Spatial models of time distract us from our existential knowledge of its character. The dying to what just was and the being born to what's just to come—*that* is time as a lived experience. And the pain of that dying is what Buddha means by the cardinal truth of suffering.

We should take care to distinguish between the necessary and the contingent in Buddha's philosophy. His ontological proposition is, I think, existentially demonstrable, even though the value-corollary which he draws from it can be debated. The existential truth that every moment is both a dying and a rebirth can be avoided only by going either above or below it. An Eleatic philosopher can discount the importance of change by looking above its particularity and multiplicity to the universal forms, relations and laws which allegedly persist unaltered. Scientific thinking, too, contains a strong Eleatic tendency, as Edwin A. Burtt has shown.[10] Theory tends to become a sedative and an escape: we fasten upon any set of concepts which reassure us by their familiarity and formal stability; we forget that they are artifacts, not confrontable realities. But it is possible to evade the troublesome paradox of existence without recourse to counteractive theories. "He slept the journey out" might be a suitable enough epitaph for many of us. Nor are theorist and sluggard necessarily so opposed as they look. They represent complementary and sometimes collaborating ways of averting the gaze from the common doom which existence necessarily entails.

The first Noble Truth leads to the second, which declares how suffering originates. The cause lies in the craving—that "trilling wire in the blood" of *Burnt Norton*—by which all finite beings, so far as they succumb to their finitude, are driven. Death does not end the craving nor destroy its effects. The Buddha likens death to a weed which infests the rice fields and sends its roots deep into the ground. Death snips off the weed at topsoil level: but the root, if undestroyed, will send up other growths. A gardener must exhume the root in its entirety; and this homely rule is a type of the third Noble Truth, which is simply the obverse side of the second—viz., that the way to remove the suffering is to eradicate the craving. That, however, is less easily done than said. Even when the root appears to have been exterminated a tiny piece of it may have been overlooked and left to propagate. A way of ensuring its thorough annihilation is required, and the fourth Noble Truth specifies the eight steps of the Noble Path by which it is to be done.

The goal of the Noble Path is *Nirvana*—a word which is sorely liable to misunderstanding by us Westerners who defensively caricature what we do not understand. Nirvana has two complementary aspects: negatively, the destruction of craving, and positively the winning of oneness with all beings through the practice of perfect sympathy. The two aspects are proper complementaries. The first without the second would lead to spiritual hardness, a seeking of one's *own* emancipation from selfhood as the goal—a contradiction in terms when you come to analyze it! The second without the first would lead to sentimentality—a warm *feeling* toward others without the rugged self-discipline that is needed to overcome the egotism which instinctively guides one's practice. In general, Hinayana Buddhism emphasizes the first, Mahayana Buddhism the second; but the greater Buddhist writings and teachers of either school have declared the indispensability of both.

Although the most prominent mention of fire in the Buddhist scriptures takes it as a symbol of *samsara*, the world of ceaseless change and transmigration, from which a wise man will devotedly endeavor to escape, it is nevertheless true of later Buddhism (as of Hinduism and many other religions) that the most special and necessary embodiment of fire— the Sun—enjoys a more positive symbolic role. Although the Buddha rejects the concept of "Brahma," which lends itself too readily to hypostatization and had evidently become an object of superstitious veneration by conservative Hindus of his day, yet most men need the thought of an Absolute, or a symbol of it, to assure them of an objective direction for their endeavors. In Chinese and Japanese Buddhism the appealing figure of Amida Buddha, lord of compassionate brotherhood, fulfilled this need. That avatar, however, was mainly an embodiment of the second aspect of the Buddhist ideal—the extension of sympathy, rather than the rigorous destruction of craving and of individual selfhood. The sun is admirably fitted to play a double symbolic role. Its essence is pure light, pure fire, in which all dross has been burned away. On the other hand its munificence is without stint: its rays spread out giving light and warmth to the entire world. Inasmuch as the sun's rays form an iconic figure resembling spokes of a wheel, the two images, Sun and Wheel, become closely associated in some branches of Buddhist iconography. The Sun-Wheel icon is often drawn with a formalized lotus flower at the hub, symbolizing the purity of the Nirvana-state, the bliss which lies hidden at the heart of all things. Its possible relation to the svastika, the snake emblem, and the three-legged Manxman has already been suggested in Chapter VII.

THE MUSIC OF THE SPHERES

The fire symbol comes into prominence in the West under different metaphysical auspices from those of the East. A livelier sense of the individual permeates the intellectual background of the ancient Greek philosophers; it kept even Plato from succumbing fully to the charm of Eleatic monism. Moreover, the Greeks of the sixth century B.C. found their main impulse to philosophic thought in the contemplation of earth and sky—an interest which maintained itself more actively and spontaneously in an age when there were no clocks, calendars or almanacs. Their cosmological speculations tended from an early date to employ two main conceptual schemata: the schema of the four primary substances (earth, water, air, and fire) and the schema of qualitative opposites. Of the three earliest known philosophers of the Ionian seaport city Miletus, two—Thales and Anaximenes— gave priority to the first way of thinking; the remaining one, Anaximander, to the second. Independently, in western Greece and at Crotona in Italy, Pythagoras, or at any rate colonies of his disciples, were in agreement with Anaximander as to the ontological primacy of pairs of qualitative opposites, although their cosmology (specifically, how the opposites should be conceived as acting on one another) and their symbolism developed along widely different lines. Two questions then arose: *What?* and *How?* The early answers to the question, *What?* need not concern us here. They become of mature interest only as they grow out of attempts to answer the *How?*

The interrelation of the *What?* and the *How?* shows itself in the difference of conception which separates the two later Ionian philosophers from each other, despite their teacher-disciple relationship. To Anaximander, the teacher, the problem was to explain how *opposite qualities* succeed each other in nature (e.g., the hot and cold of winter and summer, the bright and dark of day and night): he explains that they alternatively chase each other out of existence according to a rhythmic law of justice and reparation. To the younger philosopher, Anaximenes, the question of physical change was the question of how the *four elements* could turn into one another; and his answer was that they evidently manage it by the processes of condensation and rarefaction. Air (which he took as standard and source) thickens into cloud, water, mud, earth, stone; by the contrary process it becomes thinned out into aether and then into fire. An analogous difference of emphasis with respect to basic categories separates the two philosophical giants of that century, Pythagoras and Heraclitus.

If the well-established legends about Pythagoras may be believed he was a remarkable combination of mathematical genius, religious mystic, and wise governor of commonwealths. Although some historians have regarded this combination of talents as accidental, I believe that José Vasconcelos is right in locating the ground of their union in the principle of the Harmony of the Spheres.[11] Pythagoras' celebrated declaration, "All is number," means what it seems to mean, and also something more. In its literal sense it expresses somewhat hyperbolically the excitement of having first discovered such wonderful secrets as the length-ratios of harmoniously vibrating strings and the geometrical theorem of the squared hypotenuse. But that was by no means the entire or even the primary significance. Inasmuch as "number" (i.e., simple fractional ratios) was found to produce musical harmonies when applied to the length of vibrating strings or of columns of air in blown pipes, it came to be identified, by metaphorical extension, with the idea of spiritual harmony as well. Man's relation to man, to nature, and to the starry constellations (primordially to these last) was understood as such a harmony. But it was not a matter of conception only; for Pythagoras revealed to his disciples that on rare occasions he had been privileged actually to hear that cosmic harmony as a musical experience—the Music of the Spheres.

An advantage of Sr. Vasconcelos' theory is that it offers a reasonable explanation of how the Pythagorean number theory is related to the Pythagorean doctrine of opposites. Aristotle reports the school's table of opposites as follows: limited vs. unlimited; odd vs. even; one vs. many; right vs. left; male vs. female; at rest vs. in motion; straight vs. curved; light vs. darkness; good vs. evil; square vs. oblong. A hint of Aristotle's suggests that at least some Pythagoreans regarded the antithesis odd-vs.-even as the basic one. On Vasconcelos' theory the reason for its primacy is clear. The harmonies of octave, fifth, and fourth are produced by ratios of $2:1$, $3:2$, and $4:3$ respectively. These simplest numerical relations exemplify the basic antithesis of odd-vs.-even and at the same time produce the fairest of harmonies.

The remaining nine pairs of opposites probably represented harmonies in the social, aesthetic, and religious spheres. In some cases their symbolic meaning can be reconstructed with reasonable confidence. "Limit vs. the unlimited" was not an abstractly geometrical conception solely: it expressed also the opposition between an ordered and an unordered way of life. "One vs. many" was not simply arithmetical: it symbolized the choice between the centripetal and centrifugal ways of life—in private, finding one's spiritual unity vs. dissipating one's energies; and in politics, rule by a man of wisdom vs. chaos of mob control. The rest-vs.-motion antithesis perhaps had an analogous application. The superiority of right to left was important in Pythagorean sacrament and symbolism; that of male to female provided a sound basis of family and community life. Both terms of each antithesis, however, when rightly understood and controlled, were recognized to have their honorable place in the commonwealth of entities that is the cosmos. They are in rhythmic harmonious interplay; their rhythms were considered to be essentially the same as those of vibrating strings and air columns, which could therefore serve as their types or symbols; and the same laws of number which practice had found applicable to the one were conceived as applying to the other also. In some such manner it seems likely that Pythagoras and his disciples understood the triadic relationship of Cosmic Harmony, the Table of Opposites, and the Law of Number. It made possible their understanding of the dyadic relationship between the World-Ground of Existence and the individual things, persons, actions, events, and qualities that make up the familiar world.

The latter relationship is itself to be conceived as a harmony. The good life consists in harmonizing our individual life-rhythms and our group life-rhythms with the harmony of the world. (Harmonization is not assimilation, however; such is the difference between Greek humanism and Brahmanic pantheism.) In that most Pythagorean of Plato's earlier dialogues, the *Phaedo*, Socrates tells that on the eve of his death he was instructed in a dream to make music. With characteristic grace and light-hearted reverence he undertook to obey the command literally, but the symbolic meaning was still (and I think he recognized it so) the important one: that as the soul prepares to depart from the body and enter into the dark unknown of another life, she will fare best if she brings herself into harmonious relations with all that is best, truest, and most beautiful.

Socrates' acceptance of the dream's behest on a literal as well as on the more important symbolic level reflects the Pythagorean practice (mentioned in Chapter XII, in connection with the Watchman's formula of silence) of performing their Ethical Maxims *(Symbola)* on both planes with almost equal devotion. The full list of such maxims runs to several score, and is given somewhat differently by various writers. But some of the most typical and most generally recognized, with their probable symbolic meanings, are the following:[12]

Step not over the balance. Plutarch and St. Jerome both explain it: "Transgress not the laws of Justice."

Do not sit on the quart measure. The *choenix* was the measure of corn that was given to each slave for his subsistence. The maxim, then, evidently means: "Do not take your nourishment by the labor of another. Work to earn your bread."

Tear not the crown to pieces. St. Jerome interpreted it: "Do not transgress the laws of the city. For the laws of a city are its crown." Another interpretation current in ancient times was: "Do not spoil the joy of a festal gathering by melancholy,"—it being the custom at feasts to wear crowns of flowers. And another: "Do not speak ill of princes, nor traduce their reputations." It is likely that all three interpretations were observed by Pythagoreans at one period or another, or even simultaneously.

Stir not the fire with a sword. The interpretation given by ancient writers is usually: "Do not inflame persons already at odds." However, the widespread importance of fire as an arcane symbol suggests that this may have meant also: "Do not falsify the idea of the Cosmic Ground by applying man-made distinctions to it."

Do not wipe out the place of the torch. That is to say, "Do not extinguish the light of reason within you; at least preserve the conditions of its being lighted again."

Do not step over the tether of a bull-calf. "Do not contravene the religious ordinances of Dionysus."

Feed the Cock, sacrifice him not, for he is sacred to the Sun and to the Moon. The Cock, whose crowing ushers in the dawn, has widely been an emblem of Forthcoming Good, sometimes specifically of Resurrection. Also, by reason of his dominating ways with the hens, the Cock has been a symbol of sexual potency and hence again, from a more earthy direction, of spiritual regeneration. The Sun and the Moon probably represent masculine and feminine principles in some sense or other; the precise meaning has been lost.

When we see how the Pythagoreans held in high honor and meticulous observance the calf-rope and beans (Chapter XII), the balance, the measure, the crown, the fire, the torch, the cock, and so on—not only the spiritual meanings but the tangible emblems themselves—their devotion to certain numbers becomes more understandable. With their strongly mathematical bent they saw the world as constructed out of a progression of the first four digits: since one represented a point, two a length, three a plane surface, and four solidity. Their sum is the universally important number 10, which was expressed by a triangle composed of four rows of marks, of one, two, three, and four units respectively. But three and four had special significance: the one representing the Divine Triad and the other (doubtless with some reference to the four cardinal directions) Earthly Justice. Their sum is seven, another number of great symbolic importance, which the Pythagoreans represented by a three-dot triangle surmounting a four-dot square. Today, of course, we have lost the ancient sense of numerical significance, and we see in numbers only those mathematical properties which they possess by virtue of their place in a homogeneous series. We can perhaps still admire, however, the Pythagorean quest for a fully ordered life through bringing Tenor and Vehicle into one orbit of acceptance and veneration.

THE FIRE AND THE RIVER

No other philosopher combines more strikingly than Heraclitus a reverence for truth with an insistence upon its paradoxical and inherently elusive nature. He is enigmatic in the style of the mystics, as Sri Aurobindo has well said, because, like them, he "sought to express the riddle of existence in the very language of the riddle."[13] There is no *A B C* of wisdom; formulas are but mechanisms that stand between us and the ever-changing reality which we want to discover. For "all things flow, nothing abides"; life is a river into which "you cannot step twice, for other and yet other waters are ever flowing on"; "war is father of all and king of all"; and "this cosmos is like an ever-living fire." All things are in continual process of birth and death: "Fire lives in the death of air, and air in the death of fire; water lives in the death of earth, and earth in the death of water." Such strife is not accidental but inherent in the nature of things, and "Homer was wrong in wishing that strife might cease to be, for if that were to happen then all things would perish."[14] How in such a kaleidoscopic and evanescent world can truth be known, or even approached? The answer has both an objective and a subjective—a cosmic and a human—side.

There is in the clashing world a hidden harmony which we miss when we give our attention to the more obvious aspects of existence. "Nature loves to hide," and "The god at Delphi neither speaks nor conceals, but gives signs." The ever-living fire "flares up and dies away according to fixed measures." There is "an intelligence (*gnômê*) by which all things are steered through all things," and it is "both willing and unwilling to be called by the name of Zeus." The first part of this trenchant statement epitomizes Heraclitus' two complementary principles: (1) that a thing exists only in the act of coming out of something else and passing into something else—only in a simultaneity of being born and dying, which is to say dying and being reborn; and (2) that there is a governing intelligence in the perpetually ongoing process. Whether or not you choose to personify that intelligence by calling it Zeus, God, Apollo, Jehovah, is immaterial: it manifests itself not as an hypostasis but as a process, and a bafflingly paradoxical one. "A thing exists in agreement with itself only through differing with itself; its harmony consists in reciprocal tension, like that of the bow and of the lyre." How can man achieve the wisdom to understand a world so puzzling?

The reason why we are able to understand the process of nature is that we are part of the process. We can understand the Cosmic Fire because there is a fire-principle in our souls. When a man realizes his own nature most fully he becomes "a dry beam of light," and this state of fiery dryness is "wisest and best." To achieve the condition of fire is to achieve the harmony that comes from a controlled tension of many opposites in the soul, and it is when we are in that highly tensive state that we are best able to understand the tensions that constitute the world. It is the condition of the completed circle, "in which beginning and end are one." But that venerable metaphor puts the problem over-simply, and Heraclitus supplements it with another: "To a wool-carder the straight way and the crooked way are one and the same." Wisdom must be rightly devious in order to reach its goal. The man of reason is he who seeks to understand the Logos in things not by simplifying and rationalizing it, but by accepting every contradiction which experience offers in its raw state: perceiving that the only oneness of things is the interpenetration and interfusion of their manyness, and that the only immortality consists in the perpetual and omnipresent fatality of dying and being reborn each moment as something new. "Expect the unexpected, or you will never find truth, for it is clandestine and inaccessible." Such is the Logos in things and such is the Logos manifested as wisdom in men.

But alas, "although the Logos is common to all, most men live as though each had a private sagacity [*phronêsis*] of his own." Their souls, instead of becoming a dry light, sink into spongy wetness; they are like drunkards who are so sopped in wine that they reel along directionless and have to be guided by a boy. Instead of the Upward Way toward a state of fire, theirs is the Downward Way, whereby the soul degenerates first into moisture and at length into the inertness of dead earth. "To those who are awake [i.e., to the upward wayfarers] all is death [i.e., an ever-continuous dying and being reborn]; to those who are asleep [the downgoers], dreams [delusion]."

Although in universal perspective it is true that "the Way Up and the Way Down are one and the same," the choice between them is essential to man's maintenance of the human condition. And it is a choice that must be made anew at every moment. Yesterday's heroisms are already a faded memory; we live only by dying to them and beginning all over again. It is good not to cling but to let go. "Time is like a child playing checkers"—moving the counters at random, stirred by impulses which we do not comprehend. To depend upon time, seeking to perpetuate the past and control and foresee the future, is to become not Fire itself but Fire's victim. "Fire, when it has come upon them, will judge and condemn them." No escape: since all that exists is fire, either we become as a flame or else as a cinder. Time's path is strewn with cinders; but to be as a dry beam of light is to stand outside time's covenant. It is to have and know one's identity with the Cosmic Ground through accepting unreservedly, cleansed of hope and fear alike, the fatality of the eternally present, eternally moving moment.

FIFTEEN

Pilgrim in the Wasteland

As a CONCLUSION to these studies in the symbolic possibilities of language I want to explore certain paths of significance in, and approaching, what is perhaps the most fully pertinent single poem of our moment in history, Eliot's *Four Quartets*. It might appear to a circumspective reader, aware of the explorations already made in this field by such resourceful interpreters as Brooks, Drew, Gardner, Martz, Matthiessen, Maxwell, Preston, Grover Smith, Stephenson, Sweeney, Unger, Williamson, Edmund Wilson, Frank Wilson,[1] and many more, that scarcely anything both new and useful remains to be said. And it is true that if systematic exposition were my aim I could not help repeating a great deal of what have become virtual commonplaces of Eliot interpretation. But actually the most I hope to do here is examine several of Eliot's poetic themes which strike me as having certain possibilities of meaning beyond those already suggested. Possibilities only. Whether any particular interpretation is really justified must be left to the gradual discrimination of each devoted and attentive reader.

In discussing the philosophical meaning of any poem it is important to keep in mind how such meanings characteristically show themselves. I am not much concerned (as

should be evident by now) with the philosophical propositions that can be screened out of the poem, still less with
those that can be imposed upon it as an ideological test; but
mainly with the ideas which emerge, or half emerge, from
the poetic song and movement and imagery themselves. Philosophical ideas in poetry should be like those sculptures of
Rodin's where the unfinished human or animal figure is left
continuous with the unhewn stone. In plastic art the power
of the representation is increased by a right sense of the
medium. Analogously in poetic art the power of the idea
should be fused with the rhythmic and imagistic actuality of
the poem. Eliot's much quoted testimony "that a poem, or a
passage of a poem, may tend to realize itself first as a particular rhythm before it reaches expression in words, and
that this rhythm may bring to birth the idea and the image,"[2]
needs to be remembered in any discussion of a poet's philosophy. Dionysus skips ahead of Apollo, although it is Apollo
who lights the way. Rhythm and ideation, song and vision,
collaborate in the poetic act; and their tension motivates—
perhaps even *is*—the poem. My earlier emphasis on Assertorial Lightness—the reluctance of a poetic statement to be
meant with full logical and epistemological rigor, together
with its claim of being yet somehow meaningful—can be re-
stated as an acknowledgment that ideas in a poem must
always be understood through the poetic mode of apprehension.

Now the poetic mode of apprehension works very largely
through what I have called Metaphoric Imagining. It proceeds characteristically (although never exclusively) by fusion of elements; the poem qua poem is a particular medium
in which, as Eliot says, "impressions and experiences combine in peculiar and unexpected ways."[3] This in itself is
enough to guarantee that the philosophy of a poem is, at its
best, not a doctrinal structure but a pattern of living themes.

The poetic Eros, born of Poverty and Plenty, pursues without ever triumphantly grasping the idea; he is always arising from, never quite escaping the debris of the temporal. Accordingly my method will be not expository but perspectival. Any attempt at depth-formulation is always a succession of new beginnings; and in the pages that follow I shall explore, with no compulsion toward a total synthesis, some of the poeto-philosophical ideas and associations that have come into focus during my various re-readings of *Four Quartets*.

MUSIC, MEANING, AND TIME

Eliot's published remark that "there are possibilities for verse which bear some analogy to the development of the themes by different groups of instruments; there are possibilities of transitions in a poem comparable to the different movements of a symphony or a quartet; there are possibilities of contrapuntal arrangement of subject matter,"[4] has been sometimes misunderstood. Certain interpreters have overlooked the qualifying force of Eliot's words "some analogy." There is a good deal of misplaced ingenuity in Lloyd Frankenberg's attempt to work out the four voices in strict analogy to the four instruments of a string quartet: the philosophical voice—viola; the lyrical—violin; the narrative—violin; the apocalyptic—cello.[5] A strict analogy with music would require that we be able to distinguish two kinds of shift or transition: a shift from theme to countertheme, and a shift from instrument to instrument. There would have to be a discernible fourfold multiplicity representing the instruments, and a discernible twofold multiplicity representing the themes. Frankenberg believes he has identified a fourfold discrimination running through all four of the Quartets, and he therefore equates it, and presumes that Eliot intended it should be equated, with the four instruments. But this strikes me as a critic's conceptualization of the poem rather than a property of the poem itself. I do not discover, from a free reading of *Four Quartets,* sufficient evidence for so extreme an interpretation.

A more promising attempt at musical analysis has been made by S. Marshall Cohen,[6] who argues that the first movements of three of the Quartets are composed in something like sonata form. In *Burnt Norton* he takes the theme and countertheme to be deterministic and redeemable time; in *The Dry Salvages,* the imagistic complementation of river and sea; in *Little Gidding,* as seasonal time ("Midwinter spring . . .") and significant place ("If you came this way . . .")— which become integrated in the final coda (he says, less accurately, "chord"):

> Here, the intersection of the timeless moment
> Is England and nowhere. Never and always.

Cohen's interpretation seems to me to approximate the poetic structure somewhat more recognizably than Frankenberg's. His musical analysis of the latter two first movements is plausible enough. But regarding *Burnt Norton* I am a good deal less sure of what the theme and countertheme should be taken to be.

Burnt Norton opens with four statements of a formal metaphysical character. Their quaternity can be taken as a structural icon of the quartet-idea, which, however, is offered lightly and then allowed to disappear. But what of their intellectual content? I find that as I reread the statements in different orders, or with different emphases, their logical relationships seem to alter. Nor am I able (except by supplying connectives that are not in the poem) to bring the meanings of all four into logical consistency. Surely that is evidence that we must avoid taking their relationships in a too strictly logical way. Let us begin logically, however, in order

to see how far the plain prose method will serve our under-
standings here.

(1) Time present and time past
Are both perhaps present in time future,
And time future contained in time past.

(2) If all time is eternally present
All time is unredeemable.

(3) What might have been is an abstraction
Remaining a perpetual possibility
Only in a world of speculation.

(4) What might have been and what has been
Point to one end, which is always present.

Observe that sentences 1 and 2 are offered tentatively. The
first is softened and qualified by the word "perhaps"; the second is stated hypothetically. Regarded logically, which is to
say as propositions, they formulate a philosophy of determinism. Sentence 1 might be an impressionistic epitome of Lord
Russell's argument that it is theoretically just as possible to
remember the future as to remember the past, inasmuch as
present, past, and future are all equally and forever fixed.
The present has no independent reality on that basis; it dis-
solves into the remoteness and impersonality of future and
past. Sentence 2 declares that if all time is eternally present
in that deterministic sense, then all time is unredeemable.
But there is an altogether different sense that can be given
to the phrase "eternally present," and the search for this
other sense is one of the main motivations of *Four Quartets.*
Sentence 4 announces it. The relationship of time's phases is
now reversed. The present is now the "one end" to which all
else points. We might say, then (tentatively, as always), that
the intellectual movement from sentence 1 to sentence 4 is
from a deterministic view of time (present contained in the

past) to a more open view of time, offering, if we can but realize them, redemptive possibilities (past contained in, or intelligible only through, the present). The development is neatly paralleled by the transformation in *East Coker* from "In my beginning is my end" to "In my end is my beginning"—the first and last lines, respectively, of that Quartet.

Sentence 3 may be taken as a poetic bridge between the two opposing philosophies, since it is equally a corollary of them both. The truism that the unrealized past is unreal ("no use crying over spilt milk," etc.) would be interpreted differently according as it was based on the one philosophy or the other. Determinism would say: the unrealized past never was more than an unrealizable abstraction, for what has come to pass and what could have come to pass are identical. The redemptive philosophy would say: although other possibilities were real once, they are real no longer. "We cannot revive old factions/We cannot restore old policies/Or follow an antique drum." And yet they may still be real in a sense! And the concrete imagery which comes after indicates what that sense may be:

> Footfalls echo in the memory
> Down the passage which we did not take
> Towards the door we never opened
> Into the rose-garden.

If we are wanting a musical analogy I would be inclined to view the imagery and idea of these four lines as representing the first theme (the four opening sentences being introductory). Then, as the second theme, the doubt, the hesitant retraction, the minor key:

> But to what purpose
> Disturbing the dust on a bowl of rose-leaves
> I do not know.

The two passages have their abstract parallels in opening sentences 4 and 3, respectively. In the main body of the movement the two themes intertwine more freely, and with admirably expressive imagery, as the positive and negative sides of the rose-garden experience. On the one hand, "Quick, said the bird, find them, find them"; on the other, "the deception of the thrush." On the one hand, the main impression of the rose-garden scene ("There they were as our guests, accepted and accepting"); on the other, the counteractive implications of "dead leaves" and "drained pool." In the positive moment "the lotus rose, quietly, quietly"; but "then a cloud passed, and the pool was empty." And finally the music returns, as the movement ends, to the key of the abstract: to a restatement of the "eternal present" theme, now interpreted by the intervening imagery.

THE MASKS OF TIRESIAS

The Pilgrim to whom my chapter title alludes is not Mr. T. S. Eliot. Take him rather as the transcendental spectator, the "I" of the poem, undergoing metamorphoses, sometimes male and sometimes female, now of the present and now of the past, wavering between the concretely personal and the archetypally timeless. But wherein is the Pilgrim different from the mere Wanderer? Evidently in that the one has a sense of direction, the other not. In *Gerontion* and *The Waste Land*, the integrating Figure is identified by a name, but in these poems the purgatorial idea of pilgrimage has not yet taken form, or at best is but vaguely and impotently suggested. Let us consider some aspects of this earlier Poetic Ego, and his changing masks and scenes, before returning to the problems of the *Quartets*.

In *Gerontion* the character of the Ego (or of his major part) is announced in the title: literally, "little old man";

symbolically, the vacant, draughty consciousness of the age-
ing, sensual unbeliever who has outlived both his sophistication and his desire.

> I have lost my sight, smell, hearing, taste and touch:
> How should I use them for your closer contact?
> These with a thousand small deliberations
> Protract the profit of their chilled delirium,
> Excite the membrane, when the sense has cooled,
> With pungent sauces, multiply variety
> In a wilderness of mirrors.

The paradox of "chilled delirium" is made explicit as a need
to "Excite the membrane, when the sense has cooled"—an
idea which will reappear in the "trilling wire in the blood"
of *Burnt Norton* and (with contrary stress) in the "frigid
purgatorial fires" of *East Coker*. The old man's disintegrating
mind may be considered the theatre in which the heterogeneous fragments of character and situation are brought together in chaotic union. And simultaneously the old man is
the senescence of a disintegrating civilization, drowsily half
aware of its lost opportunities and present barrenness.

There is another speaker besides the *geron*, however.
Whose is the prophetic condemnatory voice which enters in
the seventeenth line?—"Signs are taken for wonders"—and
again in the passage beginning "After such knowledge, what
forgiveness?" Something distinct from the old man's voice
or representing merely another layer of him—his lost and
forgotten insights arising like a familiar ghost to confront
him? Both, probably. There is a dialectical drawing apart,
as in Marvell's *Dialogue between Soul and Body*, along with
a substantial and inevitable identity. The judge condemns
himself along with the criminal in the dock. For judge and
criminal are *per-sonae*—masks which each of us sometimes

wears—masks of the chameleon-like Ego which projects the poem, and which sees itself in the end "whirled/Beyond the circuit of the shuddering Bear/In fractured atoms."

In *The Waste Land* the *geron*-figure expands into Tiresias, the blind soothsayer of Thebes. Eliot's note offers two important statements about him: that as all the male characters—the one-eyed merchant, the drowned Phoenician sailor, Ferdinand of Naples—melt into each other, and all the women are essentially one woman, so likewise the two sexes meet in Tiresias; and that "what Tiresias *sees*, in fact, is the substance of the poem." But the role of detached spectator is never pure, and Tiresias himself shares vicariously to some degree. as well as observes, all the scattered experiences past and present, high and low, which the poem semi-dramatizes and brings into precarious community. The various personae of both sexes, including the self-transmogrifying "I," may be conceived on the one hand as constituting the Human Comedy which Tiresias witnesses, and on the other as metamorphosed emanations of him.

One might say there are two levels or layers of metamorphosis in *The Waste Land*—the ontological and the theatrical—symbolized by the respective phrases, "death by water" and "Hieronymo's mad againe." The former and more essential of them I will reserve for comment in the fourth section. The latter might be conceived as its subjective and histrionic correlative. The continual transmutations of all things that exist, the interpenetrating cycles of birth and death that constitute the temporal world, require of the poet their proper *mimesis*. In a classical age the "dramatic reversal" *(peripeteia)* can be unitary and formal without doing violence to a fit audience's idea of what is "necessary, or plausible." But ours is another sort of age. The contemporary dramatic poet's task stands to that of the classical dramatic poet—Eliot's to that of Sophocles, let us say—as the continuum-analysis of

the infinitesimal calculus stands to the palpable Greek geometrical conception of number. The difference has a histrionic aspect too. It is probable that the Greek actor, the
agonistes, changed his physical mask at the moment when
the *peripeteia* took place; whereas Eliot's elusive protagonist,
Tiresias, exists only through a continuous melting of one
mask, one *persona,* into another.

In the coda that brings *The Waste Land* to a close, Tiresias'
brief epiphany as Hieronymo makes a terse retrospective
commentary upon the meaning of some of the previous action. Indeed, *The Spanish Tragedy,* in which Hieronymo has
his proper being offers somewhat more of an imagistic and
allusionistic background for *The Waste Land* than is usually
recognized; and it may be profitable to digress by examining certain passages of that flamboyant Elizabethan tragedy
whose imagery and mood and sense of the mask may seem
to have influenced Eliot's poem.

The Spanish Tragedy in its main impact is a melodrama
of revenge, and our attention may go first to the scene where
Hieronymo hears Bellimperia's cry for help and rushes out
into the garden bower half dressed:

> Who calls Hieronymo? speak, here I am.
> I did not slumber; therefore 'twas no dream.
> No, no, it was some woman cried for help;
> And here within this garden did she cry;
> And in this garden must I rescue her.—
> But stay, what murd'rous spectacle is this?
> A man hang'd up and all the murd'rers gone!
> And in my bower, to lay the guilt on me!
> This place was made for pleasure, not for death.
> (Act II, Scene V)

He cuts down the hanged man, then discovers him as his
own son. His personal sorrow goes deep and is poignantly

uttered, with symbolical overtones. The dead son, Horatio, the hanged man, is briefly touched with language that might properly apply to Christ. He is apostrophized as "sweet love- ly rose" (line 406) and is praised as one perfect in virtue:

> That such a black deed of mischief should be done
> On one so pure and spotless as our son?

It may be objected that I am reading too much into these ascriptions; that they can be sufficiently accounted for by the blurring intensity of Hieronymo's grief. Nevertheless the rose was a recognized symbol for Christ to the Elizabethan consciousness. And the image of Christ as hanged to a tree has Biblical justification: "The God of our fathers raised up Jesus, whom ye slew and hanged on a tree." (*Acts* 5:30).[7] The Christian allusion is very light, to be sure; it is not urged; but taking the rose symbol, the "pure and spotless" (cf. Pilate's "I find in him no fault at all"—*John* 18:38), and the visible figure of a hanged man (recalling also a card in the then well-known Tarot pack), one is probably justified in surmising that the more alert Elizabethan playgoers would have been stirred by an intimation of something mysterious and archetypal in this agon.

Other brief touches of Christological imagery occur at in- tervals as the play proceeds. Hieronymo, hyperbolically vis- ualizing the effects of his son's murder upon sympatheti- cally lamenting Nature, tells of the blustering winds having "broken through the brazen gates of hell" (line 494)—in which the quicker members of Kyd's audience would have seen an allusion to Christ's "harrowing of hell." In a consis- tent vein, the bereaved mother Isabella fancies her murdered son sitting in the highest heaven,—

> Back'd with a troop of fiery Cherubins,
> Dancing about his newly healed wounds,

Singing sweet hymns and chanting heav'nly notes:
Rare harmony to greet his innocence,
That died, ay died, a mirror in our days.

(lines 577-581)

And later, when Hieronymo is suing the king for justice, he plays upon the Christological words "ransom" and "redeem" and the Christological idea of "showing the wounds" (lines 854, 858, 861; cf. 881).

Thus, even while the conscious motive of vengeance in *The Spanish Tragedy* is fully personal, being the rage of a father against his son's murderers, yet the outwardly motivated action still draws much of its power from dark archetypal realms beyond the frontiers of consciousness. The ambiguous relation between conscious and unconscious elements has force also in Hieronymo's assumption of madness. In the strong eleventh scene of Act III, when two Portingal strangers break in upon Hieronymo's musings to ask the way to my lord the Duke's, he surprises them with the distracted reply:

There is a path upon your left-hand side,
That leadeth from a guilty conscience
Unto a forest of distrust and fear—
A darksome place, and dangerous to pass:
There shall you meet with melancholy thoughts,
Whose baleful humours if you but uphold,
It will conduct you to Despair and Death . . .

(lines 768–774)

If the distraction shown here seems more genuine than assumed (as also in several of his other early outbursts), Hieronymo soon becomes master of his distraction—"I am never better than when I am mad" (1056)—and turns it into an instrument of the revenge he is plotting. The opportunity comes when he is asked to write a tragedy for the court's entertainment; he replies:

> Why then Ile fit you: say no more.
> When I was young, I gave my mind
> And plied myself to fruitless poetry:
> Which though it profit the professor naught,
> Yet is it passing pleasing to the world.
> (Act IV, lines 68–72)

The play which Hieronymo produces and enacts turns out to be more than a play: for he so casts the roles that Bellimperia, Horatio's bereaved mistress, must pretend to stab Balthazar his murderer; but the pretence is made a reality. And Hieronymo, triumphantly revealing the bloody outcome, boasts himself "author and actor in this tragedy" (IV, 404).

There is a complex irony in the last phrase. Hieronymo thinks himself author of the vengeful deed, but he is more of a mere actor and puppet than he knows. For his bereavement and revenge are all part of a plot set in motion by the ghost of Andrea, a Spanish nobleman whom Balthazar had slain. It is Andrea's ghost, and with him Revenge in person, who open and close the tragedy; and the play which he performs before the court is thus, to Kyd's audience, triply framed.

The Waste Land ends (except for the ambiguous Hindu benediction) with a succession of masks, the last of which is Hieronymo's cry, seemingly acquiescent but deadly as it turns out, "Why then Ile fit you"—with, as it were, the stage announcer's comment, "Hieronymo's mad againe." The Tiresias-Hieronymo protagonist confesses here to playacting, even as he had done in the voice of Baudelaire earlier—"You! hypocrite lecteur!—mon semblable,—mon frère!" But the confession of playacting is itself a bit of playacting, and therefore should not be taken with unguarded assurance. The relation of the poet-protagonist to his masks, as of the doer to his situations, is never fully resolved.

SAND, RED ROCK, AND THE VANISHING GARDEN

In the third canto of Dante's *Inferno* the Pilgrim and his guide, on entering the vestibule of Hell, come upon a group of lost souls "whirling through the air forever dark, as sand eddies in a whirlwind, their sighs and loud wailings resounding through the starless air." Vergil the Guide explains to Dante the Pilgrim that these are the wretched remains of those who lived on earth without taking sides, avoiding both praise and blame. Mercy and Justice spurn them alike: "Let us not speak of them, but look and pass on." Dante resumes: "And as I looked, I saw a whirling banner which ran so fast, it seemed as though it could never come to rest; and behind it came so long a train of people, I would not have believed death had undone so many."

The simile of sand eddying in a whirlwind is apt, it would seem, on two counts. Sand is dry and barren; it is also unstable, easily stirred to haphazard movement by every gust of wind. Eliot's allusion to the passage in describing the crowd that flowed over London Bridge—"so many, I had not thought death had undone so many"—thus implies a triple judgment against the typical individuals of our day. And let us not be complacent: the relevant pronoun in such a judgment is not "they" but "we," and more focally "I." The cowardice (*viltá*) that Dante ascribes to Pope Celestine— "him who made the great refusal"—means more strictly, as Sinclair well says, "pusillanimity, littleness of soul, the meanness of nature by which a man refuses his calling and misses his mark."[8] It is what Max Picard has named "the philosophy of flight"[9]—flight from the silent voice that stands always ready, if we will listen, to remind us of our lost direction and of the difficult but imperative way back. As a result of the chronic, unavowed Refusal we become the unstable victims of "pastimes and drugs, and features of the press"—ready to follow any wavering banner, any novel shibboleth that gains passing currency. And thus like dry sand we are barren and unproductive. What we praise as the great productions of our times are, to the undaunted vision, destructions; for to produce in any real and enduring sense would require far more than we are consistently willing to give:

> A condition of complete simplicity
> (Costing not less than everything).

The antithesis between sand and rock is a natural one, arising from the obvious physical characteristics of the two elements. The similes "firm as a rock" and "shifting as sand" express familiar enough analogies, and do not require a nurtured tradition to explain them. Yet in a culture that branches from Christian roots a sensitive mind will hear in the comparison some echo of Biblical overtones—particularly in Jesus' simile of the wise and the foolish builder:

Therefore whosoever heareth these sayings of mine, and doeth them, I will liken him unto a wise man, which built his house upon a rock:
And the rain descended, and the floods came, and the winds blew, and beat upon that house; and it fell not: for it was founded upon a rock.
And every one that heareth these sayings of mine, and doeth them not, shall be likened unto a foolish man, which built his house upon the sand:
And the rain descended, and the floods came, and the winds blew, and beat upon that house; and it fell: and great was the fall of it.

(Matthew, 7:24–27)

Biblical symbolism of the Rock is abundant and varied. The Psalmist speaks of the rock of salvation (*Ps.* 89:26); Isaiah speaks of God as "the rock of thy strength" (*Is.* 17:10); Jesus commissions Peter *(Petros)* as the rock *(petra)* upon which (we are not told in what sense) the new religious fellowship *(ekklesia)* is to be founded. More precisely relevant to *The Waste Land,* as Elizabeth Drew has pointed out, is the later passage in *Isaiah* where the prophet is foretelling the blessings of Christ's kingdom:

> And a man shall be as an hiding place from the wind, and a covert from the tempest; as rivers of water in a dry place, as the shadow of a great rock in a weary land.
>
> (Isaiah, 32:2)

But the rock symbolizes not only firmness, security, refuge. The first four verses of *I Corinthians,* Chapter 10, are of peculiar interest to readers of *The Waste Land* because of the co-presence of two significant images—immersion in water (see the "Death by Water" section below) and the drinking of spiritual water from the Rock. St. Paul writes:

> Moreover, brethren, I would not that ye should be ignorant, how that all our fathers were under the cloud, and all passed through the sea;
> And were all baptized unto Moses in the cloud and in the sea;
> And did all eat the same spiritual meat;
> And did all drink the same spiritual drink: for they drank of that spiritual Rock that followed them: and that Rock was Christ.

The Apostle's reference, of course, is to Moses' smiting of the rock in Horeb, from which there gushed forth fresh water for his thirsty people.

And the Lord said unto Moses, Go on before the people, and take with thee of the elders of Israel; and thy rod, wherewith thou smotest the river, take in thine hand, and go.

Behold, I will stand before thee there upon the rock in Horeb; and thou shalt smite the rock, and there shall come water out of it, that the people may drink. And Moses did so in the sight of the elders of Israel.

(Exodus, 17:5–6)

Why, now, is the rock in *The Waste Land* initially *red* rock? Later, in the penitential mood of *Ash Wednesday* the rock is associated with the color blue and with garden imagery. There the Lady of the Garden, the Lady of Silences

> Made cool the dry rock and made firm the sand
> In blue of larkspur, blue of Mary's color;

and when it next appears the rock itself is blue:

> In the last desert between the last blue rocks.

But that coolness, that *Erhebung* without motion, has not yet been attained in *The Waste Land*. The vision of the Madonna of the Rocks, with a grace-note reminder of Leonardo's painting by that name, is ironically inverted a few lines after the red rock passage, when Madame Sosostris pulls out of the Tarot pack "Belladonna, the Lady of the Rocks"—where Belladonna carries the literal meaning of "beautiful lady" and suggests the Madonna, perhaps also Beatrice; while complementing this is the ironic allusion to the practice of courtesans a generation or two ago of using belladonna to artificially brighten their eyes. The Rock in the wasteland maintains its semantic identity precariously, for it is qualified by such surrounding imagery as dry sand and fear in a handful of dust. On the positive side it is red because the saving grace of Christ's blood streams through

all things even in the wasteland. But we feel that the symbol
is ambivalent, that it carries other connotations balancing
the Christian ones, and that those other connotations—as the
phrase "fear in a handful of dust" suggests—may well be
pagan in character. Can we be any more specific?

I think we can. My hypothesis, for what it may be worth,
is that there is a latent reference here to the ceremony of
the Navaho Night Chant. The focal object of the Night
Chant is restoration of health to a patient or patients, although this central purpose is surrounded with prayers for
abundant rains, good crops, long life, and happiness for all
the people. "In this and other healing ceremonies," according to Washington Matthews,[10] "since the object is to guard
against death and prolong life, it is important that a life element, or what appears to the Indian mind to be such, should
be preserved as much as possible in all the articles used." The
life principle is preserved symbolically: feathers must be obtained from birds captured alive, and to secure them the
Indian must learn to steal upon the nest in perfect silence
at night. Pollen, which is to be sprinkled on the patient, must
have its vital principle preserved by contact with live birds.
The sacred buckskin, which is used for making thongs and
in other ways during the healing ceremonies, must preserve
the deer's life-force. For this reason the animal must be slain
without a wound, and its nostrils closed with pollen, so that
a certain vital element remains even though the animal dies:
one of its souls may depart, but not all.

One of the chief purificatory agencies is the sacred sweat-
bath. As the patient proceeds into the sweat-house, to which
white plumes have been affixed, the Song of the Rock is
chanted:

> In the House of the Red Rock
> There I enter;

Half way in I am come.
The corn-plants shake.

In the House of Blue Water
There I enter;
Half way in I am come.
The squash-vines shake.

On a floor marked with symbolic designs in sacred pollen dust the patient sits on spruce twigs. When he has sweated in silence for some thirty minutes two medicine men approach with careful ceremony from the east, enacting the roles of two gods, and apply sacred wands with strong pressure to the essential parts of the patient's body. A further chant follows:

At the Red Rock House it grows,
There the giant corn-plant grows,
With ears on either side it grows,
With its ruddy silk it grows,
Ripening in one day it grows,
Greatly multiplying it grows.

At the Blue Water House it grows,
There the giant squash-vine grows,
With fruit on either side it grows,
With its yellow blossom it grows,
Ripening in one night it grows,
Greatly multiplying it grows.

The pollen dust pictures are then ceremonially obliterated by being scraped from one end to the other—from head to foot when the figure is a stylized anthropomorph—and the dust from which they were constructed is gathered into a blanket and thrown away a certain number of paces north of the sweat-house.

During the sacred sweat-bath, while the evil is oozing out through the patient's pores, the strictest silence is enjoined upon him. To break silence is to lose all. There is a Navaho story of two boys, one a cripple, the other blind, who sought to be cured. As they entered the sweat-house, which was covered with curtains of blue cloud and mist and adorned on top with pictures of rainbow and lightning, they were strictly charged by the *yei* who conducted them that they must on no account talk. The lodge soon grew very hot and the boys began to perspire; presently the blind one became conscious of a faint light streaming under the curtains, and the cripple felt a stirring in his legs. Their joy was so great that they forgot the solemn warning. "Oh! younger brother," cried the one, "I see." "Oh! elder brother," cried the other, "I move my legs." In an instant the rainbow, the lightning, the curtain of cloud and mist, and the sweat-house itself vanished, and the boys were left sitting on the open ground with nothing but four stones beside them and the spruce twigs under them, the one as blind and the other as lame as ever.

The power of the story goes deeper than pathos, for what I may call the Archetype of the Vanishing Garden draws sustenance from the unplumbed depths of our individual and collective unconscious. Behaviorists have experimentally ascertained that loss of support, even in the plain physical sense, produces fright-reflexes independently of any association-conditionings. Dr. Suttie, using the methods of depth psychology, has traced the origins of many psychotic ailments to premature or over-violent "psychic weaning."[11] The individual's tragic loss of the womb's security, reënacted psychically at successive stages of childhood, has its mythic counterpart in the Garden of Eden story as well as in the broader Christian theme of mankind's continued self-ejection or self-debarment from Paradise. Even the symbolism of silence, I would suggest, is adumbrated in the Eden myth.

The tree of which our first parents ate, in defiance of Jeho-vah's command, was of the Knowledge of Good and Evil. The Creature, not content with the bounty of the Garden which is freely allowed him, dares to take good and evil into his own hands and to speak in his own way of primal matters, instead of bringing his mind and heart into the still-ness of listening and thus into the harmony of universal rhythms. And there is yet a further parallel between the Navaho and Christian versions of paradise lost. The careless boys were upbraided by all the people for having by their untimely chatter broken the efficacy of the cure, not only for themselves but for all Navahos, who thenceforth would have to supplement the healing ritual with gifts. The primal sin, in both religions, infects the entire race; the sinner plays a representative role.

The Vanishing Garden archetype is a major idea underly-ing both *The Waste Land* and *Four Quartets*. In the one poem the hyacinth garden passage followed by the sombre emptiness of *"Oed' und leer das Meer,"* in the other the rose garden scene followed by "Then a cloud passed and the pool was empty," are among the more explicit representations of it. The closing lines of *Burnt Norton*—

> Ridiculous the waste sad time
> Stretching before and after

—might express a state of consciousness parallel to that of the bereft Navaho brothers left sitting on the open ground. The co-presence of the Vanishing Garden Archetype and the red rock and handful of pollen dust imagery in one mythic pat-tern strikes me as offering not conclusive but reasonably per-suasive evidence that the Navaho Night Chant may have been one of Eliot's sources—whether conscious or forgotten I do not know.

DEATH BY WATER

The brief fourth movement of *The Waste Land* is almost purely lyrical. It contains so little of declarative force, so little assertorial firmness, that any inferences as to its meaning and relation to the poem's total statement must be drawn not from itself but from its context. Phlebas the Phoenician, "entering the whirlpool," is (by Eliot's own testimony) "not wholly distinct from Ferdinand Prince of Naples"; which means that evocations of *The Tempest* imagery are poetically relevant, and especially of the "Full fathom five" lyric. In fact, Shakespeare provides in Ariel's song a text for the redemptive possibilities of death by water as envisaged in *The Waste Land:*

> Nothing of him that doth fade,
> But doth suffer a sea-change
> Into something rich, and strange.
> (*The Tempest*, Act I, Scene ii)

But amid the stony rubbish and dry bones of the wasteland scene, where is the water to be found?

In *The Dry Salvages* the redemptive possibilities of water, although still qualified by ambiguities and dangers, are developed more positively, through the imagery furnished by a more definite locale. Sea, river, rock, tolling bell, wreckage of whale's backbone and shattered lobsterpot, all make their contributions to both the symbolism and the scene. The principal contrast is between the *sea*, whose time is a vast unshapen time measured only by the tolling bell, rung by the unhurried ground swell, and the *river*, "a strong brown god— sullen, untamed and intractable/ . . . Unhonoured, unpropitiated/By worshippers of the machine, but waiting, watching and waiting." The river has close symbolic affinity with "the trilling wire in the blood" of *Burnt Norton* and "the

fever sings in mental wires" of *East Coker*. Elsewhere I have
suggested that it might be regarded as "the physiological
correlative of the moment of illumined experience; the pulse-
beat by which we respond to the hyacinth ecstasy, to the
laughter in the garden, and now to 'the sea howl and the sea
yelp.' " For the poem plainly states that "the river is within
us, the sea is all about us." Wreckage clutters them both.
But it is in the sea that the Rock is to be found—washed by
waves, concealed by fogs, a monument on halcyon days, a
sea-mark in navigable weather, "but in the sombre season/
Or the sudden fury, is what it always was."

In the sestina with which the second movement of *The
Dry Salvages* commences, the scene, or metaphoric vehicle,
is that of fishermen setting out in their ships or boats upon
perilous seas, on an ocean always littered with drifting
wreckage and wastage. The opening question, "Where is
there an end of it, the soundless wailing . . . ?" is plurisignative. The meaning is simultaneously: "When will it stop?"
and "What is its purpose?" The question is asked twice, in
Stanzas 1 and 4, and answered twice, in Stanzas 2 and 6. As
the questions, so the answers too are plurisignative, but with
different emphases. The first answer—"There is no end, but
addition"—stresses mainly the time aspect: there is no last
moment, but a further moment is always superadded. In each
individual's life, however, there is an end in the temporal
sense—"the final addition"—for we move toward old age "in
a drifting boat with a slow leakage" awaiting the bell that
announces death. Observe that the word "drifting" sounds
an undertone which reminds of the other meaning of "end";
for to drift is to be without a purpose. In the fourth and sixth
stanzas the idea of purpose seems to me to become the
dominant one; for although the word "forever" in Stanza 5
keeps the temporal meaning alive, the teleological meaning

is given greater emphasis by such phrases as "littered with wastage," "no destination," "unpayable," and "drift."

The word "annunciation," which terminates Stanzas 1, 3, and 6, varies its meaning in harmony with the semantic shift in "end." The first two instances, "calamitous annunciation" and "Clamor of the bell at the last annunciation," suggest primarily the tolling bell which announces death; while the third instance, where the word is capitalized, evokes the idea of the historical Annunciation, the tidings brought to Mary, which marked the beginning of the Christian drama. Helen Gardner says of the sestina as a whole:

Under the metaphor of fishermen setting out on their perilous voyages, over an ocean "littered with wastage," it pictures the lives of individual men, the sum of which makes history. It finds meaning only in the union of the temporal with the eternal, in annunciations: the calamitous annunciation of terror and danger, the last annunciation of death, and the one Annunciation of history. The only *end* to the flux of history is man's response to the eternal manifesting itself in time.[12]

What is "the hardly, barely prayable/Prayer of the one Annunciation?" One has only to turn to the account of the Christian Annunciation in the Gospel according to St. Luke and read the answer. The angel's last words to Mary, in the traditional King James Version are: "For with God nothing shall be impossible." This, however, is not strictly accurate, for the subject of the sentence is *rhema*—"that which is spoken"—and the American Revised rendering comes closer to the meaning: "No word from God shall be void of power." The most lucid translation, I should think, would be: "Nothing that God hath spoken shall be incapable of fulfillment." The important point is that it is God's Word which is being spoken about. And either of these latter renderings gives full relevance, as the older one does not, to Mary's reply: "Behold the handmaid of the Lord; be it unto me according to Thy word." Here, then, is the "prayer of the one Annunciation"—no asking for divine favors, as prayer degenerately comes to mean, but a responsive yielding to the Divine Word, as in Jesus' prayer at Gethsemane, "Not my will, but Thine, be done." Miss Gardner is doubtless right in connecting it with "the awful daring of a moment's surrender" in *The Waste Land*. It is the prayer that we find so "hardly, barely prayable" today.

THE FISHER KING

The prayer, when it does come (as in the fourth movement of *The Dry Salvages*) is addressed to the Lady in behalf of "those/Whose business has to do with fish . . ." The mention of fish and fishermen in the context of sea imagery, with the ambivalent possibilities of death and restoration which they imply, revives a memory of the Fisher King in *The Waste Land*, already recognizable reincarnate as the Wounded Surgeon in the fourth movement of *East Coker*. Jessie L. Weston is right in affirming "that the Fish is a Life symbol of immemorial antiquity, and that the title of Fisher has, from the earliest ages, been associated with Deities who were held to be specially connected with the origin and preservation of Life."[13] Two aspects of the fish symbol invite attention: the eucharistic and the baptismal.

There were sacred fish-meals in pre-Christian times. They were evidently an ancient custom among the Jews, for the *Jewish Encyclopaedia* says: "The eating of fish has always been associated with the celebration of the Sabbath. From no orthodox table is fish absent at one or more of the Sabbath meals, however difficult it may be to procure." Cumont mentions the sacramental fish-meal in ancient Syria as a probable source of the Christian fish-symbolism. Among the ancient Greeks, too, it evidently had a place: for Pausanias tells of sacred fish in the waters near Eleusis, which only the priests might catch, and Porphyry says that at the sacrifices of the Eleusinian Mysteries fish were included—which I take to imply that they were also eaten ceremonially by the worshipers. How far any of these practices may have contributed to the Christological fish-symbol is uncertain. Renan thinks that fish were probably cooked and eaten at the suppers of Jesus and his disciples, and offers in support Jesus' question, "Or if he ask a fish, will he give him a serpent?"—arguing that as the serpent had already come to represent Satan, so the fish, by this metaphoric contrast, came to be a type of the Christ. A German scholar, H. Merz, offers a somewhat different theory: that when Jesus commanded metaphorically that men should eat of the Christ's flesh in order to have eternal life, his hearers, who depended on lake fish as a main article of diet, naturally turned to the ceremony of fish-eating as an appropriate way of carrying out the injunction. However, as Professor Rufus Morey remarks, whether we think these speculations plausible or not, positive evidence for them is lacking; he himself explains the eucharistic fish-symbol by the significance given from earliest times to the Multiplication of Loaves and Fishes.[14] Miss Weston goes so far as to declare that orthodox Christianity "knows nothing of a sacred fish-meal." Here, however, I think that the distinguished scholar has overstepped her evidence. She might better have said that little or no literary or iconographical evidence of such a meal survives.

May not the Roman Catholic practice of meatless Fridays have originated in a weekly commemoration of Christ's death by sacramentally eating of the symbolic fish? The orthodox form of the Eucharistic service remained as Jesus had instituted it, of bread and wine. But the Fish as Eucharist may have had its devotees also. Some evidence of such a tradition may be seen in the fragments of the *Abercius-epitaph* which were discovered in 1883, among the remains of the public baths at Hierapolis. Abercius says, describing his pilgrimage to Rome:

Faith was everywhere my guide and ever laid before me food, the Fish from the Fountain, the very great, the pure, which the holy virgin seized. And this she gave to her friends to eat, having a goodly wine and giving it mixed with water, and bread also.[15]

No sure conclusion can be drawn, for scholars are not agreed on whether Abercius was Christian or not—possibly a follower of some cult involving Orpheus the Fisher. Weston places it "outside the recognized category of Christian belief." Harnack, on the other hand, describes it as certainly Christian, although non-orthodox. A later epitaph, whose Christianity has not been disputed, which a certain Pectorius inscribed in honor of his dead parents and brothers, contains the significant sentences:

Take the honey-sweet food of the Savior of the saints, eat it with desire, holding the Fish in thy hands.
Fill thou me with the Fish—this is my longing, O my Lord and Savior![16]

The other aspect of Christian fish-symbolism, the baptismal, may have originated in the metaphor which Jesus employed in calling his earliest disciple from his occupation as fisher in Genesareth Lake: "Follow me, and I will make you fishers of men" (*Matt.*, 4:19; *Mark*, 1:17). The natural logic of this idea posits Christ as the Fisher instead of the Fish. Tertullian, who does not always follow natural logic, writes that "we little fish (*pisciculi*) are born in water after the model of our Fish (*ichthus*) Jesus Christ, nor do we find salvation except by remaining in water."[17] But earlier than

Tertullian is an Alexandrian hymn of the second century in which Jesus is addressed as the savior of mankind under two associated similes: as shepherd, and then as "fisher who entices the little fish with the bait of the blessed life."[18]

The relation of early Christian fish symbolology to the Fisher King of medieval romance is by no means clear. Yet even if it be true, as medieval scholars now incline to think, that such fisher kings as Bron and Manawyd were originally sea gods, the indubitably Christian complexion of the Grail stories makes it probable that the older Christological meanings of the fish symbol had become fused with the Celtic and Nordic myth-elements. A most significant characteristic of the Grail Fisher King is his mysterious wound (cf. Eliot's wounded surgeon), usually in the thigh or groin, and the famine or pestilence associated with it. Roger S. Loomis gives evidence that the wounds of the Otherworld King were conceived as breaking out anew annually, and argues that "the catastrophe which accompanied the wounding of the king was rather the desolation of winter; and his infirmity signifies the low vitality of natural forces, particularly the feeble winter sun."[19] That is doubtless true enough. But there is also another dimension of meaning, which Professor Loomis himself suggests in his following chapter, where he identifies Chrétien's Ile de Voirre with Glastonbury, which was also the traditional site of King Arthur's Isle of Avalon. The wounding of the Fisher King symbolizes both the winter of the calendar and the graver winter of the spirit; the Quest is not only for a return of summer, but for that state of blessedness which the Arthurian legends symbolize variously as Avalon, as the abode of Gwynne the White One, as the Ile de Voirre, as the Castle of Melwas, and so on. The wound can be healed and the life-giving waters released only if one such as Parzival, spending a night in the Castle Perilous with the restorative symbols of Lance and Cup, *can ask the right question.* In *The Waste Land* the attempts of the protean *agonistes* to ask the question (except in the Ezekiel and the Thunder passages) are neurotic, frustrated, and direction-less: "Has it begun to sprout?" "What is that noise now?" "But who is that on the other side of you?" In *Four Quartets* Eliot's questions are calmer and more comprehending, for he has passed from the wasteland of the directionless into the purgatory of the Dark Way.

SIN IS BEHOVELY

Lady Julian, from whose *Shewings,* or *Revelations,*[20] three phrases in the last section of *Little Gidding* are quoted, was a recluse or anchoress, in a cell attached to the Church of St. Julian in Norwich, England. In the year 1373, when she was about thirty years old, during a serious illness from which she was not expected to recover, she experienced the visions or "shewings" which are recorded in the one book which she has left to posterity. Beyond that, nothing is re-liably known of her life, except that she was still living in 1413.

Lady Julian's account of her experiences is bold, naïve and freshly individual, even while she professes loyal submission to Holy Church. Her unschooled efforts to bring her visions and her understanding of them into consistency with ortho-dox teaching are not always, to a critical reader, perfectly successful. But that is hardly important; she is not arguing, she is reporting what has been shown to her. And one is im-pressed throughout the twenty-five short chapters with her depth of rich feeling, her readiness to face the great para-doxes of spiritual life, her humility in the face of such mys-teries, the acuteness and constancy of her listening to the divine voice, and the quiet gentle vibrancy of her love both toward God and toward creatures.

The most troublesome paradox, to those Christians who

believe in an omnipotent God and yet dare to look candidly at the state of the world and of their own hearts, is the problem of sin. Lady Julian finds herself and her "even-Christians" (fellow-Christians) "letted" (hindered) by sin from perfectly following God's will. Why does God permit this? "Methought if sin had not been, we should all have been clean and like to our Lord, as He made us. And thus in my folly before this time oft I wondered why by the great, foreseeing wisdom of God sin was not letted. For then methought all should have been well." After Lady Julian had struggled long and troublesomely with "this stirring," the Lord Jesus appeared to her in a vision and answered her in the three words: "*Sin is behovely.*" But how and in what sense does it behoove us? In one remarkable and I should think quite heterodox passage she carries out the strange doctrine's implications to the full. "Also God showed me that sin is no shame, but worship [i.e., honor and glory] to man." And she recalls how David, Peter and Paul, Thomas of India, and Mary Magdalen "are known in the Church on earth with their sins to their worship, and it is to them no shame that they have sinned." Momentarily we are aghast. Is sin, then, a good? The writer recovers herself, and speaks more accurately in the next sentences. "Sin is the sharpest scourge that any chosen soul may be beaten with; which scourge altogether beats man and woman, and altogether breaks them, and noughts them in their own sight, so far forth that they think they are not worthy but as it were to sink into hell." Sin, then, is not itself "worshipful," but "the tokening of sin" is *turned* into glory by man's contrition and God's grace. Recovery from sin is a healing of wounds, a quickening of the soul, and this is "high, glorious and worshipful," a turning of shame into joy. "And I am sure by my own feeling," the writer concludes, "that the more each kind soul sees this in the kind and courteous love of God, the more loth is he for to sin . . . If there were laid before me all the pain that is in hell and purgatory, and in earth death and other pains, and sin;—I had liefer chose all that pain than sin."

The paradox of sin stands unsolved and stark. A fatted calf was killed for the returned prodigal, not for the son who had stayed dutifully at home. Jesus taught that there is more joy in heaven over the return of one lost sheep than over the ninety and nine which remain in the fold. And there is the penetrating irony of his declaration: "I am not come to call the righteous, but sinners to repentance." It is, in one perspective or another, the age-old paradox of *felix culpa*. If man, and archetypally if Adam, had not sinned, there would have been no need for Christ's Atonement. Is Adam, then, to be thanked? Reason boggles. We cannot know the ultimate *why* of the drama of Creation, the Fall, and the Atonement. "For this is our Lord's privy counsels; and it belongs to the Royal Lordship of God for to have His privy counsels in peace; and it belongs to His servants, for obedience and for reverence, not to wish to know His counsels." The devoted soul seeks not a solution to an intellectual riddle, but a quickening assurance that his sins are not irremediable. When we have felt the full pain of sin, and have turned to contrition wholeheartedly, *then* it is that our Redeemer tells us, "Sin is behovely," and adds the comforting words, "But all shall be well, and all manner of things shall be well."

The making of all things well comes about, Lady Julian says in a later chapter, through prayer. "Prayer ones the soul to God. For though the soul be ever like God in nature and in substance, it is oft unlike in condition through sin on man's part. Then makes prayer the soul like unto God, when the soul will as God will. And then is it like unto God in condition, as it is in nature."

But prayer sometimes seems to fail: we think that because of our unworthiness God does not hear us, and "we are bar-

ren and dry ofttimes after our prayers as we were before."
We beseech, but shall we have our beseeching? To such
doubts about prayer's efficacy God's answer came:

> I am the ground of thy beseeching.
> First, it is My will that thou have it.
> And then I make thee to will it.
> And then I make thee to beseech it.
> And if thou beseech it, how should it then be that thou should
> not have thy beseeching?

The one prayable prayer, then, is that of the tempted, troubled soul, beseeching that he may "make himself simple and
buxom to God." No other manner of prayer "makes God
supple to him"; but neither does this prayer go finally unanswered, for He whom we beseech is Himself the source
and ground of our beseeching.

THE COSMIC DANCE

> Dancing (bright Lady) then began to be,
> When the first seeds whereof the world did spring,
> The Fire, Air, Earth, and Water—did agree,
> By Love's persuasion,—Nature's mighty King,—
> To leave their first disordered combating;
> And in a dance such measures to observe,
> As all the world their motion should preserve.
> Since when, they still are carried in a round,
> And changing, come one in another's place;
> Yet do they neither mingle nor confound,
> But every one doth keep the bounded space
> Wherein the Dance doth bid it turn or trace;
> This wondrous miracle did Love devise,
> For dancing is Love's proper exercise.
> From Sir John Davies, *Orchestra* (1596)

The Dance serves in *Four Quartets* as the symbolic antithesis of "time on its metalled ways." Its relation to the para-

dox of the eternal present is clarified by the image of the
Wheel, which, like the perfect dance, turns about a central
pivot. "Except for the point, the still point,/There would be
no dance, and there is only the dance." The still point, "where
past and future are gathered," is not fixity. Its symbol is the
axle-tree, the firm center about which the wheel turns. The
axle-tree is at once still and moving. Being a physical part
of the wheel it evidently turns, and yet there is an axis at the
center of it, a mathematically pure point, which remains un-
moving in relation to the rest—"the still point of the turning world"—and which "reconciles" the contradictions of the
surrounding movement. The moral paradox which troubled
Lady Julian (or something very like it) is here symbolized
by the tapestry image of the boarhound and the boar engaged in their patterned, cyclical dance of pursuit.

The dance about the still point is only a cosmic principle;
it must be received into the self. "For dancing is Love's
proper exercise." What is Love's dance as a spiritual, not
erotic experience? An athleticism of mind is needed here;
and as a chapter ago I argued that the Music of the Spheres
and the Cosmic Fire are different vehicles for the same spiritual tenor, so now I propose that we be at pains to see the
essential identity of "the complete consort dancing together,"
the timeless moment, and the crowned knot of fire in which
"the fire and the rose are one."

The doctrine of the Timeless Moment becomes clarified
by studying Eliot's amplification of the *Bhagavad-Gita* passage in the third movement of *The Dry Salvages*. In the
eighth canto of the *Gita*, Krishna, embodied as Prince Arjuna's charioteer, is teaching his royal pupil about the nature
of the transition called death:

He who, at the time of death, thinking of Me alone, goes forth,
leaving the body, he attains unto My being. Have no doubt of
this.

O son of Kunti, whatever state of being one dwells upon in the end, at the time of leaving the body, that alone he attains because of his constant thought of that state of being . . .

The majority of beings, coming into birth again and again, merge helplessly into the unmanifested at the approach of night and become manifest at the approach of day.

But beyond this unmanifested there is another Unmanifested which is eternally existent and is not destroyed even when all things are destroyed.[21]

Eliot's version, which at one point becomes literal translation, is as follows:

> At the moment which is not of action or inaction
> You can receive this: "on whatever sphere of being
> The mind of a man may be intent
> At the time of death"—that is the one action
> (And the time of death is every moment)
> Which shall fructify in the lives of others:
> And do not think of the fruit of action.
> Fare forward.

Eliot's most significant addition is the clause in the parenthesis, a reminder of Heraclitus' aphorism, "You cannot step twice into the same river, for other and yet other waters are ever flowing on."[22] Departing from the Hindu doctrine of a sequence of definite incarnations determined by the law of Karma, Eliot follows Heraclitus in conceiving every moment as a dying and therefore (since time does not halt) a rebirth. Life and death, in Heraclitus' central paradox, are "the same"—which is to say, they are inseparable aspects of every phenomenon, and of every moment of consciousness. What matters most in this procession of contradictories is the *quality* of moment-by-moment rebirth—the degree to which one "attains to My being," as Krishna has said; the becoming like a dry beam of light, or dry shaft of fire, in the imagery of Heraclitus. Eliot's sure catalytic instinct here has been to synthesize the Hindu idea of rebirth through self-disciplined and reverent concentration upon "the Unmanifested beyond the unmanifested" (i.e., the Dark that is sought by the devoted soul, not merely the darkness of the weary round of time) with Heraclitus' idea of the relevance of rebirth to every temporal moment.

And so we are brought back to the relationship of time to the timeless, of past and future to the present—which is to say, in spatial imagery, of the turning world to the still point. The relationship is a complex and largely paradoxical one. The plain statement which concludes the second section of *Burnt Norton*, "Only through time time is conquered," is as central to the philosophical teaching of the poem as any plain statement can be. Again and again it is reasserted, in varying imagery and ever expanding context, until finally, in the four lines that open the coda to *Little Gidding* and hence to the entire *Four Quartets*, it appears for the last time in language simple, strong, and clear:

> We shall not cease from exploration
> And the end of all our exploring
> Will be to arrive where we started
> And know the place for the first time.

The end of the turning wheel is the still axis which is the *arché* of its turning. The end of the cosmic dance is the quietude of love beyond desire. The end of dying is the ever-renewed threshold experience of potential rebirth.

Notes

NOTE TO THE FOREWORD

1. Wannemunne is the Estonian variant of the Finnish Vainamoinen, the primeval minstrel and culture-hero of the ancient epic *Kalevala*, an excellent translation of which, by W. F. Kirby, may be found in Everyman's Library (2 vols.; London, Dent, 1907). In that epic the hero's status seems to be half human, half divine. Having tarried for an unusual number of years in the maternal womb, he was already mature in years and wisdom at the moment of his birth. Tribute is paid to his matchless minstrelsy. Chief among his gifts to men are fire and agriculture. He is represented as bringing the gift of fire to men by having an attendant eagle strike a flame, and as watering their vegetation by a stream that flowed from his big toe—unfortunately in such abundance as to have caused, at one time, a disastrous flood. In the main he is the great calming influence in nature. Where he has walked all is hushed; and accordingly the Finns used to refer to a calm after storm as *Väinämöisen tie*, "Vainamoinen's way."

In the Finnish version as in the Estonian, the god is associated with music.

> Day by day he sang unwearied,
> Night by night discoursed unceasing,
> Sang the songs of by-gone ages,
> Hidden words of ancient wisdom,
> Songs which all the children sing not,
> All beyond men's comprehension,
> In these ages of misfortune,
> When the race is near its ending.
>
> Far away the news was carried,
> Far abroad was spread the tidings
> Of the songs of Vainamoinen,
> Of the wisdom of the hero.
>   —Runo 3 (Kirby's translation).

It is said that the spirits of the sun, the moon, and the rainbow sit in the sky weaving as they listen to the song god, and in their delight they let shimmering strands of gold, silver, and the colors of the spectrum fall down through the air to gladden the hearts of men.

Jakob Grimm, *Teutonic Mythology* (Vol. III of the English translation, London, Bell, 1883), traces the derivation of the god's name to the Finnish word *waino*, "wish, desire, yearning"; which confirms the popular belief that Vainamoinen is the god whose song implants yearning, love, and aspiration in men's souls. Grimm's account of the Finnish version of the tale in my Foreword is as follows: "When Wäinämöinen [Grimm's spelling] touches his harp, the whole of nature listens, the four-footed beasts of the wood run up to him, the birds come flying, the fish in the waters swim towards him; tears of bliss burst from the god's eyes, and fall upon his breast, from his breast to his knees, from his knees to his feet, wetting five mantles and eight coats." The goddess Freyja laughs roses and weeps pearls in her delight.

The Estonian version which I have used was originally based upon the account by J. W. Farrar in his *Language and Languages* (London, 1878). Grimm's *Der Ursprung der Sprache* is there mentioned as the source, but in the only edition of that essay known to me the reference to Wannemunne is superficial. However, the same version is given independently by W. F. Kirby, in *The Hero of Esthonia, and Other Studies in the Romantic Literature of That Country* (London, 1895), Vol. II, pp. 81–82.

CHAPTER I.   MAN'S THRESHOLD EXISTENCE

1. The quotations are from Julián Marías, *Introducción a la Filosofía* (Madrid, Revista de Occidente, 1947), probably the most comprehensive statement of the Catholic Christian Existentialist standpoint by a Spaniard. An English translation by Kenneth Muir and Edward Sarmiento is soon to be published by Yale University Press. José Gaos, who since his self-imposed exile from Spain has been the acknowledged leader of existentialist inquiry in Mexico, has dealt penetratingly with the problem of threshold experience under the title *El Más Allá*, "The Beyond" (*Filosofía y Letras*, No. 29, January-March, 1948; Universidad Nacional de México), and rightly sees man's situation in time as an ambiguously dynamic relation between necessity (of what has been and the limits it imposes upon the future) and possibility (of what may or may not yet be). Since my present subject is semantics, not metaphysics, I must forego pursuit of that engaging problem.

2. Berkeley easily repels this type of rough-and-ready attack in the first and second of his thirteen answers to objections: Sections 34–41 of his *Treatise Concerning the Principles of Human Knowledge* (London, 1710), particularly Section 36. An excellent recent edition of the celebrated treatise is in Vol. II of *The Works of George Berkeley Bishop of Cloyne*, edited by A. A. Luce and T. E. Jessop (London, Thomas Nelson, 1948–1953).

CHAPTER II. SYMBOL, LANGUAGE, MEANING

1. Franz Brentano (1838–1917) revived the Scholastic doctrine of *intentio* in a somewhat different form, declaring in *Die Psychologie vom empirischen Standpunkt* that "the essence of an act of consciousness lies in its intentive relationship *(in der intentionalen Beziehung)*. . . . Every psychic phenomenon contains in itself something as object, although not every one in the same way. In imagination something is imagined, in judgment something is recognized or rejected, in love something is loved. . . ." Brentano's successor, Edmund Husserl, first introduced, so far as I know, the word "intentionality" *(Intentionalität)*. All consciousness has this character, he maintains. It always intends an object, regardless of whether or not that object has space-time existence. All consciousness is consciousness *of*. See Husserl, *Ideas: General Introduction to Pure Phenomenology* (Macmillan, 1931).

2. Genesis 2: 19–20. Cf. the naming of Eve, in Genesis 3:20. In quoting Scripture, I shall adhere to the wording of the King James Authorized Version whenever its influence upon later literature is in question. In other cases I shall reserve the liberty of occasionally modifying the older rendering to obtain greater clarity. A high-spirited parody of Adam's proto-semantic operation may be found in George Bernard Shaw's Preface to *Back to Methuselah*.

3. Mary Anita Ewer, *A Survey of Mystical Symbolism* (London, S.P.C.K., 1933), Preface. The primary and most general meaning of "symbol" according to *The New English Dictionary* is: "Something that stands for, represents, or denotes something else (not by exact resemblance, but by vague suggestion, or by some accidental or conventional relation); *esp.* a material object representing or taken to represent something immaterial or abstract, as a being, idea, quality or condition; a representative or typical figure, sign, or token." The ostrich as a symbol of folly, and salt a symbol of friendship (being, on the authority of Sir Thomas Browne, incorruptible) are cited as seventeenth-century examples. In the eighteenth century the more specialized meaning begins to emerge, and the *N.E.D.* quotes the following statement published in 1727: "Words are the Signs and Symbols of Things: and, as in accounts, Cyphers and Figures pass for real Sums; so . . . Words and Names pass for Things themselves." The reader will perceive that the meanings indicated by these two quotations correspond respectively to what I have called expressive symbols and steno-symbols.

4. C. K. Ogden and I. A. Richards, in *The Meaning of Meaning* (Harcourt, 1924), gave currency to the word "referent" for the object to which a symbol refers. The word *"referend"* is preferable, it seems

to me, on two counts: logically, because it is drawn from the Latin gerund (which is passive) instead of from the active participle; practically, because its plural is unambiguous when spoken, whereas the plural of "referent" can be mistaken for the word "reference." The distinction between tenor and vehicle is introduced by Dr. Richards on p. 96 of *The Philosophy of Rhetoric* (Oxford University Press, 1936), in the course of his analysis of metaphor.

5. Susanne K. Langer, *Philosophy in a New Key* (Harvard University Press, 1942), pp. 30–31. Cf. the statement by A. D. Ritchie: "As far as thought is concerned, and at all levels of thought, it is symbolic process. It is mental not because the symbols are immaterial, but because they are symbolic. . . . The essential act of thought is symbolization." *The Natural History of Mind* (Longmans, 1936). Professor Langer, in quoting this passage, takes issue with the last sentence: "As a matter of fact, it is not the essential act of thought that is symbolization, but an act *essential to thought,* and prior to it. Symbolization is the essential act of mind; and mind takes in more than what is commonly called thought." (Langer, *op. cit.,* p. 41.)

6. The story of the Thunder's Three Commands is translated by Professor Radhakrishnan as follows:

"The threefold offspring of Praja-pati, gods, men and daemons, lived with their father Praja-pati as students of sacred knowledge. Having completed their studentship the gods said, 'Please instruct us, sir.' To them, then, he uttered the syllable *da* and asked, 'Have you understood?' They said, 'We have understood, you said to us *damyata,* control yourselves.' He said, 'Yes, you have understood.'

"Then the men said to him, 'Please instruct us, sir.' To them he uttered the same syllable *da* and asked, 'Have you understood?' They said 'We have understood. You said to us *datta,* give.' He said, 'Yes, you have understood.'

"Then the daemons said to him, 'Please instruct us, sir.' To them he uttered the same syllable *da* and asked, 'Have you understood?' They said, 'We have understood. You said to us *dayadhvam,* be compassionate.' He said, 'Yes, you have understood.'

"This very thing the heavenly voice of thunder repeats—*da, da, da,* that is, control yourselves, give, be compassionate. One should practice this same triad, self-control, giving, and compassion." *Brihad-Aranyaka Upanishad,* Chap. V, Sec. 2, in *The Principal Upanishads,* edited in transliterated Sanskrit with parallel translations, by S. Radhakrishnan (London, Allen & Unwin, 1953).

Probably the syllable *da* is onomatopoeic to the Hindu ear, representing iconically the sound which thunder makes.

7. "When the work of interpretation has been completed the dream can be recognized as a wish-fulfillment." Sigmund Freud, *The Interpretation of Dreams:* p. 207 of the Modern Library Giant edition of Freud's writings. *The Basic Writings of Sigmund Freud* (Random House, 1938). "Wish-fulfillment is the meaning of *every* dream." (*op. cit.*, p. 217). Not only does Freud restrict the referend of a dream symbol to past, consciously repressed or forgotten experiences of the symbolizer; he reaches the nadir of silliness, it seems to me, by further restricting such references to the most grossly sexual aspects: "There are dreams of landscapes and localities in which emphasis is always laid upon the assurance: 'I have been here before.' But this *'Déjà vu'* has a special significance in dreams. In this case the locality is always the genitals of the mother; of no other place can it be asserted with such certainty that one 'has been here before.'" (*ibid.*, p. 394).

8. As it happens, D'Avenant does not tamper as much with this passage as with some others in the play; but the alterations that he does make are instructive. The first four lines become:

> She should have died hereafter.
> I brought her here to see my victims, not to die.
> Tomorrow, tomorrow, and tomorrow,
> Creeps in a stealing pace from day to day.

What he imposes upon Shakespeare, by the flat logic of the second line, the omission of "and" in the third, and the substitution of "stealing" for "petty," is an explicative clarity which quite destroys the cadenced suggestiveness of the original.

CHAPTER III. THE LIMITS OF PLAIN SENSE

1. Gertrude Stein, *Useful Knowledge* (Harcourt, 1928).

2. Rudolf Carnap, "Logic," in *Factors Determining Human Behavior* (Harvard University Press, 1937), p. 108. The relevant passage is reprinted in Irving J. Lee's anthology of semantic writings, *The Language of Wisdom and Folly* (Harper, 1949), p. 45.

3. I. A. Richards, *Principles of Literary Criticism* (Harcourt, 1925), p. 267.

4. I. A. Richards, "Between Truth and Truth," in *The Symposium*, Vol. II (April, 1931). This periodical was a quarterly published in New York, 1930–1933, edited by James Burnham and Philip Wheelwright, and devoted to general criticism; unconnected with the periodical of that name now being published at Syracuse University. The article by

John Middleton Murry to which Richards refers had appeared in *The Symposium* for the previous October.

5. Bertrand Russell, *An Inquiry into Meaning and Truth* (Norton, 1940), p. 294.

6. Alfred J. Ayer, *Language, Truth and Logic* (Oxford University Press, 1936), Chap. VI. Republished in 1951 by Dover Publications.

7. Charles W. Morris, "Science, Art and Technology," published originally in *The Kenyon Review*, Vol. I (Autumn, 1939); republished in Irving J. Lee's anthology, *The Language of Wisdom and Folly* (Harper, 1948).

8. Charles W. Morris, *Signs, Language and Behavior* (Prentice-Hall, 1946).

9. Cf. Thomas Aquinas' declaration that beauty belongs to the cognitive, not the appetitive faculty: *Summa Theologia*, I, v. 4, ad. 1.

As a concluding comment on some of the tendencies discussed in the chapter I would append the following observation by Coleridge: "I have known some who have been rationally educated, as it is styled. They were marked by a microscopic acuteness; but when they looked at great things, all became a blank, and they saw nothing, and denied that anything could be seen, and uniformly put the negative of a power for the possession of a power, and called the want of imagination, judgment, and the never being moved to rapture, philosophy." Samuel Taylor Coleridge, *Biographia Epistolaris*, edited by A. Turnbull (London, Bell, 1911), Vol. I, p. 18.

CHAPTER IV. THE LOGICAL AND THE TRANSLOGICAL

1. Dr. Ogden's remark was made conversationally at a gathering in New York some twenty years ago. While he was willing to admit there might be flaws in the system of Basic English as it then stood, he maintained that such flaws were remediable in principle, and that a language of limited vocabulary might eventually be achieved in which no legitimate meanings would lack adequate symbolization.

2. Hobbes' declaration is confirmed by his distinction between univocal and equivocal names. "*Univocal* are those which in the same train of discourse signify always the same thing; but *equivocal* those which mean sometimes one thing and sometimes another. . . . Every *metaphor* is by profession *equivocal*. But this distinction belongs not so much to names, as to those that use names, for some use them properly and accurately for the finding out of truth; others draw them from their proper sense, for ornament or deceit." *The English Works of Thomas Hobbes of Malmesbury*, edited by Sir William Molesworth (London, 1839): First Section, "Concerning Bodies," Part I, "Com-

putation or Logic," Chapter II, "Of Names." It is not without significance that Hobbes treats logic as a subdivision of the topic, "Concerning Bodies."

3. George Santayana, *The Life of Reason:* Vol. I, *Reason and Common Sense* (Scribner, 2nd ed., 1922), Chap. VII.

4. Christopher Marlowe, *The Tragical History of Dr. Faustus*, Scene xvi. To be sure, the "blood" image functions archetypally as well. Its symbolic role in *Richard II* and *Macbeth* will be considered in Chapter X.

5. Pound's remark was made in an article, "Epstein, Belgion and Meaning," in *The Criterion*, Vol. IX, Serial No. 36 (April, 1930), p. 470. Some months earlier *The Manchester Guardian* had interviewed Jacob Epstein regarding his sculptures in the London Underground House, and had quoted him as saying: "It was my idea to make 'Day' and 'Night' the subjects of two groups over the entrances to the building. . . . It is difficult to describe a sculptural idea, for any art has to speak its own language. Well, 'Night' is a mother-figure with her child-man exhausted and sleeping under her protection and benediction. The curved horizontal lines of the group are expressive of sleep and rest descending on tired mankind . . ." In the January, 1930, issue of *The Criterion* Montgomery Belgion made these remarks the target of an attack which drew much of its ammunition from H. W. B. Joseph's *Logic*. This was the occasion for Ezra Pound's counter-criticism in the article from which I have quoted. Pound then adds:

"When Mr. Epstein says 'Night' is the subject he means rather more. Everybody knows what 'Night' is, but Mr. Epstein or Mr. Phidias or whoever, is presumably intent on expressing a *particular* and definite complex (ideas, emotions, etc.) generally oriented by a rather vague concept already mapped out. The difference is as great as that between firing a bullet in a generally easterly direction and hitting a particular bird."

6. Quoted from *Four Quartets*, which have been republished in T. S. Eliot, *The Complete Poems and Plays* (Harcourt, 1952). The first of the excerpts is from Part II of "Burnt Norton," the second and third from Part III of "East Coker," and the last from Part IV of "East Coker."

CHAPTER V. FOUR WAYS OF IMAGINATION

1. Samuel Taylor Coleridge, *Biographia Literaria*, Chap. XIII, pp. 159–160 of the Everyman's Library edition (London, Dent, 1908). There is a lucid and thoughtful treatment of the problem of poetic imagination, with considerable reference to Coleridge, in D. G. James,

Scepticism and Poetry: An Essay on the Poetic Imagination (London, Allen & Unwin, 1937).

Hobbes' theory of the imagination as decaying sense can be found in Part I, Chap. II of *Leviathan,* and in Chap. III of *Human Nature* where he defines imagination as the "conception remaining and by little and little decaying from and after the act of sense." The two passages may be found in Vols. III and IV respectively, of *The English Works of Thomas Hobbes,* ed. by Molesworth (London, 1839).

2. Kant's word for imagination is *Einbildungskraft,* connoting by its etymology a power (*Kraft*) of making (*bilden*)—a semantic advantage not shared by the English word. Many passages might be cited from the *Critique of Pure Reason* to illustrate Kant's doctrine that the imagination works most characteristically by its pre-conscious synthesizing power. For instance: "It is only because I am able to combine *into one consciousness* the various presented elements, that I can become aware that in every one of them the consciousness is the same. The *analytic* unity of apperception is, therefore, possible only under presupposition of a certain *synthetic* unity. The thought, that the elements given in a perception all belong to me, is the same as the thought that I unite them, or at least that I am capable of uniting them, in one consciousness." From the second edition of the *Critique,* Sec. 16, based in part on John Watson's translation as published in his volume, *The Philosophy of Kant* (Glasgow, Maclehose, 1891; Glasgow, Jackson, 1927).

We should not, however, overstress the power of German etymology. William Blake seems to have arrived at his doctrine of the Imaginative Image quite independently. See, in particular, Max Plowman, *An Introduction to the Study of Blake* (London, Gollancz, 1952), Chap. II.

3. Walter Jackson Bate, "Coleridge on Art," in *Perspectives of Criticism,* edited by Harry Levin (Harvard Studies in Comparative Literature, No. 20; Harvard University Press, 1950). The word "esemplastic" is of Coleridge's own coinage, from the Greek εἰς ἕν πλάττειν, "to shape into one": "because, having to convey a new sense, I thought that a new term would both aid the recollection of my meaning, and prevent its being confounded with the usual import of the word, imagination" (*op. cit.,* p. 82). Coleridge's fullest statement of how the poetic imagination works esemplastically is the following:

"The poet, described in ideal perfection, brings the whole soul of man into activity, with the subordination of its faculties to each other according to their relative worth and dignity. He diffuses a tone and spirit of unity, that blends, and (as it were) *fuses,* each into each, by that synthetic and magical power, to which I would exclusively appropriate the name of Imagination. This power, first put in action by the will and understanding, and retained under their irremissive, though gentle and unnoticed, control, *laxis effertur habenis,* reveals itself in the balance or reconcilement of opposite or discordant qualities: of sameness, with difference; of the general with the concrete; the idea with the image; the individual with the representative; the sense of novelty and freshness with old and familiar objects; a more than usual state of emotion with more than usual order; judgment ever awake and steady self-possession with enthusiasm and feeling profound or vehement; and while it blends and harmonizes the natural and the artificial, still subordinates art to nature; the manner to the matter; and our admiration of the poet to our sympathy with the poetry."— *Biographia Literaria,* Chap. XIV.

4. Cf. Rémy de Gourmont: "The sole excuse which a man can have for writing is . . . to unveil for others the sort of world which mirrors itself in his individual glass." Translated in *Some Imagist Poets: An Anthology,* Vol. II (Houghton, 1916) from de Gourmont's *Le Livre des Masques* (Paris, 1896). Cf. also William Butler Yeats: "One night I heard a voice that said: 'The love of God for every human soul is unique; no other can satisfy the same need in God.' " From the essay, "Anima Mundi," in *Essays* (Macmillan, rev. ed., 1924).

5. John Livingston Lowes, *The Road to Xanadu* (Houghton, 1930), especially pp. 131–132.

6. Coleridge, *Biographia Epistolaris,* edited by A. Turnbull (London, G. Bell & Sons, 1911), Vol. II, pp. 153–154.

7. Martin Buber, *I and Thou* (Edinburgh, T. & T. Clark, 1937; distributed in America by Charles Scribner's Sons). Cf. Buber, *Between Man and Man* (London, Routledge & Kegan Paul, 1947), especially the first part, entitled "Dialogue." Eugen Rosenstock-Huessy's independent exploration of the role of "Thou" in experience, begun in his German writings as far back as 1916, finds expression in the Epilogue to his *Out of Revolution* (Morrow, 1938). Cf. also Gabriel Marcel, *The Mystery of Being,* Vol. I, Chap. IX, "Togetherness: Identity and Depth." The Gifford Lectures for 1949–1950; English translation by René Hague (Chicago, Regnery, 1950).

8. Alan Porter, "Song," in *The Signature of Pain* (Day, 1931). Quoted by permission of the publisher.

9. Edward Bullough, " 'Psychic Distance' as a Factor in Art and an Aesthetic Principle," in *British Journal of Psychology,* Vol. V (June, 1912), pp. 87 ff. Cf. T. E. Hulme's declaration: "Never, never, never a simple statement. It has no effect. Always must have analogies, which make an other-world through-the-glass effect, which is what I want." *Notes on Language and Style* (Seattle, University of Washington Bookstore, 1929). Cf. also Alfonso Reyes: "If all perception is already a sort of translation, this is even more truly the case when artistic sensibility

is the filter." *El Deslinde: Prolegómenos a la Teoría Literaria* (El Colegio de México, 1944), p. 13.

10. José Ortega y Gasset, *La Deshumanización del Arte* (Madrid, Revista de Occidente, 2nd ed., 1928). I have here quoted from the partial translation by Pedro Fernández, published in *The Symposium*, Vol. I (April, 1930), pp. 202–203. Another and more complete translation has subsequently been made by Helene Weyl (Gloucester, Mass., Peter Smith, 1952).

11. Reprinted from *Reflections on the Theatre* by Jean-Louis Barrault, translated by Barbara Wall for the Rockliff Publishing Corporation, London, 1951, and The Macmillan Company, New York, pp. 113–114.

12. T. E. Hulme, *Speculations* (Harcourt, 1926), p. 120.

13. William Butler Yeats, "The Tragic Theatre," in *The Cutting of an Agate* (Macmillan, 1927), p. 35.

14. The declaration of purpose which has come to be known as the Imagist Manifesto was published anonymously as the Preface to *Some Imagist Poets: An Anthology*, Vol. I (Houghton, 1915).

15. Coleridge, *Lectures on Shakespeare* (republished by Dutton, 1930). Elsewhere Coleridge declares that Shakespeare "had the universal which is potentially within each particular opened out to him." As contrasted with Beaumont and Fletcher who, as it were, "fit together a quarter of an orange, apple, lemon and pomegranate" to make them look like one round diverse multi-colored fruit, Shakespeare, like nature, "works from within by evolution and assimilation, . . . by evolving the germ within by the imaginative power according to an ideal." *Coleridge's Miscellaneous Criticism*, edited by Thomas M. Raysor (Harvard University Press, 1936).

Professor Wimsatt's remark is made in his essay, "The Structure of the 'Concrete Universal' in Literature," which originally appeared in *Publications of the Modern Language Association*, March 1947. Subsequently republished in W. K. Wimsatt, Jr., *The Verbal Icon: Studies in the Meaning of Poetry* (University of Kentucky Press, 1954).

16. *Conversations of Goethe*, recorded by Johann Peter Eckermann, entry dated October 29, 1823. An English translation is published in Everyman's Library. Cf. Goethe's declaration therein (June 11, 1825): "The poet should seize the Particular; and he should, if there be anything sound in it, thus represent the Universal. English history is excellent for poetry; because it is something genuine, healthy, and therefore universal, which repeats itself over and over again. French history, on the contrary, is not for poetry; as it represents an era that cannot come again. The literature of the French, so far as it is founded on

that era, stands as something of merely particular interest, which must grow old with time."

Cf. also Goethe's reply (July 26, 1826) to Eckermann's question how a play should be constructed in order to be effective in the theatre: "It must be symbolical, that is to say, each incident must be significant in itself and lead to another still more important." Here, as in Goethe's discussion of "the law of required change" (February 1, 1827) and elsewhere, the meaningful outreach of the symbol is seen to be not only upward to a universal but simultaneously forward to the next public situation for which it is already preparing the context.

17. Quoted by Fritz Strich, "Das Symbol in der Dichtung," in his volume of critical essays, *Der Dichter und die Zeit* (Bern, Francke, 1947). Strich comments: "The symbol is thus, in Goethe's sense, the fullest coalescence of a particular instance and a general idea." Again he declares: "In the living experience (*Erlebnis*) of a poem I become a whole man. . . . Spirit and nature, reason and sense, the essence of mankind in me and my own particular ego—these all coalesce in the *Erlebnis* of the poem, being brought together there by the poet's binding hand."

18. Carl G. Jung, M.D., *The Psychology of the Unconscious*. A translation of the new edition (Zurich, Rascher, 1943) has been published by the Bollingen Foundation in a volume entitled *Two Essays on Analytical Psychology*, as Volume VII of Jung's *Collected Works*, the entire corpus of which is undergoing retranslation to be published in the Bollingen Series.

19. Aristotle, Rhetoric, Bk. III, Chap. 4 (1406 b, 20 ff.). Cf. Quintilian, *Institutio Oratoria*, VIII. vi. 8. There is, to be sure, a good deal of sound sense in Aristotle's discussion of metaphor, despite its limitations. "Metaphors must be drawn from things that are related to the original conception, without being *obviously* so related. . . . Because the hearer expected something quite different, his acquisition of the new idea impresses him all the more. His mind seems to say, 'Yes, to be sure; I never thought of that.'" (Bk. III, Chap. 11.) So far, excellent. But when he declares, "Those ideas which can be expressed well as metaphors will obviously succeed as similes also; and similes, when the explanation is omitted, will appear as metaphors," (III, 4) he is conceiving the difference between metaphor and simile superficially as a stratagem of grammar, instead of as a difference of semantic quality.

20. Herbert Read, *English Prose Style* (new edition, Pantheon Books, 1952). Elsewhere I have employed Max Müller's word "diaphor" to signify metaphoric fusion in the sense that Read intends, but it sounds too technical to be appropriate for a discussion of poetry. Ezra Pound

appears to have meant much the same thing as Read by his self-styled "doctrine of the image": "The Image is more than an Idea. It is a vortex or cluster of fused ideas and is endowed with energy."—"The Image is itself the speech . . . beyond formulated language."—"An 'Image' is that which presents an intellectual and emotional complex in an instant of time." See Stanley K. Coffman, Jr., *Imagism* (University of Oklahoma Press, 1951), where a number of such utterances by Pound have been collected from various sources.

The German word *Bild* ("picture," but with an overtone of meaning from the verb *bilden*, "to form") has had a roughly parallel usage. Hermann Pongs, in *Das Bild in der Dichtung* (Marburg, 1927) observes that the word *Metapher* has hitherto not been so alive in German idiom as the related words *Symbol* on the one hand and *Bild* on the other.

21. Martin Foss, *Symbol and Metaphor in Human Experience* (Princeton University Press, 1949), Chap. IV, especially p. 60. Although I have found much to admire in this little book, I regret that Professor Foss has chosen, misleadingly for some readers, to follow the semantic positivists in linguistic strategy although not in doctrine; for he restricts, like them, the term "symbol" to the logically explicable kind of linguistic unit that "has as its goal the ordering of the world into clear and convenient patterns." In short, he identifies symbol with steno-symbol, and sets over against it metaphor, myth, and prayer.

22. José Vasconcelos, *El Monismo Estético* (Mexico City, 1918); *Estética* (Mexico City, Botas, 1936; 3rd ed., 1945); *Todología: Filosofía de la Coordinación* (Mexico City, Botas, 1952). The article on Eliot, "Un Gran Poeta," appeared in the Mexican weekly *Todo* in the spring of 1951.

The metaphysical basis of the union of the heterogeneous is perhaps implicit in Julián Marías' remark: "As in the world of Anaxagoras, so in life, there is a bit of everything in everything; but here as there, the decisive thing is the perspective taken, the functional articulation of the component parts." *Introducción a la Filosofía* (Madrid, 1947), p. 25.

Much the same perspectival idea has been expressed by Leonardo da Vinci, although as a painter and engineer he was more inclined to emphasize the literal meaning of perspective as a physical angle of vision. "Every visible object [he writes in his *Trattato della Pittura*] can be seen from an infinite number of places, which places have a continuous quantity, divisible *in infinitum*. Consequently every human action shows itself in an infinite variety of aspects." And he adds that the creative artist's originality consists in taking a fresh stand amid that variety.

23. "A Discussion with Hart Crane," in *Poetry; A Magazine of Verse,*
Vol. XXIX, 1926, p. 36. The discussion was apropos of Crane's poem,
"At Melville's Tomb," which appeared in the same issue. Crane continues: "Its paradox, of course, is that its apparent illogic operates so
logically in conjunction with its context in the poem as to establish
its claim to another logic, quite independent of the original definition
of the word or phrase or image thus employed. It implies (this *inflec-
tion* of language) a previous or prepared receptivity to its stimulus on
the part of the reader. . . . It all comes to the recognition that emotional dynamics are not to be confused with any absolute order of
rationalized definitions; ergo, in poetry the *rationale* of metaphor belongs to another order of experience than science, and is not to be
limited by a scientific and arbitrary code of relationships either in verbal inflections or concepts."

It might be illuminating to consider in this connection a theory of
the late Gertrude Stein. While I have never been a total admirer of
Miss Stein, it must be conceded that her method of lumbering indirection and pseudo-litany sometimes yields arresting half-truths. In one
of her more decipherable essays she distinguishes poetry from prose as
being entirely and vigorously concerned with the *noun*. "Poetry is concerned with using with abusing, with losing with wanting, with denying with avoiding with adoring with replacing the noun." The more
one reflects on this obviously incomplete characterization in relation
to the positivists' shorn epistemic, the more its tiny flame of truth begins to radiate. Semantic positivism may be conceived as reducing
poetry to an adjectival status. The crimp and curdled leaf of John
Clare's primrose is taken as a quasi-adjectival appendage of the spatio-
causal undulations that are postulated to be its real essence. But Miss
Stein spoils her case when she declares that poetry consists in loving
the names of things and keeping them alive by saying them over and
over—a procedure which she exemplifies by what is probably her most
quoted and most ridiculed utterance: "A rose is a rose is a rose is a
rose." What does this momentous tautology accomplish other than a
reductio ad absurdum of her assumption and her method? The rose is
drooping and withered after the poetess's leonine caress. There is something naïvely wrong with her belief that "if you love a name then saying that name any number of times only makes you love it more, more
violently more persistently more tormentedly." Not simply loving and
repeating a noun (indeed, she observes in the same essay that "a name
of anything is not interesting because once you know its name the en-
joyment of naming it is over") but recreating a noun out of new dis-
positions and groupings of material—this is an aspect of the poet's task
on which neither the positivists from the one side nor Gertrude Stein

from the other has properly touched. The quotations are from Stein's essay, "What is poetry?" republished in *The Language of Wisdom and Folly*, edited by Irving J. Lee (Harper, 1948), pp. 53–56.

24. William James, *Principles of Psychology* (Holt, 1890), Vol. II, pp. 576–577. A one-volume reprint has been issued by Dover Publications (1950). Although James is abstractly right in stressing the factor of *"congruity of emotional tone* between the reproduced idea and our mood," his illustrations of the principle—"the same objects do not recall the same associates when we are cheerful as when we are melancholy"—are too elementary for the purposes of poetic criticism. Such a truism needs to be supplemented by a recognition of the unpredictable emotional affiliations—sometimes hardly congruous by ordinary standards—which may erupt from unconscious sources.

CHAPTER VI. METAPHORIC TENSION

1. Allen Tate's essay, "Tension in Poetry," was first published in 1938, and later republished in his volume, *On the Limits of Poetry* (Morrow, 1948). Tate's definition of "tension" is on p. 83 of the latter volume, which also contains his other essay referred to, "Hardy's Philosophic Metaphors." Cleanth Brooks' essay, "The Language of Paradox," was first published in *The Language of Poetry*, edited by Allen Tate (Princeton University Press, 1942); republished in *The Well Wrought Urn* (Harcourt, 1947).

2. Martin Foss, *op. cit.*, pp. 57–60. The works by Wilhelm Wundt to which he refers are *Sprach-psychologie, Völker-psychologie,* and *Die Sprache.*

3. An understanding of what the plurisign is, and how related to and distinguished from the monosign, or steno-term, which it approaches as an unreached because unwanted limit, is prerequisite to clear discussion about poetry. William Empson, in *Seven Types of Ambiguity* (London: Chatto & Windus, 1930) has made a survey of prominent types of plurisignation; but unfortunately he has somewhat confused the matter by his misconception of ambiguity, which differs from plurisignation as "either-or" differs from "both-and." The one is a looseness and duplicity of reference (cf. the mention of "soft focus" in Chapter IV); the other is a controlled variation and plurality of reference in language that deliberately transcends the literal. A view similar to mine is found in Fritz Kaufmann's argument that *Doppelsinn* (double meaning) is the distinguishing characteristic of poetic language. *Sprache als Schöpfung* (Stuttgart, 1935).

4. The orangoutang and cinnamon tree similes I picked out of a dictionary of similes which I found in a library. This prompts the re-

flection that while a dictionary of similes is possible, a dictionary of metaphors is not.

5. *The Complete Poems of Emily Jane Brontë,* edited by Charles William Hatfield from the manuscripts (Columbia University Press, 1941). The stanza quoted is the first of three, but to my mind it constitutes a sufficiently complete poetic statement by itself.

6. Aristotle, *Rhetoric,* Bk. III, Chap. 3 (1406 b, 15 ff.).

7. Dorothy Whitelock, *The Audience of Beowulf* (Oxford University Press, 1951). The incident is recounted in *Beowulf,* lines 2444–2462.

8. The line is from one of Jonathan Edwards' sermons. It illustrates the nature of metaphoric action in a Biblical context.

9. Edith Sitwell, *Poetry and Criticism* (Holt, 1926).

10. Friedrich Max Müller, *The Science of Language* (1891), Vol. II, p. 448 ff. Substantially the same book as his *Lectures on the Science of Language* (1868).

11. Archibald Henry Sayce, *Introduction to the Science of Language* (London, 1880; 4th ed., 1900), Vol. II, p. 181. Sayce continues: "In no other way can terms be found for the spiritual and the abstract. *Spirit* is itself 'the breath'; the *abstract,* that which is 'drawn apart.' Our knowledge grows by comparing the unknown with the known, and the record of that increase of knowledge grows in the same way. Things are named from their qualities, but those qualities have first been observed elsewhere. The *table* like the *stable* originally meant something that 'stands,' but the idea of standing had been noted long before the first table was invented."

12. I. A. Richards, *The Philosophy of Rhetoric* (Oxford University Press, 1936), Lectures V and VI.

13. Friedrich Max Müller, *op. cit. The New English Dictionary* distinguishes also a third ingredient of our irregular conjugation of the verb "be." There is the verb stem *wes-,* from which have been derived the Sanskrit root *vas-,* the German *Wesen,* and the English "was."

CHAPTER VII. EMBLEM AND ARCHETYPE

1. *The Gateless Gate,* translated from the Chinese by Nyogen Sanzaki and Saladin Reps (Los Angeles, John Murray, 1934). The translators state that the *Mu-Mon-Kwan* (literally, "no-gate barrier") was recorded by Mu-Mon E-Kai, who lived A.D. 1183–1260.

2. Harriet (Mrs. John C.) Murray-Aynsley, *Symbolism of the East and West* (London, 1900). I am indebted to this volume for much of the information concerning the *trinacria,* as well as for several of the smaller visual designs employed in Chapter VII. The empirical

basis of some of Mrs. Murray-Aynsley's views on Eastern Symbolism is disclosed in her earlier and slighter work, *An Account of a Three Months' Tour from Simla through Bussahir, Kunowar and Spiti, to Lahoul* (Calcutta, 1882).

3. Aristotle, *Natural Science (Physica)*, Bk. I, Chap. VI. The basic syllogism on which Aristotle's principle of triadicity is based in this chapter is as follows: "Accordingly, if we accept both the previous argument [that opposites are in some way the basic principles of nature] and the present one [that opposites presuppose a substance in which they inhere, and of which they may be predicated], must we not, in order to preserve the truth of both, postulate the existence of a third something [besides the pair of opposites, and on which they act]?"—*Aristotle: Containing Selections from Seven of the Most Important Books*, translated by Philip Wheelwright (Odyssey Press, rev. ed., 1951), pp. 9–10.

4. The *uraeus* was, in secular context, the deadly asp. In Egyptian belief it was one of the scourges of those unfortunate ghost-souls *(ka)* who had not been properly instructed in the rules of other-worldly procedure which have been preserved in *The Book of the Coming-Forth-by-Day* (the so-called Egyptian Book of the Dead). From these natural and supernatural beginnings the uraeus-figure underwent a good deal of symbolic development. The Pharaoh, according to Maspero, would make his claim to universal dominion by putting on the many-colored diadems of the gods, the head-dresses covered with feathers, and white and red crowns; while "the viper or uraeus, in metal or gilded wood, which rose from his forehead, was imbued with a mysterious life, which made it a means of executing his vengeance and accomplishing his secret purposes."—*History of Egypt* (London, 1891), Vol. II, p. 31. As a religious symbol the uraeus appears to have acquired reference, by synecdoche, to the winged disc figure as a whole, although still referring more specifically to the aspen part of it.

5. Such is the doctrine put forth in the *Mahabharata*, Bk. XII, "The Book of Consolation." In Book III, "The Forest Book," it is Krishna to whom ultimate godhead is ascribed, and the three members of the Hindu Trinity are said to have sprung from different parts of his body. The archetypal pattern is evidently the same through all this. On the polarity of natures in Shiva, the Cosmic Dancer, see Heinrich Zimmer, *Myths and Symbols in Indian Art and Civilization* (Bollingen Series, No. VI; Pantheon Books, 1946), pp. 154–157. On the *lingam* and *yoni* see p. 127 and *passim* in the same volume.

6. For an account of the numerous *avatars* of Vishnu, see Zimmer, *op. cit.* Extensive references are given under "Vishnu" in his Index.

7. The classical account of the three *gunas* is found in Chapter (or

Canto) XIV of the *Bhagavad-Gita*. There are over forty distinct English translations of this Hindu devotional scripture. Those of Professor S. Radhakrishnan (Harper, 1948), Swami Nikhilananda (New York, Ramakrishna-Vivekananda Society, 1944) and Franklin Edgerton (Harvard University Press, 1946) can be recommended for analytic study; those of Swami Prabhavananda and Christopher Isherwood (Harper, 1952, and Mentor Books) and of Swami Paramananda (Boston: Vedanta Centre, 1913) can be recommended to the general reader.

8. Plato's symbol of the charioteer is in his *Phaedrus,* esp. 245 C–246 A. Lane Cooper's translation (Oxford University Press) is especially recommended. The threefold nature of the soul and the corresponding bodily seats are discussed in Book IV of the *Republic*—Chapter XIII in Cornford's translation (Oxford University Press)—and in the *Timaeus,* 69 B–71 A. See Cornford's translation of and commentary on the latter passage: Francis M. Cornford, *Plato's Cosmology* (Harcourt, 1937; Dover Publications, 1951).

9. The three panels in bas-relief belong to the western gate of the great Buddhist *stupa* at Sanchi. They are reproduced from Alfred Foucher, *The Beginnings of Buddhist Art* (London, Humphrey Milford, 1917), where they had in turn been reproduced from photographs by J. H. Marshall, the English archeologist, who carried on his main explorations in this region from 1907 to 1909. See PLATE facing p. 137.

10. John Gardner Wilkinson, *The Manners and Customs of the Ancient Egyptians* (London, 1837). A posthumous edition, revised by Samuel Birch, was published in 1878. Wilkinson's own abridgment of the original work appeared in 1854 under the title, *A Popular Account of the Ancient Egyptians.*

11. James Izett, *Maori Lore* (Wellington, New Zealand, Government printing press, 1904), pp. 27–43. Andrew Lang, in *Custom and Myth* (London, 1888), recounts a variant of the Maori legend: that Heaven and Earth were originally united but were separated by a serpent, and that the mission of the Seer (who "sees all things in one") and of the Poet-Minstrel (who "makes things one through song") is to reunite them. However, as Izett shows, the marital drama is sometimes conceived as the second, not the first step in the scheme of creation. First of all there was *koru*—which can be translated, with striking ambivalence, both "potency" and "the void." That is to say, there was empty space from eternity, but within it were the potencies of all things as yet unborn (Izett, *op. cit.,* p. 11).

12. Hesiod, *Theogony,* lines 126-128. Earth bore some of the primordial gods and natural forces "without sweet union of love"; others after connubial union with Sky.

13. *Völuspa:* done into English out of the Icelandic of the Elder

Edda, by Ananda K. Coomaraswamy (2nd ed.; London: D. Nutt, 1909).

14. *Popol Vuh: the Sacred Book of the Ancient Quiché Maya;* English version by Delia Goetz and Silvanus J. Morley, from the Spanish translation by Adrián Recinos (University of Oklahoma Press, 1951).

15. Aristotle, *Metaphysics*, Bk. XII (Lambda), Chap. vii. A somewhat different account of the Divine Mover in relation to cosmic motion is found in the *Natural Science (Physica)*, Bk. VIII, Chaps. vi, vii, ix. My own translation of both passages may be found in the volume cited in Note 3.

16. Filmer S. Northrop, "The Functions and Future of Poetry," in *Furioso*, Vol. I, No. 4 (1941); republished in Irving J. Lee's anthology cited above, in Note 2 to Chap. III.

17. Wilbur Marshall Urban, *Language and Reality: The Philosophy of the Language and Principles of Symbolism* (Macmillan, 1939).

18. W. W. Main, in *The Explicator*, Vol. IX (March, 1951), Item 36, citing James G. Frazer, *The Golden Bough*, abridged edition, 1949, p. 129, in the chapter on "Relics of Tree-Worship in Modern Europe."

19. *Thirty Poems.* Hafiz; translated by Peter Avery and John Heath-Stubbs (London: "Wisdom of the East" series, John Murray, 1952).

CHAPTER VIII. THE MYTHIC WORLD-VIEW

1. The six-line poem, "The Apparition," appears in *Birth Is Farewell* by Dilys Bennett Laing (Duell, Sloan & Pearce, 1948). It is quoted here by kind permission of Mrs. Laing and of her publisher.

2. See Note 5 to Chapter II.

3. Friedrich Max Müller gave currency to the word "mythic" three-quarters of a century ago in *The Science of Language*, Vol. II, p. 455. He employed the word chiefly to describe that early period in the life of the race when language was most imaginatively in the making—in short, for that condition of mankind which I designate "mythopoeic" and, in the next chapter, "rituo-mythic."

4. Ernst Cassirer's *Die Philosophie der symbolischen Formen* is in process of translation by Ralph Manheim. The first volume, entitled "Language," with a preface and introduction contributed by Charles W. Hendel, has already been published (Yale University Press, 1953). The second volume, *"Mythisches Denken,"* on which much of my present discussion is based, has not yet appeared; but Cassirer's own resumé of it has been translated by Susanne K. Langer under the title "Language and Myth" (Harper, 1946).

5. Maud Oakes, *The Two Crosses of Todos Santos: Survivals of*

Mayan Religious Ritual (Bollingen Series, No. 27: Pantheon Books, 1951).

6. "A myth is a story which for those who tell it and for those who receive it has a kind of cosmic purpose. It professes to relate some happening in which supernatural beings are concerned and probably in doing so to offer an explanation of some natural phenomenon."—Alan C. Bouquet, "Mythology and Literature," in *Cassell's Encyclopaedia of Literature*. Although a myth may include elements of folk tale (which Mr. Bouquet defines as dealing with relations of men and animals or with romantic adventures of human beings), "it is really concerned with them only in so far as they form part of a world which has to be explained in terms of the sacred or the supernatural."

7. Richard Chase, *Quest for Myth* (Louisiana State University Press, 1949).

CHAPTER IX. THE SEMANTICS OF RITUAL

1. The Fijian death chant and most of the attendant information are taken from Basil H. Thomson, "The Kalou-Vu (Ancestor-Gods) of the Fijians": *Journal of the Anthropological Institute of Great Britain and Ireland*, Vol. XXIV (London, 1895). I have modified the translator's English wording, in a few superficial respects, for the sake of better rhythm and readability. His account of the customs and beliefs connected with Fijian burials, while authentic so far as it goes, is not the entire story. Other manifestations, sometimes quite different, are described by the Rev. Lorimer Fison in "Notes on Fijian Burial Customs," in Vol. X (1881) of the same journal.

2. James G. Frazer, *The Magic Art*, Vol. II (which is also Vol. II of the entire *Golden Bough*), p. 142. But even Frazer's own account of the Eleusinian ritual fails to prove (in my weighing of the evidence) that the purpose of the ceremonies was more than incidentally magical. A priest and priestess representing the sky-god Zeus and the grain-goddess Demeter engaged in a mimetic ceremony of connubial union, after the priest had taken the precaution of temporarily curbing his virility by an external application of hemlock. Frazer goes on: "The torches having been extinguished, the pair descended into a murky place, while the throng of worshipers awaited in anxious suspense the result of the mystic congress, on which they believed their own salvation to depend. After a time the hierophant reappeared, and in a blaze of light silently exhibited to the assembly a reaped ear of corn, the fruit of the divine marriage. Then in a loud voice he proclaimed, 'Queen Brimo has brought forth a sacred boy Brimos,' by which he

meant, 'The Mighty One has brought forth Mighty.' The corn-mother in fact had given birth to her child, the corn, and her travail-pangs were enacted in the sacred drama. This revelation of the reaped corn appears to have been the crowning act of the mysteries."—*Op. cit.,* pp. 138–139. No doubt there is a magical element in this ceremony— the wish, namely, to secure a continuing fruitful liaison between the god of spermatic rain and the goddess from whose earthy womb the nourishing grain bursts forth. But the worshipers appear to be concerned about something more than purely tangible benefits. Their evident desire to stand in the holy Presence, and to rededicate themselves to the holy Way of Salvation, is religious rather than magical.

3. It was R. H. Codrington who, in *The Melanesians* (Oxford University Press, 1891) first emphasized the effective presence, among the Melanesian islanders, of a proto-animistic, vaguely differentiated power which was there termed *"mana."* Subsequent investigators have come to regard some such phenomenon as characteristic of many, perhaps most, primitive cultures. A good comprehensive account of the idea is offered by Irving King, *The Development of Religion* (Macmillan, 1910), Chap. VI, "The Mysterious Power."

The Iroquois Indians appear to have meant much the same thing by *orenda,* and the Sioux tribes by *wakonda.* J. B. N. Hewitt, an eminent student of the Iroquois, explains the former word as referring to the "force, principle, or magic power" which was assumed by the Iroquois to inhere in every thing and process which displayed energy or a seeming potency of energy, "in any manner affecting or controlling the welfare of man." It was conceived to operate in a manner at once impersonal and mysterious although always embodied in particular objects; to be limited in its efficacy and not at all omnipotent; local and not omnipresent; capable of being "transferred, attracted, acquired, increased, suppressed, or enthralled by the orenda of occult ritualistic formulas endowed with more potency."

The Omaha tribe of the Sioux nation, according to Alice C. Fletcher, employs the corresponding word, *wakonda,* with a double meaning. They apply it to particular objects or phenomena regarded as mysterious and therefore sacred; while in a deeper sense "it is the name given to the mysterious all-pervading and life-giving power to which certain anthropomorphic aspects are attributed." Miss Fletcher reports that the two aspects are never confused by thoughtful Omahas. When an Omaha addresses Wakonda in prayer during a fast, his address is to *the power that causes motion,* which is to say, the power that gives life; for the ability to produce motion is synonymous to the Omaha mind with life. "To an Omaha (she writes) nothing is without life: the rock lives, so do the cloud, the tree, the animal . . . There is to him something in common between all creatures and all natural forms, a something which brings them into existence and holds them intact; this something he conceives as akin to his own conscious being. The power which thus brings to pass and holds all things in their living form he designates as *wakonda* . . . He is taught that when he fasts and prays he must not ask for any special favor or gift: that which he is able to receive will be given him."

J. B. N. Hewitt's article, "Orenda," and Alice C. Fletcher's article, "Wakonda," are both published in *Handbook of the American Indians North of Mexico:* Smithsonian Institute, Bureau of American Ethnology, Bulletin 30, 2nd imp., 1912.

4. Jane Ellen Harrison, *Prolegomena to the Study of Greek Religion* (Cambridge University Press, 2nd ed., 1908), esp. pp. 3–4. Miss Harrison finds the exorcistic and propitiatory types of magico-religious attitude indicated respectively by the two early Latin inscriptions, *Do ut abeas* and *Do ut des;* and again by the two Greek words, δεισιδαιμονία ("fear of spirits") and θεραπεία ("service to and tendance of the Gods"). She quotes the orator Isocrates (*Or.,* v. 117): "Those of the gods who are the source to us of good things have the title of Olympians, those whose department is that of calamities and punishments have harsher titles; to the first class both private persons and states erect altars and temples, the second is not worshiped either with prayers or burnt-sacrifices, but in their case we perform ceremonies of riddance." Miss Harrison explains that she translates ἀποπομπαί (literally, "sendings away") by the phrase "ceremonies of riddance" instead of by the single word "exorcisms" because of the connotations of magic and degraded superstition which attach to the latter word.

5. Lucien Lévy-Bruhl, *How Natives Think* (Allen & Unwin, 1926). Chapter II is most specifically on "The Law of Participation," but illustrative and confirmatory materials are scattered throughout the book.

6. Gladys M. Reichard, *Navaho Religion* (Bollingen Series, No. 18, Pantheon Books, 1949).

7. Gertrude Rachel Levy, *The Gate of Horn* (London, Faber & Faber, 1948).

CHAPTER X.   DRAMATIC ACTION AND MYTHIC IMAGERY

1. In ethical context Aristotle discusses action in relation to the formation of good habits, which is to say virtue, or moral excellence (*aretê*), particularly in the *Nicomachean Ethics*, Bk. II. In the *Poetics* he discusses action in relation to the dramatic plot, which he conceives as the mimetic representation (*mimêsis*) of the action. Francis Fergus-

son offers a good discussion of this latter relationship, in *The Idea of a Theatre* (Princeton University Press, 1949), Appendix, pp. 229–240; cf. Part I of the Introduction.

2. The hypothesis was popularized by Nietzsche in *The Birth of Tragedy*. Analogous phenomena suggesting a connection between seasonal ritual and primitive drama in the near-East outside of Greece are described in Theodor H. Gaster, *Thespis* (New York: Henry Schuman, 1950). Werner Jaeger wisely warns against over-playing the idea: *Paideia: the Ideals of Greek Culture* (Oxford University Press, 1939), 1945), Vol. I, p. 245.

3. Philodamus, Bacchic Ode, in H. Glaster, *Thespis* (New York: Henry Schuman, 1950), pp. 103, 435; Euripides, *The Bacchae*, first choral stasimon.

4. The chthonic, or tellurian, elements in Greek religion are brought into special focus in E. R. Dodds' recent volume, *The Greeks and the Irrational* (University of California Press, 1951). Cf. several of the chapters in W. K. C. Guthrie, *The Greeks and their Gods* (Boston: Beacon Press, 1951), esp. Chap. IX, "The Chthonioi."

5. Francis M. Cornford, *From Religion to Philosophy* (London: Edward Arnold, 1912), Chap. I, "Destiny and Law," Sec. 6, "Moira as a system of provinces."

6. Toward the end of Book XIX of the *Iliad* Homer tells that Achilles' horse, Xanthos of glancing feet, prophesied his master's death, the white-armed goddess Hera having given him the power of speech. And when he had spoken, it was the Erinyes who stayed his voice, thereby restoring the natural order of things.

7. Hippocrates' criticism of other schools of medicine is found chiefly in the treatise, "On Ancient Medicine"; while the fullest surviving statement of his more positive views is given in "On Airs, Waters, Places." Both treatises are published, with translations, in Volume I of the Loeb Classical Library edition of Hippocrates (Harvard University Press). Although they may not have been actually written by Hippocrates himself, they are authentic expressions of the medical school of thought which he established.

8. Clement of Alexandria, "Exhortation to the Greeks" (*Protreptikos pros Hellenas;* often referred to as the *Protreptikon*), Chap. II. Another translation by G. W. Butterworth is in the Loeb Classical Library edition of Clement. Although Clement is too zealous a Christian to speak of pagan ceremonies without bias—"The mysteries are mere custom and vain opinion, and it is a deceit of the Serpent that men worship in turning towards them"—nevertheless he promises to describe them "in accordance with the spirit of truth, without burlesquing them as Alcibiades is said to have done." Probably, then, we can believe him

when he describes the details of Eleusinian ritual, although it seems likely that his charges of "trickery" were valid only in isolated instances. It is well to recall the more charitable judgment of St. Paul: "Men of Athens, I perceive that in every way you are very religious" (*Acts* 17:22, Standard Revised Version).

9. Harold R. Willoughby, *Pagan Regeneration: A Study of Mystery Initiations in the Graeco-Roman World* (University of Chicago Press, 1929), Chap. II, "The Greater Mysteries at Eleusis," esp. p. 59.

10. John Wright Buckham, writing in Vergilius Ferm's *Encyclopaedia of Religion* (Philosophical Library, 1945), defines mysticism as "the intuitive and emotive apprehension of spiritual reality." I would accept this with the important qualification that the intuitive rather than the emotive aspect is the one to be stressed. Mystical emotions are sham if they are sought for their own sake; the genuine mystic's desire is not for a state of feeling, but for a certain state of *being* and of *knowing*—for light rather than heat. Evelyn Underhill, whose volume, *Mysticism* (Dutton, 1910) is still the best treatment of the subject I know of, says of the mystic: "Possessed like other men of powers of feeling, thought, and will, it is essential that his love and his determination, even more than his thought, should be set upon Transcendent Reality. He must feel a strong emotional attraction toward the supersensual Object of his quest: that love which scholastic philosophy defined as the force or power which causes every creature to follow out the trend of its own nature. Of this must be born the will to attain communion with that Absolute Object."—*Op. cit.*, p. 49.

11. Claude-Edmonde Magny, *Les sandales d'Empédocle: essai sur les limites de la littérature* (Neuchâtel: Baconnière, 1945).

12. Professor Fergusson applies the phrase to *Oedipus Tyrannus*, in the work cited in Note 1.

13. The neo-Platonic belief in *rationes seminales* as the unconscious creative forces in nature, corresponding to the exemplars in God's mind, is discussed in relation to the dark forces in *Macbeth* by Walter Clyde Curry, in *Shakespeare's Philosophical Patterns* (Louisiana State University Press, 1937), Chap. II, "Tumbling Nature's Germens," and Chap. III, "The Demonic Metaphysics of *Macbeth*."

CHAPTER XI. THE GUILT OF OEDIPUS

1. R. R. Marett, *The Threshold of Religion* (London: Methuen, 1900): especially Chap. I, "Pre-Animistic Religion," and Chap. IV, "The Conception of Mana." Lucien Lévy-Bruhl, *The "Soul" of the Primitive* (Macmillan, 1928); *Primitives and the Supernatural* (Dutton, 1935). The works of Preuss, although influential upon many of these

later anthropologists, are not available in English translation. Cf. Note 3 to Chapter IX.

2. Jane Ellen Harrison, *Prolegomena to the Study of Greek Religion* (Cambridge University Press, 1903); *Themis: A Study of the Social Origins of Greek Religion* (Cambridge University Press, 1912); *Ancient Art and Ritual* (Oxford University Press: the Home University Library). Gilbert Murray's contributions are scattered through many volumes. Particularly should be mentioned: *Five Stages of Greek Religion* (Oxford University Press, 1925); *The Rise of the Greek Epic* (*idem*, 1934); *Aristophanes* (*idem*, 1933); and at least two of the essays in *Tradition and Progress* (Houghton Mifflin, 1922): III, "The *Bacchae* of Euripides," and V, "Poèsis and Mimêsis."

3. Werner Jaeger, *Paideia: the Ideals of Greek Culture* (Oxford University Press, 1939; 2nd ed., 1945). Francis M. Cornford, *From Religion to Philosophy* (Longmans, 1912); *Before and After Socrates* (Cambridge University Press, 1932); *Thucydides Mythistoricus* (London: E. Arnold, 1907). Georges Méautis, *The Mysteries of Eleusis,* trans. by J. van Isselmuden (Adyar, Madras, India: Theosophical Publishing House, 1932); *L' Oedipe à Colone et le culte des héros* (Neuchâtel: Secrétariat de l'Université, 1940).

4. Freud, *The Interpretation of Dreams:* esp. pp. 307–308 of the Modern Library Giant edition of *The Basic Writings of Sigmund Freud* (Random House).

5. *Oedipus: a tragedy. As it is acted at His Royal Highness the Duke's theatre. The authors, Mr. Dryden, and Mr. Lee* (London, R. Bentley, 4th ed., 1692). It can be read more conveniently in George Saintsbury's edition of Dryden's Works, 18 vols. (Edinburgh, 1882–1893).

6. Erich Fromm, *The Forgotten Language: An Introduction to the Understanding of Dreams, Fairy Tales, and Myths* (Rinehart, 1951).

7. Robert F. Goheen, *The Imagery of Sophocles' Antigone: A Study of Poetic Language and Structure* (Princeton University Press, 1951).

8. Liddell and Scott, *Greek-English Lexicon* (8th ed., Harper, 1897), on τύραννος: "The term rather regards the irregular way in which the power was *gained,* whether force or fraud, than the way in which it was *exercised,* being applied to the mild Peisistratus, but not to the despotic kings of Persia." The more modern meaning of tyrant began to be prominent in the Fourth Century B.C., as shown for instance in Plato's *Gorgias,* 510 B. In the 1939 edition of the Greek-English Lexicon, by Liddell, Scott and Jones, the foregoing distinction is omitted; the revisionist's motive, however, appears to have been economy of space rather than any desire of retraction.

9. Cf. Harold R. Willoughby, *Pagan Regeneration* (University of Chicago Press, 1929).

10. Francis Fergusson, *The Idea of a Theatre* (Princeton University Press, 1949), the first chapter of which is devoted to a penetrating study of the *Oedipus Tyrannus*.

CHAPTER XII. THEMATIC PATTERNS IN THE *Oresteia*

1. The main exceptions to this negative judgment are: Jean Dumortier, *Les images dans la poésie d'Eschyle* (Paris, Société d'éditions "Les Belles Lettres," 1935); E. T. Owen, *The Harmony of Aeschylus* (Toronto, Clarke, Irwin & Co., 1952); Kenneth Burke's article on the *Oresteia* in the Summer, 1952, issue of *The Sewanee Review;* and Richmond Lattimore's introduction to his translation of the *Oresteia* (University of Chicago Press, 1953). Of these four interpretations only Dumortier's had been published when I wrote the chapter. Dumortier has also pursued his method of imagistic analysis from a more special point of view in *Le vocabulaire medical d'Eschyle et les écrits hippocratiques* (Paris, Société d'éditions "Les Belles Lettres," 1935). Although the emphasis is substantially different, I have found unusual value also in Georges Méautis, *Eschyle et la trilogie* (Paris, Grasset, 1936).

2. E. T. Owen, "The *Oresteia* of Aeschylus," in *The Toronto Quarterly*, Vol. VIII (July, 1939).

3. References by line number are to the edition of the *Oresteia* (text and translation) by George D. Thomson, 2 vols. (Cambridge University Press, 1938). Different editions of the *Oresteia*, and particularly of the *Agamemnon*, may show considerable variation in the division and numbering of lines.

4. Cf. Jean Dumortier: "Aeschylus has made of this metaphor of the hunt a sort of diptych. The first panel shows Paris and Troy being hunted like wild beasts by the sons of Atreus and enveloped in a fatal snare. On the second panel we see depicted Agamemnon caught, in his turn, in the meshes woven by Aegisthus and Clytemnestra. The city of Priam and its conqueror suffer the same fate: the law of retaliation applies rigorously: eye for eye, tooth for tooth." *Les images dans la poésie d'Eschyle*, p. 76.

5. *Aeschylus, translated into English prose*, by F. A. Paley (2nd ed., Cambridge and London, 1871). Based on the Greek text as given in *The Tragedies of Aeschylus*, edited with an English commentary, by F. A. Paley (London, 1855).

6. The incident is narrated by Iamblichus, *Life of Pythagoras,* translated by Thomas Taylor (London, 1818).

CHAPTER XIII. EXPRESSIVE STATEMENT AND TRUTH

1. L. C. Harmer and F. J. Norton, *A Manual of Modern Spanish* (London: University Tutorial Press, 1935), p. 6.

2. Margaret Schlauch, *The Gift of Tongues* (Modern Age Books, 1942).

3. The illustrations from Old French and Ronsard are on the authority of Ferdinand Brunot, *La pensée et la langue; méthode, principes, et plan d'une théorie nouvelle du langage appliquée au français* (Paris, 1922; 3rd ed., rev., 1936), pp. 8–9.

4. Cf. H. H. Joachim, *The Nature of Truth* (Oxford University Press, 1906; republished, 1939).

5. Martin Buber, *I and Thou* (published in German, 1923; the English translation by Ronald Gregor Smith, published by T. and T. Clark, Edinburgh, 1937; distributed in the United States by Charles Scribner's Sons). The ideas of this remarkable little book are amplified in somewhat different vocabulary in Dr. Buber's *Between Man and Man* (German original, 1929; translation published by Routledge, London, 1947).

6. William James' views are more accurately represented not in his *Pragmatism* but in the concluding chapter of *Varieties of Religious Experience* (Longmans, 1902; Modern Library, Random House, 1936) and in three of the essays originally published in the volume *The Will to Believe* (Longmans, 1897) and republished in *Essays on Faith and Morals,* edited by Ralph Barton Perry (Longmans, 1943): "The Will to Believe," "The Sentiment of Rationality," "Reflex Action and Theism."

7. I. A. Richards, *Science and Poetry* (Norton, 1926), especially Chap. VI, "Poetry and Beliefs."

8. To be sure, some of the component statements of the verse may originally have had definite satirical meanings: cf. the *Oxford Dictionary of Nursery Rhymes,* edited by Iona and Peter Opie (Oxford University Press). That likelihood does not affect the point I am making, however, which concerns the meanings of the various statements, component and total, for a modern reader.

9. From T. S. Eliot, *Ash Wednesday:* p. 64 of *The Complete Poems and Plays* (i.e., complete through 1950; published by Harcourt, 1952).

CHAPTER XIV. THE COSMIC FIRE

1. These are the opening lines of the late Alan Porter's poem, "The Transit of Joy," in *The Signature of Pain* (John Day, 1931). The

curiously prophetic character of the poem, despite its air of playful delicacy, becomes more evident as the years pass.

2. The passages pertaining to Agni are drawn from a number of hymns of the *Rig-Veda*. For the most part I have depended upon two English sources: Ralph T. H. Griffith's two-volume translation of the entire *Rig-Veda* (3rd ed.; Benares: E. J. Lazarus & Co., 1920, 1926), and H. D. Griswold, *The Religion of the Rigveda* (Oxford University Press, 1923), Chap. VI, "Agni the Priestly God," containing numerous partial translations.

3. One or two of the details about primitive fire ceremonies have been taken from Walter Hough, *Fire as an Agent in Human Culture*, Bulletin 139 (Smithsonian Institute, U. S. National Museum: Washington, 1926).

4. James G. Frazer, *Totemism and Exogamy* (Macmillan, 1910), Vol. II, pp. 604 ff.

5. I follow the Standard Revised Version in this quotation from the Book of Malachi, inasmuch as the thing that matters here is the metaphoric content itself and not the literary influence of the King James version of it.

6. The Acts of the Apostles, 2:1–21, especially Verse 3.

7. The Hillebrandt and Haugh quotations are both taken from Alfred Hillebrandt's article, "Brahma," in *Hastings' Encyclopaedia of Religion and Ethics*. Hillebrandt's major work is *Vedische Mythologie* (3 vols., Breslau, 1881–1902; 2nd ed., 2 vols., Breslau, 1927–1929). Martin Haug is known to some English readers through his *Essays on the Sacred Language, Writings and Religion of the Parsis* (Bombay, 1862; 4th ed., London, 1907).

8. The philological connection of the Sanskrit *atman* and the German *Atem* is affirmed by Friedrich Max Müller in his essay, "The Veda," published in his *Chips from a German Workshop* (London, 1867–1875), Vol. I, p. 68. Although the form *atma* is often found in the Vedic hymns, I have used, except when quoting, the more widely known form, *atman*.

9. The Buddha's Fire Sermon, in slightly varying translations, can be found in several collections of Buddhist writings, notably Dwight Goddard, *A Buddhist Bible* (Thetford, Vt., 1938; Dutton, 1953). The Charles Eliot reference is to *Hinduism and Buddhism*, 3 vols. (London: E. Arnold, 1921).

10. Edwin Arthur Burtt, *The Metaphysical Foundations of Modern Physical Science* (Harcourt, 1925).

11. José Vasconcelos, *Pitágoras: una Teoría del Ritmo* (Mexico City, 1921).

12. A good collection and translation of the Pythagorean Symbols is

contained in *The Golden Verses of Pythagoras and Other Pythagorean Fragments*, edited by Florence M. Firth (Theosophical Publishing House, reprinted 1919). My interpretations of the Symbols are based mainly on the interpretations offered by later Pythagorean writers, notably Porphyry, Archytas, and Iamblichus, as translated by Kenneth Sylvan Guthrie (copyright in mimeograph, 1920). These writers probably reflect the interpretations of the Symbols that were current in the Pythagorean school during and before their time.

13. Sri Aurobindo [Ghose], *Heraclitus* (Calcutta, Arya Publishing House, 2nd ed., 1947).

14. The fragments of Heraclitus are available in several English translations. The most recent of them, and on the whole a very good one, is by Kathleen Freeman, on pp. 24–34 of her *Ancilla to the Pre-Socratic Philosophers* (Oxford, Basil Blackwell, 1948). Oswald Spengler's early essay on Heraclitus deserves to be better known than it is. In Augusta de Mondolfo's Spanish translation of it (Buenos Aires, Espasa-Calpe Argentina, 1947) there is an extensive and valuable "Prologue" by the late Rodolfo Mondolfo reviewing eleven interpretations of Heraclitus by eminent scholars. G. S. Kirk's volume, *Heraclitus: The Cosmic Fragments* (Cambridge University Press, 1954) has come into my hands too late to be of use in the present undertaking.

CHAPTER XV. PILGRIM IN THE WASTELAND

1. Anonymous, *On the Four Quartets of T. S. Eliot*, with a foreword by Roy Campbell (London: Vincent Stuart, 1953); Cleanth Brooks, "The Waste Land: A Critique of the Myth," in *Modern Poetry and the Tradition* (University of North Carolina Press, 1939); Elizabeth Drew, *T. S. Eliot: the Design of his Poetry* (Scribner, 1949); Helen L. Gardner, *The Art of T. S. Eliot* (Dutton, 1950); Louis L. Martz, "The Wheel and the Point: Aspects of Imagery and Theme in Eliot's Later Poetry," in *The Sewanee Review*, Winter, 1947; F. O. Matthiessen, *The Achievement of T. S. Eliot* (2nd ed., containing a chapter on *Four Quartets;* Oxford University Press, 1947); Desmond E. S. Maxwell, *The Poetry of T. S. Eliot* (London: Routledge and Kegan Paul, 1952); Raymond Preston, *"Four Quartets" Rehearsed* (Sheed & Ward, 1946); Grover Smith, "Observations of Eliot's 'Death by Water,'" in *Accent*, Vol. VI (Summer, 1946); E. M. Stephenson, *T. S. Eliot and the Lay Reader* (London: Fortune Press, 1944); James Johnson Sweeney, "East Coker: A Reading," in *The Southern Review*, Vol. VI, No. 4 (1941); Leonard Unger, "T. S. Eliot's Rose Garden: A Persistent Theme," in *The Southern Review*, VII (1942), 667–689; George Williamson, *A Reader's*

Guide to T. S. Eliot (Noonday Press, 1953); Edmund Wilson, *Axel's Castle* (Scribner, 1931); Frank A. A. C. Wilson, *Six Essays on the Development of T. S. Eliot* (London, Fortune Press, 1948). The essays by Brooks, Martz, Sweeney, and Unger have been republished in *T. S. Eliot: A Selected Critique,* edited by Leonard Unger (Rinehart, 1948).

2. T. S. Eliot, *The Music of Poetry* (Glasgow, Jackson Sons & Co., 1942). A part of the present paragraph is repeated from my essay, "Eliot's Philosophical Themes," contributed to *T. S. Eliot: A Study of his Writing by Several Hands,* edited by B. Rajan (London, Dennis Dobson, 1947).

3. T. S. Eliot, "Tradition and the Individual Talent," first published in *The Sacred Wood* (London, Methuen, 3rd ed., 1934); republished in *Selected Essays* (Harcourt, 1932 and 1950). Cf. Sister Mary Cleophas Costello, *Between Fixity and Flux: A Study of the Concept of Poetry in the Criticism of T. S. Eliot* (Ph.D. dissertation; Catholic University of America Press, 1947).

4. T. S. Eliot, *The Music of Poetry* (Glasgow, Jackson, 1942).

5. Lloyd Frankenberg, *Pleasure Dome* (Houghton Mifflin, 1949).

6. S. Marshall Cohen, "Music and Structure in Eliot's Quartets," in *The Dartmouth Quarterly,* Vol. V (Summer, 1950).

7. Peter is the Speaker in this passage (Acts 5:30). He uses the same description in Acts 10:39: "And we are witnesses of all things which he did both in the land of the Jews, and in Jerusalem; whom they slew and hanged on a tree." The evident implication of the language, that Jesus was slain first and then hanged on a tree, brings Horatio's situation mimetically even closer.

8. *The Divine Comedy of Dante Alighieri,* translation and comment by John D. Sinclair (London: John Lane, The Bodley Head, 1939).

9. Max Picard, *Flight from God* (Regnery, 1951).

10. Washington Matthews, "The Night Chant, a Navaho Ceremony," in *Memoirs of the American Museum of Natural History,* Vol. VI (1902). The prayer to the Owl God is less directly connected with anything in Eliot, but invites quotation. According to Dr. Matthews the Navahos were wont to recite it during the ceremony of cigarette rolling, while the chanter "applies pollen to the essential parts of the patient, making a motion as if bringing it from the sun, and takes pollen on his own tongue and head." The cigarettes are then transferred to the patient's hand while the following prayer is chanted responsively:

> Owl!
> I have made your sacrifice.
> I have prepared a smoke for you.

My feet restore for me.
[*Repeated for afflicted parts of the body*]
Today take out your spell for me.
Today your spell for me is removed.
Far away you have taken it.
Today I shall recover.
Today my interior shall become cool.
My interior feeling cool I will go forth.
No longer afflicted I will go forth.
Feeling light within I will go forth.
Happily I may walk.
Happily abundant dark clouds I desire.
Happily abundant showers I desire.
Happily abundant vegetation I desire.
May it be happy before me.
May it be happy behind me.
May it be happy below me.
May it be happy above me.
With it happy all around me may I walk.
It is finished in beauty.
It is finished in beauty.

While abridging and modifying Dr. Matthew's version for clarity and economy's sake, I have nevertheless quoted at such length in order to preserve the rhythmic character of the hymn, as well as the relating of personal therapy to prayer for the restoration of health in nature.

11. Ian Dishart Suttie, *The Origins of Love and Hate* (London: Kegan Paul, 1935; New York, Julian Press, 1952).

12. Helen L. Gardner, *op. cit.* (see Note 1). Quoted by permission of E. P. Dutton & Co., publishers.

13. Jessie L. Weston, *From Ritual to Romance* (New York, Peter Smith, "Observation of Eliot's 'Death by Water,'" in *Accent*, Vol. VI Smith, 1941; reprinted from the English edition of 1920).

14. My two main sources of information on the Fish symbol have been: Franz Josef Dölger, 'Ιχθύς *Das Fischsymbol in frühchristlicher Zeit*, 5 vols., (Rome, 1910); and C. R. Morey, "The Origins of the Fish-Symbol," *Princeton Theological Review*, Vol. VIII (1910). That the symbol may also have possessed magical properties is shown by Miss Weston (*op. cit.*, p. 127): "That the Fish was considered a potent factor in ensuring fruitfulness is proved by certain prehistoric tablets described by Scheftelowitz, where Fish, Horse, and Swastika, or in another instance Fish and Reindeer, are found in a combination which unmistakeably denotes that the object of the votive tablet was to ensure the fruitfulness of flocks and herds." Such may indeed have been

the case, but I would have said "probably" instead of "unmistakeably," and would think that the magical might have been one motive among others. It is unlikely that primitive man separated his utilitarian, his speculative, and his devotional interests with clear bounding-lines.

15. The Abercius-epitaph occurs in the "Life of Abercius," *Patrologia Graeca*, CXV, col. 1211 ff. Evidently the pious Christian compilers of that monumental collection had no doubts of the epitaph's Christian character. The translation is by Professor C. R. Morey, *op. cit.*, Part IV.

16. Epitaph found near Atun, 1839, now in the museum of that city. Translated by Morey, *op. cit.*

17. "Sed nos pisciculi secundum ἰχθύν nostrum Iesum Christum in aqua nascimur, nec aliter quam in aqua permanendo salvi sumus."— Tertullian, *De Baptismo*, written about A.D. 205, in answer to a certain Quintilla, who had published a polemic against the Christian sacrament of baptism.

18. Quoted by Dölger, *op. cit.*, I, 4; out of Hagenbach's recension of the hymn, as given by H. Kihn, in *Patrologie*, I (1904), 38.

19. Roger S. Loomis, *Celtic Myth and Arthurian Romance* (Columbia University Press, 1927), pp. 182 ff. Loomis quotes the thirteenth-century romance of *Sone de Nansai*, on the wounding of Joseph of Arimathaea, who becomes one of the resurrected embodiments of the Fisher King: "Neither peas nor wheat were sown, no child was born to man, nor maiden had husband, nor tree bore leaf, nor meadow turned green; neither bird nor beast had young, so sore was the king maimed." *Op. cit.*, p. 185.

20. *The Shewings of Lady Julian*, transcribed and edited from the earliest known MS., by the Rev. Dundas Harford. London and Chicago, third printing, 1925. I have drawn particularly upon Chapters XIII, XVII, XVIII, and XIX. Note on Lady Julian's vocabulary: In Norwich it was the ancient duty of the Sheriff "to be buxom to the Mayor"—i.e., obedient and loyal. (From Harford's notes to the text.)

21. *Bhagavad-Gita*, II, 69, adapted from Swami Paramananda's translation. I have previously used this quotation and the commentary that follows it, in the essay cited in Note 2.

22. Eliot's echoings of Heraclitus are not limited to the two fragments which stand as preface to the *Four Quartets*. The following of the ancient philosopher's aphorisms seem especially pertinent to the poem: the second of the prefatory mottoes, "The way up and the way down are one and the same"; "Souls delight to get wet . . . to bathe like swine in the mire . . . but the best soul is like a dry beam of light"; "In the circle the beginning and the end are one"; and (most closely

connected with the passage under scrutiny) "You cannot step twice into the same river, for other and still other waters are ever flowing on." The inner, arcane meaning of Heraclitus' "way up and way down" is intensely moral, applying not only to states of matter (rock to earth to mud to water to cloud to air to aether to fire, and the reverse) but also to the aspirations and degradations of men's souls; and it was probably connected with certain religious mysteries of life, death, and redemption, like those celebrated at Eleusis.

Index

The circumflex is placed over *e* and *o* in transliterated Greek words to distinguish *êta* and *ômega* from *epsilon* and *omikron*.